MW01689287

GOD WANTS YOU DEAD

SEAN HASTINGS

PAUL ROSENBERG

Vera Verba

www.veraverba.com

ISBN: 978-0-9796011-1-8

First Edition

Published by Vera verba, Inc.

www.veraverba.com

SEAN'S DEDICATION

After ten years of talking and thinking and jotting down notes, three people stand out in my mind as having made this book a reality instead of being just a project that I sincerely planned to do someday but never actually finished. It is to them that I dedicate this book:

To my wife, Jo, who contributed ideas, offered encouragement, and most importantly, hardly complained at all about me spending half a year writing full time, rather than doing any "real" work.

To my best friend, Alex, who kept saying that he really wanted to read this book that I had been talking about for so long, and finally said that if I actually sat down and wrote the damn thing, he would do me any favor I asked – anything up to shooting someone in the leg – he only drew the line at cold blooded murder.

To my co-author, Paul, who agreed that my ideas were worth publishing, had many of his own that fit well with mine to improve the book immensely, and put up with my mood swings and general levels of insanity long enough to see this project through to completion.

PAUL'S DEDICATION

I almost never write dedications, but this time it seems like a nice thing to do.

I'll start by thanking my wife, Ceci, who not only makes me happy, but makes me better. (And from thence making everything I do better.)

I'd also like to thank the many, many people who contributed to my voyage toward a clear mind. Some of you worked hard to get good ideas into my head, and others just happened to be who they were at the right time. Some of you didn't even realize that you contributed. Thank you all.

Finally, thank you to Sean, for inviting me on this journey. Wow. It has not only been fun, but it really has clarified my mind. Beside, working with Sean really isn't quite as bad as he makes it sound. :)

A Note Concerning Digital Copying

At Vera Verba, we do not believe in standing in the way of progress. We are happy to see new technology that allows words and ideas to move faster and farther than ever before. However, if you have obtained a copy of one of our books for free, we do provide a way for you to make a suggested donation. This sort of patronage was the business model for all art, music, and literature before copyright law existed, and hopefully will continue to be a decent model for rewarding content creation long after governments are finally forced to give up on the idea that they can change reality by passing legislation that will somehow make some bits harder to copy than others.

To find out how to contribute, please visit: www.veraverba.com/donations.html

CONTENTS

Author Introductions

Sean's Introduction – Judging by the Cover

Holding this book in your hands, do you find yourself worried that people around you might see what you are reading?

If so, why should that be? Reading a book is in no way an endorsement of the contents of that book. Reading is a quest for knowledge. There should be nothing wrong with wanting to learn why other people think differently than you, or differently than the group in which you find yourself. You don't have to already agree with everything you read – in fact it would be boring if you did.

If you are the type of person who is not intimidated by the opinions of those around you, and could bravely walk into a church carrying a copy of this book, then you will enjoy reading it. But if you are a person who would be afraid to be seen with this book, then you really *should* read it. It just might help you understand why you feel pressure to conform to the ideas of those around you.

The cover of this book was designed to attract attention – a parody of a well-known image, a shocking title, and some nudity. These elements were all meant to increase the book's fame (or infamy). However, the cover also communicates the book's central theme: Beware of Higher Powers.

Michelangelo painted the original picture on the Sistine Chapel ceiling. It depicts God's creation of Adam, the first human. In our version, God aims a gun at Adam, clearly intending to revoke that earlier gift of life.

Adam, however, has learned a trick from Bugs Bunny cartoons. He plugs the barrel of God's gun with his finger. Symbolically, this represents the human will to survive despite being born under a death sentence—and even suggests that such survival is possible.

The title of this book, "God Wants You Dead" seems hostile and blasphemous at first glance. However, it is not a statement with which the faithful can easily argue.

Western religions generally hold that though Man has tasted the fruit of the Tree of Knowledge, God has prevented us from eating from the Tree of Eternal Life. So from a theological standpoint, it seems that God does want us dead or at least wants mankind to earn immortality. And this then leads to the theological question, "When does God want you to die?"

Suicide is prohibited by most religions. But some "true believers" (Christian Scientists, Jehovah's Witnesses, and others) decline modern medical treatments. They believe that such treatments are against God's will. Although they would probably bristle at the suggestion that this as a form of suicide, they still decline certain medical help, even when the choice is clearly treatment or death.

Some people seem to think that medical science can be "too good." They feel that current research directed at extending the human life span is unnatural. They will often say that it is not good to be "playing God."

So we wonder, at just what point should the faithful believe that trying to stay alive messes up God's plan?

An even more important question this book will address is why people believe the things they do. Why do some people believe that taking penicillin will thwart God's will, while others would gladly accept an artificial heart? Why do some religions require a strictly regulated healthy diet, while others mandate the drinking of poisoned fruit punch?

We believe the answers to these and other questions can be found in understanding why and how people believe in Higher Powers. Our book explains how these Higher Powers operate and why their goals are rarely aligned with your best interests.

Please note that God is only one of many “Higher Powers” that affect people's lives. We choose to pick on God in the title, because God makes claim to being the highest of all Higher Powers. We think this makes God worthy of special attention. However, we will also examine nations, corporations, racial groups, and other Higher Powers to which individuals sometimes surrender their minds.

The title focuses on the threat of death, because it's the most extreme price that anyone can pay for faith in a Higher Power. And we maintain that an adherent's willingness to choose death is a very good indicator that something is wrong with a belief system. However, we also address the other common costs of having faith in any Higher Power.

The faithful pay a price, not just with their lives, but also with their liberty and property.

Sean Hastings

New York, New York

Paul's Introduction – Owning Your Mind

> *Men stumble over the truth from time to time, but most pick themselves up and hurry off as if nothing happened.*
>
> -- Winston Churchill

As you pass from the earlier to the later chapters of this book, you will see that it is ultimately about restoration; about restoring control of your mind to your inner self, and about restoring control of society to free individuals.

This may at first sound strange to you, but most people have limited control of their own minds. Outside influences seem to control people more than the other way around. It is also true that much greater control is both possible and greatly preferable. Unfortunately, there are many strong forces standing against this.

Please don't think of "ownership of your mind" as a trivial thing, or something that everyone would automatically want to have. It isn't easy, and some folks would rather kill than take responsibility for their own thoughts and actions.

This may affect you as well; many people experience a genuine terror when they think about having no outsider to blame for their mistakes. So, start getting used to the idea now. Giving up control of your mind doesn't remove responsibility. You can hide your head in the sand as much as you wish, but it doesn't make you innocent. You are still responsible for your actions – the things that you do, and to a lesser degree also, the things that you could have prevented.

Hopefully, you are one of the people who want to improve themselves. On one hand, we're going to make it as easy for you as we can. But on the other, we are not offering you a free lunch. If you want to regain control of your mind, you're going to have to work for it...hard. Sure, it'll be worth it, but it won't be easy.

Now, a few additional words on our seemingly blasphemous title: *God Wants You Dead.* The "God" in our title is not the big guy on the heavenly throne. It is the idea of God we are talking about – an idea that exists, almost as an independent entity, in the minds of billions. We call these shared mental patterns *Distributed Identities* and describe them as *idea-organisms.* (We'll explain this in detail in the next chapter.) These ideas are what stand in the place of the big guy on the throne, at least in the minds of most people. To make the point, please consider the following:

The guy on the throne, at least according to the Bible, is strongly in favor of human immortality. Now, what if (and this is not quite as "sci-fi" as you might think) researchers figured out how to insert an immortality gene into humans, and we suddenly attained the ability to live forever? How does that make you feel? Is it a stupid idea? Is it something to ridicule? Maybe something that is plainly wrong, against God, or maybe just against the established order of the universe?

Consider this: Such feelings are evidence of something in your mind that:

A. Is against your own self-interest. (Dying is not good for you.)
B. Is contrary to the recorded will of God.

The generally accepted record of the Big Guy on the Throne's words is dripping with references to Him not only wanting immortality for men, but of Him sending His only son to suffer and die in order to obtain this gift for us. We can argue about exactly when the Bible says this will or should happen, but immortality itself is plainly held as the highest gift of the God of the New Testament.

So, given that being immortal is both in your self-interest, and it is the stated desire of God, why wouldn't you leap immediately at the possibility? The obvious reason is this: There is an idea in your head that says that actual immortality may not (or should not) be achieved, and this idea feels more important to you than actually living forever.

So how did this idea, that dying is a good thing, get into your head? You see, immortality is not a problem to the guy on the throne, but it *is* a big problem to the God idea in billions of minds – The God Distributed Identity. This is the thing our cover refers to – the thing that wants you dead. And even if you don't believe in God, a similar higher concept of universal order, such as Nature, may give you similar ideas.

The Distributed Identities that we will refer to in this book have a strong presence in your thoughts, as the example above may have illustrated to you. In fact, you may still be deeply uncomfortable with this subject and may feel like pushing it out of your mind as expeditiously as possible. And, of course, that is your choice to make, even if it is a gutless one. If you aren't ready to take a look at your beliefs – why you believe the things you do – you might just want to put this book down now; it's going to make you uncomfortable.

Throughout our book, we will explain to you exactly what these idea-organisms are, how to identify them, and how to remove their influence over you. If you do indeed re-landscape your mind, you can achieve much more than you would otherwise. But it will always be easier if you want to just go with the flow and be average. What you do with all this information will be your choice; we have neither the ability nor the need to make you fight for control of your mind, though we do recommend it. And we have some information that we hope will help.

Paul Rosenberg

Chicago, Illinois

0
Executive Summary

WARNING: Although this book can be funny and light-hearted in many places, we start with a fairly serious summary of our ideas. If you are in a mood for a laugh rather than a lecture, feel free to skip this introductory chapter. (Come back and read it later, when you are in the mood for more serious fare.)

In fact, feel free to skip any part of this book where you are not feeling it. Each section is very different, so the next one might well be more to your liking. Or just flip through and look at all the pictures and cartoons....

They are your eyes, use them as you choose.

This book is about the past, present, and future evolution of human ideas. Its primary emphasis is on parasitic collectivist ideologies. It examines where such ideas come from, how they harm us, and how we can remove them from our own minds and from the culture around us. Finally, it tells us the amazing things that will become possible for humanity when they are gone. Not only religions, but also nation states, racial groups, corporations and other collectives are targeted for observation and criticism.

This book will probably offend you, if you hold any icons to be sacred or are a believer in any ideology that encourages group loyalty and action. When you get to a part criticizing your favorite ideology, please just try to remember that we are actually trying to be helpful. We are absolutely sure that many of your ideas are very good and can create more value in the world. However, we are equally sure that when you allow your good ideas to be bound up into an icon and used as a source of social approval, that it becomes difficult to evaluate them properly and you create a home in your mind for many bad ideas to also take up residence.

This book may also bother you if you have any strong ideas about the genres that books should fit into. It has a lot of academic knowledge in it, but it is not an academic book with footnotes or endnotes. It contains some very serious and unsettling ideas, but it also contains some stupid jokes and amusing cartoons. Its chapters and sections are numbered quite oddly and written in many different styles. The primary goal of this book is to encourage readers to step outside the patterns of thought that have been impressed upon them by their social groups; to do this we have deliberately avoided conforming to any of the patterns deemed normal or acceptable for publication in any given genre. In fact, the very idea of "genre" is somewhat of an anathema to the ideas contained in this book.

This book offers a way to look at the world that explains why even well meaning group-think so often produces bad results, and shows how better results can be achieved when people identify themselves and others as free thinking individuals rather than devotees to any icon or members of any group.

0.1 Faith

A young girl gets onto a bus. She has layers of dynamite and nails taped below her breasts. She wears a bulky coat to hide their shape. She tries to remain calm until the bus is full and reaches the center of town. She is having second thoughts. But as the bus arrives at its most crowded stop, she begins reciting the words of a Higher Power, assuring herself one last time that this is the right thing to do. Then she pulls a cord… and flies apart in a blast that instantly ends the lives of almost everyone else on the bus and even several people on the curb, along with her own.

In your language, her name translates as "Faith."

It may be almost impossible for you to understand what is going through this girl's mind when she commits this act of murder/suicide. How can she end her own young life? How can she kill strangers she has never met – people who have never done anything to harm her directly?

As incomprehensible as her actions may seem, they are just an extreme case of a type of behavior that is common to almost everyone. You probably do things that, while not nearly as extreme, are just as incomprehensible from a viewpoint of rational self-interest. Just like this girl, and just like almost every other human being on the planet, at some time you will almost certainly allow your actions to be directed by a collective ideology that has little care for individual human lives.

Two of the questions that we will explore with you in this book are:

1. How are you different from a suicide bomber?
2. How can you become even more different from a suicide bomber?

The simple answer to the first question is not particularly comforting:

The only real difference between you and the suicide bomber is the extent to which you allow yourself to make the same kind of mental errors.

More specifically, it is a question of how willing you are to accept a large number of ideas, represented by a single name or flashy icon. Can you question the individual ideas separately, once they are grouped together into an ideology, or do you feel that any given philosophy must be either all good or all bad?

This makes the simple answer to the second question a more useful one:

The less you deny your own mind, the less you believe in voices of authority without question, the less you substitute faith for reason; the less of yourself you will sacrifice to any Higher Power.

The suicide bomber is probably the most extreme example of sacrifice to a Higher Power, and as such it may be an example that does not strike home as having any lesson to teach you personally. After all, your own behavior is almost certainly not this extreme, and the Higher Powers to whom you feel loyalty may never ask for such a sacrifice. But consider that the smaller sacrifices you do make may be just as unnecessary and ill-considered, even if less overtly harmful.

It is even possible that you do not acknowledge loyalty to any Higher Powers, but before you become confident of that, please explore with us the many things that can qualify as such.

0.2 Higher Powers

We are defining "Higher Powers" as: *Icons to which people grant greater authority than they would to any individual human being.*

Such icons may be religious, such as "God" or "The Prophet." They may be historical, such as "Our Founding Fathers" or "Honorable Ancestors." They may be geographical, such as the "Voice of the Nation" or "Law of the Land." They may be natural forces, such as "Mother Nature." They may even be deliberate man-made constructs, such as a corporation. They can take many forms.

What they have in common is that none of them have any physical existence that you can touch. Even the ones that might have been real things at one time are not real, physical, things now. They are only ideas in people's heads.

It is also part of our definition that we may not speak directly with Higher Powers in the way we can speak to another human being. People may attempt to talk to Higher Powers, but few ever claim to receive answers, and we are never able to verify such claims. Any entity that verifiably talks back to you is something different than the Higher Powers we are discussing throughout this book.

0.2.1 Indirect Communication

In order to receive guidance from the Higher Powers, we must either decide that we know deep in our hearts what they are telling us, accept the word of some other individual who claims to know, or read writings which we believe contain their wisdom. In all of these cases the actual communication comes from an individual human being. Either it originates in our own thoughts (we are talking to ourselves), is presented to us by another individual, or is in the words that were written by the hand of another individual human being. It cannot be demonstrated that these communications really do originate from the Higher Power.

Such Higher Powers have great authority in the minds of the people who believe in them. When many people believe in such an entity, it can have a vast influence over our lives, though we have no direct recourse to confront it for its misdeeds.

When we surrender our thoughts to the alleged greater wisdom of a Higher Power, it becomes easy for unscrupulous individuals to manipulate us. (History certainly bears out that statement!) They can easily supply us with guidance that furthers their own ends, in the guise of words from on high. It can't be denied that this occurs continuously and wherever such Higher Powers are being given authority over individual thought and action.

Even when no individual is manipulating the voice of a Higher Power, blind obedience is still a problem. Once we give up our right to question, no improvement in our thinking on the subject is permitted. We have given up on our own judgment and adopted the judgment of another. Bear in mind that an actual powerful entity wouldn't need to be protected from examination. On the other hand, an ephemeral impostor would certainly desire such protection.

Which is worse, the commandments of a Higher Power coming from the will of an unscrupulous individual, or the commandments of a Higher Power coming from the spontaneous mutation of ideas within a group?

The first is more malicious, but it can eventually be exposed. (Think of a disgraced preacher.) But in the second case there is no identifiable source, and bad ideas that slip in are far less likely to ever be questioned.

The idea of a Higher Power, mutating like a living system, can produce bizarre commandments that no leader or individual would ever have invented.

0.2.2 Living Ideas

In this book – and we think accurately – we will be viewing ideas as living organisms; organisms that survive inside individual human minds and multiply themselves by communication to new minds. Give us a chance and we think we can demonstrate this behavior convincingly.

No, ideas are not actually living things. At least not in precisely the same way biological entities are. But these widely distributed ideas act in a very similar way, so we find the analogy to living organisms useful – even factually accurate by some broader definition of life.

Consider your ideas as living things that inhabit your mind – idea-organisms. When these ideas help you achieve your individual goals of survival and growth, they are symbiotic organisms. When they do not, they are parasitic organisms.

Blind acceptance of an unseen authority creates a fertile environment in which parasitic ideas can thrive. In such an environment, they are separated from reality, and are not held to an objective examination. This is precisely how every seemingly insane mania works, from Nazism to suicide cults.

In such an environment, the ideas that grow best are not those that align themselves with their human host's self interests, but those that direct human actions according to the survival and reproductive goals of the ideas themselves.

The most successful ideas will be those that make the host's actions (that is, *your* actions) subservient to the idea – an ideological Higher Power.

You become a tool to be used by an invisible authority that cannot be verified, and your actions become those which help that Higher Power survive and grow.

Like any living organism, these ideas must reproduce or they will die out. Because of this, they cause their hosts (people) to take actions that will increase the idea's chances of survival and reproduction, even to the detriment of the survival of the individual human hosts.

Get that again: These ideas can cause a person to do things that are against their own best interests – perhaps even things that will directly result in a person's own death.

People influenced by complex idea-organisms will labor to infect others with these ideas. They will try hard to make sure that their children have the same beliefs. They will donate money to organizations that spread the word. They will stand on street corners handing out pamphlets.

They also act to oppose competing ideas. They tend to be closed-minded and unwilling to listen to logical arguments. They will often become uncomfortable or angry when their beliefs are questioned. They sometimes ban or burn books containing competing ideas. They will even engage in bloody warfare to destroy other large groups of people who hold different beliefs.

Since Higher Powers exist on a different level than the individual, their wants and needs are based on different things. This often puts them at cross-purposes with the values and needs of peaceful individuals, which makes them dangerous to individual survival. Sometimes they will even interfere with new ideas and actions that would only serve to make all human life better.

It is important to these idea-organisms to maintain the status quo where the powers of individual humans are concerned. The environment in which they evolved included many human limitations. And it is not clear that they can continue to survive in a world in which individual human beings gain more power – a world in which certain human limitations are overcome.

Think of a field of crops that is growing well, then someone changes the composure of the soil. Will the crops continue to grow properly? Probably not – they were suited to the original soil mix. New knowledge can be like an environmental change to the idea-organisms growing in your mind. Therefore, these idea-organisms resist both personal learning and overall cultural advances in knowledge, even when this is contrary to the survival interests of individual human beings.

It seems quite likely that idea-organisms would be particularly upset about knowledge of their true natures. However, if we wish to remain true to ourselves (despite the best efforts of Higher Powers to bend us to their wills) we must try to understand the nature of these idea-organisms.

0.2.3 The Making of a Higher Power

The key factor that allows the growth of a complex parasitic ideological organism (as opposed to symbiotic ideas), is a common flaw in the way people tend to think. The problem stems from our tendency to want to categorize things. We do this in an effort to simplify our thinking and lives.

While mental categorization is a very useful tool, its miss-application is at the root of the growth of the ideological entities we call Higher Powers.

Categorization makes life a lot easier. For example, if you find out you are allergic to citrus fruits; it is very useful to recognize a pattern. You learn not to eat any fruit with a thick, waxy, brightly colored skin. It is likely to be a citrus fruit, and it could hurt you. It is useful for you to label all citrus fruits as "BAD" and to not bother trying each new one that comes along. There might be exceptions, but it is probably not worth finding out.

In the world of idea-organisms, this sort of thinking is encouraged, even beyond what is appropriate or useful.

If you read a sheet of paper with ten ideas on it, you can easily go down the list, evaluating each one. You can decide if you think each is true or not, based on its own merits.

However, if there is an impressive title that groups the ten ideas into a seemingly inseparable list, it may no longer be easy to think of each idea as separate proposition. It does not matter if the list is entitled "The Code of Gozer the Gozerian" or the "Ten Commandments of God." Once the list has such a title, it is now being presented as a single unit of thought, rather than ten separate thoughts.

There is no logical reason why the ten ideas should be grouped as one in your mind, but in order for idea-organisms to function, they must encourage this kind of grouping. For an idea-organism to thrive, its various ideas must interact and support each other. Complex idea-organisms can not exist unless your mind is willing to let many ideas work together as a single system of beliefs.

If someone asked you, "What did you think of that list of ideas I sent you?" you could easily say:

"I liked numbers five through ten all right, especially six, eight, and nine. They were my favorites. But I thought those first four were pretty weak. Maybe you should think about getting rid of those?"

On the other hand, if someone asks you what you think of "The Ten Commandments," there is more of a feeling of inseparability. You will probably feel ideological pressure to answer, "I think they are pretty good" rather than go into specific details about which of The Commandments are good and which of The Commandments could use some improvement. They are grouped together in a way that makes it hard to separate them. Logically they should be individual ideas that can each receive separate consideration. But the title of the list makes that a very hard thing to do.

This bundling of ideas is how bad information can slip in along with good. It is how complex ideological life forms, such as the Higher Powers we have described, become possible.

Complex ideologies are built of simpler ideas. In order to act as a whole unit, they must convince you that they must either be accepted or rejected as a whole unit. If you start examining the individual ideas that are its parts, the complex idea-organism falls apart. If everyone could learn to remember that they are always free to pick and choose the simple ideas that work, from any given set of ideas, while rejecting the bad ones, large parasitic idea-organisms could never survive or continue to evolve.

Remember our suicide bomber? This is exactly how she got suckered into triggering a bomb strapped to her chest. All the good ideas in her world; ideas about family, loyalty, justice, etc, got packaged together with some very bad ideas. She did not have the intellectual tools to separate the good ideas from the bad ones, so she ended up acting on bad ideas that went against her own best interests. Such bad ideas go against the interests of all individuals and are only useful to the reproduction of certain larger idea-organisms.

In this book we will try to show you how to recognize the influences of such parasitic ideas. We will discuss the dangers that occur when these kinds of ideas saturate a group and how all Higher Powers stem from collective belief systems. We will explain the strategies that these ideas use to convince you to believe in them, how to avoid them, and how to rid your mind of them.

Finally, we will show how all the rewards that Higher Powers promise (even God's offer of immortality) may be obtainable without sacrificing yourself to the cause.

0.3 Self Sacrifice

Thinking as an individual, the actions of the suicide bomber seem truly inexplicable. However, when you understand the driving forces of Idea-organisms, her behavior makes perfect sense. From the point of view of the idea-organism in her head, her sacrifice is a small one for a greater gain; a small price to pay for "the greater good."

0.3.1 The Ultimate Sacrifice

Suicide is obviously not an action promoted by our biology. It ends the ability for the genes to reproduce themselves, and is therefore something your genes would not have you do. The only possible time that suicide can be good for the genes is when the act of death is a sacrifice that vastly increases the survival chances of a large number of related creatures such as children. Related creatures carry a lot of the same genes, so the sacrifice of an individual animal can still be in the best self interest of its genes.

The same benefit of self-sacrifice can be seen in the world of ideas. It is in the best self interest of an ideology to cause a person to sacrifice her life in order to save the lives of many other people who are also hosting the same idea-organism. And in the world of ideas, a suicidal act might do more than just save other people who have those ideas in their heads. It might also actually aid in the reproduction of those ideas by calling greater attention to an idea. If the suicidal act seems noble and heroic, it can help spread the idea that initiated the suicide.

In the case of the suicide bomber, this is part of the story. However, something even more insidious is going on. Such acts are part of an ongoing war of ideologies between people worshiping different Higher Powers. However, there is actually a hidden friendly relationship between the two apparently rival powers. By demonizing each other, they actually help each other convert new followers.

0.3.2 Violence Begets Violence

The extremist aspects of two warring Higher Powers are intensified with each act of violence. One act of violence provokes retaliation, which provokes counter retaliation, until it is almost impossible to sort out who started what. The aggressive nature of ideas on each side is thus increased, and moderate ideas within each population are silenced.

As more innocent people are dragged into the violence, more ill will is created in people who would otherwise have never chosen to participate in such a conflict. Thus many additional fertile minds, ripe for infection by these violent idea-organisms, are cultivated. Suicide bombing lends itself particularly well to this process.

When the person who commits a violent act is removed from the equation, it almost guarantees that retaliation will be escalated above the level of personal vengeance, to the impersonal level of competing ideologies.

If the bomber were still alive, she could be located, captured, tried, and executed. This would give some closure to the friends and families of the victims. However, since the culprit "escapes" by dying in the act, the natural desire for some retribution becomes more widely directed towards some larger group that included the bomber. There is also a tendency for people to feel victimized if they identify with the same group as the victims. When a violent act is ideological rather than personal, people tend to feel involved, even if they do not actually know any of the people hurt. This inflation of a personal act of hatred to the level of larger groups can occur on both sides simultaneously.

One can imagine a Samoan living on the island of Hawaii in the late summer of 2001, who on September 10th was complaining about all the non-native Hawaiians on the island and telling his friends that Hawaii would be better off if it were independent from the United States. A couple days later, after the violent actions of September 11th, he might have been proudly flying a US flag, and telling his friends how he would punch out the next Arab he saw. Maybe he even joined the army. The suicide attacks on September 11th, served to strengthen the hold of the group identity, even over those in whom it was fairly weak.

Patriotic anger inspires misdirected violent retaliation that furthers the cause of violent factions on both sides of the ideological conflict.

When a Higher Power inspires a member of a group to sacrifice herself in this way, it may gain far more than it loses. The loss of one faithful believer is likely to be compensated by greater faith in many of the previously less faithful. This cycle of "violence begets violence" strengthens and furthers the goals of two Higher Powers at war. They are secret allies, helping each other enslave more minds.

0.3.3 Ants and Men

It has been said that only ants and men fight their own kind to the death or go to war. When two stags clash antlers over territory, rarely is either injured, and even more rarely is either killed. They test their relative strengths and give ground accordingly without mortal peril coming into the picture. Even where species do go to war in groups, again these clashes rarely result in serious injury or death. Most animals will not readily lay down their lives for others of their kind, no matter how large a group they are protecting.

There are some notable exceptions. One of which is that the parents of many species, especially the mother, will protect their young, sometimes even to the death. To understand why it makes sense for them to do so, one must understand that every animal is an expression of a genetic pattern, and that these genes are at the root of all behavior. So when you observe behavior in animals, no matter how bizarre it may seem to you, it usually makes sense from the point of view of the genes contained within that animal.

The genetic relationship between parents and young is easily understood. Half of the genes of each parent will be expressed in each of the offspring. Also, a mother animal will know, with almost 100% certainty, which offspring are her own. This makes the odds easy to calculate. From a gene's point of view it makes sense for a mother to lay down her life for more than two of her own offspring, or risk her life for just one, if the risk is less than a 50% chance of death.

So a mother sacrificing her life for a child or children makes good genetic sense, but how does this explain the behavior of two ant colonies fighting each other?

Truly a war between two colonies of social insects is the only sight in nature comparable to rows of human soldiers killing each other en mass. For the ants' part, they are still just playing the roles that their genes have encoded into them. And from the genes' point of view, once again, it all makes sense.

Most ants do not reproduce. Only the Queen ant and a select few male ants ever breed. The worker and soldier ants are sterile, and will not pass along their genes, except through the copies of those genes that are contained in the Queen. So, when a soldier ant sacrifices its life for Queen and Colony, the way human soldiers will sacrifice their lives for King and Country, its behavior is benefiting the genes inside of it by helping ensure the safety of the few ants that actually reproduce those genes.

In fact, because each ant colony only reproduces through the Queen, all the other worker and soldier ants in the colony can be viewed as extensions of the Queen ant. From this point of view, when two ant colonies of the same species are fighting over territory, it is really no different than two stags locking horns. The ants that die in the conflict mean as little to the whole colony organism as the occasional splinter of lost antler means to the whole stag.

So then the question remains, why do men go to war?

Human beings are not colony insects breeding through a single Queen. It is not in our genes best interest to sacrifice ourselves for our leader's whims. Certainly our individual deaths mean more than the splintered antlers of a larger animal...

The answer to this question is found in the nature of our ideas. Ideological replicators, rather than our biological replicators, often influence human behavior. Collective idea-organisms are the higher animals of the idea world. Copies of a collection of ideas (an ideology), inside the heads of each of its members, are what defines a group. These ideas act together to create group behavior and turn us into parts of a collective organism. Such a Collective will sacrifice us as quickly as the colony will sacrifice worker and soldier ants, or the stag will sacrifice the cells that make up its hooves and antlers.

When human soldiers go to war, it is because the group idea-organism that causes this behavior is defending its physical or ideological territory.

Since the idea exists in all the members of the group, it makes sense to sacrifice the warrior carrying one copy, for the many copies of the idea left in the minds at home. When two ideological organisms clash, they use human beings the way the ant colony uses soldier ants, or the stag uses its antlers. They are tools that have been specially created for just this purpose.

Collective idea-organisms turn men into tools to be used for the survival and growth of the Collective. This explains why people, who would not normally hurt a fly in their own homes, can be made to travel half way around the world, to risk death, and to kill people they have never met, in defense of their "way of life."

0.3.4 Personal Sacrifice

While you have never died for a cause (at least the fact that you are reading this, and the current level of technology as we are writing it, makes that seem unlikely), you have probably sacrificed yourself for a group in many ways, and at many times.

If you have ever done something just because you felt it was expected of you, you have sacrificed something to a Higher Power. Maybe this involved serving in the military or on jury duty, or maybe just paying taxes. Whatever it was, if you did it out of a sense of obligation rather than because of a reasoned calculation, you sacrificed to a Higher Power.

Do you tend to behave the way that is expected of you in a group? When watching a performance, do you clap when everyone else does, not necessarily because you liked the show, but because you would feel weird not clapping while everyone else is? Do you feel constant pressure to conform? Worse yet, do you pressure other people to conform?

Some people seem to have a problem fitting into groups. They are socially awkward and never seem to know how to act. They are geeky. Perhaps you know the type. Perhaps you even are one. If you are, then you lack the ability to blend into a group. This might be seen as a natural resistance to the group-think caused by Higher Powers – or as some sort of a lack of social skills. Both ways of looking at the situation are probably somewhat true. Being a geek is both a blessing and a curse. Being able to see the world in unapproved ways can be an advantage, but not sending out the right social cues can make you a target.

If you do have social skills, then you have probably made fun of such people. Maybe not recently, but what about when you were younger? Did you ever apply hurtful pressure to anyone who just wouldn't fit in? Even if you have always been nice about it, helpfully coaching people on how to better fit into a group is also a service to the Collective. Even if you have just spent some of your time talking about the virtues of some group, you have done work for an idea-organism.

Not all idea-organisms are necessarily the worst possible kind, but if you are accepting ideas without analysis, just because it's what everyone else around you also believes, then you well may end up as host to one of the very bad ones. While you may not pay with your Life, paying in terms of your time or money is also sacrificing something of yourself.

While our discussions will be relevant to all collective Higher Powers, we target God for special attention because God makes the claim of being the highest of all possible powers. This allows God to offer the most fantastic rewards in return for an individual's intellectual surrender. Believers are promised purpose in life and immortality in exchange for belief.

If you have trouble seeing that other things we call Higher Powers – the Nation State for example – are really the same sort of ideological constructs as God, ask yourself what the differences are between the following two propositions:

1. The "Chosen People" should not live among, nor should they ever do business with the "Infidels"
2. People born on different sides of an imaginary "border line" should not be able to move to live near each other, nor to do business freely.

The prohibitions that the Nation State places on free movement and trade, based on imaginary lines on a map, can be just as damaging as the results of any ideas concerning the "Will of God."

While other Higher Powers like Nation States and Corporations can't make the kinds of promises that God does by laying claim to the highest possible authority, they can still demand some truly significant sacrifices.

0.4 Picking on God

Religions, governments, corporations, and other "Higher Powers" that cause people to act as a group are all examples of collective idea-organisms. Collectives arise from the way human beings create mental identities for things in the world around them and assign icons to represent complex groups of ideas. God and Country are merely icons for such collective idea-organisms.

These idea-organisms influence large numbers of people to behave as a group. Copies in the minds of individual human beings work together the way a higher animal's component cells do, producing unified behavior. In addition, these idea-organisms may act in ways that are harmful to their human hosts, encouraging them to sacrifice themselves for the good of the Collective.

In defense of ourselves against charges of blasphemy (not that it will help), we do not believe that any true GOD would object to this line of discussion. No true GOD would need to fear examination or inquiring minds. The Big Guy on The Throne does not require protection from a couple of little guys who are just examining life on Earth and trying to find answers to problems.

In fact, we think that any god worthy of the name would have to smile upon our efforts to understand the reasons why people think the way they do.

0.4.1 The Word "God"

All the words in the title "God Wants You Dead" are highly charged. They are often misunderstood, ill defined, and/or filled with emotional response. The word "wants" is directly related to the concepts of self interest, values, and the market forces that make modern human life possible. The word "you" points directly to the concept of identity or "the self," and this is a concept that philosophers have been trying to unravel for as long as there have been philosophers. The word "dead" draws a line between existence and nonexistence, and the idea of nonexistence is one of the scariest things that a person ever has to face.

However, the first word of our title, "God," is very likely the most powerful of the lot. It may be that more people have been killed because of the idea of GOD or gods than as a result of any other idea that was ever invented. On the other hand, monotheism is also a part of the history of mankind's growth of ideas – a process that has taken us from a global population of millions to that of billions of living human beings.

So Who Is This God Person Anyway?

There are as many different answers to that question as there are people – though many of the answers are very similar.

Some people think they know God from books they've read. Others have been introduced to God by their friends and relatives. Many people talk to God on a regular basis, though only a small number of people find that God actually talks back to them. Only a very small number of people claim to have actually met GOD face to face, and for the most part, even the strongest believers in God don't believe most of those claims.

Our use of the word "god" falls into three categories. The first is "god" – a being with godlike powers. The second is "GOD" – the instance of a Supreme Being.

The third is "God" – the concept of a Supreme Being as it exists in the minds of human beings.

The first usage usually relates to belief in polytheism. Some religions past and present detail the existence of many different gods. Some belief systems even hold that it is possible for a human being to become a god, or at least possess god-like powers. We will use the word "god" to mean any being who is worshiped by those who believe in its divine powers.

The second usage refers to "THE GOD" rather than "a god." GOD is the supreme entity in a monotheistic belief system. Even in a polytheistic belief system, we might logically attribute the title of "GOD" to the most powerful god. Many such belief systems have some central figure that is the strongest, wisest, etc. We will use the word "GOD" to mean the omnipotent being that is believed to have created the universe. This is the being that we also call "The Big Guy On The Throne." If it amuses you to do so, you can think of the word "GOD" as an acronym for "Generic Omnipotent Deity."

The third usage, which is the way we use it in the title of this book, is the most interesting to us. We will use the word "God" to mean the shared concept of an omnipotent deity, as it exists in the minds of many human beings.

Even if you don't believe in the existence of GOD or gods, you certainly recognize the existence of God. The idea of a supreme being is something that demonstrably exists and has an effect on our lives. It inhabits many human minds and is capable of producing collective actions. God is an icon representing a collection of ideas with its own agenda – an agenda quite separate from the best interests of the individual human minds that host it.

In the next section we will explore the nature of the God concept as it exists in the minds of both believers and non-believers. We will show how this concept causes collective actions, and examine it as an example of a Distributed Identity.

0.4.2 The Idea of God

If you're not one of those people who really know God well, but you'd like to get to understand, perhaps the best way to do so is to look at the history of gods and godhood.

In the early days of recorded history, there were a lot of gods around. Every nation, clan, or valley had at least one, and many had several. Some people thought, "the more gods the better" and tried to get into the graces of many. If you had a good relationship with several gods, then there was a better chance that at least one of those gods would keep your interests in mind while working out things divine. This would be similar to your representatives in a modern political system. (And you know how well that works for you!) In fact, gods and political systems were once very much linked – they still are sometimes – even in some modern states. (And you probably know how well that works too...)

In those days, the leader of a nation might be closely linked to their god, often acting as the god's physical embodiment in the real world, or perhaps as the chosen conduit between men and the gods. When nations went to war with each other, their gods were also fighting, and the winners were thought to have the strongest god. Whether the winning nation's strength made its god the greatest, or the winning god's strength made its nation the greatest, was purely a matter of semantics.

In early times, the god was combined with the nation, and both were embodied in the leader.

Since the leader of a nation could be strongly associated with the god of a nation, and nations weren't as big as we grow them these days, there was a much greater range of upward mobility. If you worked hard and had a lot of good ideas, it might just be possible to become a god back then. And having achieved godhood, your descendants could often get in on the "god gig" just by right of birth. Therefore it was both possible to earn or inherit divinity.

A few thousand years ago, the god of the Jews (who later became the god of the Christians and the Muslims too when those religions evolved from Judaism), was promoted to being "THE GOD." This particular god had no single human being attached, but did have a priesthood who shared in the benefits of being the only people who really knew this god well.

This worked out well for everyone, as having a living divine entity on Earth belching and farting like any other human can be very embarrassing to a religion. It worked so well, that this particular "THE GOD," is now the GOD that over half of the people in the world are talking about when they talk about GOD. (Although there is sometimes violent disagreement about whether Yahweh, Jehovah, and Allah are the same "person.")

Not being seen allows a god to have much greater powers without the human analog constantly being bothered to perform miracles. The Priests still get bothered some, but they can simply promise to "put in a good word." They can also much more plausibly ask for money than can someone claiming to be omnipotent.

In the case of this particular god, this growth of extra powers went so far as to make him the best and greatest of all the gods. In fact he became such a strong god that many people came to believe that he was the creator and controller of everything. (OK, there were some advantages that came from monotheism, but we're having fun here, so please don't interject!)

God started out by just wanting his people to "have no other gods" before him, and ended up as "the Alpha and the Omega," the beginning and the end of everything. As "THE GOD," he was so impressive that he did not even lose face when the nation that believed in him was destroyed, scattered, and enslaved. Wherever they found themselves, and however bad life got, believers in God knew that they were the chosen people and that all was for the best.

One way that belief in God ensured this was by promising a next life in which everything would be good for the believers. This was not a new promise. Many gods had offered immortality to believers. God, however, was the big guy and could control the afterlife for everyone, even those who didn't believe in him. Whereas the garden variety god could only reward or torture his own people in the next life, THE GOD could claim that power over everyone.

Therefore, he could offer his people the consolation of knowing that not only would the next life be great for them, but also that the assholes who had persecuted and enslaved them would all be totally screwed. This was a big seller, as people like their revenge even when served that cold. It kept faith in God alive through some very troubled times.

Later, such punishment was extended, not just to those who harmed the chosen people, but to everyone who was not among the chosen. Not only did this make people very happy with their chosen status but it was also a big help in any recruiting effort by the chosen people. The original chosen people were not so interested in this. They actually set up difficult and painful barriers to recruitment, like having to learn a new language and having delicate pieces of one's anatomy snipped off. But the whole "eternal damnation for non-believers" concept lent itself so well to a recruiting drive that it was probably the major reason for the appearance of many new factions. (This lead to the birth of Christianity, and later Islam)

The other strength that this God had when it came to recruiting was that since he was the only god, if another culture already believed in a supreme being, then they must really believe in the same GOD. Thus a culture could be converted by being told that they were worshiping the same GOD as always, that they had just gotten the name wrong, and would have to change some of their methods of worship. If the culture had more than one god, invariably there was one which was the most good, most wise, and most powerful, to fit the bill.

This was much easier than the previous method of completely converting another culture. The old method seems to have required killing every last adult male and raping all the women. The new method just involved stealing and renaming a culture's holidays.

This omnipotent and omnibenevolent (all powerful and all good) being, who would eternally torture anyone who did not believe in him, was such a big hit that he was soon the centerpiece of the biggest selling religious concept in the western world. The only real competition persisted in the east where the general belief was that when you died, you came back again as someone or something else. This belief in reincarnation satisfies what appears to be a general human need for some sort of immortality, but doesn't fit well with God's eternal reward or eternal torture carrot and stick combination.

To be clear: This book is about how ideas survive and reproduce, so throughout this book we are, in almost all cases, using the word "God" in reference to the idea of a Supreme Being as it exists in the minds of people around the world, not in reference to any actual deity.

God is a concept existing in many human minds that is capable of producing collective actions. God is an idea-organism with its own agenda, separate from the interests of the individual human minds that host it. Where "GOD" and "gods" are the intangible things of faith and/or myth that deny proof, God is something that demonstrably exists and has an ongoing visible effect on our lives.

You may or may not believe in GOD, but you definitely experience the effects of God (the idea-organism) on a daily basis.

0.4.3 The Power of God

Although God is the highest of all Higher Powers conceptually, he does not have the real world clout that he once had. At one time, in most human societies, defiance of the local belief in GOD or gods would be met with a punishment of torture and death. God no longer commands that kind of power in most parts of the world.

For various reasons (some good and some bad) the authority to use violent force has almost always been centralized to a single organization that is generally called "The government." Where the government used to be controlled by religion, recently (historically speaking) a new Higher Power has risen to this peak position.

The new Higher Power we speak of is Geography. It sounds odd, when you put it that way. Geography was a boring subject you studied in school. Geography is about drawing lines on maps, and naming the areas inside the drawn borders. It seems silly that writing names on maps could give rise to a Higher Power. Silly or not, names are powerful things in the world of ideas.

Where Religion may play on people's instinctive and powerful fear of death, Nation States based on geographic borders play on our likewise powerful territorial instincts.

So the ideological power structure of the world has changed somewhat in the last several hundred years. World leaders used to claim to be speaking the will of God, or even be to a god on Earth. Now most of them claim to be speaking with the voice of the "fatherland" or sometimes "motherland." (But never "brotherland" or "sisterland," as a Higher Power will never claim to just be your conceptual equal.) Geography also calls for sacrifices from us. They are somewhat different ones than those that God would want us to make, but possibly just as damaging.

And God is still around. He is down but not out. He can still affect the decisions of most Geography-based government, even where he can no longer directly make those decisions. So when we talk about the sacrifices that God wants us to make in his name, we will also be talking about the avenues through secular government that God must use if he wants his will enforced. We will discuss how reducing the power that our governments have over us would help avoid having them used by idea-organisms against our best interests. We will also discuss other Higher Powers that use these same strategies to try to bend us to their will.

So, despite this book's title, we will not *just* be picking on God.

0.5 God Wants You Dead

The concept of God has evolved over several thousands of years. (That is quite a lot of evolutionary time for an idea, as ideological evolution moves a LOT faster than the biological equivalent.) During all that time, death has been one of the biggest and most constant facts of life.

Humans have a lot of limitations that make us who we are. All of these limitations have been part of the environment that the idea-organism called God has grown and thrived in. Remember that we are talking about a living idea with its own agenda – with its own environmental needs for survival and replication. So changing any part of its regular environment could be dangerous to God's continued existence.

Idea-organisms are creatures of culture. To protect themselves, idea-organisms must resist cultural change. One of the ways they do this is to suppress new technologies that might cause serious changes.

As interesting evidence of this, consider the fact that the people who always seem to invent new technology are the geeky types – the types that do not fit into the Collective. Earlier we talked about the fact that geeks are less in touch with the group-think of idea organisms. This makes them stand out as outsiders, unable to blend into any group. However, this also leaves their minds free of the influences of idea-organisms.

The history of technological innovation is a history of strangely geeky outsiders as the innovators. Idea-organisms suppress the creation of new ideas in the minds that host them. It takes a mind free from such idea-organisms to come up with brilliant new ideas.

To see why idea-organisms feel the need to suppress new technology, let's consider the impact that certain new technologies might have on various Higher Powers:

First, we want you to imagine what would happen to national governments, based on geographic boundaries, if a teleportation device (like a Star Trek transporter) was ever invented. Imagine a world where individuals had access to a device that allowed instant travel from place to place.

How could it not be a huge plus to human progress to eliminate travel time and shipping time for goods? Yet the idea of national borders – and hence nation states – would be threatened by this technology. You can not have a cohesive national identity, based on geographical location, when people are empowered to move freely and instantly from one side of the world to the other. We can pretty much guarantee that governments would do anything they could to suppress and control a new technology that would change or remove our concept of territory.

Your Geography-based government is already keenly interested in controlling travel. It issues travel papers to allow you to cross imaginary lines drawn on maps. It wants to make sure that you are not traveling across these lines with any personal property it would rather keep inside or outside those lines. The idea-organism of the geography-based Nation State can not allow total freedom of movement and still survive. Therefore it must strongly regulate all transportation technology, and any advances of such technology will tend to frighten it into action.

Next, imagine what would happen to the idea of Race if a technology that allowed us to instantly rewrite our genetic code was invented. You could wake up in the morning, and choose if you wanted to be Asian, Black, Caucasian, Hispanic, or even blue with purple polka dots. The leadership of groups based on racial identity would decry such technology. They would do everything in their power to stop people from using it. Such a technology would remove stupid prejudices that have long divided us from viewing each other as all just members of the same species. But those prejudices are at the core of the concept of racial identity. Those seriously infected with the idea of Race, no matter what their actual specific race, would all denounce such technology as a great evil.

If the idea of Race happened to be the highest ideological power and was currently controlling the government when such technology was developed, you can bet that the government would quickly criminalize the new technology. If the influence of Race on government was less, but still strong, the government might just strictly control the use of race changing technology. The idea-organism of Race could not survive the wide use of a technology that allowed people such freedom of control over their bodies.

Now think about the way in which Corporations are also constantly threatened by new technology. Old business models are often invalidated by new technology that gives people the power to get along without goods or services previously provided by a Corporation. When this happens, if the Corporation can not adapt quickly, it must try to influence the government to make the new technology illegal, or gain the legal right to stifle such technology for a period of time so it can adapt.

All the above examples point to exactly the sort of resistance that Religion will put up against revolutionary new medical technologies.

If human beings ever found a way to survive without eating, or breathing, this would upset the environment for all the ideas that human beings have – it would cause a lot of ideological changes. While clearly this would be something that would make human life less fragile and easier, it would shake things up a lot in the world of our ideas. So we could also say "God Wants You Breathing," which sounds a lot nicer than "God Wants You Dead." However, if human beings ever found a way to stop dying, it would be an even more serious blow to the God Idea. God has evolved in such a way as to be linked with an idea of immortality – of not actually dying when you die.

The invention of real immortality will be a bigger shake-up for the idea of God than all the previous scientific progress that humanity has ever made.

In the name of God, true believers will fight against technology that can make us all healthy and young for as long as we choose. What could be a greater boon to humanity than complete health without any infirmity or ailment? Yet the idea of God, fighting for its very survival, will resist any technology that might hurt its old business model. It will resist such technology with all its available power. Religion may not be the idea-organism currently controlling most national governments, but it will use what influence it has to fight the acceptance of anti-aging medicine.

God would certainly rather have you dead than give up a monopoly on selling immortality.

Now, think again for a moment about the question we considered at the beginning of the chapter: "How are you different from a suicide bomber?"

Does some feeling of duty to a Higher Power make you think that having advanced medical technology that could give us physical immortality would be a bad thing? Would you reject using that technology for yourself? Would you try to prevent others from using it?

If your beliefs would cause you to oppose the development or use of new life-saving technologies, for yourself and others, how different are you from those who are inspired by some Higher Power to commit suicide and murder?

1
Evolution of Higher Powers

In this chapter we will take a detailed look at what Higher Powers are, where they come from, and how they act as icons for complex idea-organisms.

In the introductory summary, we touched briefly on the idea that such complex idea-organisms could not exist if people did not commit the logical error of bundling many simpler ideas into a larger construct – a construct that requires you to accept or reject the set of ideas as a single unit. We also talked about how attaching a label or title to such a collection of ideas made it hard for people to separately consider the various smaller concepts, and to spot the bad ideas. This is exactly what an icon does, only more so.

A Higher Power is an icon that stands for a group of ideas. It lends a face, a personality, and a voice to a set of ideas. It not only helps bind an ideology together, but it also strengthens the ideas by playing the role of a very authoritative source for the ideas.

It is a logical "Error of Source" to accept ideas from authority, without examining them, just as much as it is to attack ideas you don't like by criticizing the source. However, it is still a very common fallacy, and seems to be part of the way we tend to think when we are not being very careful. (See our chapter "The Art of Thought" for more information on logical thinking and common fallacies.)

A higher power can present an icon of seemingly unchallengeable authority. Such an icon does not just pop into existence, wholly formed. The icon and the ideas that it represents are shaped by an evolutionary process. Over time, the Icon may be described in slightly different ways. The ideas change slightly, as they pass from one human being to another.

Historically, this changing with each telling would have occurred easily in ideas passed down through an oral tradition. Once the ideas were committed to writing, such changes would have occurred less frequently. But major changes could still have happened in translations to other languages, or in new revised additions authorized by some authority figure.

> The most famous example of a possible ideological mutation through translation error is the translation of the Isaiah 7:14 in which the Hebrew word "almah" was translated to mean "virgin," thus describing the miracle of a virgin giving birth. There is much debate on both sides of this, and probably for all the wrong reasons – that is, the debaters are not really interested in the truth of what was meant in the original passage, but only making their own religious or anti-religious points.
>
> The word "almah" can certainly mean either "virgin" or "young woman," much like the word "maiden" in English. And one might think that on such an important point, the author of the text would have been clearer. However, in the context that this child's birth is given as being a sign from GOD, a virgin birth is certainly more likely to have been seen as a miraculous sign.
>
> In any case, whether or not this is a valid example, there can be little doubt that such mutations can occur in written texts as they are translated into different languages.

Even when the words of a philosophy or religion are written in stone, if they are many and complicated, they are open to interpretation. This interpretation then becomes the equivalent of a new oral tradition, with different preachers saying different things about their favorite bits from their favorite holy texts.

Where such small changes in ideas are allowed, evolution can occur. The stories that impress people the most continue, and those that don't fade away. The icon attributed as the source of those stories takes on whatever aspect conveys the most authority. The more people who believe the ideas and pass them on, the more authoritative the Icon becomes. The more authoritative the Icon is the more people will pass the associated ideas on to others. The end product of this evolutionary cycle will be a unified set of ideas that act together to be as convincing as possible, represented by an icon of the most convincing possible aspect.

The evolved icon will always be one that can convincingly claim higher authority than anything you could personally hope to refute, perhaps even the highest authority you could possibly imagine.

Bad Planet ! !

1.1 Biological Evolution

In this book we will discuss at length the processes by which ideologies and icons are formed and how they survive. This book is all about evolution, but for the most part, not the biological kind. In this section we will touch on the "Theory of Evolution" as it applies to biological life forms, but only to gain some understanding of how the same process applies to ideas.

Since 1859 when Charles Darwin published "Origin of Species," the idea of evolution has raised quite a bit of fuss among folks who believe that man was created in God's physical image. (They apparently believe that God has less body hair than the typical ape, yet more than the typical woman.) However, evolution is more than just the idea that we all have distant ancestors who had a lot more fur on them than we do now, and it applies to more than just biological animals.

Evolution is the observation that any set of replicating patterns will tend to adapt to outside forces.

Evolution is a very simple idea, but it is surprisingly powerful in allowing us to explain the world we observe. This is why it is not popular with organized religions. It competes with another quite simple and powerful explanation, "Things are the way they are because God wills it."

But there is nothing about the idea of evolution that really denies the existence of GOD or gods, it only implies that if GOD had specifically wanted to create a certain animal, the process of creation started a lot further back and involved a lot more time than just molding it out of clay and breathing life into it. The idea of evolution doesn't even deny the existence of one or more beings with the power to instantly turn clay into flesh, it just points to another possible path by which this can happen (albeit a lot more slowly).

Evolution isn't really even a theory, so much as an observed fact of life. There is good strong evidence that evolution does happen. You can even do experiments yourself to see it happen. But be prepared to wait a while for results – such experiments will take many generations of animals to show obvious results. (Bacteria and insects breed fast, so it is in these species that evolution can be most directly observed.)

1.1.1 Dogs and Rabbits

If you put a fence around a yard full of rabbits, and you put a hungry dog in the yard, quite soon the average speed of the rabbits will be somewhat faster. (There will soon be one less slow rabbit in the yard.)

If you leave the dog in with the rabbits long enough, and the rabbits are allowed to breed, the offspring of the faster rabbits will tend to be faster rabbits. This is direct evidence of evolution at work. Even the most faithful evolution-denying creationist will agree that these remaining fast rabbits will indeed produce fast offspring. In doing so, they are agreeing to an example of evolution in action.

If this experiment goes on long enough, eventually our hypothetical dog will not be able to catch any of the rabbits because they are too fast, and he will starve to death. But if you had a large enough yard and even more rabbits, you could also keep enough dogs that they could breed too. Over many years, some rabbits would become dog dinner and some dogs would be too slow to catch food and would starve. Over time, both rabbits and dogs would become, on average, a lot faster.

But something additional and surprising will also happen. Wait a very long while, and some dogs and rabbits will develop new ways to eat and avoid being eaten. Some rabbits will burrow into the ground to hide from the dogs, and some dogs will lie very still and wait for a nearsighted rabbit to walk close by, rather than chase after those very fast rabbits. They will become very good at hiding quietly, and the fur of some dogs might even start to look like the grass they hide in. Wait even longer and some of the dogs will be going down the holes to catch those rabbits that are hiding, and some of the rabbits will be climbing trees. Wait long enough, and some of the dogs will be eating grass, and some of the rabbits will be chasing and eating dogs.

Leporidae Grandidentatum

Of course these kinds of highly significant evolutionary changes would take longer than your lifetime to observe – in fact they would take many, many human lifetimes.

The initial observation, that the rabbit population gets faster (on average) when the slower rabbits are getting eaten, seems ordinary and obvious. The idea that this can eventually produce rabbits that eat dogs, however, is quite extraordinary and counter-intuitive.

1.1.2 Unexpected Consequences

What happens is that the same sort of variance in the inherited traits of the rabbits – that makes some rabbits faster than others – can also lead to unexpected consequences: Better jumping ability to avoid dogs can lead to reaching the lower limbs of trees to escape. Longer claws for catching those branches and climbing those trees can also be used to defend against and maybe even sometimes kill dogs. Once the rabbits are sometimes killing dogs, learning to eat the bodies can provide more food for the new killer rabbits. Within perhaps as little as tens of thousands of years, there could be saber-tooth rabbits that have learned to seek out dogs as food rather than avoid them as a threat.

Each increase of a given trait by the evolutionary pressure of one survival strategy, can lead to a new, unexpected and unplanned, survival strategy. Each change to the population is caused by the death of many individuals. In this way the collection of animals "learns" new abilities over time – but this learning is very slow. Each noticeable stage requires many generations of breeding to improve the animal. It takes many generations of increasing survival traits and reducing counter-survival traits before any perceivable advance in survival behavior is noticed.

Genetic learning is the origin of instinctive behavior as well as body design. But this sort of learning is very slow compared to the kind humans are used to.

1.1.3 Human Learning

If a human touches something and burns his fingers, he can tell his friend that it is hot, and his friend can then exhibit avoidance behavior. Within seconds of that first human being's encounter with the dangerous object, other human beings can learn of the danger, and they can communicate it to other people who were not there to see it happen, who can communicate it to still others, and so on.

Let's compare human communication and learning to the genetic method of learning.

Suppose a new dangerous thing, like fire, appears in the environment. Through random genetic variance, some animals would be attracted to fire, and some would avoid it. Those attracted to the fire, or not sufficiently wary of it, would sometimes burn themselves. This injury might sometimes be fatal, or it might just slow them down enough that something else kills them sooner than they would have otherwise died. Over many generations of this kind of natural selection, the species would then "learn" to avoid fire.

Lower orders of life, like bacteria, have less complicated bodies and can more directly exchange genetic information. They are observed to swap genes directly. This ability, combined with a very fast rate of reproduction, allows them to adapt to changes in the environment much more quickly than higher animals can. If you drop a small amount of penicillin into a dish full of bacteria – not enough to kill all of them immediately – within a few days you will have a culture of penicillin-resistant bacteria.

The direct gene exchange and fast reproduction of bacteria demonstrates the very best learning speed that genetic information can manage. However, it still doesn't compare to the speed at which a group of human beings can adapt to their environment. Human learning can be measured in fractions of a second, not generations. It is no wonder that this amazing ability allows us to rule the planet.

So, just what is it that we are doing differently, and how did we start doing it?

1.2 Ideological Evolution

I think that a new kind of replicator has recently emerged on this very planet. It is staring us in the face. It is still in its infancy, still drifting clumsily about in its primeval soup, but already it is achieving evolutionary change at a rate that leaves the old gene panting far behind.

-- Richard Dawkins, "*The Selfish Gene*"

In his book "The Selfish Gene," biologist Richard Dawkins pointed out that the human ideas are replicators much like genes and coined the term "meme" as an analog to the biological concept of "gene." Although the actual physical structure for the encoding of ideas has not yet been fully understood (unlike the well understood DNA molecule that records the genetic code), the analogy between biology and ideology that Dawkins made is a useful one. Ideas are certainly replicators, reproducing themselves from mind to mind. They fit many of the normal definitions of living things.

1.2.1 The Jesus Fish

Here is an amusing case of evolution at the memetic level: The fish became a symbol for Jesus for various theological reasons. Christians who wanted to display their faith while driving made a fish logo to put on the back of their cars:

Some people believe that the need for God (and his son the fish) was eliminated by the understanding of evolution. In the 1980s, some believers in evolution created a parody of the Jesus Fish image depicting a fish with legs:

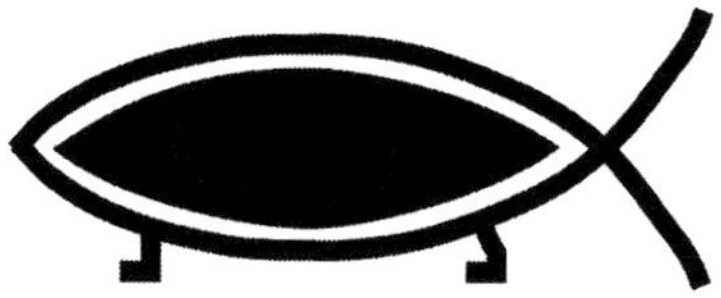

Someone else credited Charles Darwin as the man who first published the idea of species evolution, by putting his name inside the evolved fish logo:

1.2.1.1 Fishier Mutations

This started a whole slew of fish mutations, including devil fish, sharks, and this peculiar looking specimen:

This might need some explanation if you are not already familiar with the "Church of the Flying Spaghetti Monster." The church of the FSM was the invention of concerned citizen Bob Henderson in an open letter to the Kansas School Board:

www.venganza.org

At the time, the school board was considering the adoption of curriculum based on the theories of intelligent design. The argument was that students should be exposed to all theories equally. Bob's point was that if *all* theories should indeed be taught then *any* idea, up to and including Flyingspaghettimonsterism (his personal religious belief) would also need to be seriously considered by the board for possible inclusion in the curriculum.

1.2.1.2 Fish or Cut Bait

So now, thanks to a fishy idea that evolved into many different forms, if you want to proclaim your religious beliefs, your taste in food, or some combination of those two ideas like Flyingspaghettimonsterism, you can do so on the back of your car in the form of a plastic fish.

You can purchase all the standard fish at www.evolvefish.com and if you think up a new one, they might make it for you. Or you could learn how to make plastic fish for yourself. (Give a man a plastic fish and he has something to put on his car. Teach a man to make plastic fish and he can start a web business?)

Here is a fish that Sean came up with many years ago:

If you believe that Richard Dawkins contributed greatly to our understanding of replicating information systems with his introduction of the meme analogy, then perhaps you should decorate your bumper with this "Dawkins Fish" mutation. As you can see it is in the legged evolution family, but has developed a bigger brain for carrying around memes.

1.2.1.3 Family Tree

Here is a possible family tree arrangement of car bumper fish, much the way a biologist might classify existing animals based on theorized evolutionary relationships:

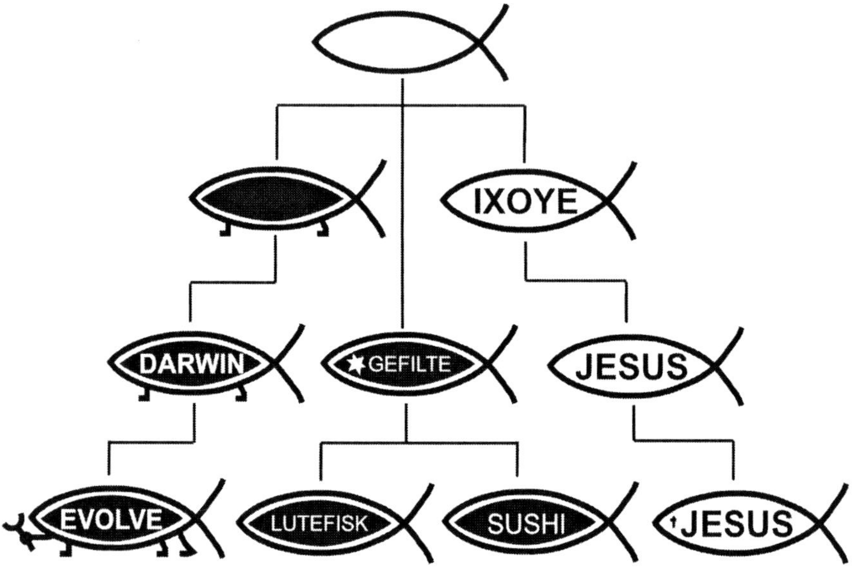

The "fish" in the example above seems to evolve in much the same way that animals on this planet have. You can clearly see three families, one religious, one evolutionary, and one related to food. This is an illusion. The Darwin fish is not a descendant of the Jesus fish so much as a competing idea borrowing memetic code from its competition. Believers in evolution borrowed the idea of a car bumper fish and cleverly added legs to make their point.

In the religious family you might find return salvos, including one with the Truth Fish eating the Darwin Fish. This is not normal biological evolution in the sense that animals of different species do not reproduce.

But it is a form of evolution. The existence of the “food fish” sub family highlights the typical evolutionary occurrence of unexpected consequences. The link between the Jesus Fish and the Food Fish family is the Gefilte Fish. This fish was clearly intended as a Jewish response to the Christian Jesus Fish. However, where Christ is linked in biblical scholarship to the symbol of the fish, the only well known fish in Judaism is an actual food dish that many Jewish people commonly eat.

Rather than continuing the religious battle of the religious fishes, this fish caused other fans of various fishy food dishes to devise their own emblems. Just like biological evolution, evolved ideological traits that come into being in response to one survival threat, often lead to new survival strategies and further evolution in totally unexpected directions.

It is important to note that many people who believe in Jesus, and might even have an IXOYE fish on their car, would also agree that evolution is a valid theory.

A whole range of ideas with constant back and forth exchange and competition exist in the world of ideology. The process by which ideological organisms evolve is more akin to bacteria than to any higher biological animal.

As previously mentioned, bacteria exchange genetic information directly and reproduce by dividing, rather than through sexual combination as higher animals do. Ideological organisms are even more fluid creatures – able to separate and recombine in whole or in parts. They do compete for ideological territory in the brains of human beings, but even that analogy isn't completely valid – as any brain is capable of holding contradictory information. What they are really competing for is not simply storage space, but ongoing thoughts and actions.

Ideas compete to cause human beings to expend their resources (time, money, etc.) doing things to promote the ideas. Sometimes this means doing relatively harmless things like buying a plastic logo and attaching it to the back of your car.

Sometimes it means torturing and killing the non-believers.

1.2.2 Survival and Replication Strategies

Your mind is a memetic structure, and your memes have certain reproductive goals. If you've ever wondered why everyone seems to want to tell you what to do, but no one ever listens to your advice, this is the reason. Your memes are trying to copy themselves into other minds, and their memes are trying to do the same. They resist your ideas (which would displace theirs) and you do the same.

Memes have evolved to resist competition from other memes. When people communicate, they are trying to put their ideas into someone else's head. People get into arguments when they have different ideas already occupying the same evolutionary niches in their minds. Seen this way, an argument is simply an attempt by the memes on each side to colonize each other's mental territory.

In addition to explaining why it's so hard to get people to change their ideas (even when it seems quite obvious to you that their ideas are SO totally stupid), looking at ideas as organisms explains a lot of other things.

For example, since your memetic reproductive strategies are different than the goals of your genes, there are often conflicts between mental and physical desires. This explains the mind/body duality that most people feel. Other conflicts, purely mental, may be described as conflicts between memes competing internally for the same resources.

Brains evolved to allow animals to react to changes in their environment. When communication of information between brains became possible, ideas began to reproduce themselves. That is, they became replicators of a new sort.

All replicators, genetic or memetic, are affected by natural selection, and this, combined with any inexactness in the replication process, is what allows evolution to happen.

For genes, sexual intercourse is the means of replication. For memes, communication between human beings is the method of replication. Memetic organisms have evolved ways of making them more likely to be communicated to other hosts.

Memes exist on top of the biological platform (without it they could not exist), but they have their own reproductive strategies. They may have a separate agenda from the body in which they reside, even though they still need that body to exist.

Idea-organisms cannot survive without minds to hold them. It is therefore not at all surprising that ideological survival and replication strategies are often (but not always) closely linked with the survival and replication of their hosts. In order to continue to survive and replicate, an idea-organism must influence its host to exhibit behavior that favors its replication.

The Idea-organism may adopt one or more replication strategies. It might offer its host some direct additional survival advantage. It might help its hosts get along and work together better as a team. Or it might just trick its host into spreading the idea, even where it is not in the host's biological interest to do so. We identify three classifications of memes based on their general replication strategy. They are called: Symbiotic, Altruistic, and Parasitic.

1.2.2.1 Symbiotic

The word symbiotic is used in biology to describe a relationship between two species that is mutually beneficial. Symbiotic memes are beneficial to the individual. They survive by making themselves useful to their hosts.

Because these ideas produce results that the biological platform identifies as beneficial, they are more likely to be remembered and passed on to others. And because they do, in fact, benefit the biological organism, the host lives longer. This gives the ideological organism more time for replication to other hosts. It is a symbiotic relationship.

Examples of Symbiotic memes:

- "Always look both ways before crossing the street."
- "Don't use lead pipes for your drinking water."
- "Make sure that doctors wash their hands before performing surgery."

Symbiotic memes can be very simple ideas. Since they provide human beings with direct benefit, they do not need to be bundled with other ideas into more complicated idea-organisms that try to hold themselves out as inseparable collections of ideas.

Symbiotic ideas can be considered individually, and are not afraid of the light of logical inspection. In fact, they welcome a chance to show that they are indeed useful. Thus they do not need any complex defense mechanisms.

People rarely get angry when someone disagrees with a simple symbiotic idea. There is usually no emotional reaction, simply logical discourse. A person might be puzzled that another is resisting a logically beneficial idea, but will not get angry about it.

If there is emotional reaction, this indicates that the idea has probably become bundled into some larger idea-organism, and is now a belief, rather than just a simple idea.

1.2.2.2 Altruistic

Whereas the symbiotic memes benefit their host directly, altruistic memes can be beneficial to a group of hosts.

These memes survive by increasing the availability of other susceptible hosts for communication. They ensure group stability at the expense of limiting individual actions – but do so in such a way that everyone is better off on average.

It is notable that these memes, as part of their replication strategy, will often call for special treatment of those who are guaranteed to be strongholds for copies of the same meme – such as the respected elders of the group. Special attention is also made to those who are most likely to be more susceptible to conversion, such as very young children.

All moral and ethical codes fall into this category.

Examples of Altruistic memes:

- "Thou shalt not kill."
- "Thou shalt not steal."
- "Do unto others as you would have them do unto you."
- "An innocent child's life is more valuable than a cynical adult's life."
- "It is better to give than to receive."

Although altruistic memes can cause individuals to behave in ways that are not necessarily to their immediate advantage, they can still be considered useful to individuals. This apparent contradiction arises from the existence of certain classical problems of economic game theory. Two such classic problems are "the tragedy of the commons" and "the prisoner's dilemma." We will not go into a very detailed description of such problems here, but we do suggest that you look them up if you are unfamiliar with these concepts.

The basic idea behind problems of this type is that there are often situations in which greater total value is gained by cooperation than through the expression of individual self interest. Or perhaps we should say greater good is achieved through cooperation than "unenlightened" or "short term" self interest. So, adopting such memes can still be in one's rational self interest, even if they sometimes limit an individual from taking actions of short term benefit.

To make this clearer – consider the first two items on the list of examples above. A society in which people do not kill each other or steal from each other, but instead engage in peaceful production and trade, will soon far surpass a society in which people do not adopt these memes. While any given individual might find short term benefit in killing another person and stealing their property, a society in which people commit theft and/or murder on a regular basis will never have the same quality of life as one where they refrain from such behavior. Living in a peaceful society is a huge benefit to all the individuals in it, the sacrifice of giving up certain opportunities for immediate gain is a small price to pay for peace.

The simpler an altruistic idea is, the easier the benefit of group agreement on a matter can usually be seen logically, and need not be taken of faith. This again is manifest in the fact that arguments against simple altruistic memes do not usually provoke anger or fear, only logical argument.

For example, if someone suggested to you that you could improve your diet by eating human flesh, you would probably not be angry. You would just point out that a lot of the benefits that people receive from being able to live in close proximity to each other would not be possible if people went around eating other people. Thus it is a benefit to you to refrain from eating other people, with the understanding that they should also refrain from eating you. (Compare this to trying to convince a Jew, Muslim, or Vegan that pork is good for them – you may well spark some hostility.)

Altruistic ideas are not quite as open to inspection as symbiotic ideas. It is often possible to logically understand that, although they may limit potentially beneficial individual actions, the collective benefit they can provide outweighs some loss of freedom. However, such ideas do sometimes tie themselves into emotional responses of loyalty and kinship. When this happens, altruistic memes can act as an anchor to start bundling ideas into a collective idea-organism, and this is when parasitic memes start to make their appearance.

While there is great overall benefit for each individual to be found in the adoption of a proper set of group altruistic memes, there is also great danger here for the group to take on a life of its own that has no care for individual values.

1.2.2.3 Parasitic

Parasitic memes are not beneficial and may even be harmful. They survive without regard to the needs of host or group. They will often attach themselves to more beneficial memes as part of an ideology. They can offer themselves as solutions to problems that have no other answer to compete with them, or they can find flaws in other biological or ideological systems to exploit.

Examples of Parasitic memes:

- "If you believe this ideology you will never die."
- "We must kill the enemy to protect our way of life."
- "Use our product and you will be more sexually attractive."

It is important to note that a parasite can produce results that look beneficial. There exist species of fluke (small flatworms) that parasitically inhabit snails. When a snail is infected it grows a thicker shell than it might otherwise. While the shell is a good defense mechanism, it has already been tuned evolutionarily to optimal thickness for the snail's survival and replication. The fluke, however, does not care about the snail's genetic goals, that might actually be easier to fulfill with a thinner shell; it influences the snail to produce a thicker shell to protect its own goals. If the snail starts to strain under the weight of the new shell, the fluke can always find other snails to infect.

Somewhat similarly, a country infected with Strong Nationalism may arm itself to the teeth, well beyond its real need for defense. This forces other countries to do the same, thus replicating the idea. If surrounding countries do not also arm themselves, when the strong nationalistic country's economy is straining under the weight of the additional defense, the nation can easily turn outward to enslave and steal from its neighbors. If all the neighboring countries are likewise infected with nationalism, bloody war ensues. The additional weapons might look like an advantage to any given country – but if nobody had them, everyone would be much better off.

Parasitic memes almost always need to hide inside a larger idea-organism to survive. When taken on their own, as a simple idea, they will be destroyed by logic. They must therefore surround themselves with a bundle of other ideas in order to survive. Sometimes they are even useful to the replication of such an idea-organism, but sometimes they just exist as a parasite inside an ideology.

The less directly harmful they are, the better they can get away with being carried along inside a bundled idea-organism. They become the equivalent of junk-DNA if they are not too harmful. They might be dead weight but it would be dangerous for any complex idea-organism to allow its component ideas to be individually considered, and this is exactly what would be required to root out the parasite.

The concept of "hype" is also a clue into the nature of parasitic memes. Ideas that sell the package without offering any true content are hype. About 50% of everything you hear is hype – this is because bullshit sells an idea and the more an idea is sold, the more you will hear about it.

Imagine two schools of martial arts. Both schools teach equally good self defense, and are equally good exercise. However, one of them claims that when you attain the highest levels (which only the master in Asia and a few of his closest disciples have ever supposedly achieved) you can do things that seem impossible. The other school makes only mundane claims about its uses. Of the two arts, the one you are most likely to hear about is the one with the extra hype attached. It's interesting. It makes people talk. Thus it does better in the market of ideas. In fact, it can actually be a worse martial art (containing fewer symbiotic memes) but still do better in the market than the more realistic discipline.

Parasitic ideas need to be helpful, or at least not too harmful, to the idea-organism in which they reside, but they can be very harmful to individual human beings. So long as they help (or do not badly harm) the idea-organism's chances for survival and reproduction, they can cause all sorts of pain and death to their hosts. Since pain and death can be good motivators for people to believe things, this can be exactly the way they are helpful to the idea-organism in reproducing itself.

In fact, as human beings have gotten better at taking care of their physical bodies, protecting them from biological diseases and parasites, the blame for most of the pain and suffering in the world has shifted to such parasitic memes residing inside complex idea-organisms.

1.2.3 Evolved Ideologies

While most memes behave like quasi-living replicating chemicals, they have also made steps towards evolving into higher ideological animals. These higher-level memetic organisms are sometimes known as ideologies. An *ideology* is a collection of ideas that work together for mutual advantage in survival and replication.

Some people, extending Richard Dawkins' meme analogy, use the word "memeplex" to describe a collection of ideas that work together. However, this is not as linguistically cute as the meme=gene thing, because very few people are ever heard to refer to a biological organism as a "geneplex." Perhaps a better term for a memetic organism would be "morganism," but that sounds too much like a religion started by a guy named Morgan. Anyway, throughout the book, we will be using the term "Ideology" or "idea-organism" to describe ideological (memetic) organisms. We know that there is no cute linguistic parallel for this word either, as no one refers to a biological organism as a "biology" or "bio-organism," but these at least have the advantage of being words that are actually in common usage, meaning roughly the same thing that we are using them to mean.

An ideology may also be sometimes called a *system of beliefs*. The word "system" is entirely accurate in this context – it is a functioning system tuned by evolutionary pressures. It is not a case of biological evolution affecting the structure of the brain (although memes can exert some evolutionary pressure in that direction as well), but a case of *evolution of ideas, caused by their competition with other ideas.* A "belief" differs from an "idea" only because it is included in this type of memetic system.

Any successful ideology will have evolved defenses that make it resistant to competing beliefs. It is easy to openly discuss the validity of people's *ideas*, and sometimes even change their minds about them; however, questioning other people's *beliefs* can get you killed. Conversions from one ideology to another are actually pretty rare, despite the MASSIVE amount of effort that some people spend trying to convert others to their way of thinking. (For example, we have spent a lot of time and energy writing this book.)

Again, *ideas* or *memes* are individual posits – mental possibilities that may or may not stand-alone. *Beliefs* are ideas that act as sub-parts of an ideology. Depending on the level at which an idea operates as part of an ideological organism; and depending upon the specific survival and replication strategies of that ideology; a given idea will be more or less resistant to change.

Evolution is a process that weeds out creatures that fail to survive long enough to reproduce themselves. In the biological sphere, this has lead to quite an array of survival strategies. The ideological world is no different.

Ideologies exhibit a wide array of belief structures that survive and reproduce in different ways. There are only a few basic ideas that seem common to all ideologies. They are, as might be expected, those most closely related to requirements for survival and replication of any set of ideas as a cohesive group.

There are three basic component ideas that all ideologies contain:

1. **Identity.** The ideology is (and should stay) a complete unaltered and inseparable whole.

2. **Morality.** The ideology is the *right* thing to believe – that not believing in it is *wrong.*

3. **Recruitment**. The ideology should be taught to other people.

1.2.3.1 Identity

Instead of being a collection of individual ideas, each of which may be separately evaluated for truth or falsehood, an ideology must maintain a single cohesive identity. This is such a common component of all ideologies that it has made its way into the thinking of almost every human being. It is the source of much erroneous thinking. The damage that this does to individuals is incalculable, but from the point of view of the idea-organisms, it is an absolute necessity.

If the human mind does not label a collection of ideas and treat it as a unit, the ideology cannot replicate itself as a unit. If the average human mind could pick and choose useful pieces from a set of presented beliefs, then no system of beliefs could ever evolve into a combined replicating entity, except where it directly benefited all its believers.

In biology, when two replicators work together for their combined benefit of survival, this is known as symbiosis. When the symbiotic relationship becomes close enough that the replication path for both creatures is the same, they can be labeled as one organism. The cells of a human being (or any animal) show an excellent example of this:

The mitochondria are an organ of the cell that has its own separate DNA. It seems that, several billion years ago, they entered another single cell life form, probably initially as parasites. Eventually they developed a symbiotic relationship, providing the vital function of supplying energy to the rest of the cell.

When this combination cell, called a eukaryotic cell, evolved into multi-cellular life forms with sexual reproduction, the reproduction path of mitochondria became so closely linked with the larger cell that it is considered to be part of the same organism. We can still see that in some ways the mitochondria are hitchhiking inside another creature, in that they still reproduce separately and make the jump to the offspring animal only inside the egg cell. They share the larger cell's reproductive path, but do not share the sexual combination of the host cell. This means that the genes of the mitochondria in your cells are inherited only from the mitochondria of your mother.

The example of the mitochondria is a good one to see how replicators can and do end up bundled together into one organism. It is a good example because the reproductive pathway is not quite completely merged, and we can still see some separation of the two replicating systems.

Something similar probably happened earlier when multiple strands of DNA (chromosomes) joined together to form the first single celled life forms. Each chromosome undergoes its own separate replication; however, they are all acting using the same cell wall for protection. They stick together as a group and divide the whole cell with them, thus giving them combined paths for replication, and allowing us to consider all the chromosomes together as a single replicating system – a single animal.

The way that human minds lump a number of ideas under one name, then reject or accept them as a whole, acts as the ideological equivalent of a cell wall. It allows groups of ideas that are self-reinforcing to become a system of beliefs that replicate as a unit – an ideology.

One might at first assume that a human mind labeling a group of things and treating it as an indivisible unit is just mental laziness; that humans just do this only to simplify the thinking process. However, it is more likely a factor of ideological evolution.

This concept of identity, acting as the cell wall around an ideological organism, is directly linked to the survival of such organisms. It is therefore plausible to believe that it is also spread by such organisms. It is certainly not an absolutely required part of the human thought process. Indeed, some human beings can be seen to exhibit it less than others, having the mental fortitude to break belief structures up into their component parts and examine these component ideas individually. (This is always the right thing to do.) However, this mental tendency to think in larger groups of ideas is reinforced by ideological organisms. It has grown along with their evolution until it has, to at least some degree, infected almost all human minds.

1.2.3.2 Morality

The second idea found in almost every ideology is linked to both the survival and reproduction of its collection of ideas. An idea-organism becomes resistant to outside attack when its host believes that the ideology is good or right – that competing ideas must be bad or evil. This also leads to behavior that is either approving or disapproving of others based on whether they exhibit belief or disbelief in the ideology. In this way, morality acts as both a shield and a sword – both protecting the idea-organism and making survival harder for competing ideas.

Morality also reinforces the concept of inseparable cultural ideas. Those who try to think a little deeper – to analyze each of the component parts of an ideology for their symbiotic value – will often feel like an outcast, with pressure from society to conform. They will give themselves away by not feeling a need to do the things that have no obvious purpose but are merely signal flags for the ideology: Wearing the right clothes, eating the right foods, singing the right songs, to name but a few examples of how idea-organisms have their hosts signal membership in the group.

Like the concept of identity, the idea of Morality has been carried into nearly every human mind. Nearly every human being has some concept of good and evil, and knows that their own beliefs are the good ones. But this is not a detailed, reasoned judgment of the merits of the ideas. Acceptance of any whole ideology as good, or denying it as evil, is a substitute for analysis. It's a fast, easy conclusion – a cheap substitute for real understanding of the merits and failings of the component ideas.

The idea of Morality can also be seen as an "on/off" switch for each ideology. It is possible for a human mind to hold all of the information of a system of beliefs without actually being a believer. The flip side of morality is immorality; one or the other is almost always present along with the information about any given ideology. It is rare for people not to have strong feelings about ideas – their own and those of other people. Rarely do people hold feelings of neutrality about any ideology.

Few people manage to ignore the higher level structure and consider the component ideas. This means that you can usually consider someone who despises a philosophy as a whole to be just as brainwashed as someone who embraces it completely. A person may know all the dogma of a certain ideology and still reject it in its entirety. It is the rarer person who can dislike a given idea-organism but is still able pick out the few good and useful ideas it has.

For example, an environmentalist might study the economics of capitalism but will see the underlying self-interest that drives commerce as being evil. He will understand capitalism but will not be a believer. The businessman may likewise understand the environmentalist argument but is not a believer. He could tell you what things the environmentalist will be for or against, and even understand why, but he would tell you that putting the interests of plants and animals above those of human beings is an evil thing to do.

In each case, all of the information of an ideology can be present, except for one idea – that the given ideology is correct – right – just – good – holy. And this idea makes all competing ideologies incorrect – wrong – unjust – evil – unholy. Once that idea is also accepted as part of the ideology, the information becomes active in controlling the behavior of the host. The host then *believes* the information, rather than just *knowing* the information. The idea of Morality is what activates an Ideology, bringing it alive, and turning a "set of ideas" into a "system of beliefs."

1.2.3.3 Recruitment

The third idea that is included in most ideologies is the desire to convert others to the ideology. The evolutionary benefits of the recruitment drive are obvious, as is the analogy to the sex drive in biological creatures. And here again, this idea has found its way into almost every human mind.

Recognizing this desire as an ideology trying to reproduce makes the world more understandable. It explains why people always seem to be trying to tell each other how to live and act. It explains why human history is one of violence towards, and torture of, people with different ideas.

The minimal level of the recruitment scheme is just that the ideology should be taught to one's children and passed on to the next generation. The maximal level is that one should go out into the world, convert as many as possible, torture people as necessary, and kill the ones who cannot be changed.

It is interesting to note that where an ideology has a weaker recruitment strategy, it often compensates with stronger identity and/or Morality. This makes absolute sense from an evolutionary standpoint. The ideology that engages in less recruitment must also lose less of its followers to outside recruitment if it is to survive. It must believe that its members are the "chosen people" and that its sacred texts must never be changed. It must strongly favor believers over non-believers. In this way, stronger concepts of identity and Morality can compensate for a lower level of Recruitment. This can allow it to survive, despite making its hosts a target for the violence that more strongly recruiting ideologies will often instigate.

1.2.4 Collective Ideologies

Once the right elements (detailed above) were in place for Ideological Organisms to hold themselves together and reproduce like simple one-celled organisms, the next step they took was one that had already been discovered by their biological cousins. They learned to work together in groups.

The multi-celled animal was an evolutionary leap made when individual cells – sharing the same DNA – learned to do different jobs for the good of a whole multi-cellular animal. This required that some cells be protected by other cells, who must lay down their lives for the good of the whole organism.

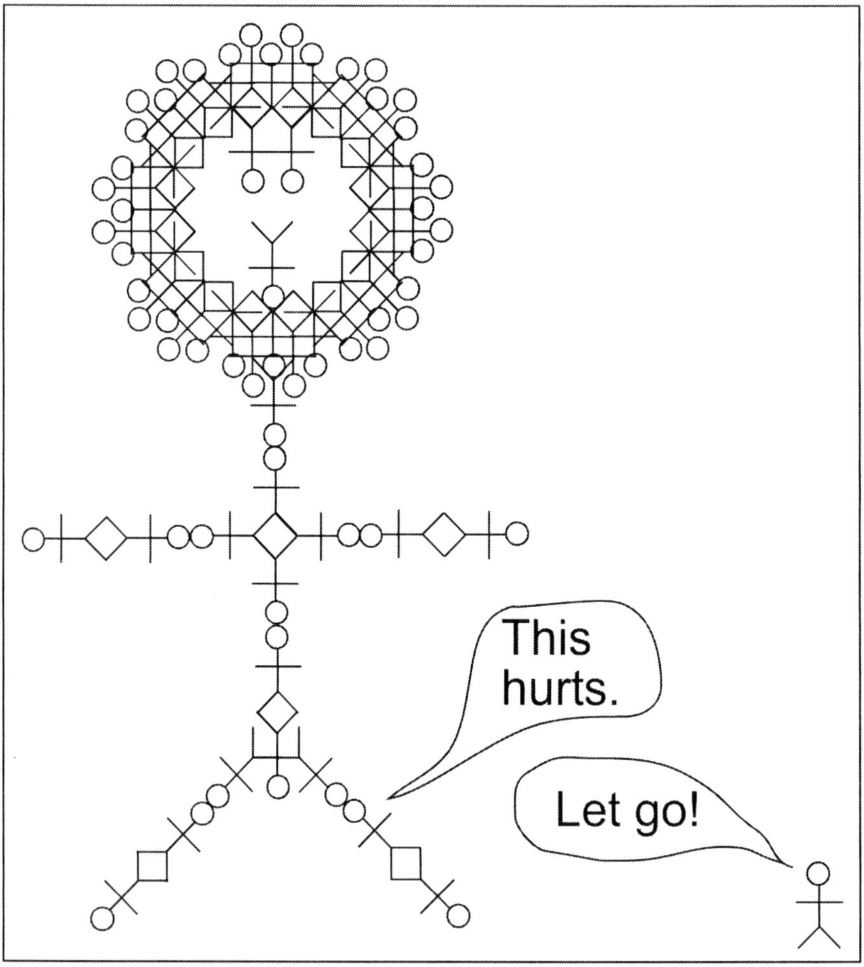

When just a few people stop believing, the Collective can get weak in the knees.

Unfortunately, in the world of ideologies, those insignificant cells that will sacrifice themselves for the good of the larger organism are actually individual people. For collective ideological systems to perpetuate themselves, people have to believe in the ideology enough to kill, suffer, or even die for the cause.

The pressure of collective thought processes is nearly always with us. Sports teams do measurably better at home with the crowds cheering for them than at away games where the collective pressure is for them to fail. When someone is upset, it makes those around uncomfortable too. There is a distinct mental pressure felt to bend to the will of the upset person and do what they want. If a larger group is upset with you, this feeling that you should give in can be almost irresistible.

In order to understand how such collective idea-organisms can get into our heads and make us do things that hurt us, we must consider the nature of our minds – how we think about things.

1.3 Identities and Icons

One of the things that human beings do with memetic information is to model the world around them. They create mental identities for the things they perceive in the world. They assign names and icons as labels by which to refer, both in their own minds and in speaking to others, to the things around them. These labels are used as shorthand to sum up a large amount of data.

Previously, we used the term identity in discussing the evolved survival and replication strategies of idea-organisms. In this section we will show how these concepts start out as useful tools for the thought processes of individual humans and are then hijacked by Higher Powers.

1.3.1 Identities

Identities are predictive models of behavior. If that doesn't make sense immediately, we're about to explain:

Your mind holds identity concepts for yourself, other people, groups, and even the inanimate objects in your environment. You use these models to help make sense of the world, to predict what will happen next, and how the world will react to your actions.

Such predictive models are a major function of the brain – maybe even the main function.

The lowest forms of life that have two brain cells to rub together use them to predict cause and effect. For example, a worm can be trained to navigate a simple T-maze. If it takes the right-hand path it receives an electric shock. If it takes the left path it finds a reward (or at least no shock if the person running the experiment is being stingy with the worm treats). Run this experiment enough times and the worm will choose the left path more often. In its brain it has learned to identify right as bad, and left as good. When navigating the maze it will have learned to avoid the sinister right path, having learned that left is right.

Higher animals (including human beings) have evolved huge brains with the ability to create predictive models for just the same reason that the worms have – but a lot more of them and a lot better. Creatures that can best predict what actions will produce which results can avoid punishment and seek out reward better than the others. This gives them a greater probability of being able to survive and reproduce, and thus these predictive traits are passed on.

Our world is much more complex than a worm's, so our identity models are also much more complex. We store identities in our brain corresponding to all the things, and people in the world around us. Starting as babies, we build up concepts of Mother, Father, Pets, Toys, etc. To some of these things we attribute sentience (the ability to think like ourselves). Some are alive but not intelligent, others are inanimate objects.

1.3.1.1 Things and Categories

The general concept of "thing" is at the root of the tree of identification. Any structured pattern of thinking starts with the "thing" concept. In language, the term used is "Noun." In computer programming, the term is "Object." Classification begins with the generic thing, and then divides into categories.

Each branch of classification shares the qualities of the branch from which it divided, it is just a further narrowing of concept. When a level is reached where a specific object is uniquely described, the branching ends. For example, consider a young girl named Anja:

> *Anja is a little girl; is a human; is a mammal; is an animal; is a life-form; is a thing.*

Working backwards, we have started by dividing "thing" into non-living and living groups. Then we have divided the living group into a plants and animals group. Then we split animals into a number of types including primates. Then we split primates into a number of types, including human. Then we split humans into adults, adolescents, and children. Finally we note that little Anja is a specific member of the child group. Bear in mind that we do this pretty much automatically without ever thinking too much about it.

This example probably makes things seem cleaner than they are. Child, for example, is a group that could also be shared by other living things, and Little Anja would actually inherit attributes from multiple other categories such as sex and cultural origin.

Here is a more complex diagram that shows the idea of multiple inheritances:

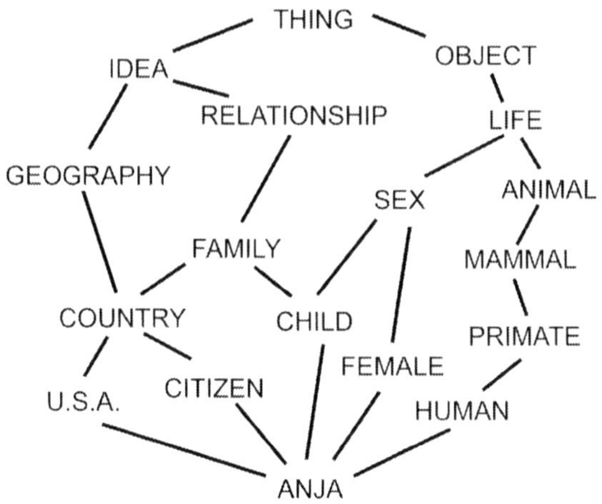

The main point however, is that all identity concepts start with the generic "thing" and move through identity classes that inherit from previous branches of the identity tree until a specific individual is described.

Everything in the world around us is modeled in pretty much the same way. This all points to the fact that there is no difference in the way the brain models the identity of a rock and a politician. The politician just has different modeled characteristics such as a control fetish and a larger ego. Both are examples of the generic Thing in our minds and share the same basic mental modeling structure to get from generic classes to specific instance.

We don't actually even know that other people have the same sort of intelligence that we do. In most cases it makes sense to give them the benefit of the doubt as they resemble us closely and exhibit similar behavior. But we cannot logically prove that they are sentient, since our only example of what it means to be an intelligent thinking individual has been self-examination.

Therefore, when we build an internal model of another person, we lend them our own concept of sentience. And if we can do this with our mental models of people, why not do it with anything?

1.3.1.2 Anthropomorphism

Anthropomorphism is the *attribution of human characteristics to non-human things*. We automatically assume that other people are sentient because we define human beings as being sentient. However, it is also easy for us to imagine non human intelligence.

Because the brain models our sense of self as just another instance of a thing, it is easy for us to project qualities that we only know of from our own minds into other objects. This allows us to imagine intelligence in a rock, a tree, an animal, or even a politician. While it may not be logical, accurate, or even useful to assign personalities to such objects, it is certainly a possibility that the mind has no trouble exploring. In fact, at least half of our children's entertainment is based upon it. We learn to do this from a very early age.

Often, the identities we associate with our pets are almost as complex as the ones we attribute to other human beings. We even build complex identities for some inanimate objects. They can seem almost alive to us. The more personal and specific an object is, the more it seems to have a personality. Does your car have a name? When it won't start is it being stubborn? We can lend a sentient identity to any object – even one that we know does not think. Associating a certain personality with a non-sentient is a normal way to remember that it might exhibit unpredictable behavior.

This seems to work, because at some level, sentience is associated with a degree of unpredictability. If you could accurately predict the behavior of fellow human beings 100% of the time, you would probably not consider them to be sentient. You would at least feel superior. You could control them by always being able to say or do the things you knew pushed their buttons. It would be like they were robots.

If you think about it, you probably apply the same robot prejudice to yourself. If you always knew how you would react to any situation, then you could write a set of rules that exactly depicted your behavior. If you did this, wouldn't you feel like a robot with no free will? In some ways, our degree of unpredictability is what makes us sentient. We are all too complex to ever create a simple set of rules, so we build more complex identity models to do the job. In effect, we lend a piece of our minds to the model we create – bring it alive with a bit of our own sentience.

You even create such identity models for yourself. In a weird self-referential way, you create your own self identity the same way you create an identity for other people and things.

1.3.1.3 Your Self

Just as the identities we create for other people and things help us model their behavior, the identities we create for ourselves help us model our own behavior.

We have a great deal of control over our own behavior, so our predictive models, in some respects, are also self-fulfilling prophecies. If you think that you are the type of person who would rush into a burning building to save a child, then there is a good chance that you will. If you don't live up to this self-image, you will either have to change it or continue pretending to be something you are not.

We constantly modify our self-images. How often have you done something and then said to yourself "That wasn't like me at all!"? When that happens, you are faced with the choice of changing your identity model to fit the facts or deciding that you will not do such a thing again. Alcoholics and drug addicts are told that the first step is to admit that they have a problem. They come to a "moment of clarity" when they can see things as they really are. They must be able to modify their self-image to fit the reality of the situation before they can do anything to change it. To some degree we are all addicted to certain sets of behavior that cloud our thinking in a similar way.

We constantly borrow from other people and things to make our own identities. We have heroes whom we try to emulate. We see people around us who have qualities that we admire, as well as those who have qualities we despise. We can imagine ourselves at our worst and at our best. Usually we try to be our best possible self.

To make matters even more complicated, we may have more than a single self-identity. Many theories of psychology have included multiple personality segments as an inherent part of the human psyche. Jung had us split into our ideal selves and our feared shadow selves. Freud said we all had an id, ego, and super-ego.

Often the group of people we are with modifies who we are. Have you ever noticed yourself acting one way around one group of people, and a different way around another? If you haven't, then you have almost certainly noticed this sort of behavior in someone else. This can be caused by a desire to fit into the given group or by feeling freer to act in certain ways with certain people. Our concept of the rules and preferences of the group is another sort of identity.

1.3.1.4 Groups

Whenever we think of a group, whether it is an organized religion, a country, a corporation, a club, or any other gathering of human beings with some common purpose or identity, we simplify it in our minds. A single human being is so complex that there is hardly room for more than one complete one in your brain (and that is you). Therefore, holding a whole group of people in mind, with all the relationships that exist between the individual members, is a daunting task.

When we think of a large group of people, the task of keeping track of every individual member quickly becomes impossible. Therefore, we tend to think of that group as a unit with its own individual personality.

If we are part of that group, the personality we assign the group tends to be like a part of our own. It is easy for us to think of how we resemble the members of the group. If we didn't consider ourselves to be members of the group, the group's personality would be more like that of a separate individual, and we would be more likely to note the differences between ourselves and the members of that group.

This sort of simplification is a natural mental process for dealing with higher-level structures. However, this way of thinking has quite probably either led to, or allowed to happen, virtually every kind of evil of which mankind is capable.

There would be a lot less war, bigotry, and genocide without first an "Us and Them" relationship. It would not be possible for people to hate one another based solely on the color of their skin without first creating a stereotype for people of that color, and then assigning that stereotype qualities worth hating.

When we meet a person for the first time (sometimes even before we meet someone) we start to quickly assemble an identity based on exhibited behavior. In order to do this as quickly as possible, we use ready-made group identities. We try to recognize what known groups the new person falls into, and use that to start a new identity model.

As we get to know a person better we continue to refine or even completely rebuild this model based upon the person's actions. The better we know a person and the more we use a specific identity model for them, the less we think about the groups into which they fit. We start to think of them more in terms of how they differ from our stereotypes, than how they resemble them. Finally they become an individual to us, rather than just a member of a group.

Separate identity models even allow a person to feel hatred for a certain ethnic group but still have friends from that same ethnic group. For example:

John White may automatically dislike and distrust any Mexican he sees, but at the same time, he might be fond of Julio Estrada, who lives next door. The reason is simple: John holds a negative model for "Mexican" but use a separate identity model for "Julio," acknowledging his positive characteristics.

The first time John met Julio, he probably started off using his "Mexican" stereotype when he thought of him. But as he got to know him better, a separate "Julio" identity grew and split off from that model. Mentally separated from the racial stereotype, soon none of the negative "Mexican" qualities remained connected to the "Julio" identity model.

If you asked John, he would probably tell you that he still does not like Mexicans, but if you ask him about his good friend and neighbor, he would say something like "Oh, that's Julio – he is totally cool." He might even use the fact that he has a Mexican friend to tell himself and others that he is not really a racist.

1.3.1.5 How You Use Identities

Imagine you are at a party, and you hear your friend Pat in the next room addressing someone as Sandy.

Your brain quickly creates an internal identity model of the thing your friend is talking to. But what is it? Is Sandy a dog? A computer? A person? Because the context is a party and there are many people there, you assume Sandy is a person.

But what kind of person? The name Sandy could be either male or female. So what do you know about this person?

Since Sandy is at the same party as you, it actually tells you quite a bit. Sandy was invited to the party, as were you. This indicates that you share a common group.

Your friend Pat is talking to Sandy, so Sandy is probably someone you might also want to talk to.

For the time being you can assign Sandy an identity based upon the group identity of "person who would be at this party" and refined by the more personal knowledge of being a "person who Pat would talk to."

You make this assessment quickly and without thinking about it.

You step through the door and find that Sandy is middle aged male, below average height, and with Northern European physical characteristics. You can now add four new pieces to the identity you are constructing.

If it happens that you hold bad feelings towards people of below average height, you may find that you already do not like Sandy. Of course you don't know Sandy, so what you really dislike is the Group Identity you have for people of below average height.

1.3.1.6 Echoes

The local identities that you have in your mind can contain their own identities. You not only store your images of other people but also everything you know about the images they have in their own heads.

For example, let's say you know two people well – Bo and Jo. Because you know them both well, you also know that they do not like each other. If each of them talks to you about the other, then you will have the following identities built up in your head:

- Jo
- Bo
- Jo's image of Bo
- Bo's image of Jo

Their dislike of each other is fed by the fact that each person also is sure that the other holds an unfavorable opinion of them. Of course they tell you all about this. So there are additional identities that you are exposed to:

- Jo's image of Bo's image of Jo
- Bo's image of Jo's image of Bo

Maybe even:

- Jo's image of Bo's image of Jo's image of Bo
- Bo's image of Jo's image of Bo's image of Jo

At some point this is just silly, but that doesn't mean that people don't go there.

The fact that you can understand Jo when she says "I know he knows that I think he's an asshole," shows that your mind is capable of storing many levels of echoed identity information.

So, the multiple levels of "he thinks she thinks he thinks..." can go pretty deep. This is particularly interesting when your own self-image is involved. One way to assess the accuracy of your self-image is to get an accurate feel for how other people see you – how they think you see yourself, etc...

1.3.1.7 Spirits

A lot of the ideas about the supernatural are probably based in the way our brains model the world. We already talked about how it was possible to assign characteristics like sentience to things that don't have them. It is possible to create such anthropomorphic mental models for things as abstract as the seasons, or as unlikely to talk to you as the sun, moon, or stars. People certainly have. Early religions were all about the idea that inanimate things had some sort of intelligent spirit.

Once you start thinking this way – ascribing spirit to inanimate objects – it is easy to relate personally to them. Is a bad storm a case of a weather god being angry at you? Does the sun rise daily only because you ask it to? Did that politician pass the bill you wanted because you voted for him?

The idea of spirit, as it relates to our mental identity models, could also account for some feelings concerning after-life. If you know a person well, and create a complex mental model for them, that model doesn't die with the person. It is all too easy to imagine that person still alive.

Perhaps they even speak to you inside your head? That complex model – which is a little piece of your mind that you have set aside, doesn't have any use any more. Maybe it gets lonely?

Our mental models are imperfect reflections of the world. Mistakes are made. This is not surprising and is no cause for shame. The best we can do is to "keep on keeping on" and try to correct any errors of thought we make.

However, some of the very worst errors of thought are not personal – they move through the minds of whole groups of people, making them very hard to correct.

1.3.2 The Distributed Identity

Let's begin this section by reviewing our progress thus far:

- Some identities you consider to be a part of yourself, representing either a model of your own actions or those of a group to which you belong.
- Other identities are models of others, representing people you know, or groups that you know about but do not belong to.
- All of these, however, exist inside your mind.
- Because we hold that other people have minds too (despite occasional compelling evidence to the contrary), we must allow for another (and very large) set of the identities: Identities hosted by other minds.

OK, given that, let us continue:

Some people know you well and will have good models of you; others may have flawed or limited concepts of what you are like. One of the stranger experiences you can have is to realize that someone you know has a very different concept of you than you have of yourself.

Some people know each other so well that they can tell what the other person is thinking. It's like they share the same thoughts. Often, the better people know each other, the more they influence each other. They become more alike through contact. This is because increased exposure allows the ideas in one mind a better chance to replicate themselves in the other mind.

When you model a friend in your own mind, you give their models extra access to your own mind. To predict the actions of others, you must understand their ideas. In understanding their ideas, you become susceptible to accepting them and incorporating them into your own mind. This is how you learn from other people.

When the ideas are good for you, this is a healthy process. When the other person has a head full of very bad ideas, it can be dangerous.

Of course, the people around you experience the same sort of interaction with your ideas. The more people you have exposed to your self-identity, the greater influence the ideas from your mind have on the population around you.

This extended effect of your mind on the world around you is what we are calling your *Distributed Identity.*

Distributed Identities are concepts of identity, shared by multiple persons.

When Distributed Identities do not encourage group action, such Distributed Identities can be thought of as public opinion or common knowledge.

When Distributed Identities influence individuals to act in the interest of the group, they create Collectives. Political parties, religions, countries and corporations are all Collectives represented by Distributed Identities.

Every thing that is known to more than one person has a Distributed Identity. Since language allows human beings to pass ideas from mind to mind, Distributed Identities are very common. To get a feel for how Distributed Identities work, we will first examine the one closest to you. That is your own DI – the ideas about you that exist in the minds of other people.

1.3.2.1 A Cloud of You

You exist both as a set of local information in a single brain and as a Distributed Identity across multiple minds and other information storage media. Every person who knows you has an identity for you that they have built up in their minds. This collection of identities is your Distributed Identity. It contains all the information about yourself that you have conveyed, through your words and actions, to the people around you.

You serve as a root or anchor for your DI. You are the best source of information about you, so you can modify people's concept about you, through your actions and words.

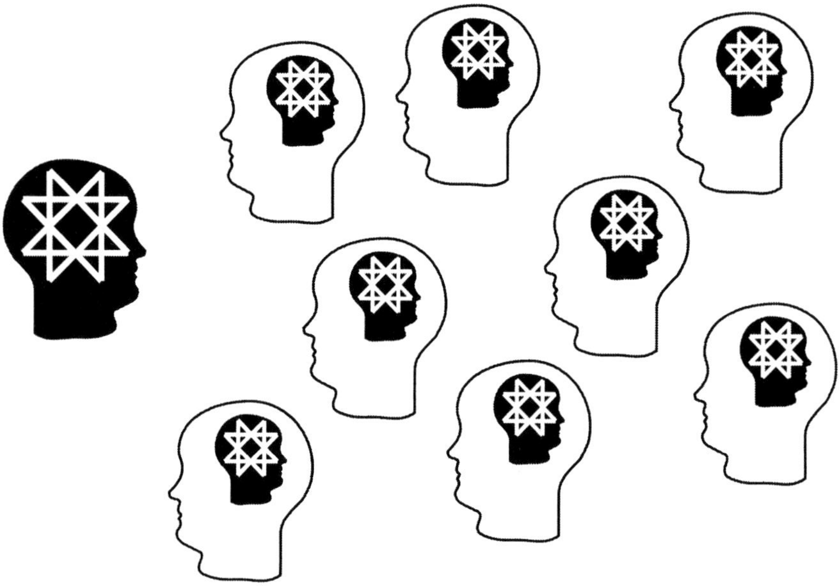

This Distributed Identity can also have a life of its own. If the people around you like you and want your approval, they will tend to act in ways that they believe will please you. In this way, your Distributed Identity can have effects on the behavior of others and make changes in the world, quite independent of your physical being.

If you were to die, and those people did not know, they would continue to do these things in hopes that you would be pleased. Therefore, even without your continued existence in the world, your Distributed Identity can continue to affect the world.

In some cases, the Distributed Identity of a person can still be around even when everyone knows the person is dead. This could be because of a sympathetic effect on people who knew the deceased. People often say, "She would have wanted it that way." As we mentioned earlier, this sort of thing may be how the idea of spirits and afterlife originated.

It could also be that the person's Distributed Identity has extended well beyond the set of people that the person actually knew directly. When identity information extends to people that the real life person doesn't know directly, the Distributed Identity really starts to take on a life of its own.

1.3.2.2 Fame

A person's degree of fame can be described as the degree to which that person's Distributed Identity has permeated the minds of people outside their immediate acquaintance. Because of the size of the DI, the famous person who is at its root becomes less crucial to its content. The public image of a famous person can often drift widely away from the root self-identity. The DI can almost be seen as re-rooting itself in other sources of information besides the actual physical person – hence the spectacle of people who are just "famous for being famous."

The ability of the human species to persistently record information in the form of written words, and more recently in reproducible sounds and pictures, lends itself to the existence of the detached DI. Books that a person has written or have been written about a person are persisting sources of identity information. In the case of actors who play roles in films, the fictional characters portrayed often have personalities widely different from the actor playing them. Fans can often confuse these characters with the actor's own personality.

The more famous a person is, the less connected their DI is to their physical existence, and the longer their DI is likely to remain in the society – even after their biological death. It is even possible for the DI of a famous person to continue to grow, and for the person to become more famous after their death. (Think of Vincent Van Gogh, for example.)

It is also possible for a DI to exist that no longer has, or never had, any reference to a single living or once living person or person. Group identities, as discussed above, are Distributed Identities. Numerous people share similar information about a group's beliefs. Those who identify themselves as members of the group carry the DI information and usually attempt to spread it. Those who know of the group but think of themselves as being outside it can also carry the DI information but they are not interested in spreading it.

1.3.2.3 Collectives

Some Distributed Identities exist throughout a population without causing any particular group action. For example, a huge number of people may have a picture in their minds of what Mount Everest looks like – it is tall, cold, and dangerous to climb. However, many DIs are about what it means to be part of a group or actually create a group of the people who have the DI in their heads.

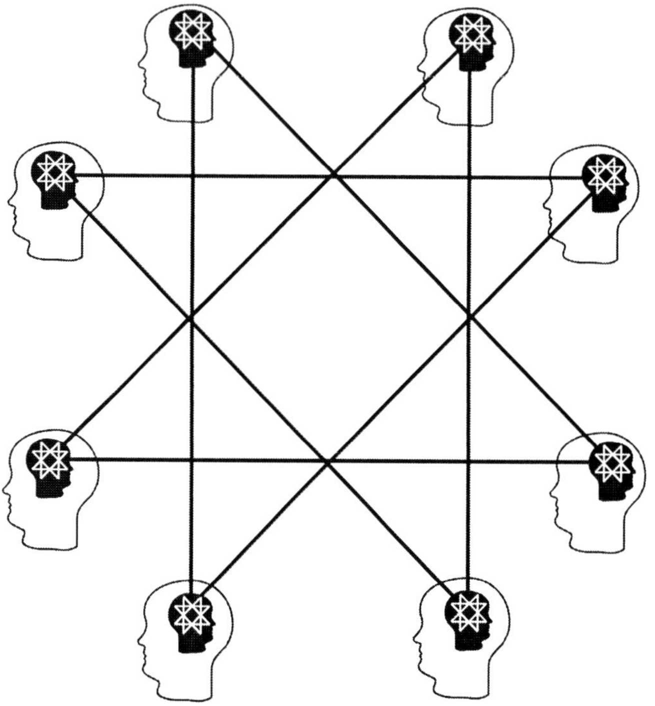

The DI of a famous political leader can invoke collective action. The "If we all work together we can accomplish my goals" ideas that the politician spreads are present in the identity of the politician and in all of the followers. These ideas can cause individuals to put the interests of the group and its leader above their own interests. Even after The Great Leader dies – the cause can go on in the leader's name.

A DI creates a Collective when it causes individuals to act as a group.

The parts of the DI within each individual become like cells in a larger organism that act together. With enough followers, smaller sub groups can form that act like organs in the body of a larger animal and each individual follower comes to be considered expendable for the good of the collective organism.

Collectives often present themselves as being necessary to protect us from ourselves. However, more human death and suffering have been caused throughout history by large scale conflicts between competing Collectives than could ever have been caused by conflicts between individuals. People sometimes kill and steal from each other because of self interest but it is group thinking that leads to theft and murder on a massive scale.

The simplest Collective is a couple, acting for "us," while The Nation State is a large, powerful, and often dangerous Collective acting in the interests of "The Homeland."

1.3.3 Icons and Archetypes

We talked at the beginning of this chapter about Higher Powers being icons for collective belief systems tuned by evolution to express the most possible authority. Sometimes such an icon starts out as a real human being whose Distributed Identity survives and grows, even long after the individual human being has died. Sometimes the identity grows from a general concept into an icon without ever having been a real thing or person. Regardless, the Icon is fine-tuned by the environment of human minds into a figure which represents a set of ideas.

These images might have once been real people. They might be fictional characters. They can be corporate logos, religious symbols, or flags. They can even be idealized images of sexual identities. (Think of Barbie and Ken). Identity images that strike a chord in our minds and command our attention are known as archetypes. Authors that write fictional works that contain some new memorable character have stumbled upon an archetype. Religious prophets whose teachings outlast them are remembered, not as the human beings they were, but as archetypical icons for their teachings.

When Christians say to themselves, "What Would Jesus Do?", they are answered by the identity concept of Jesus that they hold in their minds. This concept is a very different thing than any man named Jesus, who might have actually lived a couple of thousand years ago.

The actual Jesus may have had days where he was cranky and did not always have the right answers. He may have sometimes turned the other cheek and sometimes got angry and struck back, just like any other human being. The Jesus Distributed Identity, however, has no place for human flaws; it is an iconic archetype for the teachings of Christ. Both the Jesus icon and those teachings have undergone an evolutionary process to make them better at being part of a successful ongoing religion.

> Did you know that Jesus got angry?
>
> That he told his followers to take up their swords? That he dismissed the importance of his mother and his brothers? That he said God was away in a "far-off country"? That Peter and most of the Apostles were married and took their wives with them on their travels? That Jesus' brother James ran the church in Jerusalem rather than Peter?
>
> All of this is in the New Testament, but it has proven inconvenient for most versions of the Christ icon or the Church icon. Hence, you probably never heard most of these things... even though they are clearly recorded!

Jesus has grown into a Higher Power that is an icon for a very popular religion. This is nicely analogous to his ascending to heaven to join his father as part of the same complex multi-part being. In much the same way as your memetic/genetic division gives rise to the idea of a body/soul division, the evolved memetic entity that is a religious icon spawns the concepts of supernatural beings such as angels, demons, and gods.

A similar concept is at work in the promotion of status of certain human beings above that of mere mortals. The King or President of a nation is promoted as a living icon for that nation. The human being filling that role is still recognized as a person, but the role itself takes on the status of an icon. Heads of State throughout the ages have taken to referring to themselves in the third person, in recognition of this dual role. Heads of religions, such as The Pope, can speak either as individuals or directly for God. The office is a separate iconic identity.

In political discourse in the United States, you are allowed to have contempt for the man who is President, but you are always supposed to respect The President Of The United States. This illogical duality is an effect of the office of the presidency being an icon for the Nation State and the Nation State demanding higher status and respect than any individual human being could ever actually deserve.

Elevating a job to an icon representing the Collective can give bad leaders a huge amount of power. They speak with the weight of authority, and with the assumption that they speak for a much larger group of people, or for some supernatural force. Of course, the people who actively seek out such positions of being able to speak as a Higher Power are often not the type of people you would want to wield such power. They are probably not even believers – true believers in the Collective would probably never consider themselves worthy.

People should learn to be wary of all messages that come from such Higher Powers.

1.4 The Higher Powers

Religion is by no means the only idea that causes enforced collective behavior and individual sacrifice. God is not the only icon of such an idea. Countries, Corporations, Families, and any other sort of group you can think of, are all Collectives held together by commonly shared ideas. Such groups invariably have flags, symbols, coats of arms, and living figureheads as icons.

All such Higher Powers share a common nature: They exist as ideas in multiple minds and cause individuals to act like cells of a larger organism. They are evolved entities with their own agendas that do not necessarily coincide with what is best for the individual members of the group. They influence large numbers of people to behave as a group, and sometimes that influence can be hijacked by unscrupulous individuals.

In this chapter we have been discussing the Distributed Identities that arise from the models people create to understand the world around them. In many cases, these DIs correspond to things that are popularly considered real, in other cases they correspond to things that most people consider imaginary, and some fall in a gray area, with debate on both sides of the issue. Real or symbolic, DIs can become Higher Power type icons for a collective idea-organism and can sometimes incite violence against those with conflicting ideas.

1.4.1 The Lineup

"Number three - please step forward..."

Here are some of the Higher Powers that exist as icons for ideologies that survive and reproduce by co-opting human mind-space:

- God
- Country
- The People
- Class
- The Isms
- Science
- Conspiracies
- Race
- Corporations
- Family
- Couple

1.4.1.1 God

GOD (or a collection of gods) is an icon for a set of religious beliefs. God is the top level icon for a monotheistic religion. However, even a monotheistic religion will sometimes have additional faces for the same God, and usually also have many additional icons (devil, angels, demons, saints, and so on). A religion can also have an existing human leader as an icon, such as the Catholic Pope.

The collective idea-organism here is the religion, with God as the top level icon acting as the face of the Higher Power. God makes claim to the highest authority, the best rewards, and the most terrible punishments. However, those rewards and punishments are put off until after death. This makes God conceptually more motivating than any secular force, but with the weakness of being less immediate in that motivation.

1.4.1.2 Country

This has a dual application, to both your geographical nation and its government. The idea-organism, however, folds those both together into one semi-mythological entity. The loyalty we are inspired to feel towards our home Nation State is based on territorial and clan instincts. This loyalty is then co-opted by the government. (Think of God and Country as analogous icons, with church and government as analogous institutions, and clergy and politicians as the analogous leadership)

The Nation State has become very powerful over the past couple of centuries as geographical boundaries have replaced loyalty to royal families. At one time the leader of a nation stood as an icon of divine right of rule as a member of a royal family – now the leader of a nation is more of an icon for a geographic region.

Another icon of Country is the nation's Flag (Hence the big uproar over flag burning in the United States, which is often used by politicians to create a distraction issue.)

Like all Collectives, your country thrives on the feeling of group – of belonging – a sense that everyone born on the inside of a certain set of lines on a map is somehow one of the gang – one of us. But think about this for a moment. How many people do you even know? One hundred? One Thousand? Certainly not ten thousand. So how can a group of people that numbers in the hundreds of millions be “us”? For each person you know in a group that size, there are hundreds of thousands of strangers. Can you really identify with a group when you have only met 0.001% of the members?

1.4.1.3 The People

The icon of The People is different from the Icon of the State, but is somewhat related to the Icon of a racial group. The "Chinese People" includes people of Chinese descent, wherever they may live, whether in the political China or not. Setting the People of a nation up as an icon apart from the existing structure of the Nation State is a first step for any revolutionary change of government. This "People" icon was one of the primary factors leading to the First World War, and motivated Hitler going into the Second World War as well. It was also a major icon in the communist states of the 20th Century.

In the United States, if you are ever on trial for a crime, the case against you will read as "The people of ___ versus you." Unlike a civil case where some specific entity is against you, in a criminal case it is conceptually everyone in some geographic region that is out to get you. This must seem quite frightening to a defendant – having everyone out for their blood. Even being charged with a crime must be psychologically traumatizing, let alone being convicted and thus being put into the separate class of Criminal – an enemy of The People.

1.4.1.4 Class

This refers to social and economic classes. Such distinctions arise everywhere and at all times, as a result of people comparing themselves with others. The harshness of the lines of separation between classes has varied greatly from place to place and from time to time. An example of strong lines of distinction would be the Hindu Caste system.

In the Middle Ages, a strong class system made it impossible for a poor serf to rise to the class of nobility. Commoners were subject to one set of laws and nobility another. The United States specifically rejected the idea of nobility at its founding. However, more recently, different laws have been passed protecting politicians and policemen more than common citizens – the trend is for those who are part of the government to be treated as a separate class of people.

Marxism and its socialist variants also made much of the idea of class. In the midst of a time where upward mobility was becoming ever more possible, Communism still managed to spark many conflicts between the "haves" and the "have-nots." Thankfully the influence of Communism has waned in the wake of a couple of hundred million deaths it caused in the 20th Century.

1.4.1.5 The "Isms"

That is, communism, socialism, environmentalism, fascism, and so on. Isms are actually crosses between wannabe states and replacement religions. When they reach their goals, as in the 20th Century cases of socialism and fascism, they replace both church and state in one package.

Seldom do they last very long, but they are prone to causing huge destruction while they do exist. The isms tend to operate on the "revolution" model, endeavoring to take over and change the existing system rather than to birth something entirely new.

The "isms" also tend to flourish where religion has been dethroned and an ideological vacuum of sorts exists. In that respect, these are substitutes or replacements for the previous religion. People have a strong desire to believe in something. Wherever a large collective ideology has been toppled, you will find lots of new Isms rising up to try and replace it.

1.4.1.6 Science

It is particularly disturbing that Science can also become an icon for a Collective – a Higher Power. The basic idea behind the scientific method is that every idea is open to question, and that new ideas should always be given a fair hearing based on the evidence. This should make group-think impossible. However, human beings are so susceptible to collective mindsets that even the "scientific community" can succumb. This is why it has been said that scientific progress requires old scientists to die. It is also why the faithful followers of other Higher Powers will sometimes accuse Science of being just another religion – and they are not always wrong about this.

When science is being practiced correctly, it tears apart collective ideologies, keeping the symbiotic memes and tossing away the parasitic ones. But when Science is viewed as a single organism, and the scientists fall for this trap, it starts to be a Collective in its own right. Then it will start to make friends and enemies among the other Collectives, and the scientific method is thrown out the window.

In the past this has happened many times. Science has offered its support to many an "Ism."

1.4.1.7 Conspiracies

We might also call these "the enthusiasms." Devotion to any particular pursuit may qualify in this category – such as a belief in UFOs, mysterious old religious beliefs, conspiracy theories, and so on. These tend to operate much like the isms, but without any hope of rising to statehood and without requiring the overthrow of anything too large. One common part of Conspiracies is the idea of secret suppressed knowledge that is being hidden by more powerful Collectives.

Since the defining idea for membership in the Collective is often more an idea of being opposed to those hiding the truth, Conspiracy theories get along quite well with each other. Many of them can be hosted inside the same individual, and individuals with different conspiracy ideas can bond in their hatred of those other Collectives that are "hiding the truth."

Psssst! The government is in league with the Heinz Ketchup Corporation. They are hiding the truth about United States Defense Department experiments in focusing Chi (martial arts internal energy) using a design for the Ketchup bottle based on alien technology. The Defense Department is trying to breed a race of American super warriors, and every time a child shakes that frustrating ketchup bottle to get the sauce out, he or she is actually becoming a better and more aggressive potential soldier. We know that the prescription drug and oil companies are in on it somehow too... Don't tell anyone you heard it from us!

1.4.1.8 Race

Race can be a specialized group of "The People." It is based, firstly, upon specific external characteristics (usually skin color), and secondly upon a set of behaviors or characteristics presumed to be shared by the racial group. Race-based groups sometimes rise to the status of states and sometimes function as political pressure groups or to provide local enforcement or protection. They work very hard at compelling conformity to the group characteristics on the part of all individuals who share the race's external characteristics. This explains the American spectacle of blacks who are criticized for not acting "black."

The Race idea-organism is a good example of a Collective Identity that can reinforce itself across multiple, supposedly different, and perhaps even hostile groups. Hatred on the part of one racial group towards another race naturally creates a competing feeling of group identity to return that hate.

Collective Identities on each side encourage active hatred of the other race. They seem to be at odds with each other, but they are actually acting as weird sort of allies by helping each other recruit from a population that might otherwise be more cool-headed – less prone to racially motivated hatred or violence. One Collective Identity gives rise to the other. They actually need each other to survive and grow.

Pinks who espouse hatred of Browns serve to increase the Collective Identity of Browns. This stronger Collective Identity in turn serves to isolate Browns from any larger culture they deem to be dominated by Pinks. This happens even if that larger culture is not, for the most part, made up of pink people with ideas of racial hatred. This cultural isolation only makes it easier for Pink power groups to convince other Pinks that Browns are somehow different, and to be feared. It is a disturbing cycle – and the only benefit is seen by the Collective Identity of Race with all its many different colored faces.

Two groups playing off hatred of each other for mutual benefit to the idea-organisms is not unique to the Collective Identity of race. Religions and nations that go to war with each other receive the same recruitment benefit. Geographic nations are very similar to race, in that we cannot change our place of birth anymore than we can change which skin color we are born with.

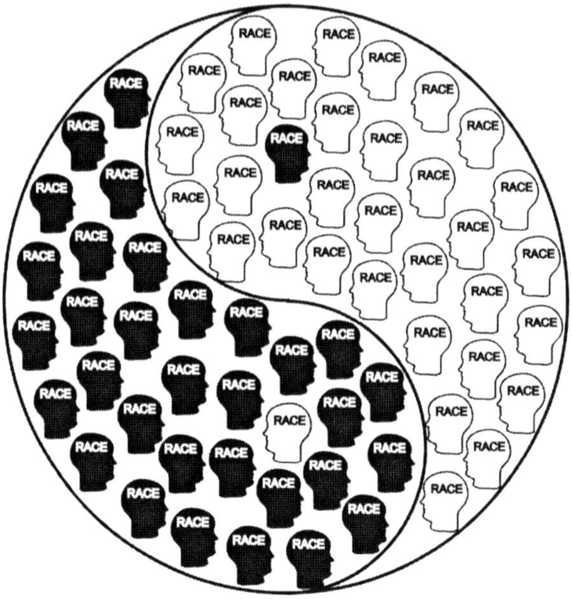

Using unchangeable personal attributes to divide people into groups, and then having these groups bond together in mistrust of each other, is an old trick that collective idea-organisms, under many names, have used again and again to survive and grow strong.

1.4.1.9 Corporations

Corporations are an interesting study. Depending upon a number of external factors, corporations function more or less as Higher Powers. The more open the general culture and the marketplace, the less corporations act as Higher Powers. But in closed markets and/or less-open cultures, corporations can have powerful identities. In Japan, for example, many people feel privileged to work for their corporations and attribute a great deal of identity and benevolence to them. In the United States, large corporations will also contain many people who treat "the corporation" as a specific entity, capable of rewarding or punishing them. Just like Religious and Racial groups, Corporations will do their best to influence the government for their own ends.

1.4.1.10 Family

The large extended family is called “The Clan” and until modern times it was a fundamental unit of humanity. Combined with ancestor worship, the Clan becomes a half-real, half-mythical entity with specific and unique virtues. As such, it can be a powerful Higher Power, even if only to a relatively small number of people. Clan-centered life is more or less opposed to the modern age, with huge markets and nearly infinite information, but clan groupings still work very well in isolated locations with small population densities.

Individual families can very occasionally reach the level of influence that the larger Higher Powers have on their members, but only with heavy doses of shame, guilt, superiority, or intimidation. The head of a family can become a powerful icon for members of the group, like a President or Pope. The size of a group does not always make the leader any less impressive to group members.

1.4.1.11 Sexual Identity

There is a Collective Identity associated with even such a broad category as sex. Biologically there are the primary sexual characteristics of the physiology of our actual reproductive systems and secondary characteristics of things like body hair, tone of voice, bone density, etc. caused by differences between XX and XY chromosomes; there are even brain chemical differences that may cause different behaviors.

These genetic differences certainly divide humans into two groups but this is only the starting point for entirely ideological Distributed Identities about what it means to be male or female. Anything non-biological that we attribute to sexual identity is part of such an ideological construct, be it the idea that boys have shorter hair, or that only girls wear dresses, jewelry, makeup, etc...

This would probably be the only example of a Collective Identity that split the entire human population into two almost equally sized camps, except that different cultures often contain completely different ideas about sexual identity. There are also some smaller Sexual identity groups that are not strictly male or female. Some of these are well known and tolerated in many cultures – while other cultures try hard to allow just two sexual groups.

As evidence that this is the same sort of Collective Identity that causes all sorts of trouble in the world, consider the reaction in some cultures to someone whose Sexual identity does not fall into one of the acceptable types. "Straights,” in some cultures, use physical violence against "Queers" because their victims' expression of sexual identity threatens their own definitions of correct sexual behavior.

In Nazi Germany, people of all sorts of alternative sexual identities were rounded up and sent to camps along side those of racial groups deemed "inferior," people who held to opposing political ideologies, and those with religions deemed unacceptable by the Totalitarian Collective. This is decent evidence that Sexual identity is in the same category as Race, Religion, or Political Belief. All of them are considered to be competition by any Collective Identity that wants complete control, because they are all examples of the same sort of ideological animal.

1.4.1.12 Couple

The Couple is the smallest possible Collective Identity. Any relationship can share behaviors that are only expressed between two people. The longer you are with someone, the more of your behavior gets defined by the parameters of what is accepted in the relationship. Sometimes you might want private time just to reclaim who you are for a while. When a relationship is ending, a lot of the trauma that you feel may be caused by this ideological construct fighting for its life.

1.4.1.13 Sub Groups

Most Higher Powers have sub-groups that specialize in one or more ways. Inside the God group are many sub-specialties and associations. Inside The State are many groups that focus on some particular aspect of The State. As noted in a few of the descriptions above, some groups that appear to be at war with each other are really aspects of a shared set of information that need each other for survival. For example, where there are only two common Sexual Identities, one for men and one for women, they are really just a part of one set of Sexual identity rules.

Each sub group, like the larger group, uses our tribal or clan instinct to make us feel better about life. Membership in additional sub groups can give us feeling of greater support. It can also make us feel better about ourselves by making us feel special.

1.4.2 The Self-Esteem Factor

All humans seek happiness – especially happiness with themselves. Probably the most attractive aspect of any Higher Power is that it offers its hosts (that's you and me) cheap and potent doses of self-esteem. If you are a Believer, then you are special. "Many are called, but few are chosen." You are one of the few, the proud.

Beyond the obvious God issues, nations always sell the idea that they have some special virtue that sets them apart. Many Italians think they are especially artistic. The French think their language makes them culturally superior. And so on...

Every political party has some provision of self-esteem to grant to their faithful. Most people hold to their political allegiance more for the self-esteem than any sort of rational conviction. In fact, if you feel a flush of anger when someone says that they're a member of the opposing party, then you can be sure that you're hosting an offended Collective Identity. Otherwise you'd simply note that you'll likely disagree with that person on some specific issues.

Once the self-esteem provision of the Higher Power is established, fear of losing that self-esteem becomes paramount. Externally-provided self-esteem operates much like an addictive drug. Not only do people become addicted to external sources of self-esteem, but they also displace other means of self-esteem. (The healthiest of which would be a reasoned conclusion – based on actual facts – that you are a capable good person.)

Once people accept the external valuation of a Higher Power, they are highly unlikely to go cold turkey. They may however, switch drugs, converting from one Higher Power to another, provided that they do it with intensity. In religion, it is a common observation that converts are always the most observant and faithful.

It is harder to build authentic self-esteem. People who accept the fast and easy esteem of the Higher Power are quickly addicted to it and will seldom go back to the beginning and start over. They feel they would be giving up too much. And not only is there the fear of lost self-esteem, but they also fear members of the old Higher Power becoming their enemies. (Often with cause)

1.4.3 Cooperation and Competition

Collective Identities exhibit various degrees of competition and cooperation with each other. Many of these ideological organisms can exist inside the same brain, and at the same time. They can sometimes make deals with each other that allow them to peacefully coexist, even as they compete for mind share. In fact, belief in more than one Higher Power often allows individuals to act more freely than they might if they were only host to one such entity. People with only one such idea in their heads can be very dangerous, as they do not act as individual, but rather as avatars for the Collective.

1.4.3.1 The Hierarchy

There seems to be a necessary hierarchy among ideological organisms. Come what may, one of them is always the "big one." Normally God is unassailable at the top but when one of the isms takes over completely, religion is likely to be outlawed and suppressed. Nonetheless, God usually reasserts itself over time, bringing down the new "ism" and reestablishing a more enduring God-State, Senior-Junior partnership.

Why must these idea-organisms be in a hierarchy? We see two primary reasons:

- 1. The surface reason is that these organisms compete. They are "programmed" to become dominant, in an effort to reproduce prolifically. They may also form partnerships with other idea-organisms, as in the usual God-State partnership, but only when that partnership is superior at maintaining a larger and more fertile population of hosts.
- 2. The deeper reason is that human minds operate on the "categorization" model. People tend to categorize every major data field and tag it with some sort of descriptor. They also tend to archive these data fields in a hierarchy of importance. (We again question whether this is an inherent or optimal condition, but it is the way humans currently operate.)

The lower collective organisms tend to struggle toward the top and to form alliances to get them there. God and Country (Geographic region) rule the roost now, and have for some time. However, both "God" and "Country" have changed dramatically over the years, to the point where the modern versions of Church and State would be almost unrecognizable to their devotees of several centuries ago. So, give the Higher Powers credit, they do adapt!

Also note that the hierarchy we are talking about can be different for different people. Any given person can host more than one Higher Power, especially where those Higher Powers do not compete too directly. For example: in the case of a church that mostly feeds on fear of death and a Nation State that mostly feeds on territorial instinct, a person can be both a patriotic member of their country and a faithful follower of their God. The hierarchy in this case is personal – if God and Country were sending contradictory messages, different individuals would have different top loyalties.

1.4.3.2 God and Country

The common relationship between God and Country is actually a very good example of how Collective Identities can both cooperate and compete simultaneously. In a market economy, people with similar wants and needs are competitors, and people with different wants and needs can trade for mutual benefit. In this same way, God and Country can actually coexist because of their differences, not because of their similarities. Similarities actually get in the way of cooperation between Collective Identities. (For example, governments and Mafias do not coexist peacefully because they both claim similar powers.) Even though God and Country seem to work in very similar ways, they can generally combine for maximum benefit to both because there are significant differences between the two.

Ideologies often use biological desires as handles to control us. The three basic bio-drivers used by geographic based government (Country) and religious group (God) are: Fear, Hunger, and Sex Drive. Refer to the table below to see the ways these handles are used. We are not saying that all of these are devoid of any legitimacy, only that these are the handles that God and Country have to use, aside from the self-esteem mechanisms discussed earlier.

	Religion	Nation
Fear	Heaven or Hell, Wrath of God	Foreign Aggression, Terrorism
Hunger	Dietary Code, Feasts & Fasting	FDA, Public Health
Sex	Marriage, Sexual Sin	Marriage, Family Values

Note that both God and Country tend to reach for the same handles. The government differs in occupying a single physical territory. Why? Because that is another basic biological instinct we have, and another biological need – we all have to sleep somewhere! National government has attached itself to our territorial instincts and needs. Religion, on the other hand, leaves off Earthly territory and claims heavenly territory. It offers life after death to gain our survival instinct as its ally.

Because of this, governments tend to focus more on man's external life and circumstances, and religion tends to focus more on man's internal life and circumstances. And, since heaven is generally considered the higher realm (even by 99% of politicians), God is much harder to destroy than Country.

And this is why God and Country tend to cooperate: The Nation State is better at the physical, God at the non-physical. When physical concerns are the greatest, the State takes the fore and is supported by God. At other times, God takes the fore and legitimizes the State – preserving it for future necessities.

When your religious and national identities conflict with each other, the resolution is uncertain. However, this can be good, as this conflict limits the actions that either Collective can require of you. You probably wouldn't let your government order you to kill your religious leader or brothers of the faith, nor would you allow your church to tell you to kill the head of your nation or fellow citizens.

However, infidels from another country... well it might not be so hard to get you to kill them.

1.4.3.3 Internal Strife

It is not uncommon for biologists to talk about the "wants" or "fears" of a particular gene. However, they are always apologetic about this, being quick to point out that this is just shorthand for saying, "The effects of the gene's expression are those which have evolved towards increasing the gene's chances for further survival and replication."

In other words, the biologists make sure to point out that the gene doesn't really "want" to cause a behavior in the same way that you or I might want to go get a slice of pizza, but that it simply causes a survival-oriented behavior because it has evolved to do so.

These biologists are wrong to apologize. Although the more familiar idea of what we mean by "wants" and "fears" is that of a human mind exhibiting desires, these mental desires are also the result of an evolutionary process.

The difference between a human and any other animal is that we contain ideological replicators. However, our ideas about what we want are no less the evolved effect of replicators than the desires produced by our genes. All "wants" and "fears," indeed all values that human beings have, are the product of evolved replicators. Some are biological and some ideological but the basic concept is the same.

There is certainly a semantic difference between saying an idea wants you to do something, and you wanting to do something because you have an idea. But if you have to choose between the two ways of looking at it, ascribing the motivation to the idea is actually a better way to examine the system logically. This is especially true because your "wants" and "fears" come, not just from your ideas, but also from your genes. Your desires arise from both biological and ideological replicators and the interactions between both types of replicators.

After all, we still observe the effect of genes driving our behavior, sometimes even against our ideological wishes.

Economists have generally taken the individual as the smallest unit from which values arise, but once you see that every value is the result of an evolved replicator, the individual human being stops being an indivisible unit. If you look inside, you see a whole economy thriving inside of each human brain.

Values are expressed by two different types of replicators: Biological and Ideological. Genes and memes struggle and bargain with each other for use of resources – and the outcome of these internal economic interactions become the behavior of the individual human being.

There is also a large factor of "previous choice" which is partially biological and partly ideological. Your biology has evolved to reduce such internal conflict by "hard wiring" neural pathways representing the winner of previous conflicts. However, in the interest of clarity we will leave that out for the moment.

Conflict between multiple ideologies and our biology explains why people are often conflicted. Humans, unlike animals, can very easily want contradictory things simultaneously. We have all experienced this, but few of us have understood the reasons as it was happening. This happens when different replicators exhibit different conflicting replication strategies, and compete for dominance.

Genes, for the most part, play nicely with each other. They are packaged together, and share the same path for replication. The ideas in a human mind, however, are not all bundled up into a single package, reproducing as a group. They can each be communicated to another mind separately, and this communication can be through our words or our deeds.

So, all of these ideological organisms are fighting and bargaining all the time for control of our words and our actions. This explains both the inner conflicts that people regularly feel and also the hypocrisy that people regularly exhibit.

1.4.3.4 Hypocrisy

When the replicators that govern your behavior are in conflict, and the behavior that you exhibit to the world is important to both, then the only choice for these memetic organisms is to fight it out inside your head. However, if one of them has a different reproductive path, then they can come to an agreement to behave one way in public, and another way in private.

Hypocrisy is most often seen exhibited in conflicts between biological drives and ideological organisms. Any number of ideological replicators can work together to set an example of a code of behavior that may go against the interests of biological reproduction. Codes of sexual abstinence or monogamy certainly work against the interests of our genes and produce significant personal conflict. However, both replication paths can be preserved if a person loudly espouses these ideas in public, while secretly following their biological instincts in private.

Hypocrisy is a fine economic bargain between two sets of replicators to divide time and resources between their respective values. It is a market solution to the conflicting desires of the replicators that inhabit a person.

Ideological replicators are probably always going to be hostile to each other in terms of public airing, and are seldom able to come to the kind of public/private bargain that ideologies make with the biological. However, private and anonymous communications do allow for hypocrisy in different communication forums. For example, a person who sings the praises of the Collective in public may secretly write nasty things about current leaders under a pen name.

1.4.4 Privacy

Without privacy, we would lose the benefits of the efficient solution that hypocritical behavior provides. Things that people do in private – and that they would not want to be seen doing in public – are the result of a compromise between replicators – ideological replicators that use a "teach by example" model for their reproduction and those that do not require that reproductive path.

Unapproved ideas use privacy to hide from dominating ideas and people often spread ideas in public that they do not really believe internally. It is part of the power of coercion that if you drive competing ideas underground, they cannot reproduce as effectively. Private communications, however, do allow the unapproved ideas some chance to continue to exist and reproduce in secret. Such unproved ideas may actually turn out to be better ideas, so to degrade private communication is to degrade progress.

All new ideas begin as threats to one of the dominant Collective Identities. Without private communication, many good ideas would be destroyed before they could prove their benefit to us. Private and/or anonymous communications are inherently necessary so long as collective force is being used to suppress new ideas.

This also points out something very interesting – it is always in the best interest for the ideas that have the best access to coercion to try to eliminate privacy. Those ideologies that are vulnerable to being destroyed by coercion will support privacy. But, they will always be in a weaker position than a user of coercion. That is, unless they can strike a public/private bargain with a biological necessity.

Then, since no ideological organism can win an all-out war against biological necessity, they must allow the public/private bargain to continue to exist – this means allowing privacy to exist.

1.4.4.1 Ideas versus Biology

One really interesting question is: Why are so many ideas contrary to our biological desires? What is the evolutionary advantage? Obviously, some advantage must exist, or the situation wouldn't be so prevalent.

One possibility is that Ideas that block our Biology, to some degree, take time away from pursuit of biological reproduction and yields more time for the creation of new and better ideas.

Or, perhaps such Ideas take hold during biological down time. Perhaps while waiting for the product of biology (that is, a baby) to make its appearance. The baby wasn't going to come for a while, so the brain may as well do something until then. Expecting parents who have said, "This baby will never come!" know what we mean here. Ideas evolve fast, and can gain considerable strength during relatively small periods of time as seen from a biological frame of reference.

Another possibility is that by controlling biological desires, idea-organisms coerce the acceptance of ideas. For example, if a male cannot get a female to mate with him unless he takes her religion, there will be a lot of converts. This is obviously an effective way to use biological drives in furthering the ideology. Biological drives can be used both as carrot and stick to promote belief of an Ideological Organism.

And, there is yet another possibility: It may be that idea-organisms began when men began to think abstractly, and that the human decision mechanism has not yet really been able to control them. (We call this the "inmates running the asylum" theory.) In this strangely optimistic view, once humans strengthen their self-reference and decision-making capabilities, the idea-organisms can be brought under control, and people will use ideas rather than being used by them.

1.4.4.2 Dueling Ideologies

For all of our complaining about religion (which we stand behind), there is one way in which it has been very useful. That is in overpowering other ideologies, typically The State, The People, and Isms. In essence, God can often act as a hedge against even worse secular collectivism. The fact that God is conceptually higher than any other icon makes it almost impossible to wipe out completely. While God is around, no other collective ideology can assert complete control.

Even in cases where the God-State alliance is strong – a different flavor of God than the one in the State alliance can act as a hedge. This works internally for the individual, making them feel good enough to pursue unapproved areas of growth and overcome peer pressure against new ideas.

Later on we will talk about how humanity makes more progress during times when different Collectives are in conflict. We will examine the history of mankind and show how a religion with a useful set of memes (memes being individual ideas in the "God" package) can actually make a great deal of progress possible – but for now let's just try to get a basic idea how this operates.

Remember... just because an idea is parasitic in nature doesn't mean that it doesn't have some useful applications. In fact, nature is full of such relationships.

For example, have you ever thought about standing up before a room of people, alone, and singing to them? To most of us, that is a very frightening idea. There is a great deal of fear and intimidation involved. What if you sing, and everyone laughs at you? Maybe it will hurt your chances of finding a good mate. Or, maybe it will make you less popular, leaving you at a serious disadvantage if a dangerous situation develops. In any event, very few of us would jump up and sing. And most of those who would may have a few less-than-great ideas contributing to their actions as well.

Now, this intimidation against singing is a very bad thing if you happen to have musical talent or are simply made happy by singing. So, if you are a person in one of these categories, you need a way around the risks of being laughed at. What to do?

The usual solution is singing at church. In fact, if you follow the life stories of American musicians, you will find that this is a huge theme. In the shelter of the God ideology, you are free to sing. In that situation, it is held as a virtue even if you are not very good. To laugh at someone "singing to the Lord" would be a sin. You are safe.

It would probably be fair to say that the majority of American musicians started this way, simply because it was the best possibility available to them. They start singing in church, then they move on to other venues once they have some adulation and some confidence. And once it appears to be a good reproductive strategy, the way is certain. But to jump right out in front of a crowd, without a hedge against collective disapproval, on the first day... not many would try and there would be a lot less good music.

Kind of makes you wonder what might have been if intimidation wasn't such a curse upon the planet, doesn't it?

Using one Higher Power as a hedge against another has been a very useful method for individuals to transcend intimidation. Transcending intimidation allows new ideas a chance to prove themselves.

1.4.5 Enforcing Mediocrity

One of the big problems with having the idea-organisms running the show is that they always prefer conformity. An idea-organism functions best when it is held by a unified group of hosts. When some of the hosts begin to differ, the organism is weakened and threatened. Any Higher Power, then, will probably act to enforce uniformity.

That means that as soon as one of the hosts begins to diverge from the norm, the Collective will work to assure that he or she is brought back into unison with the others.

From the human side of the situation this means that mediocrity will be enforced. It also enhances the sub-ideology of egalitarianism. (Egalitarianism is the idea that people should all be equal. Radical egalitarianism says that inequality is evidence of bad or criminal actions.)

From the aspect of the superior man or woman, the need for conformity means that ideological forces will push, prod and force them back down to the average level. Another option is to punish the superior individual by making them pay higher taxes or other penalties. If that does not work, they are likely to be shamed, exiled or imprisoned. Under the rule of radical egalitarians, such as communists, the superior man or woman is frequently killed.

For the sub-standard man or woman, enforced mediocrity generally means that they are to be the recipients of external support. This may be in the form of money, special attention, or some other form of support. However, in harsher situations, the sub-normal may be killed instead. The Nazis did this, as did the Communists.

Superior and sub-normal in the discussion above mean better or worse than the average in some respect that is both observable and important to members of the Collective.

H.L. Mencken famously said, "All government is a conspiracy against the superior man." You can see from this explanation why Mencken had reason to say so. All Distributed Identities are opposed to human variation. To a person with good new ideas this means the frustration and suppression of their talents, social derision, accusations of arrogance – sometimes even death at the hands of their neighbors. To the sub-normal, this means free money, pats on the head, lauding for their spiritual superiority – oh, and also sometimes death at the hands of their neighbors. (Standing out in a crowd is never totally safe.) But the general trend is to support weakness over strength.

Further strengthening the prohibitions against superiority is the emotion of envy. This grows from the human propensity toward comparison and a lack of self-esteem. Feeling at a disadvantage and lacking comfort in themselves, others envy the superior man or woman. This contributes greatly to the eventual punishment or death of a superior person who challenges collective beliefs. Never underestimate the power of envy.

If you wish to pity someone, pity the superior man. He is the source of all progress, yet everyone and everything is set in array against him. He is punished for his virtues.

You may also pity the man who is sub-normal through no fault of his own. (Those who are mentally damaged, diseased, physically miss-developed, and so on) The born sub-normal man is the victim of cruel chance. These, however, unlike the superior man, are usually spared incrimination for their differences. (Though in the bad old days it was not always so.)

The collective idea-organisms we are discussing function as barriers to new and independent thought. They enforce this by fear-compliance at the borders. If the borders are crossed, pain-compliance is next.

> Organisms want the things that they have evolved to want and fear the things that they have evolved to fear. Traits are evolved to fit a certain environment. Organisms, therefore, like to keep their environments stable. Collective ideological organisms only want what is good for the survival and growth of the collective ideology. They use the wants and fears of individuals to bend them to collective goals. The person who attempts to change some collective ideology must be judged as either a prophet or a heretic. A very risky business indeed, especially since the designation of prophet is quite often only after the person has already been killed.

History is a long story of the competition between new, innovative, symbiotic ideas and resistance from existing Ideological Organisms. The Higher Powers that evolved without these new ideas see them as a threat. Every new step in the evolution of human society can be viewed as a crime against the previous culture.

1.5 Take a Breath

OK, after having gone over all of this, we'd like to summarize briefly. New ideas need to be repeated to be understood. (Repetition is also a good brain washing technique – so be careful that you follow the logic. Just because it's in a book doesn't make it true. We are as capable of being wrong as anyone else.)

People often wonder why other people always want to tell them what to do. It might seem odd that anyone should care how another person chooses to live, and yet almost everybody seems to have opinions about the lives of other people, and many are even willing to force their lifestyles upon others.

Once you understand that ideas are a product of evolution, it all makes sense:

- Ideas are patterns of information that exist inside human brains and can be communicated (copied) into other brains.
- Ideological patterns act as replicators, similar to the biological patterns of DNA that control the form and behavior of plants and animals.
- The term "meme" (rhymes with seem) was coined by Oxford zoologist Richard Dawkins to conceptually reframe our understanding of the beliefs and values commonly accepted by members of a given community. Memes are cultural genes, the social equivalent of chromosomal genes.
- A gene is a set of instructions for making (mostly) proteins, stored in the DNA in people's cells, and replicated through sexual reproduction. A meme is a set of instructions for making belief or behavior patterns, stored in the neuronal pathways in people's brains, and replicated through imitation.
- In the same way that animals compete for physical territory, ideas compete for intellectual territory.
- In the same way that competition between animals leads to the evolution of teeth and claws, ideological organisms can also become more successful as they become more forceful.
- Ideas that were successfully forced onto people in the past are more likely to be around now than those that were not, and since they are linked to the use of force they continue to use force.
- Single ideas are analogous to very simple living organisms. Multiple ideas that compliment each other and reproduce as a unit are the equivalent of one-celled animals of the ideological world. Ideas that cause group behavior, making human beings behave like individual cells in a larger animal, are the higher animals of ideology.
- Religions, Nations, Corporations, and all other Collectives of human beings are the equivalent of multi-cellular ideological animals.
- Icons representing these collective ideologies further remove the component ideas from consideration or criticism.

- Higher Powers such as God, Nation, etc. are icons for collective ideologies.
- Just as the sum of a species' genes or genetic information is called its genome, the sum of a culture's memes or memetic information is called its memome. Just as a species has genes that promote its health and survival, so a culture has memes that do the same. And just as there can be defective genes, so can there be defective memes.
- Just as the emerging physical science of genetic engineering involves the identification of a species' genetic flaws (hopefully removing and replacing them), a social science of memetic engineering, identifying a culture's memetic flaws, removing and replacing them, may be possible.
- Just as a gene can help a species successfully adapt to one environment, then be maladaptive if the environment changes, the same applies to memes. A meme for totalitarianism might enable a culture to succeed in the Middle Ages – and cause its extinction in the 21st Century. Such a meme might have been tolerated by other cultures in the cultural environment of the previous centuries, but not now. A gene or a meme can also appear for one reason and find new ways of being useful as environments change.
- A genetic flaw can prevent an organism from being healthy, can cause its death and, if spread across its species, can cause an extinction. A memetic flaw can do the same for members of a culture and the culture itself.

One of Christianity's foundational memes as a social institution is Jesus' dictum, "Render unto Caesar what is Caesar's and unto God what is God's" (Matthew 22:17, Luke 20:25). Such a meme argues against a Christian totalitarianism and allows Christianity and secular governments to exist in tandem. This coexistence of Higher Powers has left "in-between" space for a lot more individual freedom than has existed in cultures where governments are dominated by religion, or by philosophies such as communism that do not make room for religion.

The United States of America is a country that was founded by many different groups fleeing religious persecution. This led to the establishment of strict controls to protect religion from government and also to protect government from the other guy's religion. This idea of separation of powers was even included inside the government, with different parts of the government balanced against each other. This resulted in economic benefits on a scale never before seen. None of this would have been possible without the Christian meme of the separation of Higher Powers.

Lacking this separation of Higher Powers meme is a memetic flaw of Islam. (At least from the point of view of the Individual.) Muhammad, in the name of Allah, argues forthrightly for Islamic totalitarianism. There are no words in classical Arabic allowing a conceptual distinction between the religious and the secular. For Muhammad as for Lenin, "Nothing is private." This memetic defect results in Arab culture being suffocated by religious dictatorships.

With these concepts in mind, we will now take a short look at the history of mankind with a focus on the evolution of idea-organisms.

2
A Brief History of Crime

In a funny sort of way, our thesis in this book confirms an old philosophical theory called dualism. Dualism said that man's mind and body were opposed to one another. Some dualists went so far as to say that the body was unchangeably evil and the mind good. We are not at all authorizing these ideas, but in a different way we are saying that the body and mind are often opposed. Not that they have to be, but that they often are.

As we've said (many times at this point), we humans have two separate types of replicating systems: Our bodies and our ideas. Bodies replicate via sexual recombination of DNA and ideas replicate via communication. Both are necessary for us to be the creatures we are but the two forms of replication are radically different, especially in the speeds at which they are capable of evolving.

Our bodies are very stable. Physical changes to the human animal take place only over long periods of time. The standard model for body changes is evolution – very slow, gradual changing. In fact, there have been no identifiable changes to the human body within recorded history. Biological replication systems evolve very slowly. There have been many significant functional improvements in the past hundred years or so (longer life-spans, people growing larger, stronger and smarter), but these have resulted from better nutrition and medicine, not from biological evolution.

Our ideas, on the other hand, change very, very rapidly. (Well, maybe not for Baby Boomers and politicians...) In fact, the history of mankind is really a story of ideas evolving. The major events of history are clashes between different collective ideological organisms, under the guise of Higher Powers, struggling to control the minds of the people.

Ideological organisms do care about human bodies, but only as if they were a herd of animals. In other words, Distributed Idea-organisms care about maintaining a functional group of hosts, but care very little about any specific individual. This would be similar to how a bee-keeper cares about his bees. He cares a great deal about keeping the hives growing and thriving (that's how he feeds his family), but not very much about any individual bee. So, when Distributed Idea-organisms find it necessary to compete, they are willing to sacrifice their hosts. And since this competition actually occurs in human minds, people kill each other over ideas.

When a combative idea-organism cannot get people to convert, killing them is the next choice. After all, their goal is to defeat the contrary ideas that they host. If a Higher Power can not take over the host bodies of its rivals, it can still destroy those bodies and take the other available resources – land, food, and other personal property. From the Collective's point of view, new bodies can always be created provided there is a place for them to live and food enough to feed them.

In this chapter we will start at the beginning, with theories about how it all started, and a look at history as it might be told from the viewpoint of Ideological Evolution.

2.1 Down from the Trees

We seem to be very unique creatures on the planet Earth, not just currently, but as far back as we can tell. In the entire history of the planet, archaeologists can find no evidence of any type of culture, aside from that of human beings and their ancestral cousins. We find no evidence that any other creature on this planet has ever been able to deal with ideas as we have. While other creatures operate on in-born instinct, we are constantly modifying ideas and strategies.

The odd thing is that we have yet to find evidence of Homo sapiens (that's us) doing these sorts of things more than 30,000 years ago. That's weird because we have found much older human remains, and they really don't seem much different than us. There are many possible explanations for this, but we really can't say for sure.

It is possible that extremely ancient humans were not the same sort of divided – biological and ideological – creatures that we are today. There were various human-looking creatures before that time, but no real evidence that they had capabilities much beyond that of our closest living cousins, the chimpanzees. If they were completely like us, we would expect to find the same types of things we create: Tools, dwellings, furniture, monuments, art, and so on.

In any event, it is pretty certain that humans (or near-humans) have been on Earth for several million years. It may seem strange that human beings only developed serious mental abilities in the fairly recent past, but that is because we are so familiar with what we are now. That doesn't mean creatures that looked like us were always that way. And a couple of million years is not much in terms of the development of life upon Earth; higher multi-celled animals have existed for 600 million years.

Not only do we have ancestors, who were not so bright, but we also have close cousins existing on this planet with us today, and none of them exhibit the same ability to manipulate ideas that we do. (Well, at least you can pick your friends...)

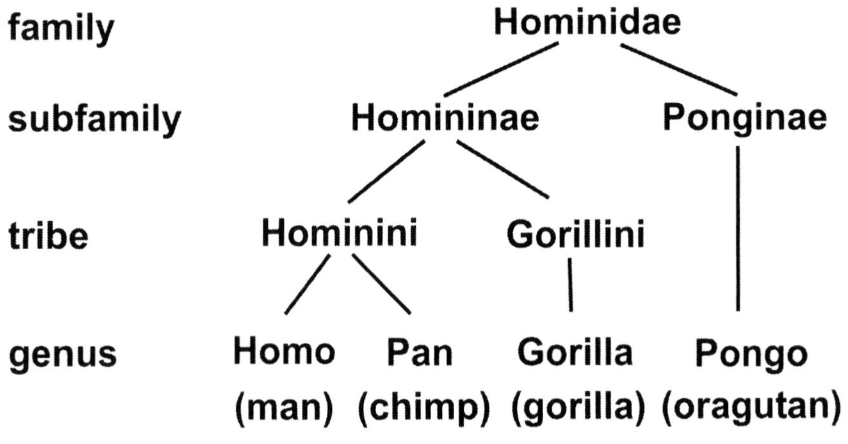

It is obvious that our thinking and linguistic abilities have given us a huge competitive advantage over all other species. We must therefore presume that evolving the biological mechanisms for hosting ideological information is quite a difficult leap to make, or it would have happened much sooner in the history of the planet.

We have only been "doing that voodoo that we do so well" for less than one ten-thousandth of the time that animals with brains quite similar to our own have existed.

What allowed us to become so different than our closest cousins and ancestors? Let's look at our family history, and see what might have happened.

2.1.1 Tribe Hominini

Early human like creatures stand out from their closest cousins, modern chimpanzees and their ancestors, in many ways. Many of our current differences from Chimpanzees and other apes, such as relative hairlessness, breath control, fat layer under all the skin, slight webbing of the fingers, etc., are shared with many aquatic mammals. This has caused some to theorize that human beings had a semi aquatic ancestor. This might also explain our upright posture as an original adaptation to keep our heads above water with our feet on the ground in shallow water. However, many other scientists are convinced that the upright gait was an adaptation to traveling long distances across arid plains and dismiss our similarities to aquatic animals as coincidence or suggest that these adaptations appeared later in human evolution.

Whatever the cause, our ancestors' body shape changed to one that allowed them to walk comfortably on two legs. This may have slowed down our top running speed, but it increased our ability to cover great distances, increased our range of vision, freed our front limbs for carrying things, and generally provided greater evolutionary advantage than the loss of speed over short distances.

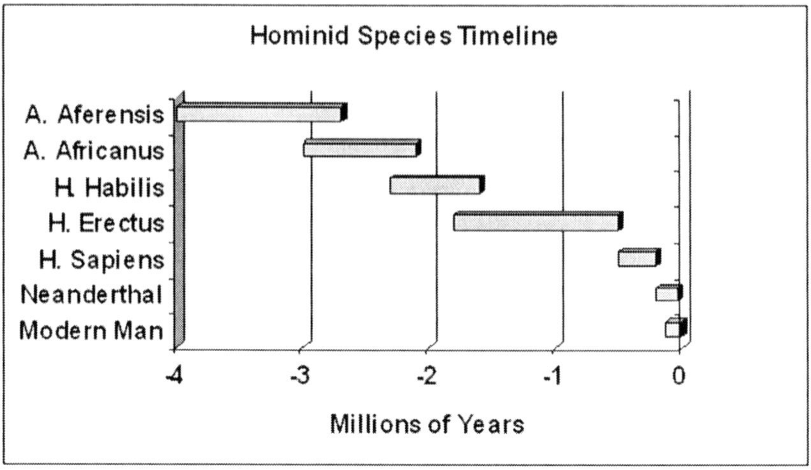

The "A" in front of the first two ancestors on the chart stands for Australopithecines, a type of hominid that developed as early as 5 million years ago, walked upright and probably carried sticks and rocks for use as tools and weapons. They were quite similar to humans in body shape, with their skull shape and brain size being the major difference between their bodies and ours. Their adult brain size was little bigger than 1/3 of a modern day human brain.

They may have used found objects as tools, but they probably did not manufacture tools for specific needs.

2.1.2 Genus Homo

As early as two million years ago, Homo habilis is our first ancestor who is confirmed to have manufactured tools, rather than just using found objects. Although there is no reason to believe that these ancestors were very much smarter than modern day chimpanzees, some would consider this first manufacturing of primitive tools to be the "dawn of man." The anthropological genus (group) "homo" (meaning "like us") indicates thinking along those lines when the Latin names were being handed out.

This was also the approximate start of the ice ages. It is not clear what early man did to change the climate. (After all, if the weather changes, it has to be someone's fault, right?) There is no real evidence that our ancestors had even yet discovered fire, or the wheel, so the theory that this extreme climate change was caused by Carbon dioxide emissions from their Sports Utility Vehicles seems... uh... unlikely. According to many biblical scholars, the universe had not even been created yet, so it probably wasn't because Genus Homo had done anything to invoke the wrath of GOD.

Maybe it is just a coincidence that the "dawn of man" happened at the same time as a massive shift in our global climate, or maybe it was part of the cause for our development. Whatever the cause, not too long into the cycle of the ongoing global freezes and thaws, Homo habilis gave way to Homo erectus, and the hominid brain started to get a lot bigger.

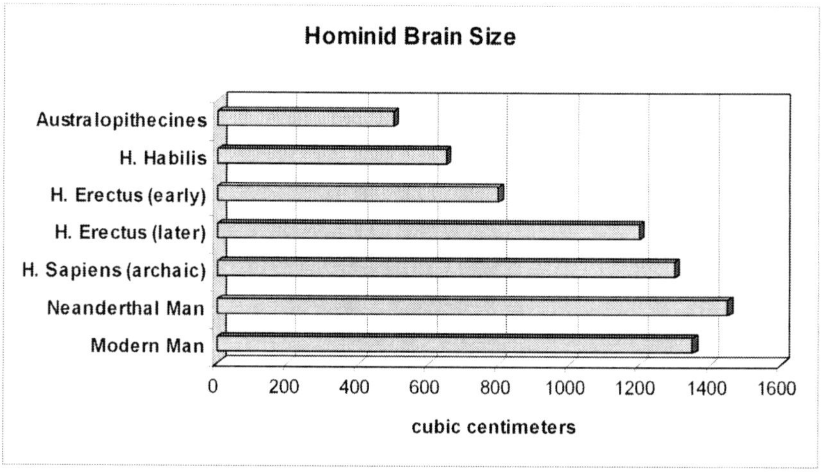

Homo erectus was an even better tool maker than Homo habilis and he quickly learned how to make stone axes. (There may even still have been a genetic component to it, like a beaver building a dam.) These axes are not the modern versions we think of today with a handle and head, but merely certain types of rocks that could be carefully broken off in flakes that produced a good edge. He may not have been conscious of why he did it in anything like the way modern man can evaluate his actions. But, he certainly made a lot of axes, and got very good at it. In fact he got so good at making stone axes and made so many of them that some scientists have concluded that he was doing it to impress chicks. Seriously. The theory is that the guy who could make the best hand axes would get the best mates.

According to Dr. Marek Kohn and Dr. Steven Mithen in an essay entitled, "*Hand-axes: Products of sexual selection?*" stone hand-axe making became what biologists call a sexual selection trait:

> *"We propose that hand-axes functioned not just to butcher animals or process plants but as Zahavian handicaps, indicating 'good genes'. Those hominids (male or female, see below) who were able to make fine symmetrical hand-axes may have been preferentially chosen by the opposite sex as mates. Just as a peacock's tail may reliably indicate its 'success', so might the manufacture of a fine symmetrical hand-axe have been a reliable indicator of the hominid's ability to secure food, find shelter, escape from predation and compete successfully within the social group. Such hominids would have been attractive mates, their abilities indicating 'good genes'."*

2.1.2.1 Sexual Selection

The most commonly used example of a sexual selection trait is the peacock's tail. It is much longer than it needs to be for any useful survival purpose, and it's a good bet that many a peacock has been eaten because its tail was long enough for a predator to catch before it could get away. One would expect natural selection to shorten the peacock's tail. However, sexual selection overrides natural selection. You see the peahen has decided that she will only mate with males that have a flashy tail (like girls who only date a man if he has a really nice car). This sexual selection pressure can lead to traits that seem to be counter to survival, but it can actually be good for the species.

The logic of an annoyingly long tail that lets predators have a better shot at you, but gets you the babes, is that by growing it you are demonstrating your fitness in all other respects. To sport the longest tail, you have to be the strongest, fastest, meanest peacock around to still be alive. This means your offspring will also be more fit, both the males and females. Only the males take this genetic risk, and that is ok from the standpoint of the species, as one live male can easily service the needs of four or five females in a season, giving them all offspring. So if four out of five males die in this sort of competition, and the one that remains has the best genes, things still work out well for the species as a whole. (That is, for the genetic replicators).

2.1.2.2 It Went to their Heads

So, according to this theory, if a male of Species H. Erectus wanted to impress the ladies, every day he would collect the necessary materials to make a new axe. What he was demonstrating then was that he was so good at procuring materials that he could make a new axe anytime and just throw his old one away. Also, the quality of the axe he made was an indication of how well his brain worked, which would have demonstrated further superiority.

STONE HAND AXES

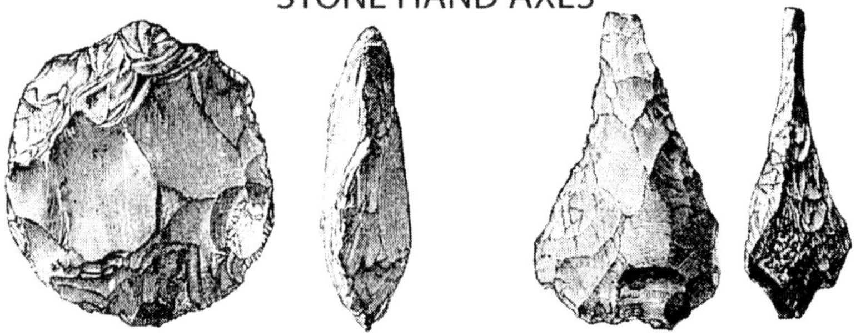

Brains grow better with good nutrition, and getting good nutrition means you are a fitter animal – just the same way the peacock has to eat a lot of the right food to grow a pretty tail. So what was really being sexually selected for was brain function. If so, the axes were probably not the only behavior that was demonstrating good brains; other behaviors such as language and musical ability are likely to have been indicators of brain function. Even to this day, men write poetry and sing songs to impress the girls. However, stone axes survive in the ground, where songs do not, and the major clue we have from this era is the truly large numbers of carefully created but mostly unused axes that have been found.

Now remember we said that brains have both environmental and genetic factors. While the female's genes might have been selecting for a trait that they thought was linked to overall genetic fitness, the males genes were cheating and evolving better brains. Better brains also seem to have been larger brains – so head size was increasing. However, a limiting factor on head size of a species tends to be the size of the skull at birth. Since the females were the ones that had to give birth to these larger headed babies, if the girls had thought this through, they might have realized that they were making more work for themselves.

Because the nature of the skull is that it holds the brain inside of it, it is a set of bones that cannot be both strong and effective for a baby animal, and still grow as much as other bones do later. Evolution has found a compromise position, with the skull starting out proportionately larger to the body than it will be in adulthood, and with the bones that make up the skull not as fully joined or as tough as they will be in adulthood, leaving some room to grow.

The size a skull can be at birth is limited by the size that a female animal can manage when giving birth. The weakness of the skull to allow growth is limited by how ready the baby animal has to be to deal with threats in the world. These both contribute to a limiting factor on how big an adult animal's brain can be.

Any mutation towards increased intelligence that would help the animal in its environment is balanced by the increased infant mortality and/or birthing problems that increased brain size, and therefore skull size, might cause. Because of this, a level of brain sophistication that might otherwise have been made hundreds of millions of years earlier, by some other animal, was delayed. The initial evolutionary moves in this direction turned out not to be beneficial, and standard natural selection can not cause change in a direction that goes against survival, even if it would eventually get to something that is very pro-survival.

However, sexual selection can, to a degree, create traits that are in some ways counter to survival. So if the theory that the guy with the biggest axe gets the best chicks is true (even though we think he might just be compensating for certain other inadequacies), then this sexual selection pressure might have been the key to pushing Genus Homo past the problem of head size to a higher level – a level of brain complexity that no other animal on the planet had ever reached.

Certainly something pushed the development of our brain, and therefore our head size, past the point that natural selection would normally be able to manage. The resulting animal, virtually identical in all respects to modern human beings, gave birth to babies with heads so large they could not even lift them for many months after their birth. Unlike almost every other animal on the planet, their infants were completely helpless, unable to even move around on their own for almost a year.

By contrast, a newborn chimpanzee is strong enough to hold its own weight by clinging to its mother's fur. When it is born, it is already as fully developed in all respects as a human baby is at approximately one year of age.

This new variety of larger headed hominid was capable of developing a much more complex brain, but at a large price in physical survival abilities. In addition to having to more carefully care for their young, the changes in pelvic structure required to give birth to larger headed babies made H. Sapiens less well adapted to running on two legs than early H. Erectus had been – especially in the case of females.

In the long run, however, a less well adapted physical body was far less of a disadvantage than the additional survival value of symbiosis with the ideological capabilities that larger brains made possible. These new hominids had almost certainly evolved the capability for structured language. They had the ability to pass new ideas from mind to mind in a more precise manner than any previously known creature. This gave rise to more complex memetic life forms than any previous creature had ever been able to host.

2.1.3 Species H. Sapiens

The first Homo sapiens were not modern man (modern man is actually a particular sub species of Homo sapiens that showed up later) but they were a lot smarter than those that came previously. Their brain was now approximately the same size as modern man. Although a bigger brain doesn't always mean smarter within a species, there is definitely some correlation across different species in brain to body size ratios. There is also some pretty good evidence that the first members of species H. Sapiens were the smartest creatures ever seen on the planet Earth. Whatever the evolutionary hurdle is to evolving our sort of intelligence, these guys were over it and leaving it far behind.

At almost exactly the same time in the fossil record that Homo Sapiens appears, there starts to be evidence of fire use, followed quickly (on the scale of time that things were happening back then, "quickly" means a hundred thousand years give or take) by advanced weaponry and complex tools like spears and bows.

This growth of technology would certainly seem to be an indication that symbiotic memes had finally arrived on the scene. The new thing that this new bigger brain was doing, was allowing for communications using a complex structured language. And structured language allowed more complex ideas to evolve.

2.1.3.1 Structured Language

Language of some sort exists in many animal species, and there is no doubt that our earliest hominid ancestors were communicating with each other on some level. In fact, modern chimps can be taught vocabularies of hundreds of words, and are almost certainly also communicating at such a level in the wild through their own sign languages. Many other species of animal are also seen to possess some level of language. However, such communication lacks a structured vocabulary. This is probably the level at which our ancestors had been communicating up until the brain growth period in which H. Sapiens first evolved.

A higher level of language structure would allow new developments to be spread and taught more quickly. As early as 200,000 years ago, Neanderthal man was probably using all the tools that you would be able to make for yourself in the woods after reading a book on survival. He was probably also able to relate his daily experiences to the rest of his tribe, much the way you would tell your friends all about the fun time you had in the woods... trying to make fire and ending up having to eat raw squirrel meat when it didn't quite work out with the rubbing sticks together idea.

2.1.4 Sub Species H. Sapiens Sapiens

The Neanderthals were a sub species of H. sapiens – as is modern man. Neanderthal man is designated as H. sapiens neanderthalensis, while modern man is known as H. sapiens sapiens.

The first genetically modern man appeared about 130,000 years ago, which was about 70,000 years after the first Neanderthals. In the past, when a new evolutionary mutation in the hominids had proved favorable, sometimes it was so good that our ancestors quickly out-competed all similar creatures living in the same environment. Other times, the two or more similar hominid species lived together, side by side in the same environments, for quite a long time. In the case of Neanderthal and Modern man, they seemed quite evenly matched at first, and shared the planet side by side for over 100,000 years. Neanderthal man actually had a somewhat larger brain, and may therefore, have actually been more intelligent, but they were the species to die out.

The end of Neanderthal man coincides quite closely and perhaps not coincidently, with the oldest known cave paintings. H. sapiens neanderthalensis may never have exhibited any sort of art or decoration of any of his artifacts – nor did H. sapiens sapiens (modern man) for the first 100,000 years that our ancestors walked the planet. Then, 30,000 years ago, something changed, and primitive man could suddenly conceptualize markings on a cave wall, or designs on a tool, or figurines of stone, bone, or wood, as representations of real objects in the world.

This was the birth of visual art.

There is no evidence that this change was a genetic one. If it was not, this would be the first evidence of memes finding a new way to transmit themselves, without the help of genes. While oral and gesture communication is almost certainly an evolved trait written into our genes, it is quite likely that nothing in our genes suggests that pigment on a cave wall could tell the story of hunting a large animal. This is the first known instance of memetic information being able to persist outside a brain for longer than the time it takes sound waves to fade away. This development may have been a product of purely memetic evolution.

Credit unknown artist - circa 20,000 years ago

It was also such a powerful development that it may well have been the factor that tipped the balance in the survival struggle between two evenly matched sub-species. Perhaps paintings helped in the teaching their children. Perhaps they recorded information about seasonal movements of prey animals – so that patterns could be figured out. If better communication somehow allowed a greater survival advantage for one of the two sub species of H. Sapiens, or even if it came to be used by both but somehow brought about greater competition as both species did better, it could very well have been the change that put an end to Neanderthal Man.

2.1.5 Regnum Sententia

(The Kingdom of Thought)

This was the beginning of the explosive growth and evolution of a new category of life. Memetic life had previously existed at a level that was analogous to pre-cellular biological creatures – like the replicating chemicals that started to form as the Earth's surface cooled. A structured language, however, gave it a chance to start evolving in ways and at speeds the planet had never seen. This is the same sort of evolutionary development that a DNA-based genetic encoding system was for biological life.

How unlikely was this to have happened? Well, consider that from the first chemical life to the development of the first animal brains took about three billion years, and that the evolution of a brain capable of acting as a platform for full replication and evolution of this new type of life took yet another half a billion years.

This was a spectacularly amazing development that led to some amazingly spectacular results.

2.2 Hunter Gatherers

As we approach historical times, our understanding of human living begins to get a bit less cloudy. We can infer more about early man from the existing archaeological evidence than we could in the case of his even earlier cousins. The information we have on the lifestyle of H. sapiens sapiens in primitive technological conditions is pretty good. It seems certain that humans lived a nomadic, hunter-gatherer existence. Archaeologists continue to find evidence of life during these times and many such societies existed recently (such as the Native Americans); because of this, we have information in the historical written record to work with, and – very interestingly – a few societies of humans living as hunter-gatherers still exist in certain parts of the world!

So, between the artifacts we find and the verifiable facts about primitive groups still living on Earth, we can put together a fairly accurate picture of what hunter-gatherer life was like. More importantly, we can get a decent picture about the ideas that guided their existence.

Let's begin by admitting that early humans were very violent. Hunter-gatherers were not happy, groovy Greenpeace members. Contrary to the popular "Noble Savage" theories of anthropology, our early ancestors tended to beat each other's heads in with axes – a lot! (In fact a lot of the oldest H. sapiens sapiens remains ever found seem to indicate murder with a stone axe to the head.)

> *Warfare in pre-state societies was both frequent and important. If anything, peace was a scarcer commodity for members of bands, tribes and chiefdoms than for the average citizen of a civilized state.*
>
> *It comes as a shock to discover that the proportion of war casualties in primitive societies almost always exceeds that suffered by even the most bellicose or war-torn modern states.*
>
> *-- Lawrence H. Keeley, "War Before Civilization"*

2.2.1 First Philosophies

Once men could actually think, they started to think about the world that surrounded them. After all, it was a mass of contradictions. On one hand, it provided you with air to breathe and generally with some sort of food and water nearby. On the other hand, there were a lot of animals that could and would kill you, some of the 'food' was poisonous, and the weather was often deadly. Add to this confusion all of the strange reproduction-related things that happen to our minds and bodies.

So, once highly-functional brains came along, questions came along with them, requiring people to formulate answers, or at least possible answers. The questions and answers tended to take shape based upon two primary things:

1. **The knowledge available.** (Which wasn't much beyond what a bare-subsistence life in the woods provided)
2. **Things that people wanted to know.** How to escape fear, pain, and sorrow. How to increase security, pleasure, and joy. How to realize their dreams of something better.

As we continue through this, bear in mind that nothing we say here excludes the possibility of an actual GOD. We can neither prove nor disprove that idea. We are just taking a look at the reasons why such an idea can and does arise, and why people are inclined to pass it along.

The things that the first religious ideas needed to explain were these:

1. **Sickness and death**. Why did my mother die? Is she just gone forever? I loved her and needed her, why did this happen? Will I really never see her again? These are damned difficult questions now – just imagine answering them for a bereft child. People were more used to death in those early days, but it seems unlikely that these questions were not asked universally.

2. **The world**. Why did water fall from the sky? What caused thunder and lightning? Why did it get cold? Then, why does it do this in cycles? Important questions, not just for the sake of curiosity but for survival.

3. **Whose fault is it?** Shame seems to be almost hard-wired into humanity, and this is a much larger problem than most of us suppose. There's a lot to say about this, but suffice it to say that as you look through history, you see men and women running as fast and far from any possible blame as they can. Obsessively. Here's a trick for you: Want to get a huge crowd of people to follow you blindly? Give them someone or something to blame for whatever makes them feel bad. Salve their shame by placing it on someone else. If you do it well, it works almost every time.

4. **Fear.** Nothing is more instinctively powerful than this. Fear of death is one of the strongest, but many others exist. Fear itself is seldom the subject of philosophies, but it is easily the most potent force in driving the demand for them.

5. **Assistance**. At moments of extreme peril, it seems a human instinct to raise our heads to the heavens and ask for help. Even in less tragic times, people find themselves over-matched by the situations they face, and wish for help from a real Higher Power. Explaining how and why this might work – and telling stories about how it did work – is very potent. At other times, however, people latch on to these ideas simply because they want something for nothing or are just too lazy to get up and work for what they want. They want an easy way out.

So, all of these factors, and certainly many others we haven't thought of, led to the first religions. After all, a religion is just a type of philosophy that focuses on what philosophers call metaphysics. Metaphysics asks, "What is the nature of existence?" and it tends to ask questions about what might exist beyond our sight and analysis. So, because these folks did not know much, their philosophy would have to include a lot of conjecture on things they couldn't explain.

It is also very easy for people to project intelligence like their own onto creatures and things that do not really have it. Earlier we discussed how even modern people think of their pets as almost equal to other people and will do things like name their cars and talk to them when they won't start. Primitive people live with fewer barriers between themselves and nature and are far more likely to project personalities onto animals and other inanimate things where they have no other knowledge to predict the behavior of such things.

2.2.2 First Religion

As best we can deduce or guess, the first religions tended to focus on imaginary beings and powers behind the things in nature that were important to primitive people. Now, this could have been as 'modern' as saying "The principle of the sun, which we do not know," rather than saying "the Sun God." But, as we have explained earlier, the simplest ideas are the ones that tend to stick, and projecting intelligence onto things is easy.

Even if the first guy to accurately describe the sun's behavior was so enlightened as to not imply personality, it would have quickly been changed by others into the more personal concept of a "Sun God," and the question became not *what* the sun did, but *why* it did it.

Death was explained as the removal of the life-force from the body. So the question of just what it was that dead people no longer had, that had previously made them walk and talk, and where it had gone, became important. The common belief arose that life force was the same as consciousness, and that the consciousness of the dead had gone somewhere.

The idea that dear departed relatives were still around somewhere was comforting. It was even more comforting to believe that they were happier – that they went to a better place or were still functioning at some higher level. While this made people feel good, the down side was that it made people devalue the human body or consider it a sort of trap for the spirit.

Ancestor-reverence (after all, they were higher and better now) fit perfectly with the human grouping of clan, and combined with ideas about the animism of trees, animals, and Higher Powers controlling the individual sources of environmental change (sun, moon, wind, rain, cold, etc.), forming the basis of a mystical world view that held sway for a long time.

2.2.3 Shamans

Once people believed in higher and more powerful forces, it was natural for them to want help from those forces. People wanted help from above (and we can guess that "above" was included because the most mysterious and powerful forces – wind, rain, sun, etc. – were literally coming from above), but they didn't know how to ask invisible Higher Powers for help in a way that might be answered.

Enter the shaman. These guys, no matter what they were called, functioned as the conduit between the Earth and the great powers above. They had to show their uniqueness in one way or another, perhaps by knowing the secret magic words, by knowing complex spells or occasionally by superior knowledge. They might also prove their unique ability to span heaven and Earth by devoting their entire lives to this work.

This early form of specialization had another feature – it made it a necessity that others gave their goods to him. You want to be in touch with the Higher Powers? You'll have to give the shaman regular food.

2.2.4 Chieftains

Who Takes Responsibility, May Rule

Tribal leaders seem to have been very common among early man. We tend to think of the tribe or clan leader as being the biggest and strongest male, and there is doubtless some truth in that. But once tools of violence were common, size and strength were not supremely important. Think about it – how would you feel about allowing a 13 year-old girl to swing a small ax at the back of your head with all her strength? Not very good, huh? Now imagine that same scenario in a place where you wouldn't receive modern medical attention – not even sterile water or antiseptic cream to prevent infection. Size and strength certainly mattered, but when even a child is capable of dealing a death blow, it isn't nearly as crucial to the power structure as you might think.

As mentioned earlier, brains – effective thinking – mattered a lot more. But so did the courage to command. And it seems likely that people of this time were just as averse to welcoming responsibility as they are now. In fact, they were probably worse. In our times, if you screw-up badly you are embarrassed and perhaps suffer some financial damage. Even in the worst cases, you could go somewhere else and start over.

In those days, being kicked out of the tribe meant a serious risk of death. Living alone was far harder than living with the tribe. Even if you are capable enough to kill an elk, how long can you eat from it before the meat spoils? Not long. In the tribe, you all share, and the economies work. Plus, hunting in groups is a lot safer.

It seems that most of the time, the bosses were chosen (or, more likely, just accepted) more for non-physical reasons. There would doubtless be many strong physical specimens who lacked the internal strength to assume risk and responsibility, much as it is today. In the end, it seems to have been the willingness to assume responsibility that determined who was to lead.

It is a shame that we don't know more about these people, but any writings they may have had are long gone. Or, more likely, it was the invention of writing that changed them into something else entirely.

2.2.5 Original Sin?

Since our chapter is entitled "A brief History of Crime" we're probably supposed to be talking about crime. Well, we haven't yet included much about crime for a simple reason: There wasn't a whole lot of it in the earliest human societies. People killed each other a lot, but aside from murders (usually more like tiny wars), there wasn't a lot of what we think of as crime. Also, it isn't really "crime" in the sense of some higher concept, until there is some higher concept of law – it is just stuff that most people don't like to see happen. (What some people call "Natural Law.")

Before farming, there just wasn't much to steal and keep. How much valuable stuff can a perpetually-roving band of a dozen people really take with them? So, there just wasn't much pay-off in stealing. And if you did steal something big, what would you do with it? Food rotted quickly and people didn't need spring, summer and winter wardrobes.

There were revenge killings, fights over women and so on (probably quite a few of them), but would you really risk your life to steal a half-basket of nuts? After all, if something goes wrong, you and the other guy (or several guys) are squaring-off and swinging axes at each other; that's just not a promising risk/reward ratio. So the only reason to steal anything back then would be if you were too stupid to find your own nuts.

Although they might bash each others heads in for many other reasons, and think that this was quite natural and normal, when it came to personal property, people were quite probably fairly civil to each other. More civilization, however, would certainly change this.

2.3 Farmers, Warriors, and God Kings

Once people invented agriculture, everything changed, and the ideas of laws and crime were inevitable. Now there were large stores of food (many types of grain), which didn't rot quickly. Then came clothing, furs, tools, and so on. (Oh yeah, and beer – now there's something worth stealing!) This stuff could be stolen and traded in the next community in the next valley.

This is when crime really began to pay.

What really made the game work, however, was that farmers were immobile. The text books like to call them "sedentary," but that's just a bit too polite for our tastes. They were stationary targets – sitting ducks – easy victims – and doubly so because farming requires special skills. The farmers worked on skills like plowing, sowing and reaping, and not on things like making bows, slinging rocks, and proper kill strikes with spears. Sure, they did some of that, but they didn't have time to keep those skills at as high a level as someone who specialized in killing things.

Hunters and herdsmen *did* specialize in killing, so these guys became the first serious crooks when marauding became a new viable occupation.

2.3.1 From Thief to Protector

Once there were a lot of farmers around who produced great wealth and were easy marks, some less-than-nice hunters jumped at the opportunity and began killing them and stealing their stuff. Of course, this tended to drive the farmers back into the wilderness. Why stay out there in the open if it's going to get you killed? And this wasn't any good for the hunters either, leaving them nothing to steal.

Then some early evil genius came up with a very interesting solution: Stop stealing everything.

However, if he didn't steal it all, he was just leaving stuff for other thieves like himself to come and steal. So he had to do something else. He has to start protecting the farmers from the other thieves. He had to start treating the farmers as if they were his property – his livestock.

(We should add here that the changeover from gathering to farming was astonishingly brutal, with various new systems for dealing with production and protection competing with new systems of pure murder and theft. As late as the 13th Century, a little improvisation in killing technique could result in one culture overrunning and violently destroying many others. Even today, this memetic dance of attack and defense technology continues. But, that is not really our point at the moment.)

The hunters and herdsmen became the warriors and protectors. They learned that if they refrained from stealing too much, the farmers wouldn't run away, and they could steal a lesser amount for ever and ever. They also learned that protecting an existing group of farmers from people like themselves, was easier than always finding new unprotected farmers. Regardless of what your history teacher taught you in the third grade, this is *really* how the first rulers came into existence.

The first criminals were forced to become the first Kings and to enforce the first laws.

Yes, we know that sounds like a very dangerous statement to make. After all, the current rulers might not like it. You might get in trouble if you repeat it.

Well, that's certainly possible, and we probably wouldn't be so bold as to write this book if we lived in a country that was less friendly to the free expression of ideas – but it's the truth anyway. Governance began as persistent theft, with the guy who led the best band of raiders becoming the boss. It was only after this point that rulers began to justify themselves as protectors. They were really just maintaining a monopoly over their human herds.

Farming was so incredibly much better than gathering that the farmers were willing to accept almost any deal that resulted in some sort of stable situation.

"You want some of my grain or you'll kill me? Go ahead and take some, just be reasonable about how much, and make sure you are the only one stealing from me. I can't afford to pay off everyone who comes along with a spear!"

2.3.2 Thug Kings

At first the life of a Thug King wasn't much better than it had been as the head of a tribe of hunter gatherers. Being able to tax farmers made life a little easier, but the business of having to protect them was actual work sometimes, and it could get you killed. Other guys with spears and bows were much more dangerous than animals that had no weapons.

The other problem with ruling the farmers was that they knew they were being robbed and tried to avoid paying the local thug what he wanted. After all, a deal made at the point of a spear really doesn't have much moral authority, does it?

So, the farmers quickly became tax cheats.

Remember, the thug Kings of that time couldn't put a freeze on your bank account or check your MasterCard records. They might also be away frequently and they didn't really have to watch the settlement too closely except at harvest time. That is when they collected their booty and when the chance of some other group of thugs trying to steal the loot was greatest. It didn't take long for the farmers to figure out how to bury some of their crops, put the beer in a cave, and so on.

Certainly the bosses tried to find the hidden beer, but they could never be sure that there wasn't more loot getting away from them. They could also intimidate the farmers, but that isn't as effective as you might think. A bit too much bullying might get some farmer really mad, and he might sneak up at night and bash the boss's head. Or a competitor might say, "Help me defeat the boss and I'll only take half as much of your crop as he did."

It was obvious, from the Thug King's point of view, that it would be much better and easier if the farmers actually liked him and would pay their taxes willingly. But, it's difficult to make someone like you when you are a parasite living off of their work. (Modern political image consultants are specialists in this skill.)

Then, another evil genius came along and invented the Priesthood.

2.3.3 The Priesthood

One of the curious things about early farmers was that they never developed the huge, universal god. You might think that this would have come a lot earlier. After all, a more powerful god is better than a limited one, right?

But if you look at a good map of an early farming city (and there are a few), you'll see that there were many little shrines throughout the city – a lot like the little store-front churches that we see now. When the gatherers moved to the farm, they took their gods with them and held to them. And they had a lot of gods. Polytheism was the natural state of affairs for a long time among these primitive farming societies.

Just as the people who had been the hunters in pre-agricultural times had adapted to the new class of farmers and the wealth they produced (by becoming thugs and their Chieftains becoming Thug Kings), the Shamans also adapted. They made a living by talking to the gods, and quickly came up with a story that said, essentially, that if you please the gods, they will help you have a terrific harvest. Well, what farmer wouldn't want a great harvest? And pleasing the gods, of course meant pleasing the Shamans.

Now it may have been that in some cases the Thug Kings would have been as superstitious as the farmers, and would fear the Shaman. However, since both Thug King and Shaman were living off of the efforts of the same people, there would have been some conflict. Then evil genius number two (whether he was a Thug King or a Shaman is unknown) figured out how they could work together.

The deal between Shamans and rulers was this: The Shamans would tell the farmers that the gods would not be pleased unless the King was getting his full and correct share of their crops. (They were, of course, allowed to continue to receive tips from the farmers in return for putting in a good word with the gods.) What evil genius number two had figured out was that the farmers would pay their taxes far more easily if they were doing it for the gods, rather than for the King, who was after all, just another man. They had Priests, who did nothing but serve their gods day and night, telling them what the gods wanted. They must know what is right!

Over time, it seems that each community combined its gods, and that the ruler – seeking the advantages of being important to a god, and not having time to become the important guy for twenty of them – engineered the unification of the local gods to one; or at least one god was deemed to be the most powerful. This was not monotheism as such, partially because there were always lesser gods and spirits, but most importantly because the city over the next hill had a god too.

The gods of other cities were not looked on as being mythical. In those days, the gods of other cities were just as real as your own; you just liked your god better because he was looking out for you. This explains why the first of the Ten Commandments is "You shall have no other gods before me." It doesn't say "I am the only GOD," because in the days when God was just starting out, everyone *knew* there were lots of gods. So God just said, "I am the jealous type. Don't you let me catch you worshiping anyone else!"

The God we are familiar with wasn't quite on the scene yet as far as our story goes.

Most cities eventually had one most powerful god, from whom both the King and the Priest derived their power. We should also add that a "city" in that era was a central safe area where the nearby farmers came to trade and for protection when threats arose. Most people did not live in the city. It was a market, temple, and castle. (Though calling any dwelling of this time period a castle would be stretching definitions a lot; architecture still had a long way to come.) The only people that lived in the castle were the King, his personal slaves, warriors and the Priests.

The King and his warriors kept busy practicing fighting, patrolling for rogues, and hunting wild game. The Priests, however, lived a life of relative leisure, as the job of keeping the sun rising every day and the rains coming in the rainy season wasn't too hard on the back. They had a lot of time to think. So it is likely that most of the ideological advances of the time came from the priesthood – the most significant being systems of counting and writing that were slowly developed in independent places around the world from 10,000 to 5,000 years ago. This association of the priesthood with scholarly pursuits has continued even to modern times.

2.3.4 God Kings

Not too long after the King's power was legitimized, came the final piece. A clever theology with the King playing a 'legitimate' role made rebellion against the King the same as a rebellion against the gods, and this made collecting taxes much, much easier. The next theological innovation, however, actually elevated the King to a level above that of other human beings.

Remember we talked about the idea of a spirit and how bodies were not necessarily thought to be so important. Well the King's body became the host for the spirit of the local god. Many farmers were probably a bit slow to accept that the gods loved the King so much that they would be divinely punished for cheating the King out of his taxes. Now, however, they were trained from childhood in the idea that the King was in some way the same as the local god. This made it seem much more likely that cheating the God King would have an adverse effect on your crops.

This new role as a living god had many additional benefits. Life for the Thug King meant having to go into battle at the head of his warriors when his farmers were threatened (or when he wanted to kill the Thug King next door and steal his farmers) and having to be careful that one of his warriors wasn't trying to kill him and take his job. The God King, however, as the Earthly vessel of a divine spirit, was not to be risked in battle and commanded absolute loyalty.

His warriors were much less likely to overthrow him now. How could they? He was a god and they were not. And if he played it right (seeming imperious and distant), most couldn't even envision taking over his position. Also, he could now pass his kingship down to his children rather than it going to the next most clever and strong guy when he died. Setting up your children for when you die is something your genes favor.

This new position as God King may have actually made the King more vulnerable to the priesthood, as they probably suspected he wasn't really a god. If he didn't do what they wanted, they might arrange to kill him – then raise his divine heir with a proper education on always doing what the Priests said. So the connection between religion and government was about as solid as you can get at this time in history. But this problem was far outweighed by an additional factor; the farmers could now be talked into fighting for their God King.

The first God King to figure this one out probably expanded his territory like wildfire. Farmers may not be the best fighters, but when the odds of the fight change from "The other guys have a handful of skilled warriors and so do we," to "The other side has a handful of skilled warriors, and so do we, plus we have ten times as many farmers with pointy sticks," this can really tip the odds of the battle. Taking over a new area and killing their King also proved the superiority of the God King over the other side's gods. Thus the farmers of the new territory would naturally convert and become part of the new army too, making the God King even more powerful.

Being a god on Earth, he did not need to fear setting up new rulers under him in far away areas, as they would never conceive of themselves as equals. In fact, he may not even have always had to fight to acquire a new city. The King of that city might be willing to take a demotion, and give up some of his cut, in order to stay alive and keep ruling his area. He might not have believed in the superiority of the God King in his heart, but his sons would be brought to the center of the kingdom and taught by the Priests, so the next generation would be believers. Only the Priests of some other god had to actually die in order to acquire a new area.

The idea of God Kings expanded faster than any one kingdom could, so soon there were many such God Kings. The mathematics of it was, if you were a leader, and did not declare yourself to be a god on Earth, your people would not fight for you as hard and you would lose out to a nearby kingdom that did. Thus the idea spread itself more strongly across a greater area, through the creation of supposedly competing cultures that were in fact just replanted cuttings of the same memetic plant. This growth pattern would be repeated many times.

> *The great strength of the totalitarian state is that it forces those who fear it to imitate it.*
>
> --Adolph Hitler

OK, now that we've insulted almost every serious power base on the planet, we'll move on to show you how the situation developed from these ugly beginnings to the somewhat less-ugly situation that we live with now.

2.4 Democracy and Empire

The first development of divine leadership, after it was more or less established and accepted, was simply to get bigger. The same formula could be applied to multiple settlements, with a few middle-managers thrown into the mix. After all, if you're a ruler-thug, what you want is more loot, more adulation, and more power. Remember, power is addictive, especially to certain personality types. To them, the purpose of getting power is to obtain more power.

So, kingdoms got larger; one King tried to take over the neighboring King's territory, second-in-command leaders tried to break off parts of large kingdoms, and so on. And this went on for a long, long time. Various religious modifications came and went, as did taxing strategies, methods of warfare and organizational structures, but the general pattern was more or less the same: Religiously-influenced monarchies.

The ideological structure remained quite stable and intact during this time. There must have been many innovators during these scores of centuries, but the overall structure was not well-suited to change. Probably the main reason was that communication was almost nil outside of the village. Ideas didn't get very far. Perhaps, if the innovator were to become an Emperor, his ideas might spread a good distance, but not many innovators also wish to kill and conquer.

There were traders during these years, but they seem to have been held in a near-universal suspicion until the late Middle Ages. They provided some communication between cultures, but apparently not enough for new ideas to spread through any other means than conquest.

2.4.1 Enter the Greeks

The Greeks were the first to play with the idea of divided governments. Why the Greeks? In part because of their geography – their terrain made control by any massive kingdom a practical military impossibility but the fact that there were many fishing settlements close to each other by boat made communications good and kept them culturally in tune. This was a likely spot for the first growth of better governmental systems. The Greeks really did a lot, and pretty quickly. If we were to suggest the innate intellectual superiority of any historical group, we'd probably have to do it here.

Whatever the cause, the Greeks began to modify the standard human collection of memes. They seem to have started like the rest of the world, with local deities, Kings and Priests, but as the nearby Greek communities communicated more, something began to happen: Their respective gods were put into more direct competition with each other without armies marching against each other to decide the theological contests.

To prove the importance of their gods, the Greeks began creating myths – stories about their gods. And – this is the big new thing – the Greeks tried to show the superiority of their god stories by how well that deity's words and actions touched and guided the inner life of his followers. Before the Greeks, a god ordered you around and made your crops grow – all external things. Now, the god addressed human values, emotions, and virtues. This was huge.

Once the gods began to compete over men's inner lives, men also were free to compare ideas. (Of course they were always free to do this to one extent or another, but they were also likely to face nasty consequences for expressing new ideas openly.)

This "open space" for ideological development allowed the first big steps into the modern age. There was no large unified power to enforce an ideological monopoly, and the gods themselves (through their Priests) were competing for intellectual superiority. Wow! What a time! People were free to innovate, to create, and to expand, not just technologically and commercially, but also intellectually and morally! Double wow!

Men began to take over the control of their own destinies – rather than doing the "not my job" thing and handing all responsibility to someone else. They considered themselves worthy of self-rule. If you think about this for a few moments, this is still a radical and scandalous idea. Self-rule... the moral right to rule one's self. The moral superiority of self-rule, the base servility of everything else; these are frightening ideas even today.

The whole development was sloppy, uneven, and flawed (slavery remained a fact of life, for example) as is always the case as systems evolve, but it was an astonishing move forward.

Once individual men decided to take over control of their own lives, they began working on arrangements that allowed it to work with larger numbers of people. This led to democracy, which has been the leading pattern for self-governance ever since.

Bear in mind that democracy is not, and never was, an end in itself. It was merely the best way the Greeks could find to coordinate thousands of self-sovereign individuals. Without a culture of people who assert control over their own lives – including taking full responsibility for their own results – democracy will never really work well.

Democracy is not a magic formula for a society to obtain more than the value of its individual members.

2.4.2 The Routinization of Charisma

The old Jesuits had a term for something that happened to fresh new developments and turned them into rigid and legalistic molds: The routinization of charisma. And this is what happened to the dynamic and vibrant ideas of the Greeks. The Romans turned the Greek charisma into a routine – a solid ideological structure.

The Romans started when some very interesting folks from the north of Italy, called Etruscans, made their way down to Rome and set up a civilization. This is where they came into contact with the Greeks. Greek superiority was significant, and over a wide spectrum of human activity. The Romans, to their credit, copied the Greeks wholesale.

Why did the Romans allow such changes to their ideological structure? Why did their current memes allow it? We really don't know; knowledge of this time is thin. It is likely that it had to do with the Etruscans, probably combined with a major military defeat that led them to question what they had been doing wrong. It may also be that a desire for dominance was a primary player in the collective Roman meme pool and that this allowed them to simply adopt the more useful ways of the highly successful Greeks. They may have just started trading with the Greeks and the ideas that came along with the Greek god-myths were highly contagious. For whatever reason, the Greek ideas of democracy, equally valued citizens, and limited government powers, were all transferred to the Romans.

However, once the Roman structure began to develop, the charisma of Greece turned a bit ugly and base. Not all of it, mind you, but some important parts.

For example, self-sovereignty: Being master of yourself implies nothing about the outside world. It certainly does not imply that you wish to subdue others. In fact, self-ruling people tend to hold very strongly to the proposition of "live and let live." Among the Romans, however, this eventually became "dominate all others."

In fairness to the Romans we must add that the general philosophy of the ancient world was focused on scarcity and accepted the fact that there were two classes of people: dominators and the dominated. So it is not surprising that the Romans would turn the economic success produced by their governmental system into outwardly directed military might.

It should also be noted that those who seek power in government do so because they like to control other people. This makes sense doesn't it? After all, those who seek other jobs do so because they like doing that sort of work, and the work of government would seem to be controlling people. If a society allows its people a lot of freedom and restricts the control that a government can exercise internally, those government officials who want to exercise more control over others must look to the outside world.

However it happened, the Romans came to believe that they deserved to rule and to conquer – and it must be said, they lived up to the challenge quite well. During the early years they held to this idea in the face of massive defeats. Where any others would have quit, the Romans persevered, adapted, and overcame. When enemies surrounded the walls of Rome, no one ever took a bribe to open the gates. This was an extremely rare showing of patriotism in the ancient world.

Rome went forth conquering and expanding until the structure could no longer sustain itself. Then it rotted on the vine.

2.4.3 Republic and Empire

It was the Republic that made Rome what it was. The political structure of the Republic was similar to the Greek Democracy, but with an added layer. Instead of the freemen voting directly, the freemen elected representatives to vote for them. This structure was much better for a large country than the Greek arrangement, which worked well enough for a city-state but was a bit limited for a larger nation.

Given the immense variability of human life and the immeasurable foolishness of politics, the Roman Republic held up amazingly well. But as one government organization after another grew up, the entire structure became huge and the votes of the people got further and further away from actually changing anything. When the Empire took over, the average person had no real hope of helping to change any law in any substantial way. Everything was done by middle structures that remained the same no matter who ran the show. (This might sound familiar to you today.)

When Julius Caesar declared himself Emperor, only those who had a real understanding of the principles of Rome were able to see how horrible it was. The bulk of the people – and their politicians and intellectual leaders – focused on the concerns of the immediate future. They decided that Caesar wasn't going to raise the price of grain too much next month, so they went along with it.

The charisma of the Greeks had come full circle and self-rule was, once again, just a dream in the minds of a few eccentric intellectuals.

Old ideas of the "divinity of the King" had still been circulating in the background, and Julius Caesar used them to become a God Emperor. Of course he was not the only god, just one of many, and of course they killed him for it, but that is not an uncommon thing for people to do to their gods.

The Distributed Identity of Julius Caesar lived on in the idea that the ruler of Rome was divine. In fact, the name "Caesar" came to be a word for divine ruler. Later emperors were referred to as "The Caesar." Even today, the word "Czar" is still sometimes used to describe a strong leader.

2.4.4 Another Cycle Runs Its Course

The Romans seem to be good examples of this routinization of charisma. It is a universal phenomenon, really, but, for whatever reason, Rome provides several good examples of it. Our second example is Christianity.

Jesus and all of his first followers lived in the Roman province of Palestine, some decades after the Empire solidified in Rome. (The name, Palestina, was a purposeful insult, deriving from the enemies of ancient Israel, the Philistines.) The religion of these folks, the Jews, was known fairly well throughout the Greco-Roman world, and it seems that the Jewish holy books were highly regarded as well. In fact, the books of the Torah (the five books of Moses: Genesis, Exodus, Leviticus, Numbers, and Deuteronomy) were translated into Greek in the 3rd Century BC, followed not much later by the rest of the Jewish holy books.

Despite the fascinations that many had for this monotheistic religion, not many became followers of the Jewish religion, at least partly because of the requirement of circumcision. (Ouch!)

We're not going to tell the entire fascinating and detailed story of Christianity here, but let us sum up: Christianity began as a reform of Judaism, or at least as an outgrowth of Judaism, and created a group of people with extreme devotion to Jesus, to his teachings, and to the original Hebrew Scriptures.

Jesus can be looked at as a powerful personality who conveyed some very interesting new ideas. He cast such a strong Distributed Identity into the world that not only did his fame survive his death, and his Distributed Identity become an icon for his teachings (as is the case with prophets everywhere), but as an icon, he was actually merged with the deity. Thus Jesus/God became a combined two part icon for the religion. Father and Son were both somehow GOD – something only possible in the supernatural world of divine spirit or in the sphere of memetics. (This was increased to three entities a few hundred years later, with The Holy Spirit being added to incorporate the understanding that

GOD is everywhere, as well as being The Big Guy on The Throne, and his son the martyr/prophet.)

If we had to choose just one group of people in history to whom we would apply the term "charismatic," it would be these first Christians. They were deeply enthralled by their ideas. When conflicts with the dominant memes came (as they'd have to), they held their ground, died if necessary, and kept spreading their message even with their last breath. Where the Jewish version of monotheism had kept to itself, the Christian version was less exclusive. They began to change the memes of the Roman world by pure ideological force.

The Roman collection of memes was surprisingly open to variable gods and the Jewish-Christian ideas were attractive and a bit exotic. With the requirement of circumcision dropped under Christianity, an adult joining up wasn't as painful.

The rulers of Rome would not likely have had a problem with this. They were mostly atheists (after all, they probably knew that they themselves were not really divine) but In order to appeal to a wide range of the population the leaders had to make the compulsory public offerings to the many gods. The Christians, however, not only refused to take part in these public offerings at all, but would also denounce them as worship of false gods. And the earliest Christians leaders were by all accounts quite impressive folks.

This made them the enemies of The Caesar, the reigning God Emperor, and led to public persecution of Christians. While this was bad for the individual Christians who became lion food, for God this was free advertising. Monotheists can go to their deaths a lot more bravely than polytheists who are not quite sure which god is going to be juggling their soul in the afterlife. Christian martyrs were quite an impressive public spectacle. They helped spread their beliefs better by being violently slain in public than they ever could by living happy peaceful lives.

2.4.5 The Beat Goes On

Over generations, the Christians began to get more of a foothold in the ideological system of the age. While attempts to slow the growth of Christianity continued, it became more and more obvious that it was a lost cause. In fact, driving it underground and slowing communication between Christians probably enhanced its ability to change and adapt to the selection pressures imposed upon it. Many brands of Christianity began to spring up, and the Christians kept making converts. Their resolve, even in the face of death, continued to be most impressive. In this way, they were surpassing the Romans in their own game of holding doggedly to their ideals.

But as generations passed and Christianity was more accepted, it came out of hiding, and controversies arose over the many variations that had evolved. Some of the old religions, such as Gnosticism, had seized on the vitality of Christianity and spun-off hybrids. Parts of these older religions were allowed to merge into Christianity. This, of course, infuriated those who were closer to the first generation of believers and caused them to break away.

By the time of Constantine (to whom we'll come in a moment), many Christians had left Rome and were living in Northern Africa. By the end of the 2nd Century the Christians had lost a lot of the charisma of their first generation and had started to be absorbed into normal Roman society – or at least this applied to some of them. Some held to the original charisma of being rebel outsiders. Others wanted official respect and privilege. Most were in-between, not knowing what to do. There were endless doctrinal challenges and feuds between sects.

2.4.6 Constantine

Constantine, as you may or may not recall, was the Emperor who made Christianity the official religion of Rome. He also moved the capital of the Roman Empire away from Rome! (Strange as that sounds) It seems that he realized that European Rome was rotting and that the future lay in the East and with new ideas.

Constantine decided to unify the beliefs of Christianity within the Roman Empire. He knew that if Christianity was going to be the official state religion, it would have to present a single set of unified beliefs. He got all the major Christian leaders together (at least all those who could be bent rather than broken, and who did not run away) and he made them all sit down to hash out their theological differences at the council of Nicea. (Now that would have been an interesting meeting to attend)

Probably the biggest issue they needed to hash out was that of the divinity of Jesus Christ. While Christianity had been taking over the Roman Empire's belief systems, some of Rome's polytheism had also crept into Christianity. Remember that in Rome the Emperor had been a god on Earth. So, early on, when the teachings of Jesus had been at odds with the edicts of the reigning Emperor, it only made sense to some of the early Christians to elevate Jesus to that same level. However, it was difficult for Jesus to be a god when he was also a prophet for the one and only monotheistic GOD.

The Council of Nicea resolved this issue by creating the idea of the Holy Trinity. God the Father, God the Son, and God the Holy Spirit were all aspects of the same God. This may also have been the result of the influence of eastern religious thought, as both the ideas of the spirit of a god being part of everyone and everything and a single god having multiple aspects are often found in the religions of the Far East. In any case, The Council resolved the dispute over the divine nature of Jesus and allowed a unified Roman Church to form.

Constantine didn't do the more authentic Christians (the ones more like the first generations of believers) any favor by merging Christianity into the Empire. Whatever Charisma remained was wiped out. In fact, one of the first actions of the official Church was to subdue the Christians in North Africa who had run from the Roman corruption of their religion. However, some fled still further, or lived in regions that were not considered worth subduing. So, even with Constantine's unification, other branches of Christianity continued to split and mutate.

The Church was now a new wing of the Roman Empire. Fortunately, the ideas of the founders of Christianity were written down and, remarkably for books in those days, accurate copies of the originals had been distributed far and wide. So, even though the charisma was effectively gone, a record of it remained. This proved very useful in the centuries ahead.

By the way, Constantine was entirely correct in his estimations. The European Empire was overrun and broken less than two centuries later. Only the Church really continued in Europe. The Eastern Empire lasted another thousand years.

2.4.7 Other Mutations

In places outside the Roman influence, the mutation of Christianity continued. It gave rise to many variations that still exist, including Islam, which today is one of the three major branches of monotheism. Islam can be seen as a linear descendant of Judaism through Christianity.

Judaism is the religion of the Torah as recorded by Moses. Christianity preserves this book as the "Old Testament" and Islam preserves it as the "Tawart." Christianity added the New Testament concerning the teachings of Jesus Christ and his apostles. Islam preserves a version of the New Testament as the "Injil." Islam further adds the Qura'n and the Haddith which record the recitations and acts of Muhammad.

What Kind of Jew are You?

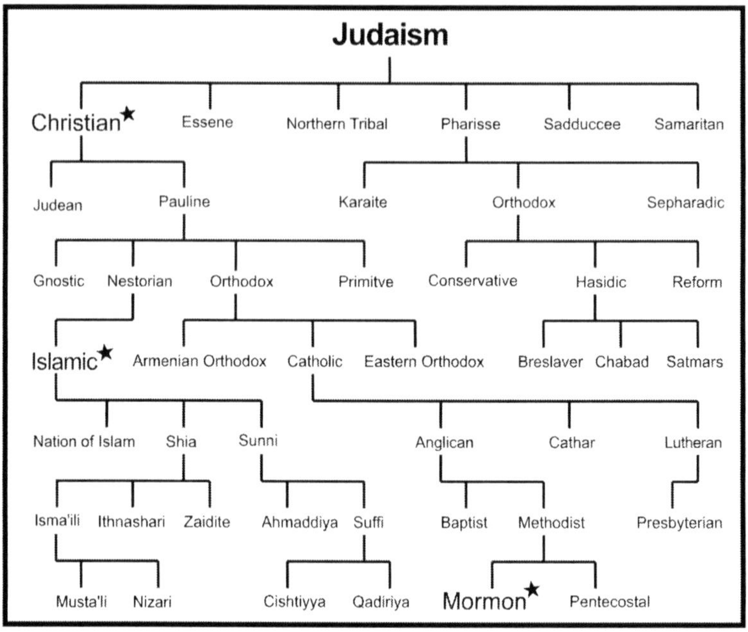

The ongoing factionation of Judaism has resulted in over half of the religious belief in the world. This chart shows a sample of existing and dead factions. A star indicates yet another new prophet and an addition of new holy books.

These correlations are not exact, as each of these books is a compilation of other books and parts of books. For example, the Catholic New Testament is the collection of gospels chosen at the Council Nicea. Some versions of Christianity still exist which chose to include gospels that were excluded by the Roman Church at that time. Islam branched off from a version of Christianity that never adopted the Nicean Creed and therefore does not include the mysterious "polytheism within monotheism" idea of the Holy Trinity, even though it does include the teachings of Jesus and his disciples.

One interesting thing to realize is that historically slow communications due to long travel times is one of the main reasons why religions tended to break apart into other religions. The teachings of a new prophet would first take root in the area where he lived and died and then spread slowly from there.

For example, the Jews who were in the area where Jesus was born and died were more likely to have become Christians than those living farther away. The Jews who were farther away and had less connection to Christ's death are more likely to be the ancestors of modern Jewish people than those who were actually there when Christ was crucified.

Therefore, when someone says that the Jews played some part in the death of Jesus, you can correct them and say:

"The people who killed Christ became the first Christians."

Christianity is really just one of many offshoots of Archaic Judaism. In fact, over half of the religious belief in the world originates with those first Jews. But you shouldn't blame modern day Jews for that either – they are the ones that have allowed their religion to mutate the least.

The family tree we have shown is complicated enough. But consider that this is really just a sampling, and that many related religions, sects, and cults (existing and dead), have not been included. Also consider that all of these religions continue to sprout new mutations regularly. Judaism, Christianity, and Islam are broad categories. Each of them has at least several popular sects with tried and true traditions. But each also has (and has always had) numerous new cults springing up with new self proclaimed prophets on a fairly regular basis. Most die out quickly, but the occasional cult grows until it is a large respectable religion.

Try to imagine (if you can) that today's familiar main-stream religions all started as weird little cults. When historical authorities threw Christians to the lions, they were just following the same sort of Collective Identity impulses that cause modern secular authorities to raid the compounds of modern charismatic cult leaders, throw tear gas through their windows, and burn them out if they continue to resist.

The Church of Rome, that dominated western ideology for the next thousand plus years, continued to fight against this sort of mutation of ideas, and was not unchanged by it. It had to continuously evolve with each new ideological change that it could not suppress.

2.5 Church and State

With the breaking-up of political Rome (in Europe anyway) and the establishment of the Roman Church, a new order had taken shape. Before long it became a firm ideological structure.

The new order featured a very powerful Church, relative to the power of the State. Or perhaps the Church might have best been viewed as the highest level of government. This might seem unusual, but the Church also had the impressive credentials of being the last part of the great Empire.

When people are living in a degraded situation, they tend to look to past glories. In this case, the Europeans found identity as being part of the Roman Empire, degraded as it may have been. That gave the Church – the last legitimate part of the Empire – great ideological power. Which, we must add, they used very well... and, once in a while, even benevolently.

2.5.1 The New Order

The Europeans of the Middle Ages were absolutely convinced that the order of their lives had been established by GOD and that to challenge it was a horrible offense. They saw a world made up of three types of people:

1. The Kings and lesser Nobles, who protected everyone else.
2. The Clergy, who interceded with GOD for everyone else.
3. The peasants, who fed everyone else.

There were always a few specialists on the fringes, such as long-distance traders and Jews, but they were not terribly many and always subject to violence if they attracted too much attention. So, they seldom made much trouble.

As mentioned above, one key feature of this structure was the meme of everyone has their God-ordained place and they should stay in it. To break out of your 'place' was a sin. This, as you might guess, ruined progress for a long time. Your talents didn't matter. It was God's will that you were born into a certain class, so that is where you had to stay. There was no upward social mobility at all. Dark times... and dark times that lasted for a lot of centuries.

2.5.2 The Rise of the Nobles

This Middle Ages structure held firm from the 7th through the 13th Centuries. There were occasional rebels who wanted to change things, but sadly, they didn't get too far. It wasn't until the beginning of the 13th Century that things started to change.

Kings of this time had great power and little accountability – after all, it was thought that GOD Himself put them there! This does not breed good conduct.

The Clergy suffered from the same perverse incentives but they were still too scary to question. Challenging them was almost a direct challenge to GOD who, according to them, would happily lock you into an eternal furnace. (Yikes!)

So when the Kings behaved badly – as Kings usually do – it was usually the nobles who suffered first. After all, it was the nobles who fought for the King and it was the nobles who had to deal with the families of their dead soldiers. It was also the nobles who were taxed by the King. Even though they passed those taxes on to lower levels, they were responsible for the whole exercise.

Eventually, the nobles got together and decided that they were getting a bad deal. It would be wonderful if we had good historical records of how the nobles communicated with each other and how they were able to overcome the 'God-ordained' problem about extending their power. But, that seems lost to us. It may have taken generations of discussions to reach this point, or perhaps it happened all at once. We just don't know. Such thoughts are not committed to writing by prudent conspirators.

We do know that the nobles of England rebelled in 1215 AD. Finding themselves in a position to demand that King John share power with them, they drew up the *Magna Carta Libertatum* ("Great Charter of Freedoms") and pressured the King to sign it. King John, facing a near-certain death if he protested, went along with the deal. He and later Kings tried to trash the deal afterward, but the nobles were strong enough to make it stick.

This gave us the first divided government since the Republic of Rome. Power was now shared by more than one group and there was a written set of rules that even the King had to follow. Divided power works because it limits the power of the ruler by requiring him to cooperate with (or fight with) other branches of power and with the citizenry. Not only does this restrain the power-hungry psychology of the King, but it leaves people to make more of their own choices, which is much more productive.

It took some time for this idea to make its way across Europe but it worked so well that it was adopted in most places. The "Our social order is ordained by God" memes have slowly changed along the way – sometimes violently and sometimes not.

While too many layers of power can be problematic (as it is now, with a government program for anything and everything), less power in more hands has worked relatively well. Concentration of power gives us the likes of Stalin, Mao and Castro.

2.5.3 The Crusades

There is a common misconception that crusades were all about Christianity trying to forcibly expand its influence into the Muslim world – that the Christians were the aggressors and the bad guys. This is only partially true regarding the Crusades. Neither side was truly blameless.

To be sure, the Crusades were sickeningly violent and vile. But, unfortunately, that's the way all war was conducted in those days. The primary opponents of the Christian Crusaders, the Muslims, were no saints either. Both sides committed horrible acts. That doesn't make any of it okay (yes, your mother was correct, two wrongs do not make a right), but neither does it make the Europeans ideological aggressors.

In fact, the truth of the Crusades is that they began as largely defensive actions on the part of Christendom.

The followers of Muhammad had been ravaging Christian lands for a long time. They did things like killing monks, requiring Christians to bear an identifying mark, applying special taxes upon them, forbidding them to display a cross, and so on. Oh, and a whole lot of spreading their religion by the sword. Actually, the very core of the Christian world was originally in Asia. And it was these lands that were conquered by the Muslims at this time. What happened to the Christian world at that time would be about the same as the United States losing its east coast to Venezuela now.

That may seem to be an extreme as an analogy; after all, we think of the United States as a single country and Europe as being a collection of nations. However, at the time, the whole idea of the Nation State didn't quite exist. There were regional place names, and rivers and mountain ranges provided borders of sorts, but no one anywhere had a sense of national identity.

There were different languages, but they were not as important as now. Language was a general problem everywhere, not a national issue. (There were many more tongues spoken than we have now. With less travel and no TV or radio, regional dialects of the same language could be quite incomprehensible.)

Loyalty was to the local nobility and to God. And the local noble family had relatives all over, with the nobles marrying their daughters off to other nobles everywhere. So another country might easily be a place where your King's sister was in charge – hardly very foreign – more like part of the extended family. Thus the sense of higher level identity that people felt was mostly from sharing God.

All of Christendom was nearly as much of an ideological unit back then as the United States of America is today, with the various countries being the equivalent of the States in the USA (which are still semi-sovereign territories). So our analogy stands.

There was certainly an ideological component to the crusades, but that is also something of a chicken-and-egg issue. It has often been said that religion is what causes wars. This is not exactly true. Wars are mostly about ownership of physical territory. That is, the theft of property, the right to reap the taxes of the populace, and, sometimes, the power to impose your ideas (only one of which might be a religion).

That said, it is true that religion plays a key role in most all wars. After all, the rulers need to convince the young males to fight and die. Religion works really well at this, just as it did in convincing people to pay their taxes. Even Stalin, a confirmed atheist and tyrant, was forced to let the Church open up and function a bit during World War II. It simply kept people more willing to die. Religion is a very good way to justify war to the people who actually have to fight and die in it.

If you have neighbors with stuff that can be taken, who you can portray as dangerously unlike your own people, you have a good recipe for war. Religion is traditionally the best choice as the publicly stated reason for war. And when two religions keep using each other as this excuse, it strengthens both of them in the minds of their people by providing a serious external threat. So this is good for both religions, and the cycle goes on.

But, back to the Crusades...

As ugly as they were, these were territorial wars, and were more or less instigated by initial Muslim conquest. Ideology mattered, but it was not the initial and instigating force, just another excuse to act badly.

2.5.4 Another Crusade

Now, if we leave the popular and simplistic idea of Crusade as an attack on Islam, we do find a wonderful example of the Church engaging in brutal warfare simply to stamp out competition.

The Crusade against the Cathars (also called the Albigenses) was almost purely an ideological thing. In the Muslim wars, ideology was used to stir up the soldiers. Here, it was actually the cause.

The Cathars were a group of Christians in the South of France that had rediscovered a form of Gnosticism. Gnosticism is an odd arrangement of beliefs and doesn't often have a lot of popular appeal. It is something of an elitist ideology. This group of folks, however, was extremely pious, which seems to have looked pretty good compared to the thoroughly-corrupt clergy of the time. (Now those guys knew how to party!)

The Cathars believed that evil was a force in all worldly things and that riches and excess were a sign of evil. They pointed to gold bejeweled crosses and elaborate churches as a sign that evil had entered the church. Pretty soon, a lot of Frenchmen were joining the Cathars and publicly insulting the Pope and the Roman clergy for their excesses. This was a direct memetic challenge. The excesses of the Church were for the glory of God. So, the dominant memes were moved to action, made their hosts angry and disturbed, and sent them to France to kill anyone who would not recant.

While there was a Collective Identity difference, personal greed needs to be addressed as well. Collectives must reward their followers as well as punishing the non-believers and the "spoils of war" are an excellent method of doing this. The Cathars were very much against property like gold and jewels but they did have a lot of land. So those who helped the Pope clear that land of the people on it (Cathar or not) were offered that land (with God's blessings).

This leads us to the only thing even remotely amusing about this Crusade. Do you remember the line from Rambo, where Stalone says, "Kill 'em all and let God sort 'em out"? Well, it came from the Crusade against the Cathars. An emissary (then called a Legate) was sent by The Pope to make sure the job got done. At one point the soldiers came to this man and asked how they could figure out who to kill. After all, they were all Frenchmen, and all looked more or less the same. "Kill them all," said the Legate, "The Lord will know his own."

This crusade is an excellent example of the effectiveness of Collective Identities in protecting their territory. The average person has never heard of this crusade, even though it was a bloody purge. These people, whose only real crime was being overly-pious, were labeled Devil worshipers who drank the blood of babies. The accusations and resultant actions were much like the Salem witch trials, but on a scale where whole cities of people were killed.

Though it remains mostly unknown today, it may have been the largest successful campaign of genocide. A few Cathars may have escaped, but certainly not very many, and those that got away almost certainly covered up their previous heritage. The Cathar idea-organism was effectively wiped out through the systematic destruction of all its hosts.

Have you ever seen a Cathar church?

2.5.5 The Inquisitions

The Inquisitions originated with the Cathar Crusade we just mentioned. The Church set up an organization, called The Dominicans, to fight heresy. These were the real scary guys of the Middle Ages. Run fast, run far.

In fairness, there were some good guys among the Dominicans, such as Albertus Magnus and Thomas Aquinas, but... if you were in any way unique and if agents of the Inquisition – who were popularly called The Black Friars – came to your little medieval village... you had better get the hell out, and fast!

The Dominicans more or less started by mopping up after the Albigensian (Cathar) Crusade. It was called the Inquisition because they went around inquiring; checking whether you were a heretic or not. And if you were... well, torture was likely.

Sometimes these acts of inquisition were worse, sometimes they were milder. (Well, "less evil" is probably a better term than "milder," but you get the idea.) They did, however, last for a long time. In fact, the Office of The Inquisition in Rome didn't close down until well into the 20th Century.

At their worst, the Inquisitions were the ideological equivalent of total war. You hold the enemy idea, you suffer horribly, and then you die. It was terrorism and brutality in service to Collective Identities – destructive and anti-human.

The Inquisitions were able to exist because of the immensely strong position of the Church in the minds of men. And this is precisely why we need to use our ideas, and never allow them to use us. Every time we serve an idea-organism, we are committing the same error that created and fueled the Inquisitions, even if the scale is smaller. And the scale of things is usually much larger these days.

Never think that we are so far beyond Holy Wars and faith-based genocide that we don't have to worry about collective idea-organisms instigating wholesale slaughter. As long as people allow themselves to think in terms of groups, this is an ever-present threat.

2.6 Exit from Darkness

In a previous chapter we have discussed the strange circumstance of one idea-organism acting as a hedge against another – allowing people greater mental freedom than they would have with just one collective idea-organism as their master. In this chapter, we'll explain how human civilization made use of this trick, leading to some of its best growth ever.

2.6.1 The West Leads the Rest

Now, before we get into the substance of this chapter, we need to start by addressing this subsection title, "the West leads the rest."

The last fifty years have been full of criticism against Western civilization, even as it has continued to make the world a much better place to live. So we had better set the criteria for making this statement and then support it:

"Lead" implies advancement. We define "advancement" as that which improves human life. How has human life been improved? How about:

- A huge increase in human life-span. (That is, not dying so quickly.)
- More food and more variety of foods. (Modern grocery stores.)
- The ability to store food. (Refrigeration.)
- Better cooking techniques. (Stoves, ovens, microwaves.)
- Healthy environments. (Central heat, central air, no open fires inside.)
- The availability of immense power, almost anywhere. (Electricity.)
- The ability to travel. (Affordable autos, airplanes, etc.)
- Sufficient wealth to allow for leisure.
- Increased knowledge. (Books, newspapers, the History Channel.)
- Increased communication. (Radio, cell phones, Internet, etc.)
- Less danger in daily life.
- More and better entertainment.
- Machines that do mundane chores for us. (Washing machines, etc...)

OK, this list could go on and on, but the point is pretty well made. Now, the proof:

Question: Where were all of the above developed?

Answer: In the West.

You can insert whatever rants you like following the last statement (Hint: we never said the West was perfect, so if you are reacting to that assumption, don't blame us), but that doesn't change the fact: Almost everything important in the last few centuries has arisen in the West. We live so incredibly much better now than our ancestors did that any comparison is ridiculous. If you live in a modern western city, even in one of the worst neighborhoods, you are richer than any King or Queen of a few centuries ago. You can afford, and have access to, goods and services that they could not even dream about.

So, we conclude that the West has certainly, and with no doubt, led the rest of the world forward. Arguing with that statement is super-duper proof that some idea-organism is fighting for dominance in your mind.

All right, with that concluded, let's move on!

We showed earlier that all of the subjects of this book, the idea-organisms, Distributed Identities, collective ideologies, unions of memes, or whatever other names we apply to them, are often parasitic in nature. They can only live in human minds and only by co-opting mind-space and brain-cycles. Further, they often endeavor to control the human animal toward their own ends, not the ends that best suit the animal.

We have also showed how some of these parasites can serve useful purposes. Perhaps these are not benevolent or completely good purposes but, given the current less-than-perfect situation, these idea-organisms (parasitic though they may be) can provide some relative benefit.

In a world where no one is free of such parasites, some can be better than others, and sometimes they can block each other, leaving room for some freedom and growth.

2.6.2 Another Modern Blasphemy

OK, now that we have defended Western civilization, we will proceed to commit another modern blasphemy by saying that much of the human growth of the past centuries has been due to Christianity.

If you are reading this book because the cover seemed sacrilegious and you are not a fan of religion, that statement may make you want to freak out. Go ahead and freak out now, we'll wait...

Are you done? No? OK, we'll wait some more...

All right, please try to restrain your emotions now, and listen to the argument.

God is the big idea-organism, the top of the Distributed Identity food chain, the biggest of dogs, and so on. That makes it very useful as a hedge against other ideas that wish to control men. The idea of God is very difficult to overpower. So... what if we could use the idea of God as a protection from other dominators? What if God could provide us open mind space in which to prosper and grow?

This is exactly what happened in the West between the 14th and 20th Centuries.

Let's take a look backward to show how this happened, understanding that we are not really contradicting the Enlightenment, or making silly claims that the Earth is only 6000 years old, or anything else of the sort. (After all, we do want to keep our secular bona fides intact!)

In the popular idea-sphere, and we think rightly, the years leading up to 14th Century in the West have been considered dark and sad. Certainly there were some people who were lucky enough to lead rewarding lives in this period, but as an overall description we think this is a fairly good one.

Chief among the reasons for this darkness was that the minds of the Europeans were held in deep superstition. The Roman Catholic Church more or less held influence over the Kings and Princes of Europe (though certainly not completely) and strongly over the minds of the European populace. The people were mainly illiterate, and were strong in the belief that the structures of their civilization had been put in place by GOD. They believed that any attempt to change them would be an act of immense evil – insurrection against GOD, almost.

The people gave the Church the benefit of the doubt at all turns and lived in an almost palpable fear of Hell. It was hard bondage.

With apologies to the many nice Catholics in the world, to understand this properly, we need to separate between the Roman Catholic Church and Christianity. And please bear in mind that no bad actions committed by Catholics of the past are to be laid to the account of any other Catholics of this time or any other. All individuals are responsible for their own deeds and collective guilt is a deadly scam. The idea that when a person who is part of some group does something bad, all people in that group are responsible is a logical fallacy caused by group thinking – a fallacy that contributes greatly to the evil done in the world.

Middle Ages Catholicism was really not Christianity as we are using the term. It was almost entirely separated from its book, the New Testament. Most of its adherents were illiterate – certainly they could not read Latin – and were fed only the bits and pieces of their book that the Roman Clergy wanted them to have. The European belief system of the Middle Ages, which is justifiably held up as a bad example, was a long, long way from being properly called "Christianity." (Where Christianity is taken to mean following the recorded teachings of Jesus Christ) It was almost completely divorced from the Christian book, dominated and subjugated by the existing priesthood, and controlled by one of the worst forms of coercion – fear of eternal torture.

We should, perhaps, add that the New Testament has no mention of the Priesthood and many passages which actually tend to revile any such institution. The history of the establishment of Catholicism, including the near-instant conversion of the Pagan Priesthood into a Christian Priesthood; "by the sword" conversions, suppressions and book-burnings of Theodosius II; the "heresy" of Donatism; the conversion of Roman holidays into Catholic holidays; and many other bizarre events make very clear the distinction between "Roman Catholic" and "Christian."

In reality, the Church of the Middle Ages was the last remaining institution of the old Roman Empire. The Church of Rome was created by a series of Roman Emperors, most famously by Constantine, but it was also significantly shaped by several subsequent Emperors.

The Church took over the secular world of Europe by a series of lying deceptions over a long period of time. If you are interested, look up The Donation of Constantine and the Letter of St. Peter to Pippin (alternately spelled Pepin) for a wild look into the Church's manipulations of the secular world. The Dark Ages were governed by a Church-State arrangement with the Church being the senior partner. (This was not a static situation and there were always many variations and exceptions but generally this was true.)

We'll back up to this point in a few minutes, but we'll continue forward a bit first.

"Christian Europe" only began to resemble the teachings of its book once that book was in the hands of the people. The first serious attempts at this were met with force by the Catholic Church. They were a bit late in clamping down on John Wycliffe in the 14th Century, but after the delay they did dig up his body, burn it, and toss his ashes in the river. Other men who worked to get the New Testament into the hands of the common people – and in a form they could actually read – did not fare nearly as well.

It finally came to a head in the 16th Century, with Gutenberg and his printing press. By this time many brave men had translated the Bible into the vernacular languages, and once they could be printed by the thousands, the suppression game was over. The Church kept trying for a long time (and killed lots of people in the process), but it was all downhill from there.

As more people actually read the Christian book, the modern world took shape. The more difficult passages of their book, such as the genocides ordered in the Old Testament, were ignored or explained away as being before the new deal with GOD that was brokered by Jesus. The new Christians turned dramatically away from the violent edicts of the old Roman Church.

New printing technology broke the hold of the Roman Catholic Church by allowing a wider readership for the actual ideas of Jesus Christ.

These changes were contagious, and soon even the Roman Catholic Church had turned away from the ideals of the bad old days. We are not saying that Protestants have been blameless. They have done lots of bad things as well, but the upward trend of humanity in the west since the scriptures were available to the common man is quite striking.

2.6.3 Backing Up – How Did This Happen?

The hold of parasitic idea-organisms on the men and women of the European Middle Ages was strong, to say the least. They were deeply affected by the Church's superstition, and had been for many generations. That's a very hard thing to break out of. Certainly there were exceptional men and women who were able to drag their minds out of the general bondage, but spreading their freedom to the rest of the people of Europe (even if they weren't killed for it) was simply too high a mountain to climb. The vast majority were psychologically unable to make such a leap.

What got them out was the evolution of a better God idea-organism. The two primary characteristics of the new idea-organism were reading the New Testament and rebelling against the authority of the Pope.

There is a lot to be said on this event, but the important things for us are these:

1. The people had a reason to say that the new version of God was better than the old. That it was far more faithful to the New Testament. They could now read it and make their own decisions on that basis.
2. The act of reading, comparing, and deciding was a method of purposefully removing the worst idea-parasites from their minds.
3. They turned hard against the biggest icon of the old idea-organism, the Pope. They kept the intangible icons of the religion, but they rebelled against a living human standing as an icon.
4. By having a better ideology and by being more faithful to it, they got a great deal of self-esteem from rebelling against previous mental slavery.

The new Protestant Distributed Identity was the perfect tool to protect people from the many influences of the Old Catholic DI. In effect, people used it as a vehicle to escape their hard mental bondage.

Then, once more or less established, the new God began to form alliances with the State. This lead to further ideological evolution on both sides, and pretty soon a new and better type of God was combining with a new and better type of State. The new world was taking shape. Economic activity began to gain respect and wealth became acceptable. Learning and free inquiry began to get a grudging respect and so on.

The situation was hardly perfect, but it was the start of an upward trend that we are still riding today – the beginning of a long movement forward.

2.6.4 The Quality of the Memes

Within any large idea-organism (such as any version of God or State) there are a large number of individual ideas. It is the qualities possessed by these individual ideas that give the overall idea-organism its main characteristics.

The new God – or the Protestant DI if you wish – proved to be extra useful for four specific reasons:

1. Its library of memes was primarily drawn from the New Testament.
2. Its library of memes specifically excluded non-New Testament memes present in the old Catholic Church.
3. The new God-State partnership was economically more productive than the old God-State partnership and at some point, economic strength equates to military strength.
4. The idea-organism was not fully-formed. That left time and space for improvements to be written-in.

The first item in this listing requires explanation. After all, the common modern-humanistic view is that anything attached to religion is poison through and through. We maintain that this attitude is just as much a product of a parasitic Collective Identity as any religious Ideology.

Logical thought allows you to look at the relative merits of each idea separately, regardless of source. A good idea that happens to be part of a religion is still a good idea. If it is bundled with bad ideas, it can be a mess to untangle, but it does not change a good idea into a bad one.

Automatically rejecting all the ideas under a given label is just as stupid as accepting them all.

As Holy books go, Christianity's is pretty good. Certainly there are some parts that modern people (including many Christians) reject. We are not saying that the book is perfect, only that it has been useful, especially for getting people out of the Middle Ages and into modernity.

While Christianity does generally claim allegiance to the Hebrew Bible (that is, the Old Testament), it specifically excludes large portions, treating them as history more than rules of faith. (Animal sacrifice, genocides, ancient rituals and so on.) This is doubly true because the crux of Christianity is that it exists as a new agreement between God and man, being mediated by the god/man, Jesus. This means that the old agreement (the Old Testament) is no longer in force. This distinction is made more or less by different groups of Christians, but it gives Christians a good excuse to edit-out "bad" passages of the Old Testament, while keeping the better parts. This ability to use the best ideas while rejecting the worst is the only defense that man can have from parasitic idea-organisms.

2.6.5 The New Testament

The New Testament itself contains a lot of useful material. No, it is not all ideal. Some passages are prone to unkind uses but there are a large number of very useful passages that reproduce some very useful memes. Consider some of the following:

2.6.5.1 Separation of Church and State

"Render to Caesar that which is Caesar's and to God that which is God's."

This tends to keep the God-State alliance from getting too strong and keeps them in a permanent balancing act. Balancing means variation and modification of both of the two Distributed Identities as moderated by their usefulness to the hosts. It means space in between where no single Collective Identity is in control, and people gain individual freedom. This is a very good thing. Neither those states controlled by religion nor states that eliminate religion; have ever offered as much individual freedom as those doing this balancing act.

2.6.5.2 Self-Reference and Integrity

"Whatever you would have men do unto you, do ye even so to them."

"With whatever judgment you judge, you shall be judged."

"By your words you will be justified, and by your words you shall be condemned."

Consider how much better this is than the old, "Obey without thinking or else" model. This model encourages honesty above obedience and suggests that people can set their own moral code provided they are not hypocritical.

2.6.5.3 Expectation of Reason

"Why, of your own selves, do you not know what is right?"

"Examine yourselves... prove your own selves."

Yes, there may be an anti-reason passage or two in the New Testament, but the command to reason exists – most emphatically from the mouth of Jesus himself. This gives any Christian full leave to use his or her mind.

"Be ready always to give an answer to any man who asks you a reason."

This makes the believer responsible for understanding. He or she must consider, understand, internalize the essential facts, and be able to assemble and present them to others. Good skills to encourage.

2.6.5.4 Compassion for the Outsider

"If a man have an hundred sheep, and one of them be gone astray, does he not leave the ninety and nine, and go seek that which is gone astray?"

"There shall be more joy in heaven over one sinner that repenteth, than over ninety-nine who need no repentance."

Considering that hatred of "the outsider" has caused enormous death tolls under many belief systems, this love for the outsider is a critical feature indeed.

2.6.5.5 Violence is Discouraged

"If a man strike you on one cheek, turn to him the other."

Violence has often destroyed value for many. This discouragement (sometimes considered a prohibition) has kept human affairs far less ugly than they might have been otherwise. Where use of force is reduced, freedom and prosperity are increased. Again, whether any particular group of nominal Christians followed this admonition is not the issue; this has always been in the primary collection of memes and has borne good fruit.

2.6.5.6 Self-Reliance

"How is it that you go to law, one against another?"

What Paul (the apostle – not the co-author of this book) is saying here, in modern terms, is this: *"Why are you suing each other in court? If you can't solve your own problems, and are running to a government to do it for you, you're no examples of my teachings."* He expects them to be a new type of human who can solve their own inter-personal problems. In effect, he says, "If you can't handle self-reliance, you're not much of a believer."

Biblical messages concerning solving your own problems doubtless contributed to the limited governmental systems of the west, and this discouragement of frivolous law suits is a lesson we can still use today.

2.6.5.7 Co-Dominance

"Love your adversaries."

Let's say you are in the construction business; so are a dozen other guys in your town; you compete against them every day... can you still respect them and care about them as human beings? This is what Jesus demands of his followers, and it is an essential and healthy thing. Without this, business becomes war. Actually, without this meme being mutually held, *everything* inter-personal becomes war, with one person or another always dominating, and the other forced to submit.

Where co-dominance is absent, anger festers, compassion fails, grudges are never released, and endless volumes of energy are wasted in posturing and scheming. (As opposed to using energy to create value.)

Where co-dominance is present, cooperation rules and massive accomplishment can and does arise.

For people to live together in a peaceful way, either co-dominance with cooperation is necessary, or tyrannical central control is required. And individual liberty can only thrive in the former.

2.6.6 The Greeks and the Jews

One very interesting thing mentioned above is self-reference. This is what bridged the gap between the two great influences of Western tradition: The Greeks and the Jews. The adherents of the Greeks and the Jews have long been at odds with each other, although generally in ways more scholarly than physical.

Adherents of the Greeks (followers of logic and science) see the Jewish group (that is, the religious ones – remember above we showed that over 50% of the worlds religions stem from the Jewish root) as being irrational. The Jewish-inspired see the Greek inspired as cold – perhaps even soul-less – lacking in the more beautiful things of the spirit.

Although these two schools of thought are seemingly at war, without the combination of both world views, we would not be where we are today.

The Greeks were the first (at least from the view of Western civilization) to begin to think seriously about thinking itself. In time, they invented logic – the science of non-contradiction. Once we have a tool for judging self-contradiction, we can eliminate our errors. This was a solid technique and made possible the clearing of many difficult paths in front of us. Not that it would be fast or easy, but that it would be possible.

The Jews, on the other hand, didn't major on the science of thinking. They developed a framework to direct, control, and train men's biological impulses.

In other words, the Greeks addressed the intellect and the Jews addressed the emotions. That is obviously a gross generalization, but it is... um, generally... true.

Training the intellect is the more straight-forward of the two. The science is clear and logic does not require long study to comprehend. We cover it fairly well in a single section later in this book. Implementing logic in a real human being, however, isn't so simple. The minds of men are full of parasitic ideologies and troubled by erratic flashes of emotion (the effects of biological replicators). The Greeks gave us tools for weeding out bad ideas, and the Jews taught us how to mediate a truce between our minds and our bodies.

The contribution of the Jews is a bit more complex than that of the Greeks, but terribly important to the overall success of the venture. (A success, we must add, that is still incomplete and is still not certain.) The Jews may have had antecedents, but this is really quite speculative. It is possible that Zoroaster influenced them. Certainly Pharaoh Akhenaten tried monotheism. And certainly the Jews were influenced by Egypt in some ways. However influenced, they are the ones that developed a successful framework for restraining and redirecting many of the most powerful emotions of men – the kinds of emotions that can create real trouble when let loose to revel unrestrained.

We must insert that Jewish ethical monotheism has evolved greatly since its beginnings. It was far harsher at its beginnings than it is now. The major innovators since Moses (presuming he existed) were the Jews of the Babylonian captivity (Ezra and Nehemiah in particular), Jesus, and Paul. Judeo-Christianity can indeed be viewed as a single library of memes that work well together.

There is a great deal to say on the subject of the structure of ethical monotheism that the Jews created. We will stick to a few highlights. Here are the big ways that this structure was important:

2.6.6.1 Monotheism

Having a single god, rather than many, does many useful things. To begin with, it centers the mind on a single judge. Secondly, it parallels human nature. Humans are individuals and now God is a single individual. This makes it possible for men to compare themselves to the highest and the ultimate and to align themselves with the high and the great.

2.6.6.2 Supreme Goodness

The Jewish monotheistic god is almost always seen as qualitatively perfect. He is ultimately wise, fair, and so on. This gives believers something to strive toward. And since there is a huge theme of the believers being associated with God, they esteem themselves as at least largely able to gain these characteristics as well. This kinship of believer with God is especially strong in the New Testament, where the relationship is explicitly that of a father and his family.

2.6.6.3 The Ethical Becomes the Eternal

Non-religious folks are often amazed (and a little impressed) to see believers get up early to go to Church, go back at night, and so on. They wonder how, with all the complexities of life, they can continually do it. The answer is simple: If you really think that the creator of the universe, the judge of your eternal soul, wants you to do it, you simply adjust your life and do it.

If you begin with a strict religious assumption, it's not hard. And that is the point here: The Jewish creation magnifies ethical choices. Acting charitably toward your neighbor doesn't just matter here and now, it creates an eternal reward. (Eternity – now there's a concept that can make your brain circuits heat up.) So, if your ethical choices are hyper-important, you care about them! This leads to improved choices, each of which may have dozens of follow-on effects to the good.

Think about this carefully – it was huge.

2.6.6.4 Forgiveness and Repentance

Since the beginning, this set of stories has glorified men who had deep changes of heart. This not only allows bad men to start anew and improve, but it removes all guilt for their past actions. There are problems associated with this from a justice standpoint, but it did make human improvement popular. Again, this was hugely beneficial.

2.6.7 Contradiction and Non-Contradiction

Now, in all of the Jewish virtues listed above, there is a troubling element: Believing in HUGE conclusions with no evidence. And that is precisely why the Jews have always needed the Greeks.

The Greeks invented the technology (non-contradiction) that moves men forward. The Jews gave it a chance to thrive. The wild impulses of the human animal were directed inside the Jews' ethical monotheistic structure, leaving openings for non-contradiction to be applied to the thoughts of men.

The combination of these two ideologies allowed man control over body and mind, with new religious and political systems that balanced larger Collective Identities against each other. This was a recipe for unprecedented individual freedom in the west and led to the realization that individual freedom could create benefits, the likes of which no one had ever seen before, or had even imagined.

2.6.8 Better than the Rest?

Some people have a real problem with the judgment, "better." They immediately jump to ugly and bizarre conclusions, assuming that anyone who does not bow down before the altar of equality is a Nazi.

The truth is that there's not a whole lot of difference between any one group of humans and another. Heck, there's not much difference, genetically, anyway, between humans and chimps!

Why did the people of the West move forward better than the others? We don't know, and we don't really care. Maybe the folks in the West were a couple percentage points better than the rest in some way, maybe it was a lucky accident, maybe there are some microbes that made a difference, and maybe it was the work of some superior being.

In the book "Guns, Germs, & Steel," author Jared Diamond makes the case that western culture overran many others because of the effects of, you guessed it, Guns, Germs, and Steel (and a few other things). But guns are certainly a product of the ideological, and not a cause. The plagues that the West bred in its cities and brought to other places are again a product of living in larger cities with denser population – an effect of the ideas, not a cause. The materials to make steel might have been easier to get at in certain parts of the world, but the will to dig it up, and the recipe to make it, are again a product of free ideological evolution, not a cause.

So why the West? Who cares? Let's just call it an arbitrary statistic that western culture has moved forward ideologically better and faster.

There is no guarantee that the West will continue to do better. Other parts of the world that have seen western progress and imitated its economic freedoms have already experienced the same acceleration of progress. Collective idea-organisms continually create an environment where people have to fight against central control. Should the West lose ground in this fight, while those following close behind on the same path do not, then the West will be quickly surpassed.

Why the West learned these cultural and economic lessons first is not important. The lessons themselves, however, *are* important. Very important.

Knowing how this increased growth and prosperity happens – realizing that it is a product of individual freedom and self-responsibility, rather than any central authoritative control...

That just might be the most important thing in the world.

2.7 Interesting Times

In a speech in Cape Town, South Africa, on June 7, 1966, Robert F. Kennedy said, "There is a Chinese curse which says, 'May he live in interesting times.'" This was probably considered to be a curse because life is a lot more dangerous when the world is in a period of rapid change. However, such changes can also bring new ideas that allow us all to live better.

We would suggest that a related blessing might be "May you live *through* interesting times." If you can somehow manage to reach the other side of such a period of change unscathed, your world may well be a much nicer place to live.

In the previous section we talked about how the old collective ideas that had enforced a world of strong central control started to change. This change started slowly, but it picked up speed. The agricultural world changed and new arrangements replaced them to create the industrial world.

Some would say that advances in farming, travel, communications, and medical technology are what bring about new forms of collective ideas, rather than saying that an off balance and changing Collective allowed this new technology to spring up without being suppressed. We won't even completely deny that view. But we will say that it is a classic "chicken and egg" problem:

Greater freedoms allows new ideas – new ideas create new technology – new technology makes new ways of life possible – new ways of life force collective idea-organisms to scramble to adapt – uncertain collective idea-organisms leave (at least temporarily) space for even greater freedoms and we are back at the beginning. Start this cycle anywhere you like and, if it can continue to overcome the limiting factors, it may pick up speed like it is rolling down hill.

New technology can put incredible evolutionary pressure on Idea Organisms. In the past, a tiny little bit of new knowledge has slain many a large powerful old idea. This is why the powerful Collective Identities fear the changes of technology.

As the pace of technological change continues to increase, Collective Identities are more threatened by new technology than they have ever been. They have to change faster than ever before to keep up. It is possible that we will reach a point when new simple symbiotic memes are developing so quickly, that complex idea-organisms can not keep up at all. They may lose control completely and forever or they may yet find a way to stem the tide of new symbiotic ideas, both technological and social. They may yet slow progress to a manageable rate, and reassert control over the world.

2.7.1 Revolutionary Ideas

At the beginning of the Renaissance the religious bosses had been enthroned for centuries on end. They were given the benefit of the doubt at all turns and everyone followed them. This predictably made them very arrogant and they behaved badly for a very long time. But, eventually the more honest guys got up the courage to question them and their power began to splinter.

As we mentioned earlier, the new technology of the printing press let people actually read the Christian texts in their own languages and this created a new

God identity which partnered with a new type of State identity, then a new arrangement came into being.

This is when technological development really began to accelerate. The upheaval of the old collective idea-organisms left room for people to think freely. The freest thinking, least infected minds developed new technologies – new symbiotic memes. The new ideas that these historical geeks developed changed the world even more, and continued to keep the Collectives in a state of flux.

Also at this time, a very important new meme came out of the darkness and into the light of day. This was the nobility of commerce and of commercial success.

2.7.1.1 The Commerce Meme

Before this time, commerce was widely considered a dirty thing. Here is a story that illustrates the point:

> *A certain monk reported an important vision. He had been praying in his local church and opened his eyes to see demons everywhere. They were sitting on people's shoulders, waiting in every corner of the church, and generally trying to distract anyone in any way possible. There were hundreds of them. Horrified, the monk left the church and walked into the market square. There, he looked about and saw but one lone demon, sitting high on a pole and observing the people buying and selling. Seeing this, the monk was thoroughly distraught and prayed bitterly to God for an answer. How could it be that the church was full of demons, but the market had only one? Soon enough, the answer came: The demons had to flock to the church, because that's where people were being turned god-ward. In the market place, the answer continued, the devil already controls them all, so he needs only one demon to observe.*

This story was well-known, and the interpretation was widely accepted. But once the old grouping of ideas in the old dominant Collective Identity was broken up, this meme was subject to question. And, as people saw soon enough, having enough food, land, houses, clothing and provision was rather nice, and commerce seemed pretty good at getting all those things.

While anti-commerce memes remain today, and outbreaks of such thinking can still occur and devastate whole nations, compared to the dark ages, we are all fat happy capitalists.

2.7.1.2 The Science Meme

Under the old ideological regime, religious leaders had gone so far as to say that they knew everything about everything. Once they were shown to be wrong, their empires of fear cracked and the vast oceans of non-thinking obedience began to dry up. The need for those who claim to know the mind of GOD to be able to produce all the answers is the root of the war between science and religion. It was not just the Catholics that were opposed to new discoveries; a lot of Protestants hated them too.

As this began to run its course, religion got kicked to the back seat. In this void, science was able to function with much less intimidation. There was some science under the old system, but it was restricted and maligned.

Think of it this way: What if you were to develop a better form of money? Would the powers that be let you use it? Maybe. but only on the peripheries. However better your currency might be, it is not theirs, and the legitimacy of their money may not be questioned. You may not compete with it directly. Why? Because... well, shut up! There's something wrong with you!

Get the picture?

Like commerce, science provided excellent results and found a safe place in the new collection of memes that was forming. The religious memes did not want to let go, but as their best hosts began to die, and the new hosts were less receptive (having already seen a different vision of life on Earth), there was no real option left. They continued to exist strongly in some places, but fewer and less-strongly as time went on.

2.7.1.3 Wars and Geeks

It has been noted by many people, at many times, that scientific breakthroughs and new technology happen more quickly during times of war. Some have even concluded that war is therefore somehow good for us. This wartime surge of innovation may be the best evidence we have that collective idea-organisms spend a lot of their energy slowing the creation of new technology.

A war means that the Collective is competing violently with another Collective. During such time periods, it is reaching for any advantage that it can. It can not afford the safe route of suppressing new ideas that could be dangerous to it – instead it has to give its freest thinkers the opportunity to devise new technologies for killing people and destroying things – but also healing people, rebuilding things, communications, transport, etc.

The individuals, throughout history, who create new technology, have been those who are not as strongly molded by the Collective into standard pathways of thought. These people are the poorly-socialized geeks. They don't always know how to talk to members of the opposite sex, or blend into a group of people when it is best to be unnoticed, but their minds do some strange and wonderful things.

Free from the chore of thinking about correct social behavior with whatever large percentage of the brain that normal people use for this – the geeks can explore new ideas. They can see new ideas clearly for their relative costs and benefits to individuals, without the distortion of the Collective's desires.

In times when Collectives are not fighting for their lives – such people are too dangerous to be allowed to create and communicate new ideas freely and are suppressed or even killed. When the Collective is fighting for its life, it either does not have the time to devote to such suppression or recognizes the need for the production of new value that these people can create – even if it might be dangerous.

A whole book could be written on the topic of "war and geeks" – starting maybe with Archimedes who is famous for running through town naked in the excitement of scientific discovery yelling "Eureka!" He was also instrumental in building many new war machines to keep the Greek dream of freedom alive against outside invaders. Da Vinci, likewise known for many personality quirks, produced useful weapons for renaissance warfare. Tesla, a key man in the invention of radio and electricity, was renowned for his bizarre mannerisms.

Every time you look into the history of a great mind, you almost invariably find that the person was also a serious eccentric. Such people have only been tolerated in times of war, or times of greater freedoms in the gaps between colliding collective idea-organisms. In many cases, once these people won the day for their side, and the Collective moved back to a state of stability and stricter control, these heroes were once again persecuted.

Alan Turing was by all accounts a very odd fellow indeed. He was also a key figure in bringing victory to the Allies in World War II. By breaking Nazi codes, his work provided crucial information that could very well have made the difference in winning the war. After the war was over, the British government "rewarded" him by forcing him into experimental hormone therapy to try to cure his homosexuality. These hormone treatments caused him to grow female breasts. Turing became distressed and eventually killed himself.

The societal upheaval of war can create the freedom of thought necessary to allow free thinkers to exist unmolested and to advance science and technology. Fortunately, this upheaval does not always have to be war – the new ideas that such people create can sometimes keep society churning long enough for the next generation of thinkers to do the same. This cascade of freedom and invention is what we find ourselves in today. It produces an environment for freer exploration of technological ideas – much like a war does – but without all that annoying screaming, dying, and blood.

It is not a coincidence that the historical start of this cascade of new technology has been given a name that sounds like it was a war – it has been named the "Industrial Revolution."

But despite the general progression towards the creation of more and stronger symbiotic memes, and fewer and weaker parasitic ones, collective idea organisms continue to adapt in order to survive. They keep finding new ways to re-assert control. With the upheaval of older forms of the Collective Parasite, new contenders have evolved quickly to fill some of the same ideological niches.

2.7.2 Lines on a Map

One important subject we have just barely mentioned is the Icon status of local geography.

The land people live on has always been special to them. These feelings certainly increased when human beings invented farming – when the larger part of our food came from seeds planted in the ground. Even before that we had territorial instincts much like any other animal – hunter gatherers almost certainly had strong feelings about their hunting grounds. You can still see it today, as "The land where our fathers died", "Where our brave ancestors spilled their blood", "Where they tamed the wilderness," and so on.

Now, those may in fact have been good things, but it was not the dirt that made your ancestors great. If they were great – it was due to their own virtues. Dirt is for walking upon and for growing things. Warm memories about things that happened in a certain place are nice, but glorifying dirt is stupid.

Be that as it may, the local geography always developed into something of an icon for the people in the area, and helped them feel connected and unified. This is, of course, good for tax collections. (It is also good for military defense, another book-length subject that we'll leave alone.)

Note that land was more important both before and after the medieval rule of Church and State. The strong icon of the Roman Church suppressed and co-opted almost every other icon – The Land was no exception. This return to geography was in some ways a return to the norm and, in retrospect, it seems a lot healthier not to have a purely ideological entity like a church empowered above the ruler (even if the ruler is usually an idiot). Allowing an abuser to control the bodies of men is bad enough, but to have an inhuman idea-organism control their minds is much worse.

The sanctity of the land made a comeback and moved up in the Distributed Identity hierarchy. Until the industrial revolution, that is. Then everyone started to flee the sacred valley and move to the unknown, cold city; a place with absolutely no relevant mythology. Distributed Identities were a mess over this for some time.

2.7.2.1 The Map IS the Territory

Previous to the industrial revolution, building a larger kingdom entailed taking over a series of small, rural power centers. Now there were huge urban power centers and with all that manufacturing, specializing, and inventing going on, these cities were very, very powerful. That made all the Kings uneasy, although they, too, grudgingly adapted.

The new unit of collective rule would be the nation-state, complete with a modernized set of collective ideas.

Before the Industrial Revolution, people knew "where they belonged," even if the rules did change from time to time. Now, the farm boy often moved to a completely new place, where he knew almost no one and lived a radically different life than anyone in his family had ever lived. The nation needed an identity much larger than what was necessary for the local valley. If not, a neighboring nation – which had unified itself with a strong Collective Identity from border to border – would be able to defeat your country militarily.

The first part of the new national myth was simply to extend the local land icon. After all, the folks on the next hill were pretty darned similar to you – and the next hill after that – and the one after that... Pretty soon, the name of your individual valley mattered less and the name of your nation mattered more.

Just as the agricultural King needed a priesthood, the new national leaders needed people to encourage the loyalty and support of their people. In some places The Priesthood remained in this job for some centuries. In others it fell away. In the cases where the Church fell from favor, a variety of replacements were drawn in: Intellectuals, artists, orators, psychiatric associations, teachers unions, and many others.

All of this was made solid by the ideological organisms in human brains. As mentioned earlier, these always prefer stability. So once in place, the new order had its own roots. Today, the concept of the nation-state is considered unquestionable. It is that which is, was, and ever will be... except that it *was not* only a short while ago and almost certainly *will not* be forever, and upon real examination, has only some arbitrary lines drawn on maps as its justification for existence.

We are not saying that the nation-state is a particularly bad choice for now. An idea of national identity, confined to geographic borders, actually reduces the chance of expansionist warfare. After all, if our borders are somehow sacred, it wouldn't be right to change them by absorbing our neighbors. But, notice that seriously considering that the nation-state has not really been around very long, and may just be a temporary concept, is something that probably causes you a little mental discomfort. Uh huh, that's right, evidence of the Collective Identity in your head sitting up and taking notice of what you are thinking, unwilling to have its legitimacy questioned.

2.7.2.2 Vox Popular

Along with changing sources of legitimacy for this new world order, the mechanics of governance changed. The old order, based upon farm communities and the old methods of publishing and enforcing the King's commands, began to vanish. A new "city model" began to form.

A middle class composed of merchants, traders, supervisors and engineers appeared and grew steadily. Wave after wave of farm children came to the cities for good jobs. Banks, courts, meeting halls, merchants' associations, central markets, warehouses, barge terminals and more began to appear. The world took its modern form. However troubling these changes were, they were based upon science, and Science had a very powerful and respected place in the new hierarchy of memes. The changes would go on and everything else – short of questioning the state itself – would have to adapt.

Before this time, the idea of "divided power" meant divided among the nobles or perhaps divided with the clergy, but it did not mean divided with the peasants. At this time, the Greek dream of individual rule was "remembered" and divided government evolved into representative democracy, with the people of each area choosing and sending a few of their own to capital cities, in order to pursue their interests.

Yes, we all know that representatives don't always represent terribly well, but this was a significant change nonetheless. For the first time, the great masses of little people were a force for the ruler to reckon with. This was especially true as communications technologies improved and newspapers and mail became common – government actions were at least partially open to scrutiny and discussion.

Power shifted to the masses living in the cities. That meant that rulers were now in the popularity business. Getting huge numbers of people to vote for them determined their status and power. This was particularly true of the more industrialized nations, and since such states waged war better than others, the model proliferated.

Politicians had to learn to balance group against group and to figure out what the masses really want, what they are afraid of, and what made them like or dislike a candidate. Politics (rulership) became a manipulation contest. This led to a lot of work being done – purposefully – to strengthen the basest of human manipulators: Fear, envy, status, dominance and shame.

In modern times, Distributed Identities associated with the basest instincts are somewhat stronger now than they "should" be. Not only politicians, but corporate marketers and manipulators of all types, use the same mental hooks. Let's go through just one example, regarding how people tend to vote:

> Joe Half-think is watching TV, and a commercial comes on. The politician, dressed impressively, is warning him that another politician is getting ready to "slash spending" on the program that "we all rely upon" and that he'll give "your" money to his rich friends! This is called (in highly technical terms) Triple Sucker Bait. There is fear of losing something very important and maybe of a granny reduced to eating cat food. There is outrage at the bad politician stealing what it rightfully yours. Finally there is envy, that there are people richer than you and that they are getting a good deal. Now Joe isn't going to let them get away with it – so he votes for... a complete liar who doesn't even believe it himself.

If this wasn't how people voted, negative ads wouldn't work and you'd almost never see one.

Every time you hear a scary political slogan you are being played for a sucker. And, it gets worse! There are sets of memes that pump cheap self esteem into people because they are a member of a certain political group. (Demogogic, Repellican, whatever...)

Power thrives upon this, even though it is almost entirely fraudulent. Politicians take mountains of money away from people to spend it on imaginary fears that they create from scratch! The problems will never actually be solved but that really doesn't matter. In fact, if the problems ever *were* solved, they'd have to revamp their entire business structures.

Finding or creating an unsolvable problem has become a political specialty.

Being the boss is what matters. And the way to do that is to deal in envy, fear, and cheap self-esteem. Remember – it's now all about lines on a map. Keep the people jealous of their neighbors on this side of the line, afraid of those strange people on the other side of the line, and proud to be surrounded by the best lines ever to be drawn on a map.

If you do it right, you can become and stay rich and powerful. If you can actually make yourself believe your own lies, at least when the cameras are on, it all works even better.

And the crime goes on.

2.7.3 Enter the Isms

As the Industrial Revolution has spread and continued and the idea of the Nation State has risen, scientific knowledge has advanced and religion has lost some territory. This has happened slowly at some times, rapidly at others, even reversing upon occasion, but religion has been on a downward trend.

Because Ideologies are competing for territory in human brains, such a big idea as religion losing its strength creates something of a vacuum, or at least a gap. Perhaps it would be better to call it a memetic ecological niche that is going partially unfilled. As the Church controls less and less mind-space, other idea-organisms move in and fill the vacuum. There is some space for them to get started, but with even a reduced version of God still in a top place, and with The Nation State right up there next to it, these new memes have to begin first on the fringes, then – maybe – move to better positions.

2.7.3.1 Communism

Perhaps the most "successful" of the new breed of idea-organisms (which we have called the "Isms") found its niche by competing directly with commerce. Communism (or Socialism, its first stage) seeks to displace commerce in the modern mind, then to extend those gains all the way to Statehood.

Notice that one of the first things this ideology did was to create a derogatory label to place upon commerce: *Capitalism.* Free commerce is not about capital (that is, stores of money) it is about free human action and the creation of human value. But the idea of "capital" implies unfairness, stirs envy, and directs the mind completely away from the virtues of commerce. This has proved to be Communism's great tool.

Once it had booted commerce and was rooted in enough minds, Communism began to adapt in whatever ways would get it maximum power. The Bolshevik variant proved best at this. It waited for an opportunity to arise, and then seized power with extreme speed and force. The Bolsheviks took over the existing machinery of the Russian State and violently forced all other memes out of business.

This was the Inquisition on steroids. People died in mind-numbing quantities – only because of the ideas they held.

But because the Bolshevik pattern worked, other communist groups followed the pattern, and soon Socialism controlled major areas of the Earth. Something like 200 million people died in the ideological warfare that accompanied this Inquisition. In this example, better than any other we have, we see that human bodies are of no real importance to the idea organisms. If the easiest way to insure ideological supremacy is to kill everyone who disagrees – so be it; new bodies can be grown.

Once in power, Communism has shown itself to be the deadliest idea-organism ever to poison the Earth. In Cambodia, where the utter disregard for the human may have reached its peak, the ideology killed a third of the population in only a few years. These numbers are on par with the worst biological plagues in history.

In a head-to-head comparison, socialism exceeded the Church of the Middle Ages in killing people by a stunning margin... even as compared with the height of the Crusades or Inquisitions.

Despite Communism being the current, undisputed, death toll record holder, the anti-capitalist, anti-commerce memes remains strong. Go to most any upscale cocktail party and start talking about the utterly astonishingly and anti-human acts of Communism... but be ready to be scowled at and probably to be called some very ugly names. And you may expect that it will be otherwise seemingly intelligent, educated people who will become angry and call you the worst names, rather than engaging in reasoned debate on the topic.

Regardless of intelligence and status, anti-commerce memes have been firmly planted in many people's minds and tied to their self-esteem. Therefore it hurts the hosts to hear such ideas called evil. To these people, letting go of these ideals would be like pulling off a piece of their souls.

But, with over 200 million deaths on its hands, in a matter of decades... what else can you call Communism but evil? To pass over all of those purposeful deaths – purely for the sake of a disembodied idea... Dear God! What kinds of monsters can subservience to a collective Ideology make us!?

One of the most frightening thoughts for a couple of guys that are writing a book about collective ideas is that this was pretty much all Karl Marx did. He put some thoughts on paper about how government and economics worked, and how maybe it would work better someday. The big theme of his "Communist Manifesto" was really just the idea that the world would be a nicer place if people would just share the wealth. By committing this seemingly nice idea to writing, he killed over 200 million people.

So now here we are writing a book about political ideas, and it occurs to us that we don't want anyone to die. So we thought a clarification of our thought might be a good idea:

UNDER NO CIRCUMSTANCES ARE ANY OF THE IDEAS IN THIS BOOK TO BE TAKEN AS MEANING THAT ANYONE SHOULD BE KILLED – OR EVEN HURT A LITTLE. WE ARE DEFINITELY NOT GOING FOR THE DEATH RECORD HERE.

There – we feel better now. Oh, wait a second, let's add:

MARX PROBABLY FELT THE SAME WAY, AND YOU SHOULD ALL STOP KILLING EACH OTHER OVER WHAT HE WROTE TOO.

Oh, and:

JESUS ALMOST CERTAINLY ALSO FELT THIS WAY ABOUT HURTING PEOPLE.

Actually Jesus was quite specific on the topic, and it didn't seem to work for him... Damn.

Well, we have at least tried to keep it somewhat light hearted. Maybe if Jesus had told more jokes or drawn cartoons, not so many people would have died? Hopefully we will manage to keep our death toll well below his numbers...

2.7.3.2 Fascism

Fascism was a very unique idea-organism. It was actually a bid to directly replace the Nation State.

The State, as it exists in modern times, rests on the support of its citizens, more or less. These citizens reside primarily in or near cities and find their identity not only in their DNA, but as members of a scientific, industrial, modern world. Fascism was something of a return to the past in that it placed "The People" – the DNA group – at the top of the hierarchy of importance.

This "People" ideal said that The State was fraudulent, built upon a foreign base of money and the interests of Jews and other "peoples." With this idea more or less established, Fascism sought to replace the previous form of State. It promised to be more faithful and helpful to the "people" and demanded (not 'asked') vehement support from the people. If you didn't support the People, you were an evil traitor.

You can probably see that this was an ideology that was perfectly positioned to demonize outsiders and, most unfortunately, it did so quite well. It was also an ideology that pretty much needed to be expansionist in order to survive and the resulting war (World War II) killed some 65 million people.

2.7.3.3 Environmentalism

This is the big, new Ism. Modeled more or less after socialism and using many of the same strategies, this has risen rapidly in the last couple of decades, though more so in Europe than in the United States.

In defining what we mean by the Environmentalism idea-organism, we can say that we are referring to that which goes above and beyond the simple altruistic meme "try to minimize your impact on shared resources." As we have seen with other Ideologies, Environmentalism may have some symbiotic and altruistic memes, as well as many parasitic memes bundled together.

Remember that these new Isms are the product of old collective idea-organisms trying to adapt to a world that is rapidly changing and advancing. Slowing that change is a priority for modern collective Ideas. The two main ideas that enable progress are Commerce (creating and allocating new value efficiently) and Science (producing new ways to create value). Where Communism/Socialism attacked only Commerce, Environmentalism is also going after Science – and, very cleverly, it has learned to do this by putting on the clothes of Science.

Environmentalism may be the last shot for collective idea-organisms to hang on in their current form. It seems to be a clever enough adaptation that it could conceivably stop Western Progress – and it already has a strong hold established in Europe and is growing in the Americas. The reason for Environmentalism's greater success in Europe is primarily that religion memes have been much more removed from the European host-pool than they have in the US. This left a larger void to be filled by a new Ideology. Notice the way that followers of this ideology exhibit similar behaviors to what the religious Europeans used to display.

For example, service to nature replaces service to God. It's the same passion and the same devotion – just a different icon. (The scary part is where they try to enforce their dogma.) Environmentalism is a theology where nature replaces God. There are even versions that have an icon that makes this more explicit: Gaia the Earth Goddess. But even where this religious icon is not as explicit, the idea of a "natural order" is virtually equivalent to a "divine plan."

Adherents in the US display the same characteristics as the Europeans, and tend strongly to be non-Christians. But in the US there are still many fewer of them, as a percentage of the populace.

Environmentalism seeks to directly replace the religion meme, and seeks an alliance with Science, which is still strong (even though under attack by a few neo-tribalists). This alliance with the idea-organism version of Science is quite a two-edged sword for Environmentalism, since when science is practiced correctly, it cuts idea-organisms to shreds – but it is proving to be a fairly effective strategy for now. In order to make this work, Environmentalism must influence Science away from the scientific method – make scientists more concerned about whether conclusions are "good" than whether they are true.

On one hand, science is very useful to Environmentalism. By publishing scary, scientific-looking papers, getting scientists to sign petitions, and so on, Environmentalism got a free ride toward respectability. On the other hand, the actual scientific results are not nearly as impressive as the press releases.

Some of the original leaders of the movement have already shown themselves honest enough to admit their scientific errors, and have publicly turned against the collective ideology. Of course they are branded heretics by their former comrades. Fortunately, it's a lot less dangerous to be a heretic than it used to be.

Like all collective idea-organisms, Environmentalism has offered its share of horror stories concerning the fate of the world if its leader's directives are not followed. The current enviro scenario is the battle against global warming, but other disaster scenarios have been tried and failed to get as much attention – seas dying from toxins, holes in the ozone layer, genetically modified food monsters, and even global cooling. Ideological evolution is constantly searching for the scariest possible scenario to gain the most attention and win mind share.

Global warming is surprisingly meek for the attention it has received – its strongest claims seem to be that the seas will rise a couple of feet over the next hundred years. This is hardly end of the world stuff.

The degree of the claimed danger is not really the issue though. The issue is the bad thinking that goes into the arguments to avoid the claimed danger. Here are some important questions one needs to answer before trying to control the actions of other people in a "good" cause:

1. Is there really a problem?
2. How much value will the problem cost people in the future?
3. Will the proposed controls really stop the problem?
4. How much value will these proposed controls (including the power to enforce them) cost people now?
5. How does value lost now compare to future lost value?
6. Will collective controls now open the door to more controls later?

Instead of any real attempt to find real verifiable answers to these questions, Environmentalism makes its case for collective control over individual action with the same methods that have always been used by collective ideologies of all sorts – fast speaking, quick zingers, and the age-old "excluded middle" trick. ("Either you support our plan, or else you are in favor of sewage in Baby's soup!") The worshipers of Nature use the same logical fallacies that have served, and continue to serve, Gods, Countries, and Corporations.

The people that use these tricks may even know that they are stretching the truth – but they believe that it is in a good cause. This is the same as church and state lying to you for your own good. It is the same as communist revolutionaries killing now for a better world later. Environmentalism is just another idea-organism trying to control as many minds as possible – and as such its adherents know that they are righteous and can do no wrong.

Environmentalism is also attempting to absorb other Isms. The newest variation in Environmentalism's strategy is that it is increasing its infiltration of Nation States by making use of the groundwork laid by socialism/communism during the 1960s when socialists (now usually called Progressives) invaded existing state structures. This adaptation, rather than the not so scary global warming scenario, is probably the main reason for its recent rise to greater power.

This is a slow revolution via the Trojan Horse model, in which Environmentalism is infiltrating existing structures by absorbing Socialism. There are a lot of socialist types who are installed, able and willing to influence what they can towards any promising socialist cause. Environmentalism has tried to become such a cause.

Maybe we should just call this the *Sixties Strategy*. But, whatever the name, it has proven to be very effective. Marxism, for example, has been as completely discredited as an idea can be, but it remains King in the University. Socialist types are ensconced there and they promote whatever ideas make them feel young and revolutionary. The icon of Nature seems to be providing what these people need.

> A group called FEE (The Foundation for Economic Education) exists to combat the anti-commerce memes that are still spread in United States Universities. They promote the teaching of economics through student seminars, and the publication of free market literature of all sorts. According to their website at www.fee.org, FEE's mission is "...to offer the most consistent case for the 'first principles' of freedom: the sanctity of private property, individual liberty, the rule of law, the free market, and the moral superiority of individual choice and responsibility over coercion." – Sure sounds good to us!

Whether the socialist/enviro alliance will gain strong control over any Nation States is an open question. Environmentalism seems to be gaining power with its current strategies, but Science may reclaim its nerve and dethrone it, or a few good winters could do the job.

Things could get quite entertaining. If the scientists do a bit of thinking, they'll figure out that environmentalism is anti-technology, and if we'll have no technology then we'll have no use for science. The more thoughtful scientists have already figured it out, although plenty more are still running around looking for easy grant money.

Hopefully the death toll from this one will not even be measured in the tens of millions, but in the crazy world of collective ideological organisms... Well... Now that we think about it, the death toll on this one is already pretty high if you include the banning of DDT and the resulting malaria deaths. (DDT was banned in a mania following the first big Enviro book, "*Silent Spring.*") In the book "State of Fear", Michael Crichton wrote:

> *Since the supposed ban, two million people a year have died unnecessarily from malaria, mostly children. The ban has caused more than fifty million needless deaths. Banning DDT killed more people than Hitler.*

In addition to obvious deaths, there is the much more difficult issue of reduced production. You never know where and when a little extra convenience and comfort might give someone the intellectual free time to develop a cure for cancer – or to make any other major new technological breakthrough. We can't know what specific value is not created because of artificial restrictions. But since we are on an exponential upward growth curve, intellectually we can know that any artificial restrictions have exponentially growing costs going forward.

Body counts are obvious, but they may be the smaller part of the cost we pay when we let collective idea-organisms restrict our freedoms. We may pay a larger price in lost opportunities; geniuses who are ignored, dreams that are never realized, value that is never created – useful world-changing technologies that take longer to invent or are never invented at all.

2.7.4 The Long Arm

Another recent collective icon to make the list is the concept of "The Law." This may seem a strange thing to call an icon, but it actually has all the right parts and effects people's thinking just like any other Collective Identity.

The Law or the concept of Law Enforcement has its roots in an older concept.

2.7.4.1 Justice

Remember Lady Justice? She carried scales with which she weighed each case, and wore a blindfold so she would not be swayed by the sight of those who were being judged. She was a slightly different icon, for a somewhat different concept than The Law. She represented the idea that the scales would always be balanced, that all evil would be punished, no matter whom had committed the evil. Whereas enforcing The Law implies forcing the actions of each individual to conform to a set of collective rules – just or not.

> *That standard of justice is what Max had always been after. He hated to hear his business called 'law enforcement.' "Law enforcement," he used to say, "is a cheap substitute for justice. Half-justice at best, and frequently much less." The further he rose in the ranks of the FBI, the more he was forced to do 'law enforcement,' and the less real justice he could pursue.*
>
> --A Lodging of Wayfaring Men

The idea of punishing evil presupposes that we know evil when we see it. This is not too much of a stretch. The whole concept of "law and order" is to have a society in which all the things that can go wrong are minimized. We know when something has gone wrong. Therefore, we know what we are trying to minimize. If we believe that punishing someone will reduce the "wrongness" in our world, then we do it.

We try to create a system that maximizes reward for those actions that create value for everyone and maximizes punishment for those actions that detract value for everyone. This is not just true at the societal level – but personally as well. We give feedback to those around us, concerning what is and is not acceptable behavior. When situations are extreme enough, this feedback can and does take the form of violence.

Our sense of justice is based on the idea of Natural Law, which is the law we feel in our hearts to be correct. (This is properly based upon self-reference, but "know in our hearts" is how it is traditionally explained.) The things that really bother us, to the degree that we would be willing to use violence to stop them from happening, are the things that we consider illegal under a system of natural law.

Now, since different people have different ideas about what really bothers them, it seems like society might be stabilized by finding some normal average of what the people believe to be wrong. That idea is that we should write down the things that, on average, society feels so strongly about that violence will be used to stop or punish someone doing them. This is done for two reasons. First to keep weirdly insensitive people from doing things that are, on average, considered bad, and warn them that society will object violently to these things. Second to warn weirdly sensitive people against reacting violently to a thing that, on average, society does not care enough about to prevent with violence.

While this *seems* like a good idea, it is where we start to lose our concept of justice, and replace it with the idea of "Law Enforcement." We stop thinking in terms of what is right and wrong, and start thinking in terms of legal and illegal. If it is written down as "illegal" it must be bad – and we know this not because of certain results, but because of a label that has been assigned.

Goodbye Justice. Welcome your new icon, The Law.

"We definitely got her on brandishing this deadly weapon. Do scales count as drug-paraphernalia?"

2.7.4.2 The Law

Once a list of things that society will not tolerate is written down, it has the unfortunate tendency to take on a life of its own. Earlier in the book we noted the difference between a list of individual ideas and a list with an impressive title like "The Ten Commandments of God." The deal is the same here. When you have a list of rules that people are expected to live by, and you label it as "The Law of the Land," it stops being a list of separate ideas and becomes an indivisible unit which requires your respect. The moment it is thought of in such a way, it is harder to criticize individual bad laws that happen to make the list.

Somewhere the paradigm shifts, and it stops just being an informative list that tells anyone who reads it what the things are that members of a society, on average, would be willing to use violence to stop. Instead it becomes a list that, if you can get something written into it, allows you to cause society to use violence in the way you want it to. And boy do Collective Identities like to be able to direct societal violence where it will do the most good for the idea-organism.

Law starts as a way to *identify* bad ideas and ends up as a tool to *enforce* bad ideas.

It changes into a system where, once something is written on the list, society is obliged to use violence to enforce it, even if the average person in society would not think it to be a thing worthy of violence. This means that if you can get something put on the list, you can harness the full power of collective violence to your cause. This is true, regardless of how much any specific member of society, or society members on average, agrees that your cause is worth using violence to achieve.

The list of laws can become something sacred. And when the list is sacred, challenging any part of it is sacrilegious. Even if the list is not considered sacred, it is hard to keep it from expanding to things that only some people care a lot about. If someone wants to put something on the list that society on average does not favor, but would not normally think worthy of using violence to stop, people are not likely to object much.

It's hard to stand up and fight for everyone's right to do something that you personally find distasteful, even when you don't think it is worth initiating violence to stop or punish the people who like doing it.

The list of "crimes" always ends up being a lot longer than it should ever be.

Once the law has morphed into this form, it is sometimes known as positive law, in contrast to Natural law (which is sometimes called negative law). The positive-negative distinctions come from the idea that Natural law is there to stop people from doing bad things. It warns you that you must not do things that will get people mad enough to hurt you. "Must not do" is what makes it "negative" law.

The other system is positive law, which can compel your actions. Rather than just preventing you from doing things that bother others, it can require you to take actions that may bother you. "Must do" is what makes it "positive" law.

Natural law is about telling people not to piss off other people, positive law is about telling people what they have to do (and, hence, it often pisses people off). It is also the ideal mechanism for Distributed Identities to enforce themselves as a Collective. (Ironically, we observe that positive law has many negative effects.)

Positive law is a list of rules which must be obeyed – even if those rules aren't things that folks would normally care enough about to use violence to enforce. In order to have these rules enforced, the Collective needs a special group of people willing to use violence to make other people do whatever is written down – because it is their job and they are just following orders.

Unfortunately, it has never been terribly hard to find people who will enforce rules without questioning them.

2.7.4.3 Law Enforcement

Collectives are often divided into different organizations. This represents the same advantage that multi-cellular biological organisms have. Different cells can specialize and group themselves into an organ that provides certain services to the larger body. Each cell still contains the same genetic material, identifying it as part of the same organism, but each is differentiated to perform a certain function based on its location in the body. Likewise, each person in a Collective may be hosting the same basic ideology, but their roles can differ depending on the organizations to which they belong.

Organizations for the purpose of law enforcement are just such an organ.

While the rules of proper conduct in the minds of the people may vary, the purpose of a law enforcement organization is, theoretically, to keep societal norms of behavior in line with the laws of the land. This enforcement causes feedback to the minds of the people and brings their mental ideas about what is acceptable in line with the written law. Although the idea of law is to have a system in which the people's ideas of right and wrong give rise to the codified rules of behavior, an opposite pressure becomes felt, and what is written in the codified law affects what people think of as right and wrong. The Law becomes a powerful icon that can be used to enforce collective behavior.

2.7.4.4 The Law as Icon

The rise of The Law as an icon, started out, as all such things seem to do, with only good intentions.

When John Adams declared his preference for a "nation of laws, not men," he was talking about a nation in which all were equal before the law. (Remember that Lady Justice has a blindfold for this purpose.) But when you think of that phrase from a standpoint of ideological organisms, it sounds a little creepier. Taking individuals out of the equation and letting the information systems rule is exactly the bad thing we are talking about throughout this book.

Once The Law is an icon of high authority, with specialized organs to enforce it, these enforcers are often given different rights than normal people. When this happens, you have divided the members of society into separate classes.

1. Law Makers
2. Law Enforcers
3. Law Breakers (Criminals)
4. Potential Law Breakers (Everyone Else)

In a democratic system, this becomes somewhat circular, with the first and last classes on the list being somewhat blended together. The idea is that by some system, all the people can influence the making of the laws. This is a big step in the right direction, but there can still be problems.

Ideally there should only ever be one class of people, all of whom have equal rights. But as long as only certain special people are allowed to enforce the laws, they are effectively a separate class with additional rights that others do not have. And as long as those who break the laws are forever after treated differently, they also become a separate class with fewer rights than others. (For example: In the United States, if you are convicted of a serious crime, you lose your right to vote – thus becoming a lower class of citizen.)

Granted, the Law Breakers class will likely be filled with a lot of total scumbags. However, in a society that expects its people's morals to follow what is written in law – rather than the other way around – anyone who fails to bow to the Icon and tries to maintain their own ideas of right and wrong may be labeled a criminal. When this happens, they lose their ability to try to change the laws of the society.

Even if they happen to be right, who is going to listen to a criminal?

This is all great stuff from the point of view of a Collective Identity that wants to control everything within the society, but from the point of view of individuals who want the best set of rules for a society based on what works best for people, not for collective ideologies, it totally sucks.

Are you infected with this Distributed Identity icon? Think about how you feel about this statement: "You need not have any respect for The Law – you just have to respect other individuals." If that statement bothers you, it is because you are hosting a DI called "The Law." Actually that statement works pretty well for testing your feelings about any idea-organism. The word "respect" is a BIG deal for an idea-organism.

2.7.4.5 The Law at War

The icon of The Law and the idea of Law Enforcement have worked so well for the Collectives, and have grown so much in recent times, that the United States doesn't go to war anymore. Instead it has police actions. In this way, it makes it clear that other nations will follow its rules and be pressured to think as it chooses. It does not invade them and take their territory into itself. The concept of geography as icon may actually have gotten too strong for that to happen. So it has adopted the concept of Law and cast its military into the role of global police force.

In some ways, this makes the idea of "The Law" the current King of the mountain, and it is quite possible that the concept of "International Law" will eventually grow to be the controlling ideology of the planet. It may start out as just an imposition of the will of the most powerful nation states, but if they remain constrained by their sacred borders, an icon of International Law could break away and start running the whole show on a global scale.

Ironically, at the same time the military of the United States has become a global police force, back home it has become normal to sell bad law enforcement by declaring it to be a "war." The current biggest, most futile, exercise in impractical law enforcement is called "The War on Drugs." But we will talk more about that, and the nature of The Long Arm of The Law, in the next chapter.

3
Your Money or Your Life

In the previous chapter we reviewed the history of the world with a focus on the evolution of ideological life forms. The best parts of history are stories of new symbiotic memes and how they have helped mankind survive and thrive. The worst parts are stories of war between competing collective ideologies and the damage that parasitic memes inside these Ideologies have caused.

In this chapter we will take a look at modern forms of collective idea-organisms. We will examine the ways in which the Collective bends the individual to its will and makes sure that some large part of individual productive effort gets channeled into the survival and reproductive goals of the Collective. This channeling of resources takes the form of a loss of value for individuals everywhere. It is a price paid in property, liberty, and sometimes even lives.

While it is true that God claims the highest authority, the Geographic Country (Nation State) is actually the strongest player in controlling peoples' lives in our time. Although the State's moral authority may not be as great as God's, it certainly has more guns, bullets, and policemen than God currently commands.

The collective forces we are mostly talking about in this chapter are the governments of Nation States, where such government can be defined as the organizations that makes the claim that they have a legitimate right to maintain (and use) a monopoly of force.

We will also discuss how the various idea-organisms in a society compete for influence in the government – for a chance to use this legitimized violence toward their own ends.

While reading this chapter, keep in mind the things we have talked about previously concerning the nature of icons as faces for collective idea-organisms. Worship of these icons is what allows behavior in service to the group that would never be tolerated on the part of lone individuals:

Murder is wrong, but the Nation State is allowed to kill.

Slavery is wrong, but the Nation State can direct your actions – make you do work without compensation.

Theft is wrong, but the Nation State can demand that you contribute property.

Those who look favorably on the Icons of the Nation State believe that since their Country is good, any action taken in its behalf must also be good. Those that carry out these actions feel blameless because they act in service to a Higher Power – they "know" that they are the good guys because their icons are good. While they would never kill, enslave, or steal from another person for individual gain, they believe that it is alright to do such things on behalf of a Nation State.

This same logical error, that allowed the Church of The Middle Ages to commit atrocities, now allows powerful Nation States to turn greater technological capabilities to the task of even greater stealing and killing – limited only by the need to keep a certain level of stability for host human beings to stay productive.

I WANT YOUR
MONEY

3.1 Killing the Goose

We have already discussed how The West took the lead economically when gaps between the competing/cooperating idea-organisms of Church and State left room for individuals to have greater freedom of thought – and hence to create new value. The paradox from the Collective's standpoint is that if the wealth that such free thought creates could be turned towards the "right" goals, the idea-organism could strengthen itself and replicate itself forcibly to other nations. However, that same freedom of thought makes it hard for the Collective to guide its hosts to such actions. For the Collective, this is a classic "you can't have your cake and eat it too" scenario.

Let's take a look at how the degree of central authority affects the nature of a collective:

3.1.1 Strong Central Authority

One man with a gun can control 100 without one.

-- Vladimir Lenin

Ideas are more powerful than guns. We would not let our enemies have guns, why should we let them have ideas?

--Joseph Stalin

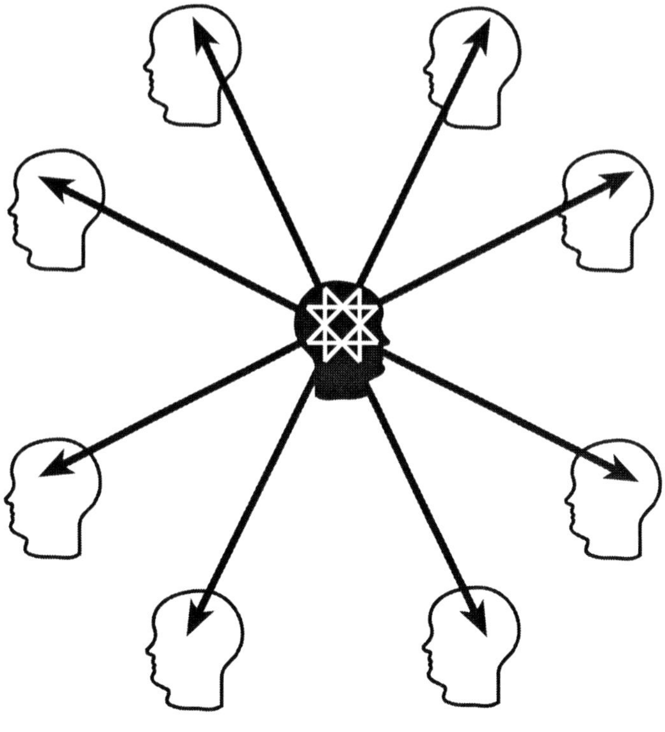

The idea behind a Collective with strong central control is that all "important" decisions are made at the center of things. Information comes in from all points and central decisions are communicated back to the people that need to take action. Authorities at the center are presumed to have the best possible information and thus the best chance to make exactly the right decision.

When information speed was slow and the world was not changing as fast, having a central hub for decisions might have been the best solution for the survival of a group of people – but that has definitely changed as the technology has increased and everything is moving faster.

3.1.2 Weak Central Authority

That government is best which governs least.

-- Thomas Paine

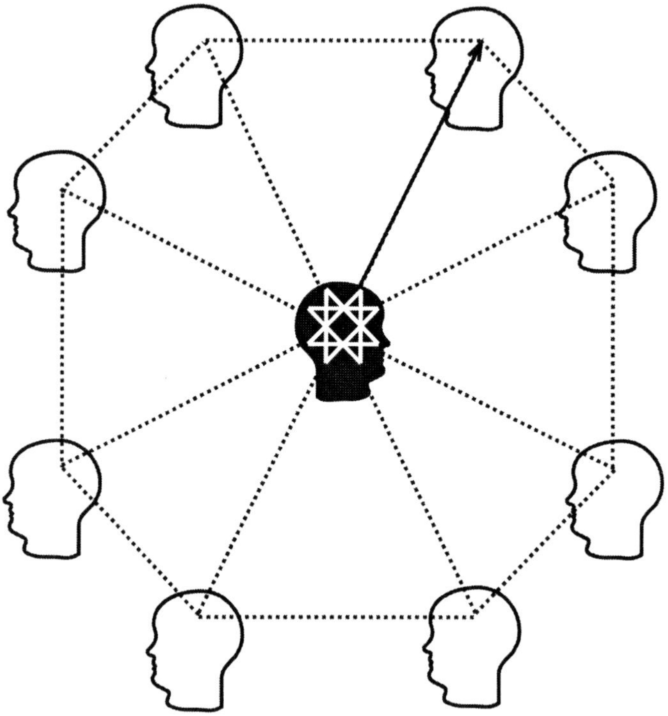

Weaker central authority makes better decisions faster. In such a system, the central authority only rarely gives orders, and only when a threat to the power of the central authority is perceived. No attempt is made to control every action. People are allowed to think and act for themselves. In such a system the center acts as a distribution point for the best possible information.

A reasonable amount of information must also be passed from person to person, bypassing the central authority; this insures that the center can not completely distort the truth. Without this independent communication, a slow creep towards stronger central authority is almost guaranteed. Limited central authority is therefore possible only with communications systems that allow a wider range of person-to-person communication. Decentralized communication systems lend themselves to supporting the concept of Free Speech, which limits the growth of control by central authority.

3.1.3 No Central Authority

> *That government is best which governs not at all; and when men are prepared for it, that will be the kind of government which they will have.*
>
> -- Henry David Thoreau

> *While the state exists there can be no freedom; when there is freedom there will be no State.*
>
> – Vladimir Lenin

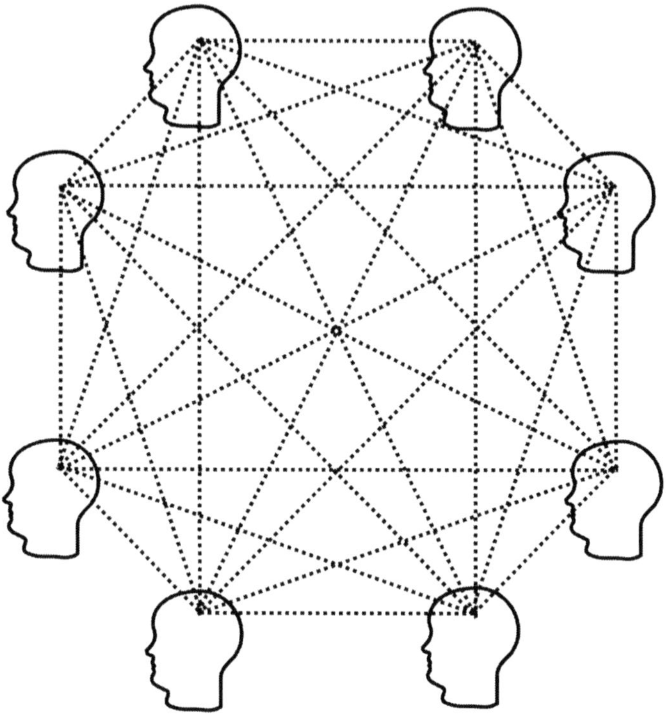

If people are allowed to act on their own ideas, and anyone can communicate ideas with anyone else, then no single authority need ever decide what the mandated solution is. A good idea can be communicated more quickly to everyone, and many people will implement it. At the same time, others are free to pursue better ideas and try new things. This allows a better idea to come along at any time, even to replace an already good one. This is both a faster path to a good solution and a never-ending process of producing even better solutions.

The less central authority is allowed, the faster and better all solutions become. And those solutions continue to improve with each discovery of new information and/or innovation.

3.1.4 Communications Systems

Decentralized systems are only possible with fast, unregulated, person to person communications. Not surprisingly, this sort of peer to peer communication is resisted by any existing central authority. Central authority will especially resist technology that allows any arbitrary individual to broadcast information to a large numbers of interested parties. Such systems allow ideas that are against the central authority's purposes to germinate and spread very quickly.

The better and faster a Collective's communications systems are, the weaker its central authority becomes, while at the same time benefit to individuals increases. Good for individuals, very scary for a Collective.

Note that in the "No Central Authority" diagram above, information may flow from any individual to any other individual, without any center point of control. This is precisely the type of communication system that has grown first and fastest in the West with the advent of modern telephony and the Internet.

3.1.5 Just Choke It A Little Bit

The Collective is always forced to allow some level of individual freedom. A weaker Collective Identity makes better decisions and can adapt to external threats faster, but a stronger Collective Identity can better subvert human resources towards its own needs. This is the delicate balancing act that any Collective Identity must manage carefully.

The goose that lays the golden eggs must not be allowed to fly away, but if the collar is too tight, it can choke to death.

Unfortunately, there is no good feedback system when the Collective starts to go bad. When it starts to choke the goose too tightly, the goose will get angry and pecks at it. (Yes, let's way overstretch this metaphor.) Then, the Collective will push back at the goose by squeezing harder.

Now, in real world terms: When people start to feel overly controlled, they'll start to subvert those controls. This gives the Collective's bosses an excuse to declare emergency measures and to call on their people's loyalty to the group, "in this time of crisis." The reflex will be to impose tighter and tighter controls until either all out civil war or internal coup results. The other possibility is that the Collective will be destroyed from the outside because it has grown weak from internal strife, or because it failed to keep up with the innovations of freer systems that are competing with it.

Individual human minds may be smart enough to recognize when things are heading in a bad direction, but the Collective is not, and therefore neither are those who unthinkingly serve it. When central control increases to the point that free individuals become powerless to change the system, things have started to go down a bad road – one which almost always ends in a great deal of human misery.

3.2 Controlling the Market

A large part of what collective idea-organisms do involves economic manipulation and control. This is a good point of attack for control of all human behavior, as the exchange of value is what makes all modern human lifestyles possible.

The things that free individuals value differ from the things that the Collective values. The desires of collective idea-organisms affect the market significantly, making it – on average – produce results that are worse for individuals – resulting in less overall human value.

Collectives have great influence. And when they use this for their own selfish purposes, it distorts the market and disrupts the efficient allocation of resources... at least as those allocations of resources correspond to the best solution for individuals.

And before we get into this, we should be careful to explain that trading is THE central mechanism for human survival, at least for survival beyond bare sustenance. Without free trading between humans, we could not have anything more than what we grow in our own back yards. No water purification, no sewers, no refrigerators, no heaters, no car, no air travel, nada. If you think self-sufficiency sounds romantic, go try it for a while. (You have no freaking idea.)

Trading is simply what people do, unless someone forces them not to. Label it capitalism if you must, but it's really about free trading. And this is the thing that allows humans to specialize and to increase production. There is enough 'stuff' on this planet for all of us to have many mansions. The problem is making use of it. Free trade is the best method ever seen for efficiently allocating scarce goods to where they can create the most value for people.

3.2.1 The Collective Desire for Monopoly

Collectives, as we have said many times now, behave like living organisms. And if you look at nature, you will see animal eating animal, with never a guilty thought. Animals are, from our standpoint, fully amoral. We don't attribute malice to the bird that eats the worm, do we? There is no morality implied – the bird is amoral – it is hungry and it eats what it can find.

Collectives have an amoral desire to feed to expand and, like animals, they will do this to whatever extent is possible.

Humans are, to these organisms, raw material. We are hosts and we are creators of more power. We are things to be used. It's not that the Collectives are actually malicious; it's that they are wholly amoral. They want to be the bird, even if it means that we are the worms.

The basest of economic instincts is to presume what economists call a “zero-sum game.” That means that there is only so much money (or whatever) to go around. The name comes from the Game Theory side of economics. Think of the game Monopoly, which has a strictly limited amount of money in the game's bank.

Here's an example: You sit down with some friends to eat a pizza. Let’s say that there are twelve pieces and four people, so you each can have three. But if you are really hungry, you might want a fourth. In order to get a fourth slice of pizza, for yourself you have to take one slice of pizza away from someone else.

The zero-sum game is how primitive human societies always looked at wealth. And it is also how collective idea-organisms still look at wealth. "More" must be obtained by taking it away from someone else.

The alternative to the zero-sum game is called the *positive-sum game*. You can think of a positive-sum game as one where, unlike Monopoly, additional money can be put into the bank during play.

A positive-sum version of the example above would end with the person wanting more pizza getting up and making another pie (or driving to the pizzeria to get one). Additional work produces additional pizza.

Positive-sum is how modern economies work. (They could have worked like this in the old days too, if everyone hadn't kept trying to steal everything within their reach.) When they started selling microwave ovens, did people stop buying gas or electric ranges? Of course not. The people who sold microwaves didn't have to steal "slices of pizza" from the range makers; they simply "made their own pie." Positive-sum economics presumes that humans can create wealth – that scarcity can be overcome.

If you look at economics this way, you'll find a never-ending set of strategies by the Collectives to maximize their advantage in the market; a market that they presume to be zero-sum.

3.2.2 Disapproval and Prohibition

There are two ways in which collective values can work to repress unwanted (by the Collective) ideas and actions. The first way is through expressions of collective disapproval, the second is through use of collective Force.

Collective disapproval may not sound as strong as using force, but in many ways it can be just as effective. Since no one is compelled by force, it is not really a distortion of the free market, but rather an expression of the values of the Collective, within the free market. It is, in our opinion, a good idea to ask, "Do we want our market to reflect the values of parasitic ideas?" If the answer is "no," certainly it would be hypocritical to try to use any sort of force to prevent it. Education concerning the nature of collective idea-organisms would be the only right answer.

3.2.2.1 Collective Disapproval

If you live in a place where certain actions meet disapproval, you will tend to modify your behavior, even if there is no other bad consequence to be faced. In fact, knowing that the people around you disapprove of your actions can make you feel physically bad.

In most cases, it is the ideological that must bow to the biological. This is because ideology can change a lot faster than biology. So, the pressure that the biological exerts on the ideological occurs over more "generations," and produces more change. The ideological cannot exist without the biological, nor exert direct change on it. However, human beings have lived with ideological replicators long enough that some backwards pressure on human bodies to have occurred. Rather than any specific ideas enforcing changes in our bodies, our biology has responded to make us feel a fear of being different than the group.

The reason that this is a biological survival issue is simple enough. Up until very recently, from the standpoint of biological evolution, human beings could not easily move around the planet nor exist in a fairly anonymous way in a big city. The survival of a human being was, to a great degree, predicated on the ability to work well within a small group – a tribe. In fact, this structure is seen in other animals too, and almost certainly predates human thought processes by hundreds of millions of years.

Amongst a small group, disapproval can be as deadly as any weapon. If the rest of the tribe believes in the Sun God, and you express your belief in the Moon God, they may stop taking care of you. They do not need to actually crack your head open with a rock to seriously hurt your chances for survival. If they only stop sharing food with you, you're in trouble. If they decide not to back you up when a big cat comes hunting for some man flesh... well, you're dinner.

Once ideological organisms catch onto this (and remember how fast they adapt) pressure is put on the biological replicators. The resulting mutations cause people to feel bad when they are in some way different. This is likely the source of the quite physical reactions associated with embarrassment and shame. The biological pressure to change your ideas can be so severe that some groups can condition people into believing almost anything. (I know you don't think this could happen to you, but it really can – your body will betray your mind in a minute. All your body cares about is physical survival and reproduction – your genes don't know and don't care what strange philosophies might be bouncing around inside your skull.)

Biology adapts slowly. So, even if you live in a culture where different thoughts will not lead to being shunned by the tribe and starving to death, your body still sends chemical messages warning that not blending in is a bad thing. And, since ideologies may still use the direct method of brute force against the non-believer, those chemical messages may still be giving you good advice from a physical survival standpoint.

3.2.2.2 Collective Force

While the expression of the values of Collective Identities bends the free market away from what it could be if it reflected only individualistic values, it is still a working market system. The use of force in the cause of the Collective doesn't just bend the market, it breaks it.

There is a huge difference between a group of people expressing disapproval – even refusing to associate – and that same group of people authorizing the use of force to make a person behave the way they want them to. Morally, it is similar to the difference between paying for something you want and taking it at gunpoint.

And there is no doubt that the market is indeed the target of collective idea-organism interference. A currency (like dollars or Euros) allows for the fluid exchange of goods and services. It is targeted in cases of prohibition. The first step towards fully prohibiting goods and services that do not further the goals of a Collective is to prohibit the exchange of money for them.

Where a society is not yet restrictive enough to be able to ban all unapproved sex, it can often ban the exchange of sex for money. Where it can not yet remove the right of individuals to put anything they want into their own bodies, society may still make the sale of certain substances illegal.

Where such restrictions are not yet possible, the market can still be skewed by taxing goods and services that the Collective disapproves of. The mathematics are fairly simple from the point of view of the Collective – if some activity is an unwise use of resources, coupling it with a direct contribution to the collective coffers can cancel the sin. In religion this took its purest form in the purchasing of indulgences for sins; in the secular world, the form is taxation. (Which are sometimes even called "sin taxes.") But even though this is a lesser measure than criminal charges and punishment, the Collective must still have a means to enforce such rules.

However, the biggest hit to the market comes when the Collective starts to enforce its rules through physical violence or the threat thereof. Doing this invariably requires a new class of people with different powers to act as the enforcers. This can be trouble even to the Collective that spawns this new organization.

The first problem is as old as the first police department. It is summed up by the Latin Phrase, "Quis custodiet ipsos custodes?" which means, "Who will watch the watchmen?" This group of humans is clearly free to break the rules as long as they stick together as a group and fail to police themselves.

That policemen are free to break the law is not so bad all by itself – at least not from the Collective's standpoint. Just as it is okay for the televangelist to sin in private as long as he keeps many others toeing the collective line, it is okay for the cops to be robbers as long as they are all doing more good than harm. The harm comes from the fact that any group assigned to such a task will evolve its own group identity.

The higher-level Collective is, in fact, spawning a lower level Collective to act as one of its organs. Such lower-level Collectives must, by their own evolutionary logic, do more harm than good, both to Individuals and to the Collective that spawned them, because they must redirect as much value as they can to their own survival and growth, and this value is leeched from the higher Collective and taken from individuals.

However, some of this harm to the Collective is canceled by the advantage of specialization. Much like biological animals have specialized organs that perform certain important functions, the evolution of Sub-Collectives can be a net gain for the overall Collective. It is however, important that Sub-Collectives identify themselves strongly as such, or they can actually grow to compete with the overall Collective. (Think military coup)

3.2.2.3 Enforcement Agencies

Let us take a look at the life cycle for a new agency of prohibition:

The agency is being created for some reason. Some good or service exists in the market that is deemed to be damaging to the collective "way of life." Let us call our prohibited thing "Behavior X." If the Collective perceives it to be a large enough problem we can jump right to the creation of the new agency, but if not, it might be something that needs study first. So a panel of one or more qualified people is put together to study the problem.

The panel gets together to decide if it has a real problem to work with. If it decides not, then it winds up, and everyone has to go look for a real job. However, if the panel wisely decides that Behavior X is a serious enough problem to require prohibition, then, as the "experts" on the evils of Behavior X, everyone on the panel gets a job that lasts for as long as the Behavior X problem continues to exist.

So an agency is created to fight Behavior X and it is given a budget to hire the initial employees (perhaps the original "experts" and many of their friends and relatives). The Anti-X Agency (AXA) must then come up with a plan of action to combat Behavior X and put it into effect. If the plan is immediately successful in wiping out Behavior X then AXA has no more purpose, will receive no more funding, and all the employees of AXA must go look for a real Job.

As long as Behavior X continues to be a problem, AXA might continue to exist. If the problem of Behavior X grows or is perceived to grow, AXA will receive more funding, and more employees (perhaps more friends and relatives) can be hired. With more employees comes more sub organization, and pay bumps for the new department heads (those same early employees).

So the main job of AXA is most definitely not solving the problem, but rather scaring everyone into believing that the problem is worse than ever. On the other hand, AXA can not be seen to be losing the battle, or it might be replaced by some other agency, so it must seem to be always winning the battle. Also, we have new departments all fighting the same way to survive and grow. Eventually there will be sub-departments, and so on.

> *Big fleas have little fleas, upon their backs to bite them. And little fleas have lesser fleas, and so ad infinitum.*
>
> -- Old proverb

What we have described is the evolutionary process by which a parasitic organization takes up residence within a larger collective. The final product is an organization that spends its time and money showboating and scaring you, always claiming to be winning the war on Behavior X while at the same time claiming that the problem is also somehow worse than ever. They are forever claiming to need more resources from us in order to fight this horrible problem, and ever reminding us what a horrible problem it still is.

> The "War On Drugs" is the most obvious example of this sort of organizational budget growth, and the spending of that budget to further scare the public. It becomes all about the money, and not at all about protecting people from anything. In the United States, laws have even been passed allowing drug enforcement agencies to take private property directly from citizens, and the citizens can only get it back if they can prove that it did not result from "drug money." This is exactly opposite from the right of Due Process guaranteed by the U.S. Constitution that requires proof in court before any property can be taken. As usual the Constitution (the supposed highest level of law) is ignored by The Law.

That sounds pretty bad, but it's even worse when you consider that most of the agencies in your government are probably operating like this. This evolutionary process weeds out agencies that are efficient enough to solve the problem they are asked to solve, or ones that fail to keep the problem in the public mind, or ones that don't overreach their original mission. And since the public grows used to something that stays the same and stops caring about it, only problems that continue to grow worse will continue to stay in the public mind. So your government ends up as a large collection of agencies that manage to do just the opposite of what they are set up to do. Instead of solving problems they make them gradually worse – or at least scare you into thinking they are worse.

The message from your government is a fairly constant one: "You are in more danger than ever as we continue to make you even safer!"

3.2.3 Values and Vices

Values are quantities (like numerical values) that we assign to things in the world, according to how much we prize or despise them. We might not use numbers, but we do say, "I like that a lot" or "I hate that!" By saying these things, we are assigning values to those things.

Now, this is important: We express our own values when we reason, decide and choose. But if we simply follow others and Authorities, it is some idea-organism that is expressing its values, and we're just an unpaid spokesman.

All expressions of values can be seen as the extension of some replicator or combination of replicators. For example:

> If you like candy, it is because certain genes cause you to be predisposed to the taste of sugar.
>
> If you prefer boxers to briefs, it could be that that your body is more comfortable that way, and/or, it could be an ideological question of taste.
>
> If you wouldn't be caught dead wearing white after Labor Day, then it is certainly just a question of ideological replicators expressing a strong value.

Vices (depending a bit on how you define them) are things that individuals value but the prevailing Higher Powers do not like. Ideologies would rather have you do only things that increase the ideology's chances for survival and replication. Any time or money you spend doing something that does not further the Higher Power's ends is a waste of time, and is certainly something to be discouraged – those are resources that could be put to work serving the Higher Power's needs.

Depending on the level to which a Higher Power is bothered by an action, vices will receive some level of tolerance. They can never be eliminated without eliminating the underlying replicators, and if those replicators are in any part biological, there is not much chance of this – yet. However, there is certainly a level of discomfort that a Distributed Identity can impose on its host to suppress these behaviors.

It can also push its hosts to suppress such actions in others. This can represent a net win for the Higher Power, if it does not spend too many resources in discouraging the behavior. In fact, if a host is good enough at discouraging resource wasting in others (from the Collective's standpoint), it matters little if a host engages in those same behaviors privately. This may, in fact, be a common sort of compromise that can be made between the replicators that must share a single body.

This would certainly explain why televangelists always seem to get caught with a pre-op transsexual prostitute, while snorting cocaine off his-her boobs, and listening to death metal music – or some other such blatantly hypocritical behavior.

Those who fail to practice what they preach, are always the ones preaching the loudest.

3.2.3.1 Sex

From the viewpoint of the Collective, sex is a good thing – but only to a point. Sex leads to babies, and babies have very impressionable minds that are quite likely to end up hosting a copy of the resident collective idea-organism. Occupying the mind of a child is much easier than attempting to colonize the mind of a non-believer and evict the native ideas, so the Collective is very big on unprotected sex for the purposes of producing children.

So if the Collective is all for sex, why does it seem to have so much to say on the topic, to the point that it often seems to be against it?

Well, for one thing, the Collective needs sharp hooks in order to motivate people to do its bidding. If it can convince you that you need to have a special public ritual that is accepted by the Collective (marriage) before you are getting any, then it has enlisted a powerful biological drive to its cause. If, on some level, people are made to believe that they can only have their fix of regular orgasms with the approval of Church and State, and if they were not good worshipers/citizens that these pleasures could be denied them, the collective Higher Powers end up with a lot more enthusiastic believers.

Also consider that there exist quite a few sexual behaviors that can give people their orgasm fix, yet are guaranteed to produce no offspring: masturbation, oral sex, anal sex, gay sex, sex using contraceptives. Wow – look at that – that list, plus any "extramarital" (non Collective authorized) sex and incest (which can produce birth defects) would be almost exactly the list of sexual behavior that we find is routinely discouraged by Higher Powers. Coincidence? Nope. The Collective definitely likes healthy babies.

Beyond this, there is the guilt factor. This is extremely useful to Collectives. Not only is guilt very powerful, but it is an emotion. That means that it does not need reason in order to function. Think about this: Collectives need people to sometimes act against their own self-interest. How are they supposed to do that? Encouraging people not to think is one popular way, but humans don't always comply with that. So, the only other path around reason is emotion. And guilt is a strong one. Now follow us here...

The sex drive is the most basic, hard-wired, immovable force in humanity (well, after the need of air, water and food, maybe); it's what keeps the race alive. It is the one thing that is most difficult to restrain. So, if you make people think that the sex drive is evil and must be restrained... and they basically cannot do it except by heroic measures... then you have a super-duper, never-fail way to create guilt!

After that, getting people to act contrary to their own interest is pretty easy. Make them feel guilty and make them feel that they owe the Collective the action you seek, and they'll do it. This has worked like a charm for all of recorded history.

Finally, also consider "gay" sex – an act that produces no offspring – and think about why the Collective reacts the way it does to the idea of gay-marriage. That is the idea of condoning a sexual relationship that does not produce offspring. If you think of it in these terms, it's not the homosexuality *per se*, that is the trigger. The Collective would probably react in much the same way to talk of a new kind of heterosexual marriage that was to include only oral and anal sex. Many Collectives are specifically about demanding only reproductive sexual behavior.

3.2.3.2 Drugs

Various chemical substances are known to distort various functions of the human body. Some of these can be used for medical reasons to produce beneficial results. Some make people feel good, some bad, and some just interestingly different. Some are poisonous substances that can kill even in low doses. Many fall into more than one of these categories at the same time.

So what causes some of these substances to be labeled a vice by the Collective, while others are considered harmless or actually approved of?

As with the issue of sexual behavior, the major discerning factor is the question of "Does this behavior serve the needs of the Collective, or does it waste resources that could better be applied elsewhere?" Of course it is not that cut and dried, because we are dealing with an evolutionary process with constant random mutations. Also, advancing technology is constantly uncovering new substances that have different effects on the human body. Since it takes a while for a new thing to be evaluated, the general answer is: If it's new it's bad, until it is proven good. If it's old, we will try prohibiting it every now and again anyway to see if that makes things better or worse.

Alcohol is one very interesting case. It has been with human beings for a very long time, and its value as an anti-bacterial agent has, in the past, helped many cultures avoid water-born diseases. Before chlorinated and fluoridated water, people used to drink watered down alcohol, rather than straight water. Straight water could kill you. Alcohol can also be harmful to people and it can cause behavior that meets with collective disapproval. (Loss of inhibitions caused by alcohol might be looked at as a temporary suppression of the parts of the brain that hold our models concerning approved collective behavior.)

It has a long history of changes in its status from Prohibited to Mandatory and everywhere in between. Some people say it's bad, some say its fine. Of course, the real issue is not whether any given substance is good or bad, but whether we should allow people to do things that are bad for them.

Imagine a world where, instead of ingesting small amounts of poison to feel differently, people found they could get high by hitting themselves in the head with hammers. Of course everyone would have their own hammer type of choice. Tough macho guys would use sledge hammers. Fancy young ladies would prefer small hammers made of crystal. There would be an ongoing debate between the ball-peen and claw-hammer crowds, concerning the quality of the buzz obtained.

In all meaningful ways, it would be the same world as ours. People would certainly become addicted to the released endorphin from all that hammering. Sometimes they would overdo it and hammer themselves to the point of seriously injury or even death. Some would have to go to rehabilitation centers to kick the hammer habit. There would even be some fatal car accidents because hammer heads were driving while still dizzy from too many blows to the skull.

And just like our world, certain groups would probably even try to make certain types of hammers illegal, and jail the people who used or sold them.

Of course, one difference would be that when you called up a friend on a Friday night, you would say, "Let's go out and get poisoned!"

Making any drug (be it alcohol or heroine) illegal in an attempt to prevent voluntary destructive behavior, makes just as little sense as outlawing certain types of blunt objects because people are choosing to hit themselves in the head with them – or certain types of rope because people are choosing to hang themselves with them.

Actually deaths due to recreational strangulation/hanging and auto-erotic asphyxiation have been increasing in the United States. Is it only a matter of time before the purchase of something as mundane as rope becomes heavily regulated?

3.2.4 Censorship

Another group of things that Collectives are very keen on controlling is any idea that it finds dangerous. And it does make some sense for the collective idea-organism to attempt to restrict control of all media channels. But, as we pointed out earlier, tight control on information flow can also seriously hurt the health of the Collective. The areas that do tend to get censored regularly are closely aligned with commonly prohibited behavior. Once again it's a case of Sex, Drugs, and...

3.2.4.1 Rock and Roll

The ideas of young people are always of great concern to the Collective Identity. Those youth are the next generation of true believers, and must be infected with the values of the Collective if it is to continue to survive. However, there is a gap between the experiences of adults and younger folks. This leads to a rise of a separate, sub-DI. This is the DI of the new generation. You know the ones who always know everything that matters, and know that their parents are completely out of touch. While these kids almost always grow up to adopt most of their parent's culture, not all of the ideas packaged in the previous generation's DI cross the generation gap to the next generation. New ideas can and do replace the old in this turnover. This is a place where the old ideas are really fighting for their lives.

Music often spreads these ideas, and the adult who stops to listen to the lyrics of their children's music is often shocked. This leads concerned mother's groups to lobby for mandatory labeling of music. This, of course, also applies to magazines, comic books, video games, and any other media targeting youth. Sometimes the leisure entertainment of the newest generation goes so far (by the standards of the older Collective) that it is banned.

3.2.4.2 Pornography and Other Spectator Sports

Because of the link between sexual behavior that is not approved by the Collective and sexually stimulating information in the form of text, pictures, and video, it does not seem too odd that the Collective wants to censor erotic media. Sometimes it even tries to make it out to be an addictive drug. To contrast the way the Collective Identity acts towards pornography, consider for a moment the parallels between media that deals with sexual situations and media that deals with sporting events.

Where the Collective frowns on sexual media, it highly approves of sports media. Where a father giving his son an adult magazine might be considered evil, a father giving his son a magazine about baseball would be considered quite wholesome. They would seem to be entirely different things. However, they are actually very similar.

Sports media targets the tribal instinct in human beings in exactly the same way pornography targets the sex drive. Both produce adrenaline rushes that can be considered addictive. Both give a person a sense of participating in something exciting where they are not actually participating. Rather than actually going out and engaging in real sexual behavior, a person can use pornography to receive vicarious gratification of the sex drive. Likewise, rather than actual engaging in tribal behavior that involves actually fighting with some other tribe, sports allows a vicarious outlet for those drives. Just as a person can sexually fixate on a media icon, rather than actually falling in love with a person they know, so can a sports fan experience a sense of hero worship over a sports idol, rather than falling under the influence of a local cult leader. In this way, both mediums are "gaming" the biological system – deferring biological needs that might lead to consequences that they are not ready for by faking out their biological replicators.

The reason the Collective reacts unfavorably to one and favorably to the other should be pretty clear. The impulses that the individual is redirecting in the sexual arena are impulses that lead to production of more hosts for the collective DI, while those that are being redirected in the sporting arena lead to the production of competing smaller collective DIs that could grow to offer competition. It may be that by encouraging the creation of harmless Fan DIs that have no teeth, the Collective is avoiding the formation of a more dangerous type of DI.

> This may also explain why the Collective seems to have no problem with the standard plot of an action adventure movie – or television show, in which the hero stands as an individual against the Collective. This type of entertainment also serves as an outlet for impulses that could break apart a Collective's control if channeled into real life actions. If you can vicariously be in on the fight against the Evil Collective with your favorite action hero, you don't need to fight for freedom in real life – you can be a good tax-paying citizen.

Perhaps when the University of Michigan "battles" Ohio State in the "Big Game," this diffuses a regional rivalry that could otherwise eventually turn into an actual armed conflict between the two states. The whole concept of organized sports and the vicarious sense of self-worth that fans draw from watching their team win, might be what allows Nation States to be as large as they are now without breaking up into smaller regions fighting each other for the sake of regional pride.

Local jurisdictions regularly buy their professional sports team's new stadiums, spending large amounts of local tax dollars. One would think that the higher level Collective would see this as a waste, unless the resources expended doing this were far less than what might otherwise be lost to local armament and internal conflict without this mechanism for diffusing such local DI tensions.

In addition to all this, actually playing team sports serves another important purpose – preparing young men for war.

Playing sports is different than watching. Rather than the "tribal" unity, it is a "team" unity. This prepares young men for battle in many subtle ways: Making sound decisions on the fly, rising to adversity, instinctively helping your teammates, grace under pressure, seeing many actions at once and integrating them, and so on.

This is very much in the interest of the Collective, and sometimes in the interest of the human as well. Just because warfare is essentially evil, don't think that it is always a waste of time. If you are being attacked, war skills are necessary; very much necessary. It is a fool's conceit that he can talk an irrational thug out of violence. And if your DIs don't like the sound of that, remember that history proves it – over, and over, and over again.

3.2.5 Taxes and Tithing

OK, we just explained that unwanted behavior (from the Collective's standpoint) can be deterred by expressions of disapproval or through threat of collective force. Similarly, resources needed by the Collective may be obtained by asking for donations, with expression of approval towards those who donate and disapproval towards those who do not, or alternatively, by threatening the use of force against individuals who do not contribute. Contributing to the Collective coffers without fear of force we'll call tithing, where force is used to obtain the payment it is called taxation.

Just as with prohibition of goods and services, the use of force to obtain funds damages the creation of value that free market exchanges might otherwise produce.

Normally, every free exchange of value creates additional value. This happens because people will not freely choose to trade unless they value what they receive more than what they are giving up. If both parties in an exchange value what they receive more than what they gave up, additional value is created (or released) in the exchange.

This additional value doesn't come out of nowhere – it isn't magic. It is a factor of goods or services being supplied where they do more good. For example, you have heard the phrase, "He could sell ice cubes to Eskimos," which is funny because Eskimos live in a very cold climate. The phrase, "He could sell ice cubes to Polynesians," wouldn't have the same exaggeration-based humor, because Polynesians live in a hot area, and could really use the ice. Therefore if Eskimos traded ice with Polynesians in return for pineapples, each would have received something that they valued more, and thus new value would have been created. The new value comes from moving something from where it is not highly valued to where it is.

The great strength of the free market is providing goods and services to the people and places where they are most needed, producing the most additional value.

Unfortunately, not only does taxation take value out of the hands of people who can presumably do more good with it than the Collective, but the taking of it, no matter how it is done, also creates a deadweight loss in transactions that don't happen. This takes value out of the market, and thus reduces the average value of everyone's lives.

Ten out of ten economists agree that if the free market can provide given goods or services, having the government provide the same, funded by involuntary taxation, is a bad thing to do to the economy.

Taxes can be taken from people in many ways.

3.2.5.1 Income Tax

The idea behind income tax is that you give some percentage of money that you earn to the government. This form of taxation may have originated with the custom of tithing some percentage of one's income to one's church. It is a pretty good system from the standpoint of collecting the money because you are asking for money from the people that are making money.

The deadweight loss that occurs due to this form of taxation happens because people need to make a certain amount of money for it to be worth their while to do a given job. Since they must pay the government part of this money, the bar is set higher on the salary that an employer must pay for any given job. This means that there will always be employers and employees who can not quite hook up on the price that the employer can pay.

In a nation with income tax, jobs go undone and people remain unemployed. Without the income tax, this work would get done and economic value would be created.

3.2.5.2 Sales Tax

The idea of sales tax is that on any economic transaction involving money, the Collective takes some percentage. Again, like in the case of income tax, this leads to deadweight loss in transactions that do not occur due to the higher prices that are required of a buyer for the same goods. Buyers that would have made a purchase at the untaxed price will not necessarily find any value in the exchange at the taxed price.

3.2.5.3 Inflation of Currency

Sometimes called a "hidden tax," a Collective that controls the issue of currency can fund itself by simply printing more currency. This causes everyone's currency to actually be worth less than it was previously, but it is not so obvious that value is being taken. Deadweight loss is caused here by the fact that prices will always be somewhat higher than they would otherwise be to reflect the knowledge that money is losing value over time.

> Think of it this way: Everything in the United States has a certain amount of monetary value. And, there are only a certain number of dollars in circulation. So, let's say that your factory is worth 0.01% of all US dollars. Now, if Congress goes out and prints up 20% more dollars, your factory is worth only 0.008% of all US dollars. The long, slow result is that the dollar has lost about 99% of its value since the Federal Reserve Act that allowed Congress to print up money with relative impunity. (Not that any other countries are much better about this. Many are much worse. This always happens when politicians take control and the currency is uncoupled from real value, such as gold, silver, or any other real world goods or services.)

On the plus side, this form of taxation causes no additional deadweight loss in the overhead for calculation and collection of the taxes that requires work for no economic benefit whatsoever.

3.2.5.4 Other Possible Tax Revenues

A few other ways to tax occurred to us while writing this, but since governments never stick to just one method of taxation, even if the ways we came up with might be better, it would be VERY irresponsible for us to publish them and give the Collective new ideas about how to take your money. This is particularly true since each new type of taxation causes additional unplanned consequences and requires additional compliance costs.

If the government could be convinced to only have one type of tax, it could raise the level of that tax such that it would be the same revenues as the current multiple tax systems. The boon to the economy of not having to deal with the compliance costs of multiple systems would be significant.

It has also been shown that in some cases reducing tax rates can actually increase tax revenues. When taxes are decreased, the amount of damage that taxation is doing to the economy is decreased. This can stimulate more economic activity and actually result in higher tax revenues.

This was famously illustrated by a diagram called the "Laffer Curve" named after an economics professor who sketched it on a napkin for some politicians. These politicians went on to argue publicly that tax revenues could actually be maximized by lowering taxes. While this can indeed be true, any argument that starts with the premise that our goal is to maximize the amount of value put into the hands of the government does not sit well with us.

3.2.5.5 Government Fees

It also is possible to have a system of taxes in which people pay only for the government services they voluntarily use. Sometimes called "Consumption Based Taxes," these are the most free-market friendly form of tax there is, and might not even be called taxes, per se.

However, if private parties could offer the same services legally, and the choice to use government or non-government services was voluntary, then the government service would just be another competitor. In that case why have government service at all?

The fact that government services are almost always protected monopolies, or are not voluntarily purchased, means they need not, and therefore will not, offer the same value as a non-government service organization.

3.3 Good Enough for Government Work

Wealth is created through individual actions and transactions between individuals. Not only do Collectives use this newly-created wealth for their own ends (at the expense of individuals), but wherever the Collective intrudes on the free market – requiring and prohibiting economic behavior by threat of collective force – the result is always inefficiency. Not only does such market interference cause economic deadweight loss by repressing actions that would otherwise create value, but governments often intrude to the degree of completely taking over whole industries. Let us look at a typical path by which this happens.

3.3.1 Regulation

The first intrusion of the Collective into any industry is the start of regulation. This begins with information coming to light about how this industry could be better. Perhaps it could make safer products – perhaps it could be less polluting – the claim is that there is something this industry could be doing somehow better. Always, this is mixed with a certain amount of fear, envy or outrage to better sell the idea.

The free market would normally take care of this problem, as new information gets to customers and they look for a competitor in the industry that does this thing better. If it costs more to do this thing, then people decide if it is worth it to them by how much they are willing to pay. This is a signaling system that works perfectly, given perfect information.

Regulation can only be good if the regulators always have better information and always act benignly. Neither is normally seen to be true.

In the name of making the world a safer place, the Collective creates regulations concerning the industry and creates a new agency to enforce these new prohibitions of economic behavior. Now, much like the cases we have previously talked about concerning agencies of prohibition, this agency begins to grow and branch out. It increases the number of regulations and the degree to which it enforces these regulations.

The cost of any good or service offered by the industry has already started to increase in response to the cost of compliance with regulations, but this additional drain on the economy is only paying for the additional cost of doing business, it is not paying for the cost of enforcement. The money that pays for this new agency has to come from somewhere. If the people had been willing to voluntarily pay more for this better safer industry, the new agency would never have needed to exist, so they certainly are not going to be happy about paying the additional costs plus oversight and enforcement costs.

Licensing is the usual next step as a means of both raising revenue and exercising greater control over the industry.

3.3.2 Licensing

So the next step, if this industry "needs" to have oversight, is to make it pay for it. A new oversight tax is then implemented in the form of licensing fees. And to justify these fees, additional levels of oversight are added in the form of verifying the suitability of anyone trying to get a license. This means that before any new player enters this industry, they will have to have a stamp of approval from the Collective.

There is even a religious example of licensing. Actions of individuals are controlled by a church through the concept of Sin, in much the way the government regulates through the concept of Law. Churches used to allow people licenses to sin – called Plenary Indulgences. They would allow the rich to buy the right to act as they chose. (The church was issuing a "license to kill" before James Bond's agency, MI6 ever existed.)

The interesting thing here is that when this occurs, there may already be a free market organization (that is to say, one that can not get away with using force and thus has to provide real value) that has already been certifying members of this profession. This organization may call itself a school and provide training followed by certification, or it may just call itself a rating agency, but it is in the business of giving consumers additional information when it comes time to choose from many competitors in an industry. More than one competing rating industry may even (and likely does) exist.

The government (the Collective that can get away with using force) doesn't like competition, so if it's going to go into the rating industry, it is going to want to get rid of these competing organizations. The easiest way is to just absorb them (see below), making them part of the government. This is done either by actually declaring them governmental, or by cementing a relationship with one of them such that its credentials are accepted, and all other agencies credentials become worthless. In exchange, the Collective assumes control of all policies for the previously free-market rating agency, which now has a product that is legally mandated.

You might expect the actual professionals in this line of business to complain about this – maybe go on strike or something, but it turns out that they like the situation. You see, the harder it gets to satisfy the government to get a license to be in the industry, the less competition there is.

The natural laws of economics say that when demand is restricted, prices go up. This means that the people lucky enough to already be in this line of work are now making a lot more money – more than enough to afford the government licensing fees. If they are really lucky, the government will not only shield them from competitors, but they may also decide that their services are necessary for everyone, and make it mandatory for some or all of the people in the Collective to become customers.

The AMA (American Medical Association) is an example (just one of many) of a government supported trade union in the United States. The government puts the task of licensing of doctors into the hands of the AMA. It then carefully restricts the number of new doctors that are allowed to practice each year, and thus makes sure that the cost of medical care is kept high. This high cost benefits the members of the AMA financially. It is also used by the government as a political tool to justify greater regulation of medical matters. This is the same system used by every union, trade association, or guild, since this form of Collective Identity first evolved.

3.3.3 Absorption

When everyone is forced to pay more than they want for a product they do not want (does that sound familiar?) then the government does its final trick. It has already infiltrated this industry on all levels, so it is no big move to just declare it to be a government service. They combine everyone in the business (if they want to remain licensed to practice) into a single non-competitive government agency. In a final bit of bitter irony, if the Collective is not strong enough to do this without explaining itself to the people, it claims that it is doing this to reduce the rising costs that are hurting this vital industry, and to protect it from the perils of the free market.

In the United States, the airline industry is right on the verge of this level of governmental control. These days the Geography Distributed Identity is very strong in the form of the Nation State, so travel is a highly suspect thing and prone to strong control. The railroads have been an effectively nationalized industry in the United States for many years, and it is quite possible that the U.S. Government will find the necessary excuses to do the same with the airlines. The hobgoblin of terrorism is already moving things in that direction.

3.3.4 The Finest First

The first private businesses to be absorbed or replaced by any government are justice providers. Living in a non-frontier area (as you almost certainly do) the idea that a police officer could be anything but a government employee may seem ridiculous to you. This is a Collective Identity talking – there is no conceptual reason why a system of privatized justice can not work.

In the United States today, security guards and bounty hunters employed by bail bondsmen are all that is left of private justice providers. But in the early days of the United States, private cops were well known. The Pinkerton National Detective Agency, established in 1850 was the largest police agency (public or private) in the country during the late 19th Century.

In theory, the only thing that separates a government authorized police officer from any other citizen is a government monopoly on the job of serving warrants. This certainly need not be the case – at least in theory. A government that only consisted of legislatures and courts could exist, and when some person or group wanted law enforced, they could pay any of multiple private law enforcement services to do it.

The Framers of the United States Constitution saw "policeman" as just another job like "plumber." They likely did not think of a policeman as having to be a government employee, or even someone who had to be licensed.

Today, in the US, law enforcement agents are almost a separate class of citizen, with many special laws protecting them. It is illegal to impersonate a police officer – much as a serf in feudal Europe was not allowed to dress like a noble. It can even be more illegal to physically defend yourself against a large armed and armored man who breaks into your house in the middle of the night, than to do harm to a defenseless little girl in her own home – that is if he has a badge and she doesn't.

Under such a system, when you felt you had been wronged (let's say someone stole your car) you would obtain a warrant from a court and could go to a police agency to arrange a deal with them for trying to recover your property and/or bring the alleged criminal to justice. A private insurance company could be involved to pay you for your loss and pay a police agency to try to recoup their loss – also saving you the trouble of having to negotiate with the private police agency.

There is no reason why such a system could not be made to work. In fact, there have been such systems at various times and places in history. The reason they do not last, and the reason you have all sorts of objections to the idea popping up in your mind, is that such a system does not allow for a lot of the laws that various idea-organisms would like to have in place. Control of law enforcement is the first place that idea-organisms attack to gain control over the actions of any group of people.

A government monopoly over law enforcement is the gateway thug.

Until this is allowed, government can not control any other industry. Until this is allowed, there can be no enforcement of laws concerning victimless crime. If there is no victim, who would complain?

Laws based on immoral behavior – drug laws, prostitution laws, gambling laws – are all the product of idea-organisms. They are all attempts to force ideas of some code of behavior on people that don't think the same thoughts. Laws that mandate any business to be licensed or operate a certain way are likewise a product of the need of the Collective to control things. Immorality laws and economic controls are both examples of laws that regulate otherwise voluntary behavior and contractual exchanges of value between consenting individuals.

Collective idea-organisms can not assert serious control over individual behavior until you have a government designated law enforcement agents going around looking for people who break the rules, rather than a justice provider responding to actual complaints. The out of control growth of government agencies and bad legislation all starts with the monopolization of justice – the change over from Justice Providers to Law Enforcement Agents.

3.3.5 Consequences

Real world observation and experimentation shows us that everything is more expensive and lower quality when the Collective does it. But why should this be?

Perhaps the waste lies in the transfer of value from individuals to the Collective – like the waste one sees in any transfer of energy from one form to another. Perhaps it is lost in the costs of the battle between individual and collective interests – the cost of taking it away from the individual. Maybe it is the cost of the damage done by the parasitic memes that get bound up in the Collective idea-organism? Whatever the reason, everything is at least twice as expensive when the Collective does it. That is why when they do something, they are the only ones allowed to do it. Free market competition would be more efficient and would make the government look silly.

To hide the fact that it is more costly, the price is often partially deferred into general taxes. Thus people are left paying only somewhat more for somewhat worse product and services, but separately, paying a higher tax bill. The tax bill may even look reasonable as a line item, after all it *is* a charge concerning a very vital industry, and the government *is* the only provider, so it *seems* reasonable...

The progression from freedom to control continues mostly without interruption. This progression, like all progressive control by the Collective, is very hard to stop and seems to be almost always one way. Given enough time, the Collective will first regulate and then take over any industry. It will start with those that are most vital and move on to all of them. It is almost always a one way journey towards more central control.

> *Government's view of the economy could be summed up in a few short phrases: If it moves, tax it. If it keeps moving, regulate it. If it stops moving, subsidize it.*
>
> -- Ronald Reagan

3.3.6 Deregulation

When things start to get bad there will sometimes be pressure against central control and talk of free markets performing better. At such times a government may be forced to do a feeble experiment in deregulation. This will be done by removing some controls, while leaving others in place, in such a way that is guaranteed to choke the industry.

One example might be opening up a free market in the suppliers for that industry, but continuing to fix prices for the end product. When the market for supplies rises temporarily above the level where the end product can be produced and sold for a profit, the industry starts to die and the government will move back in and declare "deregulation" a failure.

In 1996 the California State government announced that it was "deregulating" the power industry. However the actual legislation enacted included rules about who could own power plants, who could sell power to whom, time limits on power contracts, and strict pricing controls – while other California laws made it a practical impossibility to build new power plants as demand increased. California was experiencing regular blackouts by 2001 and "deregulation" was widely criticized as the villain of the story – never mind that the State's scheme more closely resembled a communist 5 year plan than a free market.

From then on, politicians can point to the failed experiment in "deregulation" whenever anyone suggests that free markets might actually work.

God help us!

3.4 How Bad Laws Happen to Good People

When talking about law, it is necessary to remember what we discussed earlier, that there are two differing philosophies of law:

Natural Law (also called Negative Law) is based upon the idea that you are free to do whatever you want, except things that are specifically forbidden, because they hurt other people. This was expressed in the Common Law as the idea that, "Your freedom to swing your fist only ends where my nose starts."

Positive Law is characterized by legislation from authority, and is based upon the idea that an authority can make things forbidden or mandatory.

> *Legislation, the deliberate making of law, has justly been described as among all inventions of man the one fraught with the gravest consequences, more far-reaching in its effects even than fire and gun-powder. Unlike law itself, which has never been 'invented' in the same sense, the invention of legislation came relatively late in the history of mankind. It gave into the hands of men an instrument of great power which they needed to achieve some good, but which they have not yet learned so to control that it may not produce great evil. It opened to man wholly new possibilities and gave him a new sense of power over his fate. The discussion about who should posses this power has, however, unduly overshadowed the more fundamental question of how far this power should extend. It will certainly remain an exceedingly dangerous power so long as we believe that it will do harm only if wielded by bad men.*
>
> -- Friedrich A. Hayek, "*Law, Legislation and Liberty*"

Natural Law is much better for the individual. Positive Law is much better for the collective idea-organism.

Under natural law, the local policeman is a Peace Officer not a Law Enforcer. His job is to keep life moving forward safely and productively. Under Positive Law, the police officer is employed by the state to detect crimes. In the former case the cops respond to requests from people who think something is wrong and they try to make it right. In the latter case the cops go looking for people who may well think that what they are doing is right but the government has made it wrong.

Natural Law was the original Common Law of England, which was then passed to the entire English-speaking world. Over time, layers of legislation have brought the English systems of law closer to Positive Law, but so far the foundation is still holding somewhat firm. In many places, the foundation of the legal system was actually Positive Law, but the success of the Anglosphere (English-speaking) countries has encouraged many to emulate the Common Law, at least in part. This gives us a world of mostly mixed Natural and Positive Law systems.

For the balance of this section, we'll be talking about a mixed system with a Natural Law basis but a layer of Positive Law instated by later legislation, as is the case in most of the United States. The roots in the English Common Law system still provide protection and value to individuals but collective idea-organisms are often able to use the layer of positive law for their own ends.

3.4.1 The Law of the State

Law enforcement organizations play a key role in any Collective. The laws of a society can be thought of as the society's genetic code. While the rules of conduct in the minds of the people may vary, the purpose of a law enforcement organization is, theoretically, to keep societal norms of behavior in line with the laws of the land. Different organizations are often charged with enforcing different sets of laws.

As we mentioned previously, such organizations are also the products of evolutionary pressure. They usually come into being as a result of some perceived problem that they are charged with solving. If they actually solve the problem, then they are no longer useful and will eventually disappear. If they seem to be too ineffectual however, they will also tend to disappear. This naturally leads to the existence of a collection of organizations that look very busy, but never actually solve any problems.

The other thing that an organization must do to successfully survive is to provide feedback in the society that perpetuates its own existence. They must continually exaggerate the magnitude and threat of the behavior that they have been charged with modifying. For example: Witch hunters would soon be out of a job if they did not regularly find witches to burn (whether they were there to be found or not) and exaggerate the power and danger of the witches that they defeated.

The end product of this is that the successful law enforcement agency must put on a good show of fighting a "war" against a problem that is always growing, and claim the need for more and more resources and power to combat the “growing threat.” They will also continually lobby for more laws for them to enforce and greater protection for the existence of their organization under the law.

3.4.2 How Far Shall It Go?

At one time new laws were hard to come by. Legislators had to travel long distances on horseback, discussion took time, voting took time, and getting the new laws to each little town took a very long time. But now, with jets, email and FedEx, new laws happen fast – in response to short lived media hyped issues. Worse, politicians are always trying to prove their worth by pointing to the new laws they enacted! Laws are multiplying, and that is NOT a good thing. More and more "victimless crimes" are being legislated. Where does it all end? How do we stop legislators from legislating?

> Actually, we do have one good example of how to keep legislators from making new laws.
>
> In the United States, during the presidency of Bill Clinton, the U.S. Congress spent a very large amount of its time discussing oral sex instead of passing laws. It seems that Legislators find sex scandals more interesting than creating new restrictions on our freedoms. A presidential sex scandal would seem to be a recipe for less legislation.
>
> This same time period produced huge economic growth and a boom of new technology companies. Coincidence? Maybe. But perhaps it is an experiment worth repeating.
>
> We would suggest that freedom loving people everywhere should try to vote in such a way that different branches of your government are always controlled by different political parties. (Political gridlock is our friend.) Furthermore, trying to elect politicians who you believe will find themselves in juicy public scandals seems to be a very good idea.

One example of police activities against victimless crimes is now called the "War on Drugs." Literally millions are imprisoned for non-violent drug offenses. Granted, many of these drugs are essentially poisons and taking them is stupid... but do we really need to throw millions of kids into jail to prove that we are righteous?

Perhaps you can see from our drug war rant that there is another element here: Once "the law" exists under the legitimacy of the collective DI, it is very hard to change. After all, "It's The Law!" and "If we don't respect The Law, we'll have anarchy!"

None of this is to say that there is not a legitimate place for a system of law, that snorting coke is good, or that we should allow people to sell these poisons to children on their playgrounds. But, once these ideas become "The Law," they have the legitimacy of a revered icon, which makes them very hard to question or to remove. This is a mistake and the “war on drugs” is just one great example where it stands out.

Legitimizing laws for any other reasons than their effectiveness at producing greater value for individuals is an error. A law is NOT good because it is part of "our system;” it is only good if it produces good results.

To respect a law for anything but its direct benefits to us is not really respect, it is worship.

3.4.3 Are Any Laws Good?

We have been complaining a lot about central authority and the controls it places on individual freedoms. However, this may contrast sharply with the idea you might have in your head that some kind of law is necessary or good. Most people agree that there is too much law, and that a lot of it is ill-considered, but almost no one thinks there should be no law at all.

So when is law a good thing, and why?

Earlier in the book we talked about some memes falling into the "altruistic" category. These are ideas that stabilize a society and create an environment that is safer for the breeding and exchange of the local memes. Since societies with bad laws can certainly lose out to those with good laws, the evolutionary pressure is for the laws to promote the continued existence of the society. Since society is made up of people, this can't help but do some good for some people some of the time.

However, for a law to be, on average, a good thing, it must create more value than it removes in restricted freedoms. (All laws restrict human action in one way or another.) This is actually a hard thing to measure.

It is important to understand that law does not directly produce value. Human behavior naturally produces value and sometimes – to a lesser extent – losses. The best law can do is to minimize the losses. If the losses it eliminates are greater than the costs it imposes, then it is a good law. If the costs of enforcement are greater than the losses it is preventing, it is a bad law.

The problem with tabulating all of this is that counting the losses that a law prevents is almost impossible. Once people know that there is an effective law in place, some of those who might otherwise do nasty things will think twice. So, any calculation of the avoided losses has to be based upon guesses.

Someone who wants law to be justified will guess very high; someone who is not too fond of law might guess low. Collective idea-organisms want lots of law to channel all behavior and thought into pathways that will not produce competing ideas. So those infected with such idea-organisms will always be guessing on the high side.

All of this leaves the people who want government and law to expand endlessly in the advantageous position: How can you actually prove that it wouldn't be worse? You can't. You may be able to show that it is highly unlikely to get worse, but the big government types can make powerful appeals to fear with simple arguments. The minimum government types have to appeal to reason and to use fairly complex arguments about the economics of free thought and action. The maximum government people don't have to use arguments anymore complex than, "Without this law, no one will be safe!"

So, what is the right amount of law? The answer is, "We don't really know." We do, however, know that law can impose huge costs upon a society. It is very likely that when the costs of law are high, they outweigh the losses that law is supposed to prevent.

Some accepted system of resolving disputes will always be a useful thing in our complex world, simply because people will always disagree over things. It is better to have a responsible third party solve the problem than have people fighting about it endlessly. (It might be ideal if people resolved their own disputes, but we're talking about reality now, not what people "should" do.) There is reason to believe that such a system of law need not be put into the hands of a central authority – that there are ways to create a sort of free market in laws and justice. But even if this is a possible system, getting from where we are to there could be quite a trick.

In his book "*The Machinery of Freedom*," David Friedman discusses the possibilities of free market legislation, law enforcement, and courts. He says:

> *In such a society law is produced on the market. A court supports itself by charging for the service of arbitrating disputes. Its success depends on its reputation for honesty, reliability, and promptness and on the desirability to potential customers of the particular set of laws it judges by. The immediate customers are protection agencies. But the protection agency is itself selling a product to its customers. Part of that product is the legal system, or systems, of the courts it patronizes and under which its customers will consequently be judged. Each protection agency will try to patronize those courts under whose legal system its customers would like to live.*

It is also important to remember that the enforcement costs of law can be very high, but are often completely ignored, as if they were inevitable. Enforcement costs are not just paid in dollars, but in lives lost and in liberty surrendered. The ongoing costs of imprisoning a significant percentage of society can be incalculable. In many cases, the costs of fully enforcing a law may actually be infinite. Unfortunately, that still does not stop enforcement agencies from trying to do the job.

The sensible thing to do, then, would be to have the minimal necessary law, and the most efficient administration of that law.

Bear in mind that very limited systems of law in the past produced excellent results. The English Common Law, the Lex Mercatoria (Law Merchant) and others did a fine job, with enforcement costs that were a tiny fraction of what we pay now. In addition, these systems of law easily adapted, largely because they were not under strong government control. (How many times have you seen a legislature erase a law that wasn't working? Ever?)

In some cases, a law that provided benefit at one time no longer works in light of new technology or other changes in a society. Of course this will not stop enforcement agencies from trying to enforce it and from continuing to hype the necessity of the job they do. (Consider the costs of trying to enforce copyright law since the invention of the Internet.)

Whenever the costs of enforcement can be seen to be continually increasing, it is a very good sign that the law being enforced is no longer a good one by any reasonable definition. Whenever more people are being punished every year for breaking a law, rather than less, this is a good clue that something might be wrong with the law. Keep in mind that punishment itself is a cost – especially from the point of view of the person being punished. If your first thought here is "But they are criminals!" you are thinking in terms of Collective Identities again. The existence of the law in question is all that has made them criminals. Without that law, they are law abiding citizens.

If it is a bad law, then considering those who break it to be criminals is a bad thing.

In 1897, a bill was introduced into the Indiana House of Representatives that would legislate the value of Pi to be a rational number. No one in the State Congress seemed to be bothered by the fact that this law was attempting to contravene a known mathematical law of the universe in which we live. (Apparently the idea was that it would be of benefit to the majority of people, who do not understand how irrational numbers work, if irrational numbers simply did not exist.)

Several possible alternative values were considered to replace the irrational value of Pi, which is, in the real world, approximately 3.14159..., including either 3 or 4, for people who could only deal with whole numbers or 3.2 for those that had mastered their decimals but had not learned how to round them off properly.

While it did not actually become law, the bill did pass in the House by a vote of 67 to 0 before dying in committee in the Senate. It may have failed to become law only because the Senate was very busy and there were many matters, more important than saving people from irrational numbers.

Also it was probably unclear to the Senators how this law would have put any money into their pockets. (Although one would think that these politicians would have welcomed the promotion to legislating the laws of the universe rather than just the laws of Indiana.)

3.4.4 Is it Worth Killing For?

The idea behind law is to write down what things society will not tolerate – what actions society is willing to use violence to punish. The problem is that once you have such a list, it allows anyone who has a way of adding things to that list to focus collective violence on things they don't like. So we end up with laws that are violently enforced, even if the majority of people would say that the "crime" is not something worth using violence to prevent.

One of the ways that bad law comes about is through the "binary thinking" that Collective Identities encourage. People who succumb to binary thinking feel that something must be either good or bad – this leads gradually to a legal position that all behaviors should be either forbidden or mandatory.

To allow a free society, people need to stop voting for legislation that makes things that they like mandatory and things that they don't like forbidden. They need to instead ask themselves the question "Is it worth killing for?"

All the big crimes, that people are *sure* should be illegal – murder, rape, assault, theft, and the like – are crimes that you know are worth fighting and possibly killing for. If you saw someone doing any of these things, you would have no problem initiating violence to stop it. Or if you did not feel up to the task, you would have no problem with the idea that someone else would initiate that violence to prevent the crime. It would not bother you that the person doing the evil deed might be hurt or killed. You would probably even believe that preventing or punishing such a crime would be worth the risk of the person coming to the rescue as well, perhaps even if you were that rescuer.

Now think about all the victimless crimes against which laws are regularly passed and violently enforced. Would you feel right breaking down someone else's door and physically assaulting them to prevent them from eating or smoking one plant but not another? What about the behavior you engage in privately – if someone else did not like what you are doing at home, should they break down *your* door?

The Collective is quite willing to risk individual lives in enforcing a wide array of laws – controlling all the behavior it can. Individuals are much less willing to risk violence than collective idea-organisms. Probably because individuals have only one body and it is precious to them, where as the Collective has many bodies, and they each individually mean very little to it. Would you personally risk violence to ensure the enforcement of all the laws you claim to agree with?

The only correct test of whether a law is worthwhile or not, is to ask yourself, "Is this worth violence? Is it worth the risk that someone will die over this?"

The problem is, when it comes to voting on laws, you have to either vote Yes or No. Well, actually, you can abstain, but trinary logic is not much better than binary logic in this regard. So when you are a congressman, and someone introduces a stupid bill to prevent some sort of private act of sexual perversion or unhealthy (but quite voluntary) behavior, you are presented with three choices:

1. **Vote YES**, even though you would not really think it is worth having such a law that will be violently enforced, perhaps resulting in deaths, to prevent such voluntary consensual behavior.
2. **Vote NO**, even though you don't really like the behavior, and then have your political opponents forever after publicly label you as being in support of something you actually disagree with. (See how the legislative system supports binary logic? You are either with us or against us!)
3. **Abstain**, and let others decide the vote.

The correct answer is of course #2, but every time you choose that route you are giving your political opponents more ammunition. Do it enough and soon you are no longer a congressman. You will be replaced by someone willing to vote YES or abstain on such issues. This is true unless the people who are doing the voting can think more clearly than the usual binary Good/Bad – Us/Them mindset that the Collective encourages.

As an individual citizen you face the same issue. With binary thinking, you can not publicly speak out against overreaching laws without seeming to support those things that the laws are trying to ban. It is very difficult to have to say "I am not in favor of it, but I don't think there should be a law," even though retaining a free society requires that we all do just that – and often.

Because this is hard to do, many issues not actually worthy of violent enforcement, become law. First the behavior becomes unpopular through collective disapproval. Then someone infected strongly by a collective idea-organism proposes legislation. Then people have trouble not agreeing that something unpopular should be illegal.

Every behavior eventually becomes mandatory or forbidden as the Collective grows in power. This is how totalitarianism comes into being.

> *First they came for the Jews, and I didn't speak up because I wasn't a Jew.*
>
> *Then they came for the sick, the so-called incurables, and I didn't speak up, because I wasn't mentally ill.*
>
> *Then they came for the Catholics, and I didn't speak up because I was a Protestant.*
>
> *By the time they came for me, no one was left to speak up.*
>
> -- Poem based on speeches by Pastor Martin Niemöller

3.4.5 Bad Breeds Bad

It is also worth noting that creating one bad law often leads to more bad laws. There are two related reasons for this. One is the "slippery slope" effect. The other is the effect of seeing "The Law" as an icon.

3.4.5.1 Slippery Slope

Most people are quite familiar with the "slippery slope" phenomena. And it is a hard thing to resist. The only defense against it is to stand strongly on principles and never give in to incremental erosion of our rights. This is hard because your opposition will always have the position of seeming more reasonable than you. They will always be suggesting just a small change in existing laws that does not reduce freedom too much, and *might* help solve some problem.

> *It is seldom that liberty of any kind is lost all at once.*
>
> -- David Hume

The most insidious part of this is that this slow creep of more and worse laws can happen over generations. If every generation allows just a little more law, and gives up just a little more freedom, over the course of a few hundred years, freedom can become slavery. There is a noticeable "ratcheting effect" that happens – in which Laws can not be rolled back.

3.4.5.2 Ratcheting

The "Law as icon" problem we talked about previously is the cause of this "ratcheting effect" which keeps bad laws from being repealed. The Law is held as something semi-holy, so once something is called illegal it has then been assigned a sinister quality beyond its actual relative merits or demerits. Even if the prohibited behavior was just barely thought bad enough to make illegal before, the additional bad feelings that calling it "illegal" generate act to "lock it in." Something illegal must be bad, so trying to repeal a law must then be a bad thing to do. This makes adding laws to the system a one way procedure. Add to this a political body that must justify its own existence by always doing something new, and you can expect the growth of law to be a constant one way process.

While the "slippery slope" is a problem – there is also something worse going on. Deciding whether something should be legal or illegal is ideally a process of logical reasoned debate. Of course it never is – it is usually all about the use of emotional appeal and various other logical fallacies – but that is not what we are discussing now. What we are trying to point out is that even when people do try to think logically about new laws, existing law gets thought of as being a given.

In logical terms, existing laws tend to get thought of as axioms rather than theorems. That is, they are held as givens that can not be disproved; because of this, once a bad law is passed, it can be used logically to create more bad law. For example:

In the United States, immigration is a big issue. No one will argue that past waves of immigration helped build the country, but now immigration is resisted. One of the "logical" arguments against immigration is that, when unskilled people come to our country, we will somehow have to support them with our tax dollars – paying for their schooling and health care. Therefore, we should not let people immigrate here that might take more out of "the system" than they put in.

This sounds plausible, but you could also look at it from another standpoint. You could acknowledge that immigration was a good thing in the past – and was part of the great success of the country. Then you could decide that if welfare makes immigration a problem, it is the concept of welfare that must be flawed. An argument that puts two concepts – immigration and welfare – into opposition with each other should open each concept up to inspection of its relative worth.

However, if the Icon of "The Law" makes the existing law seem unchangeable, then one bad law can "quite logically" produce many additional bad laws to terrible effect – for example, shutting off a country to any influx of new productive members.

Laws that are unchangeable, even when they have unforeseen consequences, can be horribly damaging to a society. It is a VERY bad idea to take a logical system like law and then set things up so you can only add theorems – never remove them – and never try new axioms. Such a system will just paint you into a corner over and over again, and produce more bizarre and draconian laws in each attempt to patch each previous mistake that can never be undone.

3.5 Praxeology and Other Big Words

Praxeology (PRAKS-see-OL-uh-gee) is the more general study of human action that grew out of the narrower field of Economics. Initially, Economics sought only to quantify and explain the production, distribution, and consumption of goods and services, but it eventually became clear that all aspects of human values and actions feed into these issues. Praxeology, therefore, arose as an overarching attempt to explain all values and actions that feed into the market of goods and services.

One of the common starting points of Praxeology and Economics is the assumption that individuals make rational, self benefiting, choices – if not always, then at least on average. This starting point has been useful in explaining many observed market phenomena, but has certainly fallen short of explaining a great deal of what we observe as human behavior.

We believe that the reason Praxeology has fallen short of its goals is actually fairly simple: Praxeologists have not taken into account the fact that market pressures do not arise from individual human beings, but rather from replicators – genetic or memetic.

Because human beings are creatures of both biology and ideology, they are uniquely able to have desires that conflict with each other. Where the actions of most all biological creatures are driven solely by their genetic code, human beings play host to additional ideological replicators. While genetic replicators are forced to mostly play nicely together, because they succeed or fail to reproduce as a group, memetic replicators can work directly against the wishes of the host's genetic code, and against other memes in the same host's head.

When religious fanatics strap on bombs and blow themselves up, it is clear that the desires of their ideological replicators are overriding the desires of their biological replicators. The value pressure that the religious replicator is creating inside the individual is, at least temporarily, overriding the individual's biological desires for survival and sexual reproduction.

Since there are conflicting market pressures inside individual human beings, the assumption that individuals are the source of value is an error.

Praxeology and its subset, Economics, should in fact, be viewed as subsets of information theory. Since it is these replicating patterns of information, and the ways in which they interact, that actually create the values, it is the propagation and interaction of these replicators which must be studied to understand patterns of human interaction.

To understand the human animal's behavior, a couple important questions need to be answered:

1. How do the various wants of the many replicators that influence a human mind add up to produce an individual human being's behavior?
2. Why does the biological desire for continued life sometimes give way to actions that are sure to result in death?

3.5.1 The Animal Inside

Let's start out by making some educated guesses at what goes on inside the mind of an animal in governing its behavior. Human beings can be thought of as animals with an additional level of replicating ideological information. Many animals are quite capable of quite sophisticated learned behavior; they just are not as good as people at communicating what they know to others. Our theories about how animals process the world around them should give us some insight into the first level of motivation that affects human behavior: the purely biological.

The brain has evolved as an organ for storing and processing information collected by the nervous system and every animal with a brain as complex as that of a flatworm or better has the ability to learn from its environment. Without the ability of animals to learn, all useful behavior would need to be encoded specifically in the animal's genes. With the ability to learn, general patterns of behavior may be genetically encoded and applied to specific situations. When they work well or poorly, they can be used again or ruled out for the given situation.

For example, pretend you are a very simple animal that may have just a few genetically encoded behavior patterns, such as Fight, Run, and Eat. Past evolution may well have also specifically linked these behavior patterns to certain things that have existed in your ancestors for a long time. Perhaps:

Fight if attacked by animals in group A. Run if attacked by animals in group B. Eat animals in group C. Ignore animals in group D.

This genetically stored information happens through the very slow process of natural selection. Potential ancestors that were first inclined to try to fight, run from, or eat the wrong animals, died and did not pass on those inclinations. However, those that were inclined towards the more correct response lived and passed on information about correct choices, thus preserving the encoding of specific behavior in the genes of you, their descendant.

But beyond this genetic memory, animals have evolved the more familiar kind of memory. Genetic memory is no help in new situations that ancestors never dealt with. Information is important for survival, and while passing on lucky first guesses to your descendants certainly improves the species, being able to remember bad guesses that did not quite kill you, so you can try a better guess next time, improves you, right now.

Let's say a new animal – one that has not yet coexisted long enough with your species to have made an impact on your genetic code – comes on the scene. Your first instinct might be to eat it because it looks something like a species from group C, although it is red instead of blue. So you give it a nibble, but instead of feeling full and happy, you get very sick and have to go lie down in pain for a while. You won't be eating that animal again, best to file it in category D to be ignored.

Just that easily you have learned something, and no ancestors had to die to put that information in your head. So what happened? Well, your genetic code was helping you out again. It is always there doing its thing. Your genes built you a body that has internal states, including 1 – Full and Happy, and 2 – Sick and in Pain. Your genetic inclination is to prefer state 1 over state 2. Your mind has the evolved ability to associate past events with the internal states they have produced. This allows you to think first and see if the thought of an action provokes any remembered response.

The next time you see one of those little red animals, your genetic inclination is still to gobble it up, but your mind does a test run on the idea of eating the animal and finds a connection to the feeling of being sick and in pain. When you think of eating the little red animal, you actually feel a little sick. When you think of eating its blue cousin, you actually feel a little full/happy. Your mind is alerting you ahead of time to the likely outcome of your potential actions, based on the results of your actual actions in similar past situations.

We started by talking about economic values, so it might seem odd to discuss how animals learn what to eat. However, these are in fact primal economic values. The animal is clearly exhibiting "wants" in its behavior system. It genetically wants to eat certain potential food animals, with a memetic override that it has learned that certain animals are poisonous. The combination of genetic and memetic information is used to assign high value to the little blue animals as food, and low value to the little red animals. This valuation is the beginning of an economic system.

But we wanted to look at Praxeology, the study of human action, not figure out why animals avoid poison food. So what is it that humans do differently? Or more to the point, the question should be, "What do humans do additionally?"

3.5.2 What it Means to be Human

Even non-human animals make use of learned behavior. It is much faster than genetically encoded behavior, as it can help you tomorrow, rather than helping your decedents long after you are dead. Even the smallest worms with the tiniest of brains can do it. With human beings something is different.

You never see other animals doing weird things like building metal boxes that can fly all the way to the moon, just to go there, make speeches, bounce around a little bit, and come home with a sack of rocks.

So far we have explored two levels of information that produce values and actions: First genetic replicators that evolve to produce values based on natural selection, and second, memetic encoding of values based on experience. The next level is that of communicated learning. Only a few animals can do this at all. Human beings excel at it.

Communication of memetic information allows one human being to pass learned behavior and values on to another, and another, and so on. In theory this means that only one human need experience the potential negative consequences of a learning situation and can then pass the learned information on to everyone else.

Let's take a look at these three levels of knowledge as regards to the way they help a creature avoid a potential danger to life and limb:

3.5.3 Genetic Learning

Fire is hot and can burn you – perhaps badly enough to kill, or wound you enough that something else can kill you more easily. This is why most animals fear fire and will run away from the sight, sound, or smell of it. But in order for animals to have this knowledge genetically, fire had to kill a lot of animals.

The first animals to encounter fire had actions that varied randomly according to their genetic makeup. Some of them moved towards the fire, some ignored it, and some moved away. The ones whose genetic makeup happened to encourage them to avoid fire had a big natural selection advantage. They were much more likely to survive, while their less lucky kin roasted alive. Those animals that lived to reproduce spread the "fear of fire" gene to their offspring, and with enough repetition of this process, eventually only animals with some fear of fire exist today.

3.5.4 Memetic Learning

Animals with memory have an additional advantage. Even if fire was a brand new thing that had not been learned by their genes, if they happened to guess wrong the first time they saw fire, and moved towards it, or ignored it, it is still possible that they lived through their burns. If so, the next time they saw fire, they associated it with those painful burns and ran away. A smarter animal, capable of somewhat more abstract thought, might even be able to learn the lesson without getting burned, simply by seeing other animals get burned.

So in the case of animals capable of memory and learning, the number of animals that have to be killed for an entire population to learn something is vastly reduced.

3.5.5 Communicative learning

The big trick that human beings do so very well (and that a few other animals also do, but not quite so well) is the ability to encode life experience and pass it from one to another. If a group of human beings encountered fire for the first time, the first one to move towards it and get burned might die, or not, as in the case with any other level of animal. But the first human to get burned, and all those that see it happen, can then communicate this experience to other human beings.

The value judgment that fire is dangerous can be communicated throughout the whole of the species based on one learning experience. In the best case scenario, a dangerous lesson can be learned by all human beings without anyone ever having to die for that knowledge.

3.5.6 Putting it Together

Let's recap these three types of learning and see how they compare in learning the lesson that fire is hot:

- **Evolved Genetic**: One or two thirds of the entire species must die through repeated encounters with fire for the lesson to be fully learned.
- **Experienced Memetic**: One or two thirds of any group of the species may die the first time that fire is encountered by that particular group.
- **Communicated Memetic**: One or two thirds of some particular group of the species may die, the first time fire is encountered, but later groups encountering fire may have learned the lesson without danger.

So with just genetic learning, a new threat is likely to kill some large percentage of the population that exists at the time. With Memetic learning, it is still likely to kill a significant percentage of the population. However, with experiences communicated perfectly between members of a species, the overall percentage that needs to die from any new threat becomes negligible.

Of course communication is not perfect. For it to be perfect, not only would good information need to be distributed to everyone instantly, but there would need to be a mechanism that insured that only good information would be communicated, and that bad information would never be distributed. Because people can communicate misinformation, not only do other people not listen as much as they might, but they are also reluctant to believe. Even if you tell a person the fire is hot, until they see it burn, or even better, feel it burn, they will not really "know" it on some level. This is what people often refer to as the difference between "book learning" and real experience.

When we first talked about memory, we indicated that memory associated experienced situations with existing behavior patterns like fight, flight, or sexual reproductive behavior. These behavior patterns are also analogous to feelings like fear and anger. Because communication can be wrong, learning by experience often generates mental links to strong feelings that learning by communication does not.

So even though, as we explored above, communicative learning has the potential to be far more beneficial, human beings are far more likely to hold values and take actions based on their individual experiences. Things that they have learned through actual experience are more likely to be actively connected to strong feelings that influence their behavior. The exception to this is during the early years of development.

During the early years of development, a child is sheltered from experiences that might be harmful and has as much communicative learning as possible. The evolutionary advantage of this is significant, because the child is surrounded by adults with large stores of both communicated and experienced knowledge to share with the child.

During this time, the slight skepticism and resistance that causes an adult to favor existing knowledge over new ideas does not exist. It is therefore possible for misinformation to enter a child's mind unchallenged, to later be protected by this skepticism as an adult. However, the bad information that can be propagated this way is outweighed by the huge amount of useful information that can be learned quickly.

To prevent a cycle of misinformation, children must be taught to use critical reasoning skills, so that they can later review and question their early beliefs.

3.5.7 Economics of Ideology

Once communication from human to human became possible, something very interesting happened: Information held in the brain was no longer just a useful trick of the genes to allow our species to react more quickly to changes in the environment than we could through genetic evolution. The information that passed from brain to brain was now a new kind of replicator, and it could actually compete with genetic replicators. It could evolve to produce values and actions that promoted its own replication, even where those values and actions might conflict with those selected genetically.

Let's return to our example of reaction to fire. The idea that fire is bad and should be avoided must link to biological fear mechanisms to increase the amount of attention the human mind gives it. If it finds additional ways to create that fear, perhaps joining forces with an idea that, "There is an evil fire god that hates us!", it is even more likely to be passed on to other human beings with some urgency.

A competing idea, "Fire might be useful if we just understood it better," might be defeated by further linking to senses of anger and group loyalty. People who failed to loudly decry the evils of fire might be suspected as being in league with the fire god. They would no longer be considered good members of the group. When such persons were discovered, we would surely want to impale them on a spear quickly before they might summon the fire god to destroy us.

With such strong linkages to biologically evolved feelings and behavior patterns, the anti-fire idea is now entrenched, and unlikely ever to be defeated by communication of competing ideas. (Whenever anyone tries to challenge the idea – we impale them!) However, over in the next valley is another group of humans where the idea of the evil fire god never took hold and random new ideas about fire were given a fair hearing. Those guys are now cooking their meat to avoid parasites and disease, keeping dangerous animals away, and not freezing to death on cold nights.

Clearly they are in league with the evil fire god and must be destroyed! Unfortunately, when we get there to kill these heathens, there are more of them still alive, they are healthier, and they have learned to harden the points of their spears with some evil fire magic.

It looks like we are doomed – the evil fire god will surely now devour the world...

OOPS!

What the hell just happened?

We started out looking at the sources of information that weigh into human values and therefore human action. It all seemed fairly straight forward, with new knowledge found to contribute to our survival and reproduction being accrued three ways: genetically, through individual experience, and passed on from those with greater experience to those with less.

It all sounded good – then suddenly we were a bunch of technophobic fanatics trying to destroy what was obviously a much better way of life, rather than embrace the additional value it could clearly give us.

The problem here is that while human actions will attempt to maximize the best value for human beings, replicating ideologies create values and actions that maximize what is best for these ideological life forms. While it is not in the best interest of human beings to expend their lives trying to stamp out competing ideologies, it is very much in the best interest of the ideology to have them do so.

Ideally, we would have a tool to quantify the degree to which the values of ideologies skew the market. Only with such a tool will Praxeology be a complete science. Until then, it can only describe the action of human beings pursuing rational self interest, and not the combination of human self interest and the self interest of replicating information with its own survival and reproductive urges.

Perhaps groups of ideas that propagate as a unit should be considered individual actors in the economy. Corporations certainly fit some of the criteria for being ideological collectives, and also exist as legal economic entities. Churches and governments might also be viewed as such. However, the necessary work that has not yet been done in Praxeology is the explanation of how an individual human being can exist as a self-interested party, an employee of a company, a member of his church, and a citizen of his country, with each of these identities applying its own values to influence his actions. Each of these ideological constructs pays its host with the value of self-esteem, in addition to any more tangible rewards, in exchange for taking actions that further the ideology.

We are certainly no economic wizards, but we have come far enough in thinking about these entities to identify the difference between replicating ideologies (Idea-Organisms that have their own agendas) and ideas that are useful to one's own self interests. Identifying such idea-organisms is simple. They need to replicate a complex set of ideas as a whole, so wherever a complex set of ideas is contained under one label without questioning the parts individually, there you will find a complex idea-organism – one that has evolved its own survival strategies that do not necessarily take into account the interests of the human beings who believe in it.

Perhaps some clever economist can someday find a way of indexing the degree to which a given population has succumbed to this sort of thinking – quantifying the degree to which a group of ideas with a label on it has become inseparable. This might correlate quite nicely with the deadweight loss of value found in the economy, as value is stolen from individuals and used to further the end of higher ideological powers.

As human beings, we are creatures of ideas. Often those ideas are useful tools, but sometimes they can get the better of us. The key is figuring out where ideas that are part of ourselves leave off and where foreign parasitic ideas that are trying to use us for their own ends begin. But before you can weed out the bad ideas, you need to decide what your core values are.

You have to discover yourself.

4
Finding Yourself

In this chapter we will be discussing the nature of the Individual. What we are searching for is The Self – the inner core of being – what makes you you.

This is no easy task. The nature of "self" has been a subject of philosophy throughout history. It is as hard a question as the answer to the ultimate question of life the universe and everything (which we will also tackle in this chapter). Perhaps the two are related, because wherever it is that the self leaves off, that is where everything else starts. However, to even divide the world into the "me" and "not-me" categories is quite problematic, because all we have of the outside world is our perceptions of it, and our perceptions would seem to be part of ourselves.

We can find a clue in the classic example of the young person who intends to go traveling to another country, and when asked why, answers, "I am going to find myself." Although we might jokingly respond, "What makes you think you left yourself in that particular country?" we actually do understand what was meant.

You really can find yourself in traveling. When you go to another place and immerse yourself in another culture, with another language and another way of life – many things will have changed. If you take stock of all the things that have not changed, they add up to being you. When almost everything else is different, the things that are the same are either things that are common to all human beings, or things that you brought with you.

If you have managed to truly adopt another totally different culture, then you have replaced all the outside influences of your old culture. The parts of your being that did not change is your inner ideological self, as it exists without the influence of any Collective, and your biological self. This is the real you. This is the self that Shakespeare meant when he wrote "To thine own self be true." If you can rid yourself of all adopted culture, what remains is a pure Individual.

Well, almost. There are group identities beyond that of the culture of your country and some of them may be very similar from country to country. No doubt you will still feel the pull of your racial and sexual identities, as these cling pretty tightly to your body and are very hard to get rid of. And of course, you still have your body. We are not saying that it is impossible to live without your body, just that we don't think anyone has ever actually managed it. But that doesn't mean that you can't resist its control over your mind.

When you are not giving into your genes – eating, sleeping, having sex, using drugs, etc... and you are not giving into collective idea-organisms (worrying about how other folks judge your actions) that part that remains is the real unique and individual you. If you can learn to control or at least bargain successfully with your body and resist the pull of the Collective, the real you can thrive and grow.

Of course, it may be hard to separate your Ideal Self from the wants of your body, or your own ideas from those of other people you know. After all, we are creatures of both biology and ideology and this divides us against ourselves sometimes.

4.1 Genetic and Memetic

We exist as creatures caught between two worlds. We are part biological and part ideological; part genetic and part memetic. What this means is that, unlike almost every other living thing on the planet, we are not just the product of a single package of self replicating information.

Instead of counting on our genes to pass good survival behavior on to our offspring, we use the information pathways of memory and language. While other animals, especially those closely related to us and those we have domesticated, may also learn things and pass them on to their young, we have embraced this newer and faster way more completely than any other species. The linguistic centers of our brain have evolved to play host to a different sort of evolving information system, and this has set us apart from other animals. It has also, in some ways, divided us against ourselves.

4.1.1 Urban Jungle

To gain an understanding of the difference between the two worlds we inhabit, start by considering the biological world separate from mankind. Imagine yourself standing in the unspoiled tropical rain forest. It is a place full of life, everywhere you look you see life in color; green, yellow, and brown plants, multicolored animals, birds, lizards, and insects. You are also surrounded by sound; buzzing, hooting, hissing, and growling – animals communicating their desires and warnings to each other. There is nothing around you that is not natural, a product of biological life; the ground you stand on is filled with worms and insects, and even the dirt is a mulch of once living plants and animals.

Now imagine yourself in the center of a large active city. Here you are also surrounded by sights and sounds; lights flash, horns blare, engines growl, music is playing. Plenty of signs of life here, but something is different; almost nothing around you is biological; it is a landscape of stone, metal, and plastic. Most of the sounds you hear emanate not from the biological noise makers of the forest, but from the constructed voice boxes of horns and speakers. The bright colors are not those of colorful animals displaying themselves in warning or to attract a mate, but lights, billboards, and brightly colored clothing. The ground you stand on isn't real stone, but manufactured concrete.

Not everything in the city is artificial, but even natural materials have been altered. Where you see wood it has been cut, shaped and polished. There is also animal material here, but most of it has been treated and sewn into clothing.

There is a living animal – a dog – but it looks nothing like what you would see in the forest; it is wearing a collar and its body looks oddly proportioned, almost as if it has been altered to look interesting, and not in a way that would make a life in the forest easy for it.

The dog is being lead on a leash by a woman. She walks towards you. Most of her is biological, but certainly not all. She is clothed and wears jewelry. She has makeup on her face. Her hair color doesn't look real. Even some of her permanent skin markings are actually tattoos.

Are those breasts even real? You can never be sure without touching them.

Photo credit: Sean Hastings 2007

4.1.2 Natural or Artificial?

The city scene is so different from the forest, and yet so similar. Both places are certainly lively, but are both alive? In fact they are, but clearly not in precisely the same sense.

So what is the difference?

One distinction that comes to mind, in comparing the forest to the city, is the idea of what is "natural" versus "artificial." The word "artificial" means the same as "created" but even in the forest we see things that are created; beavers build dams; birds build nests; spiders spin webs. Are these constructions the same as the buildings of the city?

What makes a beaver dam natural but a hydroelectric plant artificial?

One could define this as simply "One is made by man, and the other is not," but that evades the real question. What makes the works of man different than those of other animals? Why are we different? Why isn't the human animal considered to be every bit as much a part of nature as any frog or a tree?

In search of the answer to these questions, consider that everything you see around you in the forest is in fact a complex ongoing chemical reaction. All the life you see around you is made up of cells and each cell contains some very complicated organic chemical that are capable of doing some extraordinary things, including producing other very specific complex chemicals. Under the right circumstances, they even reproduce exact or nearly exact copies of themselves. These chemicals, called RNA (Ribonucleic acid), and DNA (Deoxyribonucleic Acid), are the basis of the self replicating systems that are generally referred to as life.

There are many repeated patterns around you in the forest: trunks, leaves, wings, legs, tails, eyes, etc. Each of these patterns is built from a blueprint found in the DNA at the center of the cells that make up the plant or animal. The repeated behavior of the animals is also encoded in their DNA. Birds of the same species sing messages of warning, information about available food, and songs of courtship. Because they share the same patterns of DNA, animals of the same species share genetic knowledge of the meaning of their communications. A tree frog does not need to learn how to speak tree frog language – it is born with that genetic knowledge.

The physical constructions of some animals are also embedded in the genetic code – encoded in the DNA. The beaver's dam, the bird's nest, and the spider's web, are all constructions that the animal does not have to learn. They are patterns, like those of animals' bodies, refined through natural selection, and passed down from the animals ancestors in the genes. Even though these structures are not in any sense a part of the animal's body, they are as much a result of the animal's genetic code as head, legs, and a tail.

This does not mean that animals can not learn. Any animal that has evolved even the most primitive central nervous system has some ability to store and retrieve information. As we have mentioned before, even a very simple animal can be trained to always turn right when it comes to an obstacle by giving it a small electrical shock whenever it tries to turn left. It will soon remember that right is the right choice and that left is somehow sinister. So not all of the information that generates an animal's behavior is genetic – some of the animal's information is stored in its nervous system, its memory.

So what is it that humans do that is so different? Very few animals take the next step. The most notable examples are our closest cousins, the rest of the simian family. What they do is teach their peers new skills. When a monkey discovers a new way to do something, it can explain these skills to its fellow monkeys. When it observes something, it can tell its friends about it.

A monkey has some facility for language and communication of new information. This differs from birds calling warning to each other, and even from tigers teaching their cubs to hunt. New behavior patterns, proven to be successful for survival, can be adopted and passed on to other animals immediately, not just to offspring through a long period of natural selection.

In a system that passes information through language, the evolutionary selection process works on the ideas, the new information, rather than the animal itself. Good ideas can be repeated and bad ideas discarded without the selection process meaning the death of the animal. The genetic code stops being the sole method of evolving new behavior.

So this is the real difference between our deep forest scene and our city center. The information that is used to build the trees and animals is all stored in the genetic code and expressed in the form of plants and animals, while the information that builds skyscrapers, roads, and cars is stored as language and expressed as ideas in people's heads. In the forest, the birds and animals make noises that communicate information to members of their own species who share the same genes; in the city, when signs flash messages and people speak, they are passing ideas. Where plants and animals can pass information that triggers pre-coded behavior patterns, people can pass information that can actually rewrite the code for each others behavior patterns.

4.1.3 Biology and Ideology

When people talk about the distinction between natural and artificial, they are really speaking of the difference between the expression of biological and ideological information. What we do, that other animals do not, is make significant use of a new system of storing information that is much faster than the genetic code.

A man can try and discard dozens of ideas in an afternoon. An animal species must see a dozen new genetic lines of subspecies born and die out in an uncertain number of generations to learn the same thing. Even then, these negative examples are not really learned, as those same new sub-species lines might just as easily come into being later with just as little success. The genetic code has no memory of past mistakes but a man can remember which ideas are bad (and why) and tell everyone else in the world that he wants to – if they will listen.

When one looks at it this way, it is not at all surprising that the world has changed more in the thousands of years since these new ideological information systems came into being than in the billions of years that biological information systems have existed. It should come as no surprise to see these ideological systems supplant and control the biological ones. Just as throughout the history of the planet before us, better, faster, stronger biological systems dominated and replaced those that came before. We are now seeing a better, faster, stronger system take over. This is the natural order of things.

Prior to the existence of DNA, the most interesting chemical interactions were growing crystals that slowly replicated a pattern. DNA was faster and brought us a myriad of plants and animals that moved and hunted and exhibited all sorts of interesting and wonderful behavior. Now we are seeing the next step. Information systems that are even faster are making the planet even more interesting and wondrous.

So we exist as creatures of both biology and ideology – a half breed, or stepping stone between two distinctly different types of living information systems. This division is really quite clear to us, as it often puts us at war with ourselves. Our body might want to eat the cookie, but our mind says we are already too fat. Our body wants to have sex with someone we find attractive, but our mind says that it is socially unacceptable to do so.

This division is evident in all attempts of mankind to define ourselves. Psychologists talk of the different parts of the personality. Freud postulated the Id, Ego, and Superego. Jung spoke of the Anima and Doppelganger. Poets speak of the war between the hearts and minds, and having the guts to act. Priests tell you that you have an immortal soul, separate from your physical self. Other animals just don't seem to have these problems with being made of different parts that want different things.

4.1.4 Good, Bad, or Ugly?

There are even some people who see all the works of man as bad things. They have a sense of loss that the artificial is replacing the natural. They have the idea that the biological is good and the ideological is bad. This is the same as if some of the members of the first tiny species of wriggling things in the primordial soup bemoaned the fact that their species, with its new capability of moving about, was knocking down all the beautiful but fragile little chemical crystal towers that grew around them.

A modern scientist, able to study that primordial ooze, might also see the chemical crystals as pretty, but would find them far less interesting than the new life forms. The scientist could recreate the crystals easily enough, but would be hard pressed to reproduce that first spark of life that started the evolution of the little wriggly ones.

The small wriggly environmentalist would mourn for the crystal, simply because he was too close to his own kind to see how much more interesting he was. He would be unable to conceive of what further beauty and grace would later evolve in the form of the animals that would follow after his kind. Likewise, the human environmentalist is blinded to the beauty of his own species – the beauty of the things that human beings produce and might one day become.

Imagine an environmentalist's nightmare, an active oil refinery; big metal holding tanks and cooling towers, a complex array of metal pipes, and smokestacks with flames shooting out the top. The sight of such a place might make an environmentalist cry.

Now imagine the exact same scene, but imagine that human beings did not produce that refinery. Suppose it was just recently discovered, and was found to be created by some sort of animal. Let's say a rare species of giant insect built this incredible factory to convert raw organic materials into a burnable form for heat to incubate its eggs.

The scene hasn't changed at all, but now nature lovers would flock from around the globe to see such a sight. It might be declared the most wondrous natural phenomena anyone had ever seen.

Photo credit John Mullen - used with permission

Environmentalists would still be moved to tears, but they would be tears of another sort. They would marvel at this incredibly beautiful thing that nature had produced. They would be enchanted by the amazingly unique species that could produce such a complex structure.

Now try another way of looking at our species from the outside. Imagine you are some sort of intelligent space creature that was born and lives in the depths of space. You have traveled from star system to star system and seen millions if not billions of planets. On many you have seen beautiful geological formations of complex crystals. On some there has been organic life and on a few even complex animals that you have been fascinated to study.

One day you find something absolutely brand new to your experience. You approach a planet that is fairly close to a normal sort of G-type star. There you see what you might think to yourself is the most beautiful sight ever to grace your many optic organs. Every other planet you have ever seen close to a star is brightly lit by the star on one side and dark on the other.

This planet is different. The dark side of this planet sparkles with its own light.

Data; Marc Imhoff, NASA GSFC & Christopher Elvidge, NOAA NGDC. Image: Craig Mayhew & Robert Simmon, NASA GSFC.

The shapes of the land masses are clearly made visible by a myriad of little points of light. What could cause such a thing? Is it Geological or Biological? How could it be either? Neither has ever produced such a thing in your extensive past experience. There is something wonderful and new at work on this planet.

Once you trade the word "artificial" for "ideological," the idea of labeling the phenomena that result from ideology as inferior to that of geology or biology becomes self-defeating. Your philosophy that reveres the natural over the artificial is itself an artificial idea. Your appreciation of the beauty of nature is ideological.

Plants and animals don't know that they are beautiful; they just are. Beauty is in the eye of the beholder – a human beholder. Plants and animals lack the ideological capacity to appreciate the beauty of their own species. Only human beings have the ability to see themselves as either beautiful or ugly.

Why would you want to limit yourself to using just half of that ability?

And so what if we are still somewhat ugly now? So were those little wriggly things that appeared at the beginnings of biology. As the first proto-creatures of ideology, it is quite likely our destiny to evolve into something much bigger and more beautiful yet.

Of course there will be growing pains along the way. We still have a long way to go, and a lot of questions to answer.

4.2 The Ultimate Question

In his book "The Hitchhiker's Guide to the Galaxy" (which you really should read if you have not already); Douglas Adams has great fun with the question of "Life, The Universe, and Everything." He tells us of an advanced race of aliens who build the ultra-mega supercomputer "Deep Thought" to answer The Question. Needless to say they were not happy with the answer when they finally got it, despite it being entirely complete, factual, correct, and concise.

4.2.1 Answers

Many others have stated The Ultimate Question of Existence in many different ways and come up with many different answers. Most of these answers sound more profound than Deep Thought's answer, but all convey a similar lack of real information.

Answers to the Ultimate Question all fall into one or more of the following categories:

1. "It can not be known."
2. "You do not really understand the question."
3. "You can not really understand the answer."
4. "Give me all of your money."

Zen Buddhism is a fun school of thought that actually has a special answer for annoying questions like this. Their answer, which incorporates the concepts of paradox and un-provability, is "mu." This means something like, "The question un-asks itself." While we kind of like the approach of coming up with a new word to provide a definitive answer to the whole category of otherwise unanswerable questions, we'll stick with a more honest approach in answering the Ultimate Question of Existence.

So are we going to give you the answer? Of course we are! In fact, we'll give you more than one of them!

Paul's answer to the ultimate question of existence was: "I don't know, and that's OK."

Sean's answer was this: "I know that I don't know."

While Paul's answer is a bit more comforting (at least to Paul), Sean's is actually more useful.

Being aware that you don't know is an important thing. Sean's thinking goes something like this:

"I know that I don't know."

"I am also quite sure that you don't know either."

"I am even fairly confident that no one knows, and that no one ever has known; but, I don't know that for sure."

"I am somewhat less convinced that no one will ever know, but that is something that I will probably never know."

"The one thing I am really, really sure about is that I just don't know."

"And you can quote me on that!"

This may seem to be an entirely unsatisfying, even if somewhat amusing, answer. It is not, however, the dead end that it seems to be. We may not know and understand everything, but we do understand our current position.

Think of it like this: We find ourselves at the top of a massively thick stone tower looking down into a thick fog with no way to see the base. From this position, however, we can verify the stability of the structure, reverse-engineer parts of the structure immediately below us, and then build higher. The question of precisely what our tower rests on may remain open, and may trouble us, but it need not prevent us from building toward greater heights – at least not if we can verify its stability first.

The answer "I know that I don't know" actually provides us with a bit of solid ground on which to stand. It may not be the ultimate answer (which would, of course, be most welcome), but it is a useful one. We suggest that you forget about the bottomless abyss of the Ultimate Question of Existence; if that answer ever comes along, we assure you that you'll notice.

It is much easier to stay on track if you remember that you have settled that issue already – that you have given it due thought and that you know definitively that you don't know the answer.

This differs from a simple "I don't know" in that when someone else claims to know the answer, you can be quite a bit more skeptical; this answer indicates confidence in your lack of knowledge. It indicates that you have already given the matter some considerable thought, rather than having a gap in knowledge to be filled by the next person who comes along claiming to have more knowledge than you do. You will require some serious explanation and evidence from them.

4.2.2 Philosophy, Religion, and Science

(Oh My!)

The three primary avenues that people take to discover the answer to the Ultimate Questions are philosophy, religion, and science.

Regardless of which avenue we choose to find an explanation for everything, we always end up face to face with the fact that we can find no final, provable answer. This is highly unfortunate for the consumer of philosophy, religion or science who is looking for an elegant, provable answer. On the other hand, it can be highly fortunate for a vendor of philosophy, religion, or science who wants an area to work in where there is little or no chance of ever being proven wrong.

Philosophy seeks to find the answer through reasoned argument, science through detailed observation, and religion through inspiration. In actuality all three of these are viable avenues, but only one of these, science, is ultimately reliable. That is not to say that philosophy or religion can't supply important information, but only science can provide verification.

OK, a few additional words on philosophy, religion and science:

4.2.2.1 Philosophy

Philosophy includes a lot of different ideas. Plato and Aristotle were, in many ways, quite at odds with each other and it hasn't gotten any better from there.

The philosophers who have tried to explain everything (or at least more than can be seen on Earth) generally used reason and inference.

Plato, for example, was very big on the existence of a great "pattern above," a superior realm, of which the Earth is but a dim shadow. Plato's means of proof for this, however, were more than a little fuzzy. (It's our guess that Aristotle was driven to the study of non-contradiction [logic] because of such squishy ideas from Plato. We're also guessing that Plato was not amused.) In any event, philosophy has never really made a serious assault on the question of Life, the Universe and Everything. Its highest achievement may be Descartes' statement, "I think therefore I am" proving only the existence of the self.

4.2.2.2 Religion

Religion – at least our Judeo-Christian type – handles this in a very interesting way: It sets God outside of nature. By placing the creator, controller (to some sects) and judge outside of the visible universe, it guarantees that we cannot know the answer to Life, the Universe and Everything by normal means. Granted, there are a few verses in the New Testament on "the spirit teaching you all things" but providing a complete answer to everything is actually not a primary Biblical theme. However, the answer to all questions is present in religion: "As God wills it!" Proof of this answer, however, is not available.

4.2.2.3 Science

Science is really just a tool for verifying things, but it is very good at verification. The results of science experiments may sometimes be fabricated, distorted, or exaggerated, but the tool itself is reliable. It may be slow, it may be limited, but it works. That's why we use it, and that's why we hold it as a final judge.

Sometimes inspiration can allow you to leap tall buildings in a single bound, but other times this proves to be only an illusion. So, we recommend that you welcome the insight, but then be careful to prove it before you try to leap. At the end of the line, everything must be verified in order to be trusted.

Both inspiration and verification are valid when used properly. The "war between science and religion" is actually a relic of the late Middle Ages, when scientists came up against an unthinking religious establishment.

We rely primarily on science. (But we really do like inspiration, when it works.) The problem with science, of course, is that it is slow and plodding. It provides answers one at a time. This, honestly, is most disappointing. There is so much to be answered and science is so slow in getting to most of the answers. Well, that stinks, but it's the best we've got. It is better to plod ahead slowly than to sprint back and forth on misdirected paths.

4.2.3 And Why Do You Ask?

Let's take a short detour into psychoanalysis, and ask another important question: Exactly why is having the ultimate answer so important to you? (And, we admit, to us too.)

Obviously knowing an ultimate answer would be a very useful thing, but in our experienced judgment there is a lot more to this than just getting some useful information. Some reasons we think people are engrossed with such questions:

1. **Discomfort with unanswered questions.** People want everything in place, so they don't have to keep their minds at the ready and to engage in ongoing analysis. They want simplicity. We'll avoid the deep reasons for this right now and simply point out that simplicity is a bad goal to seek. The real world is complex and simplicity can only be had by reverting to a pre-modern world view. If you want simplicity, you'll have to swallow a lot of superstition along with it.
2. **Pre-packaged answers.** People are mentally lazy. They want short-cuts and easy answers. A final answer for everything has obvious appeal. It is the ultimate shortcut around thinking, analyzing and verifying the real world. As a public service, we remind you that being offered something for nothing is the one sure evidence of a scam.
3. **Because everyone else asks.** Most people do frighteningly little original thinking. Mostly, they just remember slogans. Questions about ultimate truth are just one of those things that they have received from others and keep re-asking when the right situations come up.

4.2.4 Do We Know Anything?

Being firm and comfortable in our findings that we don't know the ultimate answer, that you don't either, and that nobody may ever know, we ask this: Do we know anything at all?

Here we get some satisfaction. The answer is: We actually know a hell of a lot!

Presuming that you are reading this book outside of a primitive jungle, just take a look around; mankind has learned how to produce food in a stunning abundance, we have learned how to transport ourselves at amazing speeds, we have learned to live in comfort, to educate ourselves, to discover the inner mysteries of all sorts of substances, to understand ourselves (at least partly) and to develop methods for continuing our discoveries.

Mankind has had a lot of knowledge for a very long time. The general knowledge held by mankind has grown so much in the past few centuries that it is amazing. We might not understand the most primary roots of all our technologies (due to our imperfect understanding of Life, The Universe, and Everything) but we know plenty enough to do a lot of important and amazing things.

Even when we don't always know *why* something works, we do know it works.

Now, a quick aside: If the preceding paragraphs created in you a need to scream, "Oh yeah? What about wars, destruction, starvation, murder, and global warming!" you might want to start thinking about a few idea-organisms that may be in your mind and fighting for their continued dominance. We may not be perfect, but we are unquestionably and emphatically the most amazing species ever to live anywhere, or at any time that we know of, and our pace of improvement is only increasing. If that plain fact offends you, something that doesn't have your best interests at heart is influencing you. The truth is the truth, whether your Distributed Identities like it or not.

Is this arrogance? Perhaps it is. Maybe we should be asking ourselves, "Just who in the hell do we think we are?"

4.3 The Question of Identity

All the choir of heaven and furniture of Earth – in a word, all those bodies which compose the frame of the world – have not any subsistence without a mind.

-- George Berkeley

The concept of Personal identity can be seen as either an axiom or foundation of Western thought. Many philosophers have thought long and hard (which is of course their chosen job) on the issue of Personal identity. During this thinking, many related questions have been raised and answered to various degrees of satisfaction.

4.3.1 Questions and Answers

Some such Questions that have been posed on the issue of Personal identity are:

- "How do I know that I exist?"
- "What makes me today the same person as me tomorrow?"
- "Who and/or What am I?"

Some answers to these questions might be:

4.3.1.1 Existence

Rene Descartes is widely credited as having definitively answered the question of existence, with his famous statement: "*Cognitio Ergo Sum*" (I think therefore I am). This gives philosophy a nice starting point, by being able to claim that the self exists. It may seem obvious, but nothing is obvious to people who think long and hard about it – so it's nice that the philosophers seem to have gotten together on this one, and have allowed you to confirm your own existence.

What would you ever do without these guys? You'd be walking around not knowing if you existed, that's what! So be sure to thank the next philosopher you see. If you want to get one a gift, they tend to like alcoholic beverages...

4.3.1.2 Persistence

The second question is known as the question of persistence. It seeks an explanation of how we can identify with the person we were as a child, and with the person we will be in old age. This is especially interesting, considering that both of these people would be seen to have very different personalities, and would exhibit very different behavior, if they could be compared side by side with the person we are right now. These people are not just separated by time, but also, for the most part, composed of entirely different physical matter. Despite that, we feel very strongly that our past and future selves were and will be the same person as we are now.

A possible answer to this question, sometimes credited to John Locke, is what as known as the "memory criterion," which says that a previous person is the same person as you, if you remember being that person, and that a future person is you, if they will remember being you now.

This is a fairly reasonable and useful definition of self. It does exclude some period of time, in early childhood, that you can not remember, as well as some period of time in the future when your mind may be failing, and you forget your previous life. This is not so bad for our definition, however, as we would expect things to get fuzzy towards the beginning and ending points. After all, we know there was a time in the past when we did not exist as ourselves.

Where this break of identity occurs: Child, Toddler, Infant, Birth, Fetus, Embryo, Zygote, Sperm and Egg cells, will always be a fuzzy issue. We also expect a time in the future when we will cease to exist. Where exactly this occurs, Old Age, Senility, Vegetative State, Death, Corpse, Ashes and Dust, is also a fuzzy issue. Why not then, answer these questions in fuzzy terms of memory, since memory gets fuzzier as we go back or forward, in some fairly direct proportion to our ability to identify that previous or future person with the person we are now.

We should further amend our definition to "the potential for remembering," rather than "actually remembering" since we do not spend all of our time actively recalling past events. This means that while you were busy thinking about what you wanted for lunch (mmmmm, French fries) you would not stop being the you of yesterday. This also cleans up such issues as occur during sleep or other unconsciousness. A person in these states could be said to still have potential to at some future time remember their past selves, and might be then allowed to keep the same concept of identity.

4.3.1.3 Composition

What exactly makes up The Self is the hardest question of all to answer.

Some philosophers, pondering this question, undo all the previous progress gained in thinking about the other two questions, and arrive at the conclusion that they don't actually exist after all; that The Self is an illusion. Some, alternatively, conclude that they are all that exists, and the rest of the world is an illusion. Some even try to contemplate how both those seemingly contradictory ideas could be true at the same time. Many others try to find a middle ground that makes more intuitive sense.

We are going to try to fall into that last group, even if our ideas on the topic will be a little different than most.

We think that it is best to be practical. "I think, but I am not," does not seem to be very useful, although that doesn't stop it from being the core of a lot of Eastern philosophy, with talk about being nothing or having no head. Likewise, the idea of Solipsism that holds that you are GOD and the whole world is your dream, while probably good for the ego, doesn't seem very productive. So we are going to opt for a middle of the road solution – we maintain that only some small part of the universe is you and the rest of everything is your environment.

This seems to be a fairly reasonable and intuitive answer. However, it is a good bet that we will not be providing an answer that is going to sound reasonable or seem intuitive to you. If it was easy, all those guys who think long and hard about everything wouldn't be coming up with all that crazy shit about the self and/or the rest of the universe all being an illusion.

Let's start by taking a look at what you mean when you say the words that you use to identify yourself.

4.3.2 Me, Myself, and I

The Concept of identity is all about self reference. The brain is a tool for creating maps and models of the world. Some part of identity is the red dot on such a map with the label, "You Are Here." This means that there can be many types of identity, based on the type of mental map you are considering.

The first layer of identity is about location relative to other things.

4.3.2.1 Body Sense

Keeping track of the body relative to other things in the environment is something that the brain has been doing for multi-celled animals for the past 500 million years. Relating the body to information about the world outside of the body is, quite probably, the big reason that biological life found this whole "brain" concept to be evolutionarily useful.

After a half billion years of evolution, you can now navigate a dark room that you have seen before, and touch your finger to the tip of your nose with your eyes closed (unless you have been drinking too much). Of course these are things very much like what other animals have been doing for almost that same half a billion years.

There may be some things, however, that you can do with your body sense, that animals can't, or at least don't get much of a chance to do. The sense of self in relation to environment is more fluid than people realize. We can project our sense of self out from some center to include things in our environment. We can also think of ourselves as being somewhere else than we actually are.

When you drive a car, you find that your sense of self awareness in space increases to encompass the whole vehicle. You think of the corners of the car as being "my corners" and have a sense of how your control of the car translates to its motions through the surrounding environment. This awareness is particularly useful for parallel parking, as you need to have a feel for the size of your vehicle and exactly how close it is to the other cars that you are parking between. (But try not to think about this process when you are actually parking your car. It doesn't help you actually do it. Sorry.)

Similarly, if you have ever done any martial arts weapons training, a weapon, when used properly, becomes an extension of your arm. You have a feel for where it ends, and how far you can reach with it, just the way you know how far you can reach out and touch something with your own hand. Even with a projectile weapon like a firearm or bow, getting a feel for the range of your projectile, as if it were an area you could reach out and touch, is a useful illusion to have. One way to do this is to visualize the curved path that the projectile will take as it flies and falls – think of that path as an extension of the weapon and yourself. (This one actually does help if you think about it. Sorry again about the parallel parking thing – if you hit someone, feel free to leave a note saying it was our fault.)

Your sense of self can also be reduced from your whole body to just part of it. Think about when your arm falls asleep, and it seems to be not part of you, but something separate from yourself. People who have actually lost a limb sometimes experience their sense of self ending at the stump, other times they experience what is known as a "phantom limb" that they feel is there, even though the limb is gone.

A phantom limb is even useful to them when it comes to wearing prosthetics, as it makes it easier to quickly start using the new artificial limb as if it was their own, without the years of training that a martial artist may need to feel that an external object is a part of his body. This left over body sense allows them to easily extend their sense of self into the artificial limb.

You can even project your sense of self well outside your body. A video game is a good example of this. As you move around a simulated maze, fighting simulated monsters, you project yourself into that maze and identify with your simulated body. Your identity is projected into the video game. Likewise if you have ever operated a remote control toy car, airplane, or helicopter, you may have noticed that it becomes easier to navigate it successfully once you can project your sense of self into the remote object.

Some people even claim the ability to send their self out of their body and to experience remote environments without going there. Although we find the evidence for any actually extra sensory perception to be unreliable, it is understandable that since our minds seem to have no problem projecting the sense of self outside our bodies in some cases, that some people who try to do this deliberately, will find that their minds fills in the missing details, such as sight and sound. Just as a phantom limb will often feel pain, or itch, some people's minds may feel obligated to add sensory details when the sense of self is projected elsewhere without any actual sensory information being available.

Some of this sense of projecting self is almost certainly also used in modeling the behavior of other people. We try to think, "What would I do if I were in his shoes?"

4.3.2.2 Behavior Models

We touched on the concept of identity and behavior modeling in an earlier chapter and discussed how we can model the minds of other people, our selves, and even fictional characters. Now that we are trying to pin down the elusive concept of identity, we need to come back to this topic and look at it from another angle.

One of the interesting things about our sense of self identity in terms of being a predictive behavior model for our own actions is that it can be wrong. A person may believe that they will react a certain way in a certain situation, and they can then surprise themselves. Even more interesting, is the fact that other people who know that person can actually know that that person has an inaccurate model of themselves. Other people can have a better mental picture of the total person than they do themselves.

For example, you probably know a guy who claims to be a tough character. He might say things like "If some guy ever pulled a gun on me, I'd just take it away from him and shove it up his ass!" But you know that if he was ever actually confronted by a mugger with a gun, he would just hand over the cash, and might even wet himself.

Having done what the Twelve Step Programs call a "searching and fearless moral inventory" - I am forced to admit that I am neither a pirate nor a ninja.

Or how about the girl who talks about how much she hates a particular guy, how arrogant and full of himself he is, and how she can't understand what his current lady sees in him. She may really believe that she doesn't like him, then she ends up kissing him at a party, and then they are dating.

Part of the reason that self image does not always correspond to self reality, is that it fails to take into account the desires of biological replicators. What your genes want can be a very different thing from what your self image says you want. Your identity is stuck in your body, but it need not always exist peacefully with your body. You may often be at war with yourself.

The reason it is sometimes possible for external observers to more accurately predict your behavior, than you can yourself, is that they are seeing your whole body as you. From the inside, you have the illusion that you are a separate entity from your body, and that you control it. From the outside, you and your body are all one combined system.

Another issue is that you can have ideological organisms in your head that are quite well entrenched in your psyche, and have a great deal of control over your behavior, but have not actually penetrated your sense of self. Even though your identity is an ideological construct, it can be at war for control of your body with other ideological constructs that have found their way into your mind.

For example, you may really want to travel and see the world, but your family obligations keep you in the same home town where you were born. Your inner identity wants one thing, but your identity as a good member of your family wants another. This leaves you constantly unsatisfied if you stay put – or feeling guilty if you chose to travel. The existence of two warring identities guarantees that you will never be completely happy.

Some people can even develop multiple personalities with access to different memories. Most people, however, only experience this to the lesser degree of having different faces they put on for different groups of people, different friends, family, lovers, co-workers, etc.

The thing that saves the attempt to pin down self identity from being a totally lost cause is the fact that we have self reference. Some piece of our mind can consider what is going on in the rest of our mind, and can choose to resolve conflicts between different ideological constructs and biological desires. If we bother to think about it, that is. This self examination is not always easy or automatic, and it is a skill requiring hard work and practice to acquire, just like any other skill.

In fact, it is clear that a lot of people don't bother to ever use self reference, reacting to their environment without ever considering the reason for their actions. This has been noticed by many philosophers.

> *An unexamined life is not worth living.*
>
> -- Socrates

If you have self reference, it allows more control of your actions. You can decide when to react, and when to stop and think. But who is this person inside us who makes the decisions? Who is the Decider?

4.3.2.3 The Homunculus

Attempts to peel away the layers of identity come up against a problem known as the homunculus fallacy. (Homunculus is Latin for "little man.")

The problem is this: We can keep digging deeper into our minds, looking for "the decider." Then we can ask, "Is this the actual inner person? But, can we go deeper?" It's a lot like saying that the universe was created by GOD, then asking where GOD came from. We can say that some smaller part of the whole mind is the real Self, but we still end up with: Is there a person inside of the person?

The only way out of this setup is to say that identity is an illusion or trick that we play on ourselves. That would mean that there is no real decider, but simply a record of previous decisions that plays off of itself. Hmmmm...

In reality, however, we *do* have levels of self reference that allow additional levels of decision and can let us break out of repetitive behavior. We can decide to decide differently, or decide that what we thought we knew was wrong. This may sound like a paradox – and in fact it is exactly that.

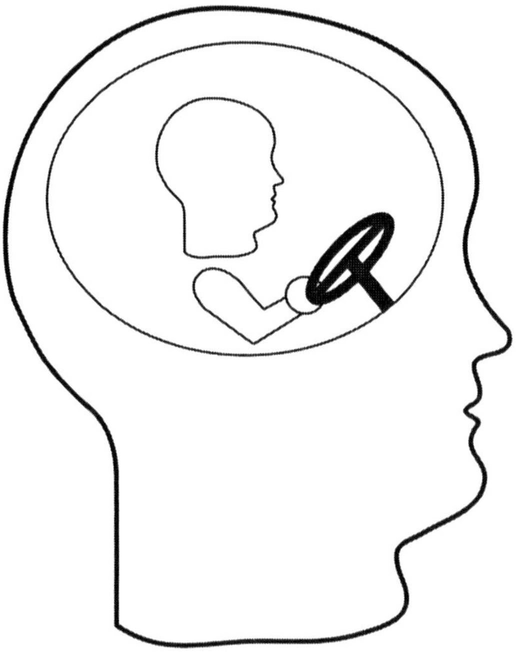

Mathematician Kurt Gödel is famous for his proof that showed that no system could ever be entirely complete or consistent once it was powerful enough to produce self reference. The human mind starts out with self reference built right in, so we should not expect to be able to ever entirely pin down the question of identity. It will always be a paradox – so we suggest that you learn to love it and move on.

Mental self reference, overseeing all the other functions of the brain, binds us into a whole that is greater than the sum of its parts. This paradox is the magic of consciousness.

The total sense of self that we feel is a combination of several things:

- **Body sense**. The things we can control and feel. Our ability to experience the world around us.
- **Identity Models.** Of ourselves and other people, objects, and abstract concepts.
- **Tendencies**. Behaviors that have become habit based upon previous thoughts and actions, real world conditioning, and repetition.
- **Self Reference**. Our ability to turn our thoughts back on themselves.

This last item is exemplified by our ability to ask, and even answer, the question "Who am I?"

4.3.2.4 Free Will?

Whenever people start to think about the nature of identity or intelligence, the issue of free will usually comes up.

If, as we talked about above, our decisions are a product of pre-existing behavior models we have created through previous experience and learning, then how is this any different than a computer running a program?

The simple answer is that it isn't different, but that this is nothing to be concerned about.

If you take a look under the hood of human consciousness, you find a machine, and if you could fully understand this machine, you might no longer believe that the things that it does are some sort of magic. So what? This doesn't mean that you don't have free will. You make your own decisions. It doesn't matter that "you" can be reduced to a number of systems that do real things in the physical world to produce these decisions. Those systems are still you.

People who deny the existence of free will say that if you cannot make a different decision than the one you are programmed to, or that if you do it is because of some sort of random error, that you are not free. However, they do not offer any way that their fuzzy definition of "free" could ever be realized.

You are a collection of evolving ideological systems. The decisions that you make may be a direct product of those systems and any deviation from that may just be random errors. This does not make you any less free, or any less you. It makes you an evolving information system. You do not have an outside perspective to show that your actions are predetermined – thus you have free will from your own perspective.

You have free will unless you define free will as being something you can't have. And even if you do that, it doesn't change anything about whom and what you are. Your mind is the product of an evolutionary process, just like your body. You are an evolving/learning information system.

To understand Free Will is to understand that you are not a programmed robot, but rather that you are the program inside the robot – you are a program that can re-write itself

4.3.3 Final Thoughts on identity

Let's review what things are and are not your self identity.

4.3.3.1 "I" Ain't Got No Body

Although body sense is a component of identity, your body is not. As we pointed out, your body sense can be projected into other things, and even remotely – it is not always attached to your body.

While the technological means to do so have not yet been developed, your total sense of identity can in theory be detached from your current body. The proof for this is in the fact that it can be easily imagined. There is a whole genre of movies in which characters switch bodies. These movie plot lines are only possible because we can separate our sense of identity from our bodies.

Try a thought experiment. Let's suppose that someone has, during the night, somehow switched the mental process of John and Susan. John's body would wake up in the normal bed, but its head would be running Susan's mental processes. The first thought inside that head would be the thought's of a mind thinking it was Susan, and the thought would be "How did I get in John's body?!?" it would most certainly not be "How did Susan's mind get in my body?"

The mental processes are the identity. If they could be duplicated, then the identity would be duplicated. So in our search for the core of self identity, we can ignore the physical body and just consider it to be the most immediate part of the environment that the Self exists in.

The self is an information system.

4.3.3.2 "I" Ain't Got No Group

Despite feeling a sense of identity within the framework of some group of people, this is not your self identity. You might think of yourself in terms of being a citizen of a particular country or as a member of a certain church. But these are not you; they are group labels you associate with. If you allow these things to define who you are, then you give up control of your identity to whoever can make decisions for the group.

If you decide that part of being you means being a good Catholic, then the Pope can change your identity by redefining what it means to be a Catholic. If you decide that part of being you is being a good American, then the President can change your identity.

Identifying with a group moves part of your identity out of your own head, and into someone else's, where you have no control of it.

If you want to control your own identity, you need to make sure that you do not identify with a Group identity. If you like the individual ideas that a group holds, feel free to incorporate those ideas into your sense of self. But do it one idea at a time. That way if someone tries to change the definition of the group, they can not automatically change you – you get to reconsider each new idea separately and decide if you want it to be part of you.

So in our search for the core of self identity, we can ignore group affiliations. To insure that you control our own identity you should reject such labels, and consider the individual ideas that the labels try to package together. (Yes we keep saying this over and over – but it is really that important!)

4.3.3.3 So What's Left?

If you separate yourself from your biological urges (easier said than done) and from your automatic acceptance of new ideas from your group affiliations (hard again, but doable with a little mental discipline), what do you have left?

- You have your sense of the things you can control in the world around you. This is primarily your control over a physical body, but is not that body. It is an information system.
- You have your knowledge, both direct experience and learned from others. This includes your behavior models for other people, and even yourself. This includes information about groups – but ideally, does not place you inside any group.
- You have a record of previous thoughts and behaviors, and certain adopted tendencies and habits of thought and action.

- You have your mental processes, including self reference, your ability to use and rewrite your behavior models, and your ability to use and rewrite your tendencies and habits.

If you can (using your self reference) stop unwanted biological impulses from affecting your behavior, remove the negative effects of Group Identities, and re-write your tendencies and habits the way you want them, then your actual self will come to closely resemble the internal identity model of your Ideal Self.

4.4 Your Ideal Self

The challenge of living up to your ideal self image is a life-long process. It is not a goal to be achieved once. It is not a test that you can pass or fail. On any given day, you will act in ways that are closer or farther from the self you wish you could always be.

Do not be overly discouraged when you slip, nor overly self congratulatory when you manage to overcome fears and tendencies that usually distract you from your aim. Take it one day at a time. Keep at it.

Consider the goals of a person trying to lose weight and become more physically fit. He might eat better and exercise more for several weeks, then one day, slip up and give in to his cravings and eat a pint of ice cream. If he puts it behind him, and continues for another few weeks of healthy life style, his momentary failure of willpower has almost no affect on his goals. However, if he decides that he has failed, he will resume his previous ways of overeating and minimal exercise and soon all his previous work will be undone.

Likewise, if the dieting man should reach his target weight, and declare himself a success, he may decide that he is done, and can stop his efforts to be healthy – again it will only be a few more weeks before all his work is undone.

The quest for "intellectual health" is no different. You should never assume that you are beyond falling into bad ways of thinking and you shouldn't be too upset over past failures. If you realize that you have slipped back into bad ways of thinking or acting, don't be afraid to admit you were wrong. Don't kick yourself too hard. Just renew your concentration on deliberate, chosen thinking and behavior.

Changing over from letting someone else do your thinking for you, to thinking for yourself is hard, but not as hard as Higher Powers would have you believe. Maintaining that change over time, against the constant onslaught of voices telling you to surrender your mind, is the harder part. You will find yourself slipping. But if you re-evaluate yourself honestly and often, this is not a serious problem.

But first you have to decide just what ideas make up your ideal self. You need to know what your principals are in order to make sure that you keep living up to them. You have to decide just what it is that you really believe.

4.4.1 What to Believe?

The first thing you need to do is take an inventory of your mind and all the ideas in it. You must decide if each is good, bad, or unknown. The good ideas you will include in your model of your Ideal Self. The bad ideas you will recognize as things to be avoided. The rest of the ideas end up in an "I don't know" pile – where you can occasionally pick them up, dust them off, and rethink them when you have the time.

Remember that collective ideologies are a product of bundling ideas together. So, when you evaluate any idea, remember to be sure that you are accepting or rejecting that idea solely on its own merits – not because of any other ideas it might be commonly associated with.

Anytime someone offers up a new idea, or a change to an old idea, it automatically goes into the "I don't know pile," regardless of who it is offering the idea. When you have an opportunity to spend the mental time and effort to think it through, you will do so; until then it is an "I don't know."

If you want to lend greater credibility to some people, and less to others, feel free to do so, but do not let it affect your reasoning. The only purpose to labeling some people as "wise" and others as "foolish" should be the speed with which you get around to thinking about new ideas from them, and the amount of time and energy you are willing to spend on it. If someone you have previously labeled as Wise offers up a new idea, you might start thinking on it sooner, and give it more time before dismissing it, than you would a new idea from someone you think of as foolish. But do not let those labels overshadow your own personal reasoning.

(OK, there are exceptions. In a life-and-death situation, you might not have time for analysis. If there's a question, you have to go with the answer that comes from the most reliable previous source. Ah well, real life can be sloppy. But take the time when you have it. Think for yourself! Question what you are told!)

Also, do not be afraid to think about an idea and decide that you still don't know, and put it back in the "I don't know" pile. If you do this a few times, you might even want to put it in an "I know I don't know pile," that is seldom, if ever considered again, unless you are really bored (or very drunk).

Furthermore, feel free to rethink ideas that you have decided are true or false, when you have the time, or when you get new evidence. Do not be afraid to be wrong. Admitting that you are wrong just proves that you are not a robot doing the programmed bidding of someone or something else.

So where do you get the ideas to start with?

You already have a lot of ideas in your head. Start with them. You have collected your memes from a number of sources, among them, the following:

4.4.1.1 Heredity

We inherit genetic traits from our parents via DNA. DNA is really just a set of templates for building about 30,000 proteins. The full scope of the information that can be transferred in those 30,000 proteins is largely unknown as we write this. It could be much less than we had formerly expected or it could be more. Right now, our knowledge of heredity is still limited, even if it is radically better than it was a generation ago.

It is, however, certain that we inherit a lot of behavioral tendencies from our parents. Some of those tendencies certainly impact on the ideas we hold, so we know that there is a bleed over from the genetic to the memetic. The reverse is almost certainly also true.

The very structure of your brain comes to you via heredity, so it is certainly possible to inherit propensities toward certain ideas. Idea-organisms have been part of our environment long enough to have exerted significant evolutionary pressure on our genes. Since it is not always safe to stand apart from the collective, the genetic tendency to think in terms of groups has been selected for over many generations; those who were not drawn towards the collective would often have failed to pass on their individualistic genes because they were prematurely killed by those with a stronger group mentality.

4.4.1.2 Modeling

Beginning in infancy, we gain a tremendous number of ideas, habits and tendencies by copying other humans. In most cases this involves observing and copying your parents and siblings, though other humans will generally suffice in their absence – later we begin copying friends and heroes – even fictional characters from books and movies.

Actually, modeling (copying) is a very efficient way of learning. It includes its own safety system – if someone else is doing it with success, then it is probably safe for you too. Because of this, we tend to do a lot of modeling.

4.4.1.3 Traumas

Unfortunately, trauma is one of the best methods (maybe the very best method) of changing human behavior. Here we can easily cross the line from meme to a semi-permanent physical change. We'll avoid an examination of psychological techniques for reprocessing and clearing traumas, but less severe learned behaviors are also gathered from traumatic events and there is quite a bit of overlap.

4.4.1.4 Displacement and Replacement

We are complex and very capable beings. We are more than capable of self-organization at an unconscious level. Frequently, an uncomfortable void in our area of our psyches will be filled by something replacing the missing piece.

For example: We contend that the removal of religion from European culture in a radically short period of time (a single generation in many cases) caused an unpleasant void in the general European mind. A variety of pseudo-religions have been arisen in to fill this void.

There are many other well-proven variations of this, including the transference that so frequently arises in psychotherapy.

4.4.1.5 Key Experiences

There are probably a handful of moments in your life that have had a profound effect on you. This is, more or less, the reverse of trauma. Unfortunately, it is not often as powerful. (This is probably because being afraid has strong survival value.) These experiences, if positive, tend to verify the value of the memes associated with them, resulting in them being strongly accepted. This is useful, though the memes are often accepted without sufficient examination.

4.4.1.6 Conditioning

Conditioning may not be the end-all of human behavior, but it does cover a lot of territory. Again here, conditioning provides memes that are not vetted properly. Among the strongest conditioning is that of family or clan.

In the past century or so, the conditioning of institutionalized schooling has displaced a good deal of family conditioning. Whether this is a good thing is quite a separate subject but, when the caretakers of children implant a specific set of ideas for most of a child's waking life between the ages of five and adulthood, we can expect significant results.

4.4.1.7 Choices

The choices you make can have a profound effect upon your life from that moment forward. In effect, many choices put you on one or another path, to the exclusion of all others. In other words, important choices change the lay of the land for many future choices. Choose wisely and with all possible information.

4.4.2 Examining Memes

"Don't put that idea in your head! You don't know where it has been!"

The big problem with picking up memes is not that the memes are wrong. In fact, many of them are helpful. The problem is that we don't do it intelligently. Because of that, it takes extra work to identify, analyze and remove or modify the meme.

Memes such as "look before crossing the street" are very useful. Others are inglorious wasters; memes of this type would include worrying, complaining, shame, need for dominance, victimhood, blame avoidance, cheap self-esteem, envy, inordinate fear of losing, presumption of ineffectiveness, the assumption of a zero-sum world, fear of change, and others.

Even when memes are helpful, there is a problem that is often associated with them. People do not analyze them for value but adopt them simply upon another's insistence or example. We think that this is also harmful, though in a secondary way.

It is a long accepted fact of neurology that neural paths (such as circuits within the brain) that are more-often used grow to become better pathways. Some of you will remember the old electronic adage, "Current tends to take the path of least resistance." That is what happens in our brains. Accepting a set of control instructions once, without analysis, makes us more likely to do the same thing a second, third, and fourth time. This is not a useful habit – being far to close, literally, to "flying blind."

Memes or susceptibilities that you inherit are certainly not analyzed and chosen, they are accidents of birth. These are especially difficult because you got them automatically. And they may or may not be useful. If you were lucky, you inherited more good than bad from your parents. If you were unlucky, you got more un-useful than useful. But in either case you had no choice, and in either case you got them unvetted (without being analyzed). Verifying and/or improving the group of memes you got is a good idea.

Memes obtained via modeling are a bit less problematic, since you chose them for some reason. However, they may also have been obtained at a time (i.e., when you were three years old) when your critical analysis was far from well-developed.

Memes gathered via trauma are nice in that they can be easily identified and difficult in that they can be hard (but not impossible) to eliminate.

Memes that are obtained via replacement are interesting and sometimes especially difficult. Not only are they accepted sometimes uncritically, but they may also be deeply interlocked with a number of other memes. If a vacuum gave rise to this meme, the things that drew it in have roots. Usually this manifests itself in the meme being a source of self-esteem.

For example, many people hold to political opinions, not so much because they have invested a lot of critical thought, but because other people will say good things about them. Wrong as a meme associated with such a situation may be, uprooting it would involve having to reestablish the person's self-esteem. Yes, it can be done and should be done, but a lot of people will never do so.

Any simple symbiotic or altruistic memes can be reconsidered with little work. Bundled ideologies offer most of the problems, but can also be a source of some good ideas if you can break them apart and analyze each idea separately.

4.4.2.1 Borrowing Ideas from Ideologies

Now that you know you are allowed to pick and choose from the components, those collective idea-organisms that are still in your head are not nearly as dangerous. Feel free to metaphorically poke at them with a stick.

Break them apart. Consider each piece on its own merits.

Are you religious? What did your favorite prophet say that GOD told him?

What about science? Ideas that can be demonstrated to work would seem to be the most useful of ideas.

What about the philosophies of people you disagree with? If a lot of people believe something, chances are that it contains some symbiotic ideas and some useful simple altruistic ideas for maintaining a peaceful culture. It almost certainly also contains a lot of parasitic information, but any ideology that is more than 50% parasitic will probably die out fast, so those that stick around almost always have something good to say too.

> The anti-religious are just as at fault for bundling ideas as the religious. Have a conversation some time with a devout atheist and bring up a religious parable – for example the story of Solomon suggesting splitting up a baby to see who cared about the child most. Some people are so adamant to deny the religious that they will not even accept such a reasonable parable that shows an excellent truth, simply because it originated from the Bible. Rejecting an idea based upon the book you find it in, is just as bad as accepting it for similar reasons. It might be even worse, as this is really letting your ideological opponents control what you think – allowing yourself to be defined by their beliefs.

Certainly don't be quick to accept all the ideas of any Ideology, but also remember not to reject, out of hand, the components of competing Ideologies. There may well be nuggets of gold in that heap of dung.

So how do you tell which ideas are good and which are bad?

4.4.2.2 Recognizing Parasitic Memes

Before you can revise the memes in your mind, you have to recognize them. Until you know what is influencing you, being able to change is made considerably more difficult.

We said earlier that parasitic memes behave as amoral entities, and seek their own advancement rather than the individual's. That means that they don't want you to think, to analyze, or to accept or reject them based upon their usefulness to you as an individual. Until you notice them, they will control you.

> *None are more hopelessly enslaved than those who falsely believe they are free.*
>
> --Goethe

Here is a list of clues that a meme is seeking to replace reasoned thought in your psyche. A parasitic meme is usually evidenced by the following:

- You have the impulse to disregard facts. For example, someone brings you an idea and you don't want it to be true, regardless of fact. In such a case, there is either a meme fighting to remain dominant, or an underlying mental routine that is being stretched. (We'll talk about these underlying routines shortly.)
- You feel that because someone rich, famous, wise, powerful, etc. said it, it must be true, or because a lot of people believe it, it must be true.
- You get angry at someone for pleading their case, rather than simply disagreeing with them. Again, this is evidence of a meme not wanting to be challenged or the underlying structure wanting to remain inviolate. Notice that reason is being pushed aside, and that your obedience to the parasite is being enforced by discomfort.
- You choose a conclusion first then assemble evidence second. Notice that reason and proportion feel like enemies in these situations.
- You have the will to oppose or hate something before you even understand it.
- You want to be right, and have "your side" win the argument, rather than wanting the truth to win the argument.
- You believe that it is important to convince other people of an idea. Perhaps you even think that there is urgent reason for others to accept this idea as soon as possible – that those who doubt are actually putting themselves, and perhaps even you, in danger.
- You believe that you must either accept the idea, or you must accept some other competing position that you know to be flawed. You believe that there are only two possible choices, even when the positions presented contain several different ideas. You don't seem to be able to break these sets of ideas up and examine the ideas individually.

All of these are evidence of bundling of ideas from an Ideology with parasitic components. When you realize that this is occurring to you it is a good clue that you should throw out the whole ideology and start carefully rebuilding it from simple individual ideas again.

Just because emotion or urgency is attached to an idea, certainly does not make its false, but it is a good sign that more than just logic is going on. Try to remove the hype and reconsider each idea rationally. Until you can think about an issue with a cool head, it is unlikely that you are reaching the correct conclusion. You may be pushed into illogical thinking or emotional non-thinking. The examples on the list above are all cases of emotional reaction or of a logical fallacy.

The example, just prior to the last one on the list, is a demonstration of a fallacy called "Appeal to Consequences." In the next chapter, "The Art of Thought," we have provided a list of the common fallacies of logic. You may wish to look at these carefully. Any logical fallacy can be evidence of a less-than-benevolent meme seeking to trump reason in order to extend its own existence.

The last example on the list above is a situation in which binary logic is being forced on you. Parasitic ideologies often try to provide false binary choices. It's another example of the "You're either with me or against me" scenario. This is sometimes referred to as the fallacy of the excluded middle, and is a standard idea-organism tactic.

Idea-organisms use a combination of multiple ideas under a single identity and require you to accept all ideas in an Ideology or reject all of them – even the good ones. This false binary logic can allow two bad ideologies to use each other as the "only other option," and force everyone into one camp or the other.

Always try to be very sure that there are not more possible positions than just two – that there isn't a third option, or even any number of possible combinations of ideas that you had not realized could be separated. Not all propositions are truly statements of binary logic. There are often possible middle cases. Sometimes there is a whole continuous array of choices. Not only that, but sometimes where a single continuous axis is presented, there may even be an additional possible axis, or multiple additional axes, turning the possible viewpoints into a 2 or more dimensional continuum.

4.4.2.3 Multiple Axes

A famous example of presenting multiple axes (independent scales of measurement) is the Nolan Political Quiz – also called "The World's Smallest Political Quiz." (Take the quiz at www.theadvocates.org/quiz.html)

The political spectrum in the United States is often presented as a Right to Left single axis, with the Republicans on the Right and the Democrats on the left as the only viable choices.

David Nolan presented two axes, one representing government control in economic matters, and the other representing government restrictions of personal freedoms. He showed that with these two axes, Libertarians were at one point of a square, demanding freedom of both economic and personal matters, and that this was the opposite corner from Fascism in which both are controlled.

In this layout, Democrats and Republicans occupied the other two corners, each half way between Libertarianism and Fascism, each allowing freedom in one arena while restricting the other. From the Libertarian perspective, each of the two major political parties in the United States had it half right and half wrong. This is actually a pretty likely state of affairs, and not at all a matter of chance.

When two ideological entities are pushing binary logic – working together to restrict your choices to one or the other – both will have to be equally about half symbiotic and half parasitic.

If the population is going to be split roughly evenly between two ideas, each of the ideas must have some merits. If an idea-organism is going to control people in some respect – bend their actions to its own ends – it can not allow complete freedom. Based on our theories of how idea-organisms work, two such competing but complimentary political parties, each espousing freedom in one domain, while controlling people through the other, would be an entirely expected state of affairs. This is, in fact, what we often observe.

It is certainly not an uncommon state of affairs to have people split down the middle on a given issue. Usually such an issue is really more than one issue. Each side of such an issue will be unwilling to see the merits of their opponents best arguments and each also unwilling to see the flaws in their own worst arguments.

People are convinced by collective idea-organisms to think in terms of only two possible choices, or a single axis. Even when they try to think logically, they find that the weakest points in their philosophies are supported by the stronger points. This shouldn't happen logically – as they should be able to separate the points into independent issues. Then they could abandon their weaker points while keeping their stronger ones.

You may not have noticed yourself doing this, but you have probably noticed it in other people. When you are having an argument with a member of an opposing political party – just when you are making a good point concerning some issue – the other person will often switch to a separate issue upon which your two parties disagree with each other – and quite probably one where your arguments are not nearly as strong.

Since both of you have always been encouraged to think in terms of only two possible sides, you each feel obliged to defend all the points of your Ideologies. To admit the weakness of one idea seems to invite the defeat of all. Therefore, switching from one issue to another seems like a reasonable argumentative tactic, and logically unrelated ideas are used to support each other.

If your minds were free, each of you could admit to each other the strengths and weaknesses of each different issue. In the end, if you did not feel bound to one indivisible ideology or the other, together you could build a brand new Ideology from just the strong points of each.

Mental slavery to all the points of any given Ideology creates divisiveness, where as free examination of individual points within any "set of ideas" allows people to find common ground and make intellectual progress.

Once your mind is free of the need to think in terms of large bundled groups of ideas, you will often notice the idea-bundling of others – perhaps even find it amusing. You might be arguing about some issue with a member of one of the standard political parties and making some good points. Suddenly the other person will switch to a totally different issue to attack you on. The funny part will be that you will suddenly find yourself being attacked on a point you entirely agree with, with the other person having the absolute expectation that you disagree. In the party member's mind the two issues are linked, and they can not understand how you can disagree with one of their points but actually agree on another. This may even upset them more than if you were in disagreement on all points, because you are not just questioning their set of beliefs – you are questioning the idea that their set of beliefs is so special as to be one of only two possible ways of thinking.

This is an opportunity to help the other person open their mind. Point out what they just did and why the two ideas are not linked. Discuss the way that political parties bundle ideas, promoting the idea that there exist only two sides rather than many sides of many issues. Explain how this causes people who accept a two party system to always be wrong on about half of the issues all the time.

Political parties are, of course, a huge artificial collection of issues that are often entirely unrelated. Thus, no one who has a free mind would ever identify themselves as a member of a political party – not even the Libertarian Party. Doing so puts other people (the people who speak for that party) in control of your mind. We would highly recommend thinking as a libertarian with a small "l", but suggest that you resist the urge to think of yourself a Libertarian with a large "L". Don't be a party member. Be an individual with your own ideas.

Political parties are certainly not the only case of binary logic or single axis thinking being forced on people. The concept of multiple idea or multiple continuous axes can be applied almost anywhere.

For example, many people think that belief in GOD or gods is a binary logic or single axis sort of issue. The binary position is just **Atheist** or **Theist**, while the somewhat more complex single axis model runs like this:

Atheist – Weak Atheist – Agnostic – Weak Theist – Strong Theist

This is more complex, and therefore likely more realistic, but does it really cover all the possibilities? Consider the concept of "Agnostic." Some people actually identify themselves as a "Strong Agnostic" or "Weak Agnostic," where a strong agnostic claims that not only do they not know if there is a GOD but that you don't know either – they are sure that it can not be known.

How does this fit into the above axis of faith? The answer is that it doesn't – not without adding another axis. A more realistic picture of any person's theological position can be obtained in two axes.

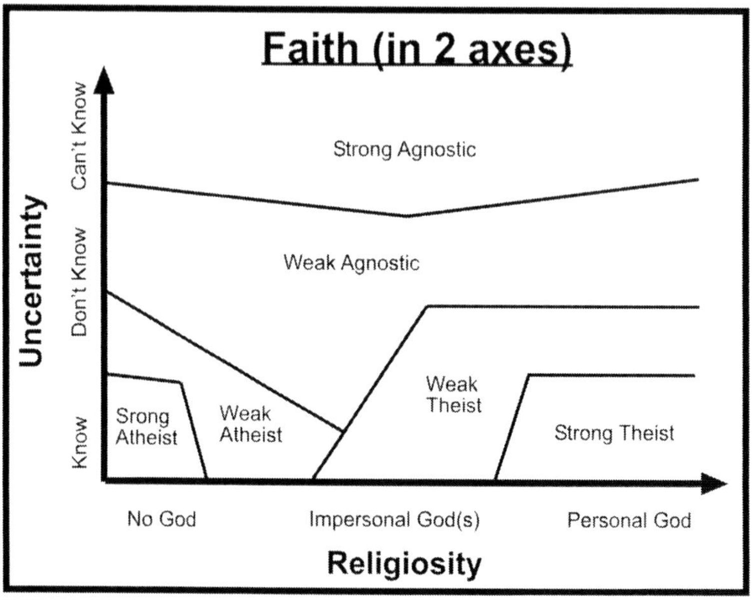

To find your position on the previous graph, simply ask yourself two questions – one for each of the axes:

1. **Religiosity** – What is your best guess concerning the involvement of a creator in the universe? Assign a ranking from zero to ten. Zero being no creator. Ten being a creator who pays constant attention to your every action and thought. (For example – if you believe that the universe was created, but that the creator is not an old bearded man who sits on a cosmic throne watching everything we do, but rather something more like the extra-dimensional equivalent of a kid with a chemistry set, you might assign yourself a "5" for religiosity.)
2. **Uncertainty** – How likely is it that you don't know and/or can't know the nature of the creator of the universe? Again zero to ten. Zero means you are absolute certain that your picture of the universe is correct. Five means you don't know, but someone somewhere might, or might be able to find out. Ten indicates that you believe that no one can ever know the answer.

You do not have to stop at two axes – the more different issues on the nature of faith that you add in, the clearer your picture of the real world possibilities becomes. For example one might add an "Evangelism" axis. This would distinguish Strong Agnostics who keep to themselves, from the ones that ring you doorbell on Saturday morning and want to talk about how sure they are that it is impossible for you to know whether or not there is a GOD.

We could even assign a different axis to each of the standard qualities of GOD – we might want to know just how Omnipotent, Omniscient, and Omnibenevolent does each person think GOD really is? There are also many more possibilities than just Theist or Atheist, and many more possible answers to the question of creation than "Let there be light!" or the Big Bang. For example, some people believe that we all exist in a computer simulation – how would they fit into your definitions of Theist or Atheist?

There are even some good reasons to believe that we might exist in a computer simulation. Observed laws of Physics look very much like computer programming tricks to save memory and processor usage. The speed of light sets a maximum speed at which information can propagate. Heisenberg's uncertainty principle, based on wave/particle duality, shows that the Universe holds off on resolving answers about reality until the last possible moment. (This is known as "lazy resolution" in computer science.) Such a theory would imply some sort of creator. But a GOD? One would expect a GOD to have better hardware and not need to resort to such resource conserving programming techniques.

It has even been pointed out by noted transhumanist, Nick Bostrom that if we expect such simulated worlds to ever be possible with our own technology; we are predicting that the number of simulated worlds will someday be far greater than the number of real worlds. And if the number of simulated worlds that will ever exist is much larger than the number of real worlds, then the odds are highly in favor of us actually being in a simulation right now.

So there are a lot more possible ideas out there on any given topic than are easy to keep straight in your head. Allowing your mental models of other people to have a true range of ideas and beliefs gets very complicated very quickly – it is easier to label people and put them into broad categories. But that is not an accurate picture of the real world.

Pretty much any simplification you allow in your thinking becomes a handle for the idea-organisms to steer you into some alternate version of reality – one where you end up working for their survival and replication rather than your own. From the point of view of the parasitic idea-organism, the simpler your view of reality is the better. If you see only one answer to any question ("All things are as the Great Whatzit wills it!") that is ideal. If you see only two possible sides ("You are either a faithful follower or an infidel enemy!"), that is good too.

Once you start allowing in-between positions, it becomes harder for idea-organisms to manipulate your actions to their own ends. When you start seeing Ideologies as being made up of multiple separate ideas, rather than an insuperable whole – and realizing that each of these individual ideas might have many in between positions – then your mind has the tools to discover and remove parasitic memes.

Parasitic memes give you a simplistic, inaccurate view of the world. Symbiotic memes, on the other hand, are always working towards giving you a more accurate picture of reality. Unlike parasitic ideas, symbiotic ones survive and thrive by being useful accurate ideas about how things really work.

4.4.2.4 General Principles

When picking and choosing your ideas, it is easiest to spot symbiotic memes – ideas that benefit you are of course the ones that you want to collect. A few simple guidelines are worth noting:

- Don't be afraid to try new ideas
- Continue to test your old ideas repeatedly

If new ideas are better, use them. If old ideas don't work, don't make excuses for them. Don't be afraid to admit you were wrong.

Altruistic memes that create good environments for human interaction and mutual assistance are very useful, both to have in your head, and to encourage in other peoples' heads. This is a dangerous game though, as this is the borderline of where idea-organisms start to form, and before you know it, you can be working for your ideas, rather than the other way around.

Let us present what we think are some good general guidelines to follow, in order to have good altruistic memes, without allowing idea organisms to creep in.

- Keep them simple – If it's complex, try to break it up into smaller ideas.
- Equality of rules – rules you enforce on others should also apply to you.
- Try to maximize overall creation of value and minimize overall loss.
- Do not believe that anyone or anything is a Higher Power than you.

4.4.3 An Ideal Higher Power?

Having mentally leveled the playing field, before we eliminate the concept of Higher Powers, we should make sure we are not losing anything in doing so.

Part of the process we are advocating involves always considering each idea on its merits, neither accepting nor rejecting any idea without some thought. Therefore, we should make sure to squeeze any useful juice out of the Higher Power concept before we discard the skin.

One thing that the Higher Power concept seems to have going for it is its usefulness in managing behavior modification. This need not always be involuntary brain washing by a Collective, but can sometimes be voluntary mental hygiene. When the person in question really wants to change bad behavior that they feel they have no control over, the idea of accountability to a Higher Power seems to allow them to regain control of themselves.

Let's look at a couple of examples of making use of proven successful techniques based on Higher Powers while making sure that your Higher Power is self contained and therefore can not be used by others to externally manipulate your behavior.

4.4.3.1 WWMISD

You've seen the WWJD bracelets, haven't you? WWJD stands for "*What Would Jesus Do?*" They are tools to remind people to match their actions to an external standard.

Here's how we borrow this tool and adapt it to our uses (and, yes, this is ideological evolution at work):

Once you have an idea of what your Ideal Self should be like (and this is, arguably, the real value of the Jesus bracelet – reminding you to think about how an ideal person should act) you can make reference to this Ideal Self regularly, to bring your actual behavior into line with your concept of ideal behavior.

This is valuable to you! Do this: Form an image of the person. Take your time – weeks or months if you have to. Think about the person as you nod off to sleep at night. (Trust us; this is the right time to do it.)

We call this mental image your "Ideal Self." Don't worry, you can always modify this Ideal Self if you get better information, or just change your mind down the road. Just start working on building this identity. Make changes as necessary.

Once this image is in place, in any situation, you can stop and ask yourself, "What Would My Ideal Self Do?" Maybe this sounds silly, but it is a very potent tool. Use it. Apply it in creative ways.

Try it and see.

4.4.3.2 The 12 Step Program

Another of the success stories of self help programs based on reference to a Higher Power has been Alcoholics Anonymous. This organization has helped many people learn to live successful lives despite problems with addictive behavior. Its 12 step program has been translated to help people successfully overcome many other behavior problems that they have felt otherwise powerless to deal with. This includes drug addiction, over eating, gambling, and many others addictive behaviors.

This success should not be ignored, despite an integral part of the teaching of such programs being the idea of accepting a Higher Power.

This idea that a Higher Power is necessary to the process makes it hard for individualists to buy into the workings of a 12 step program. However, we have stated that we are determined to accept the results of experimentation – to not reject anything that might be useful. And this has been shown to be a useful tool. We will neither accept anything on faith, nor reject anything that is proven useful based on our own ideology.

Ideology should always adapt to fit the results of real world experiments – never the other way around.

Let's start by taking a look at the 12 steps with an eye towards memetic engineering while keeping in mind the reasons why we might want to discard certain ideas that lend themselves to turning a collection of ideas into an idea-organism.

These are the original 12 steps of Alcoholics Anonymous:

1. *We admitted we were powerless over alcohol—that our lives had become unmanageable.*
2. *Came to believe that a Power greater than ourselves could restore us to sanity.*
3. *Made a decision to turn our will and our lives over to the care of God as we understood Him.*
4. *Made a searching and fearless moral inventory of ourselves.*
5. *Admitted to God, to ourselves, and to another human being the exact nature of our wrongs.*
6. *Were entirely ready to have God remove all these defects of character.*
7. *Humbly asked Him to remove our shortcomings.*
8. *Made a list of all persons we had harmed and became willing to make amends to them all.*
9. *Made direct amends to such people wherever possible, except when to do so would injure them or others.*
10. *Continued to take personal inventory and when we were wrong promptly admitted it.*
11. *Sought through prayer and meditation to improve our conscious contact with God as we understood Him, praying only for knowledge of His will for us and the power to carry that out.*
12. *Having had a spiritual awakening as the result of these steps, we tried to carry this message to alcoholics and to practice these principles in all our affairs.*

Ok, so let's take a look at what we have here and see if we can separate the meat from the fat.

We can throw step 12 out right away. It is clearly a replication effort by this collection of memes. If you want to spread the word, and it makes you happy, go ahead – but never believe that it is a necessary step for your own personal salvation. Just because we personally happen to get off on it and go around writing books, doesn't mean that you also have to spread the word to stay happy.

You can be quite content in your own life without the need to bother other people with the "good news."

Now the main idea in the rest of these steps seems to be that if you can't do it yourself, you will need the help of a Higher Power. At first blush it would seem that there is no way to fit this into our theories that put the self at the same level as, or even above any Higher Power. However, there is something we can try.

Remember that our Ideal Self is who we want to be, not who we actually are. So in a very real way, our Ideal Self is something apart from us that we can ask for guidance and help.

Unless you believe that GOD is actually speaking to you, your concept of God is no different intellectually from any other identity model. It exists in your head. It is part of you. When you think about what God would want you to do, you are consulting and internal mental model. Your concept of Ideal Self is the same kind of model and should therefore be able to serve as exactly the same purpose.

Consider that seeing the divinity in the words of a prophet or messiah is only possible if we have divinity within ourselves to begin with. Otherwise we could not recognize the truth and beauty of the gospel. Why think in terms of an external divine person? Why not just pick the ideas that seem divine to us, and include those ideas in our Ideal Self?

If you can do this, then you will no longer be under the influence of anyone who claims to speak for a god or GOD, but you will continue to have access to the same internal guidance that God can provide. You can receive the same sort of guidance from your Ideal Self without sacrificing your individuality.

So let's rephrase those 11 remaining steps in terms of our Ideal Self as the Higher Power, remove the repetition (it looks like someone was padding to get 12 steps – not sure why), and see what we come up with.

1. Conceptualize your Ideal Self.
2. Decide how you are and are not living up to your Ideal Self Image.
3. Admit these faults in internal conversation with your Ideal Self and also to another real world person.
4. Ask your Ideal Self to remove your shortcomings, while first being ready to believe that this will work.
5. List all the people you have harmed, and make direct amends wherever possible, in a way that will not hurt them or anyone else.
6. (Lather, Rinse, and Repeat steps as necessary)

This would seem to get to the meat of the matter, without allowing anyone or anything else a hook into controlling your mind.

Step 4, would seem to be the most iffy, but we will offer some more detailed ideas about how to actually change the patterns of your mind in the next chapter.

There is good experimental evidence that human beings can be conditioned to believe or do anything, given the right external stimulus. It should be possible to do the same from the inside – set the habits and patterns of behavior that you want to have. Why not at least give it a try?

5
The Art of Thought

In the previous chapter, we talked about deciding what to believe in and about creating your Ideal Self. In this chapter, we will talk about the tools of logical thinking and how they can be used to move from simple core beliefs to more complex ideas without making errors of logic.

When you were a child, and your ability to reason was not fully developed, you tended to accept everything that other people told you. Maybe you believed in Santa Claus, the Tooth Fairy, or the Boogey Man. As you grew older, you developed the power of reason and you gained mental defenses against new ideas. The more mature your reasoning processes became, the more skeptical you learned to be concerning the things other people told you.

"Let me down! You have the wrong man!"

You have learned to look for people's motives, and see why it would serve their own self interest to have you believe what they are telling you. This is certainly a good defense against future exposure to bad ideas but how much was stuffed into your head before you gained the ability to reason things out for yourself? How many things do you believe now, just because you heard them from someone before you realized that person capable of lying or of being wrong?

There are probably people whom you trust without question, at least on certain topics where you believe they have more knowledge than you. You don't stop to ask yourself what's in it for them – either because it is too much work to figure it out for yourself or because you have been taught to trust them without question. These experts could easily be lying to you – but perhaps even more frightening is the idea that they are passing on false information that they believe to be true, because they heard it from experts that they trusted. Information that is accepted on faith, without proof, can be passed down this way through generations, with falsehoods creeping in unnoticed and unchallenged.

You may well still believe in certain icons that are no more substantial than Santa Claus.

The only defense you have is to think for yourself. Whenever you accept or reject an idea without giving it any real thought, you are being lazy and denying the power of your mind. But as we have discussed previously, with a little bit of hard thinking, you can smoke the culprits out and deal with them as you choose.

If you do not have the time or the inclination to do any hard thinking, then you should probably be asking yourself why that is. Are all the ideas you accept without critical thought simply so unimportant that it is not worth the time? Or are you letting ideas go unchallenged that could make a great difference in your life? Maybe even the difference between life and death?

Isn't it time you thought about freeing your mind?

5.1 Free your Mind

The idea of Higher Powers is a very hard one for some people to get past but until you can, your mind will never be your own.

The big problem here is that people tend to identify themselves in terms of groups. They think of themselves as members of a group rather than as individuals. The key to individual thinking is to make sure that your internal models of yourself and all the people in the world around you are free from illogical grouping. Not everyone can do this completely.

In the worst case scenario, one group idea assumes control over all others, leading to fanatical behavior. In the "best" case no ideas of groups are present at all – but this leads to difficulty interacting with the vast majority of other people who have shared world views that include information about groups.

We will describe these various levels of group modeling like this:

- Fanatic Head
- Group Head
- Idea Head
- Geek Head

5.1.1 Fanatic Head

The mind of a fanatical devotee to some philosophy (in this case a religious fanatic) might be modeled like this:

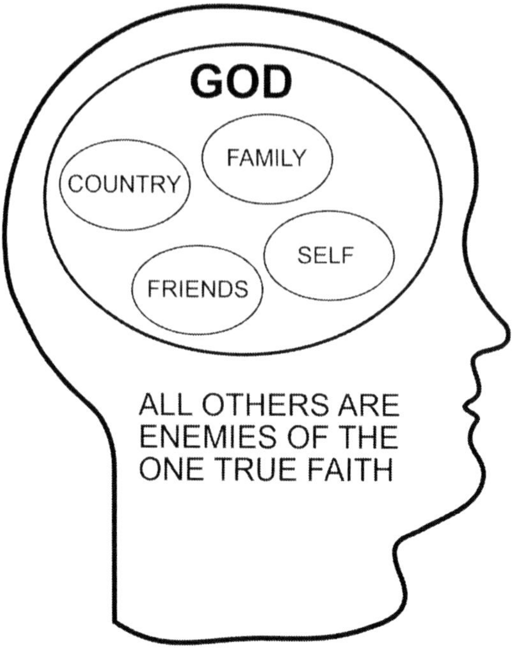

To the fanatical mind, one philosophy is all consuming and dominates every aspect of life. Groups of countrymen, family, and friends are thought of only in terms of how they also relate to that single Higher Power.

This makes the commandments of that Higher Power almost impossible to ignore. To be rejected by the icon of the one true faith would be to lose all sense of personal identity and all sense of belonging to *any* group. Failure to obey any command for any reason is risking becoming an enemy of everyone you know – even an enemy of yourself.

5.1.2 Group Head

Next we have a more common sort of mental model of self identity. Group Head is better than the previous Fanatic Head. Having more than one co-dominant philosophy competing for his attention allows him some space in the gaps for personal thought and ideas. But there is still a big problem with this model of self.

You will notice that Group Head accepts all the beliefs that are defined as being a part of the various groups to which he belongs. They are all fully contained inside his sense of self. Also, he rejects all of the philosophy of his enemies.

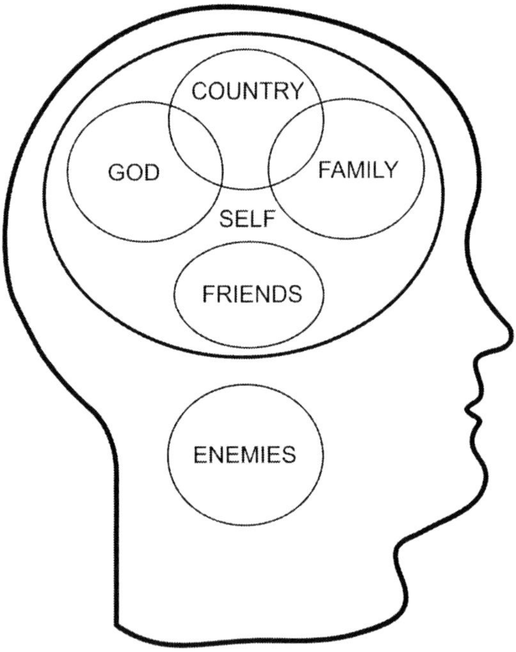

If his enemies make a discovery that could benefit him, he will automatically reject it. If his allies jump to some stupid conclusion, he will be forced to jump with them. (Yes – you have to drink the poison fruit punch. Sorry, but it is the will of the Great One! ... No – not Wayne Gretzky – the other Great One...)

There is a better way to model your Ideal Self. It is more complicated, and thus a little harder, but well worth the effort.

5.1.3 Idea Head

Instead of accepting the beliefs of any group into yourself, you can be aware of the individual ideas of any given philosophy, and then accept those that you deem correct and reject those that you think are incorrect.

In this model, not only do you have room for personal thought and ideas, but all the ideas in your sense of self are completely and truly your own.

Idea Head is aware that some other people share some of his ideas. He knows that many people may even identify themselves as part of a group based on ideas he also holds dear. But his ideas are still his own and no one else's to control.

Idea Head is free to change his mind about things without consulting anyone. He decides for himself which ideas are true and which are false – which are good and which are bad. He is his own person, answering only to himself.

The Idea Head model has several important features that are different from the previous model:

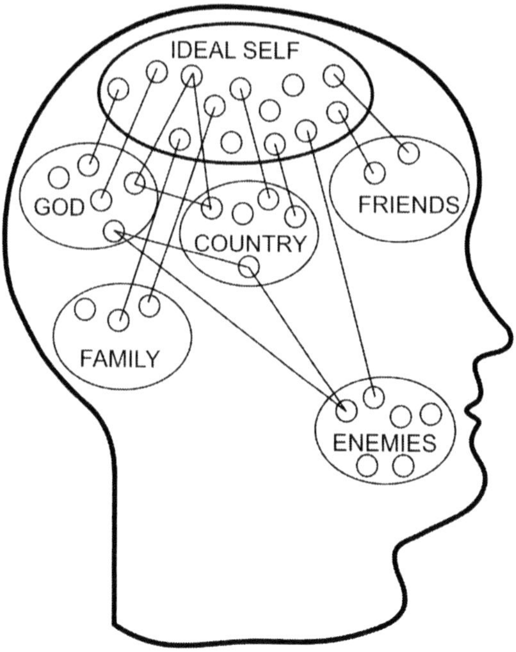

- You are considering ideas one at a time, rather than whole bundled groups of ideas. (We have talked about how this protects you from idea-organisms and their parasitic memes.)
- You can share many ideas with Groups that you have good feelings about, such as your Church, State, Family, and Friends – but all of their ideas don't have to be the same as yours. You can admit that these groups can be wrong about things sometimes.

- You can have very different ideas from people that you have negative feelings about, but you can still have some ideas in common with them. You can admit that your enemies can be right about some things sometimes.
- Even more interestingly, you can see that some ideas you disagree with (maybe the idea that strong collectivist thinking is a good thing) can be shared by both the groups you like and the groups you don't like. You can see that even groups you have strong good feelings for can share some philosophy with groups you have strong bad feelings for.
- Most importantly – your self-concept is equal to your images of other people and groups. It is neither made up of other philosophies, nor contained by other philosophies. This allows you to place yourself above, or at least on an equal level with, anything that would previously have been a Higher Power.

The most accurate way to think is to completely ignore the concept of groups and have a separate mental model for every individual person and the ideas they hold. It is possible to have a mental model of the world that does not even have broad group concepts such as "Enemies." However, this is a very difficult way to think and since other people commonly think in terms of groups, it makes relating to other people more difficult.

But you should be willing to at least give it a try now and then to see how it feels.

5.1.4 Embracing Your Inner Geek

We mentioned before that people who don't seem to fit into groups seem to make all the great discoveries. This is because they do not model themselves or those around them in terms of groups. They are not good at following every fad because they need to take the time to think every new idea through. They don't just automatically do what the people around them do. They neither accept nor dismiss new ideas without thought.

This allows them to do new and wonderful things sometimes.

However, there is a price. The drawback is that Collective Identities have learned to persecute people that don't display the correct outer signs. People are forced to host the Collective mind in order to survive or learn to camouflage themselves well.

Society can make it very hard for you to think for yourself. It can be costly, and sometimes even fatal. It is a hard choice, but we believe it is worth doing it, for the sake of what you can be if you free your mind.

We cannot guarantee that you will be great just because you learn to think for yourself, but we do guarantee that you will not be great until you embrace your inner geek. You will never have any great new ideas if all your attention is devoted to keeping track of what you are supposed to be thinking.

You can not be great until you are no longer afraid to appear foolish.

But if you are going to place your own ideas at an equal level to the prophets and philosophers of the ages, if you are going to stop letting other people tell you what is right, you may first have to clean up that mess inside your head.

When was the last time you did any mental house cleaning? Odds are you are in need of it.

5.2 Cleaning House

Now that we have some idea of how to recognize parasitic memes and how to choose the memes that are good for us, let's take a look at how we can do a little bit of mental house cleaning.

We are all influenced, sometimes heavily influenced, by the idea-organisms we carry around with us. But we also have the power, if we choose to work at it, to revise our collection of memes – to weed out those ideas that are not beneficial to our goals. You are the decider, if you wish to be. In other words, you can be free, if you wish to work for your freedom. Fighting for your mental freedom may not be easy, but it is available to you if you want it.

5.2.1 Changing Your Mind

All of our outer actions begin as thoughts within our minds. Without signals from the brain there is no movement of the muscles, whether those muscles are our biceps for strength, facial muscles for speech, or abdominal muscles for sex. Our inner world is what gives birth to our external circumstances.

No, this is not New Age hocus-pocus and there is no magic involved. Our internal mental machinery is the cause of our every action and this is what produces our results in the outer world. Changing one's mental systems can directly change the sort of results one is able to obtain in the world – whatever the field of endeavor.

This being said, there can be serious obstacles facing us, some of which we may not be able to surmount. A war, for example, can completely ruin the development of our outer worlds, no matter how great our inner workings may be. But, external obstacles aside, our inner world is where all of our results are born. So, if we can fix-up our internal worlds, we can make serious changes in our outer results.

Here is a harmless experiment you can do to prove to yourself that change is possible, and to see how long it takes to accomplish: Fold your hands. You know... interlace your fingers. Next, check to see which hand is on top; usually it is the left index finger that ends up on the top of the pile. Now, reverse the order – if your left is on top, put the right on top, or visa versa. This will probably feel uncomfortable. For the next several weeks, make yourself use the reversed order. No exceptions allowed. At the end of that time, you should be doing it automatically, and soon the original order will feel almost as uncomfortable as the reverse order does now. We suggest that you do this right away and prove to yourself that it works, and also as a proof to yourself that you are committed to actually making some changes. (Such symbolic gestures are no small thing in the fight for you mind.)

Almost every modern self-help book or seminar endeavors to upgrade your mental universe in order to improve your results in the outer world. And these efforts are not essentially misplaced; as we've said previously, your inner world gives shape to the results you produce. (This is assuming that external obstacles remain at a manageable level.)

There is nothing wrong with most of the success seminars, but they do not directly address problems associated with the ideas in our heads. Instead, they do it by delivering examples and inspiration to their students. This is fine, but it only works part of the time. If a student will focus on their lessons with great effort and consistency, they will probably get improved results. There are, however, more direct and effective ways to do the same thing.

That said, a warning is in order: When you start tugging at deep old ideas in your psyche, the experience can be painful. Here, "No Pain, No Gain," is true. But if you're willing to do the necessary weeding, your new, improved brainscape should prove to be much more useful than the old one.

We will go through several methods of revising your memes in this chapter. All are of use and all can be used at the same time. Remember, we are talking about your personal happiness and effectiveness here; for us, at least, anything that helps us along this path is something that we desperately want.

5.2.1.1 Force

The first method of changing your memes is simply to apply force against them. It works like this:

1. You recognize an idea-organism that is sharing brain space and you want to get rid of it.
2. You decide, resolutely and even violently, to remove it.
3. You keep yourself vigilant, watching for any appearance of this idea's influences.
4. When you notice it, you immediately and forcefully shut it down. You refuse to think that way and you replace bad thoughts with other thoughts and ideas.
5. You continue doing this for as long as is necessary.

To remake your mindscape by force, you start at the ground level and work your way up asking yourself where each belief you hold comes from. For each belief that you find, imagine for a moment that the opposite is true. Does it make you feel uncomfortable? Is it possible that you only believe it because it is uncomfortable not to – not because you have good evidence that it is true?

It is important, not only to know *what* you believe, but to know *why* you believe it.

Now, the above method requires concerted time and effort. On one hand, we want to make this easier for you if possible. But on the other, if you're not serious about cleaning out the center of your being – if you don't care enough to work damned hard at it – then why the hell are you even reading this book? (It was the cover right? We know, its funny – but now its time to try to get serious for a while.)

This stuff ain't for lazy people, amigo. If you're not willing to drip sweat over this, then maybe you shouldn't even bother. You can live a lazy, semi-conscious life and might even get through it without too much pain, especially if you lose your memory when you're old so you don't have to think about what could have been.

When re-landscaping your brain, it is generally best to go one step at a time, or at least not too many at a time. This leaves you with enough energy and doesn't require you to keep too many targets on your 24-hour radar screen. It also means that you are picking targets carefully. It is also possible to change multiple memes at once, though this can be problematic.

Changing many memes at once is generally called changing paradigms. The word paradigm refers to a pattern – a structure of ideas through which we view the world – a group of memes that we accept as useful for understanding the outer world.

The most commonly effective method of changing paradigms is religious conversion. This is accomplished in the following general steps:

1. Dissatisfaction with the existing pattern of life. ("I'm not living right.")
2. Polarization of the choices. ("Eternal Heaven or Eternal Hell.")
3. A definite, unalterable decision. ("I give myself to Jesus for all time.")
4. A new set of ideas. ("Now I live by the Word of God.")
5. Continual support. (Gathering continually with other believers.)

These actions make it possible for a person to change a lot of memes at once; sort of a batch change. The quality of the results from this process is primarily a function of the quality of the new memes. Because the new memes are generally not carefully vetted, the person may pick up some less-than-useful ideas at the same time the old ideas are being replaced.

People who have been deprogrammed more than once seem to be the most rational. A single religious conversion can change one fanaticism for another. After a second conversion, people tend to get a sense that many whole collections of ideas – contradicting each other – can seem equally true. This makes people suspicious of such collections of ideas, and thus more resistant to the effects of parasitic idea-organisms.

One way to help free your mind is to deliberately adopt a new Ideology, then deliberately trade it for another.

Even deep unconscious habits can be changed by the force method. Generally, it takes at least a few weeks of diligent effort to see results (much like the folding hands example) but then the results come quickly and surprisingly easily. If you have ever broken any bad habit (quit smoking or whatever) then you have already done this.

When using the force method to remove idea-organisms, you will probably find yourself instinctively using some of the other methods. Autosuggestion – that is, speaking – is probably the most common. Go with your instincts. Talk out loud if you feel like it. (May we suggest that riding alone in your car would be a good time to do this, rather than in a crowded office.)

If some other action seems instinctive to you, try it out. As long as no one gets hurt, who cares? It might be very useful. Any deliberate effort is helpful, whatever the mechanism. Even if it doesn't work, it gets you used to the idea of deliberate effort – this is very important.

Also, when using any method of meme reorganization, you will find various associated ideas and images wandering around through your consciousness, as if they were looking for a new place to stay. These are memes that were somehow attached to the idea-organism you are removing, and they are floating around searching for moorings. They may be useful or not. This is the perfect time to analyze them and to give them a place, consciously, or to kick them out with a minimum of effort required.

5.2.1.2 Teleology

Humans are teleological. That means that we operate naturally by first seeing goals then moving toward them. This is very convenient for us, once we understand it. (There are also philosophical and religious studies of teleology, which are not the subject of our discourse here. This is about teleological motivation.)

You can see teleology in your physical movements: You first see your friend across the room, and then decide to move towards him or her; you don't plan each step you take, rather, you see the goal and move toward it, with your interior circuitry taking care of the details. The same thing happens to us on the larger scale of seeing a condition we wish to reach. By seeing the final state, we set our internal gears into motion for reaching it.

5.2.1.2.1 Seeing Your Goals

To use the teleology mechanism, you must develop a clear picture in your head of what the payoff looks like. What exactly will you get at the end of the line? What will your internal circumstances be? What will the external circumstances be? Spend your time envisioning this. Daydream about it; look at it from every angle; feel it, know it, and allow it to evolve into its own organic form. Once you can feel the prize in your hand, your mindscape will begin to modify itself to match the goal.

If you do this well enough, you will not only imagine the goal, but you will begin to expect it. This is when things really start to change. Remember this: *You don't get what you want out of life; you get what you expect.*

We're not going to marshal a bunch of studies to support this statement, but it is true nonetheless. Sure, a war or a bunch of contrary ideas that you hold to rigidly may stop this process, but humans simply tend to get what they expect. This is not to say that there is any magic at work here, but it is what tends to happen.

If we had to guess, we would say that the reason this happens is that humans are capable of a great deal more than they realize. This means that expectations are both motivators and limiting factors. People get what they expect because when they get there they stop – they do not proceed any further. So, setting your expectations high and keeping them in mind is important. Also, when you get there, setting new goals and expecting to also reach them prevents stagnation.

This is probably the great strength that religious people find in prayer. They regularly talk to God about the things they want, and they expect that this will allow them to achieve those things.

Do the same with your Ideal Self. We strongly suggest some serious analysis on your part. What do you really expect? If you find yourself expecting things that you don't really want, kill those thoughts. Command your mind to do it your way. Then, start expecting the best things. Meditate on them. Talk to your Ideal Self about them. But don't hope, and don't wish. See them in your hand. Spend time seeing them in your hands, in your life. Grow to expect them. Know that your Ideal Self can get them for you. If you do, you are likely to get them.

Expectation comes from visualizing the goal in sufficient depth, with a near-constancy, and as an expression of authentic desires.

As we said earlier, if you can visualize your goals clearly enough, your psyche's ecosystem will reorganize itself accordingly. Here, again, you'll find assorted memes, newly disconnected from their moorings, floating along and looking for harbor. Again, this is the perfect time to deal with them consciously.

You may also find certain Distributed Identities barely hanging on, and a type of discomfort driving you to pluck them off their moorings. Go for it. If they don't make good sense, pitch them. (If they really do have a use, they'll find their way back soon enough anyway, so don't sweat pulling them off.)

5.2.1.2.2 Seeing Yourself

Now, here is another key point: We have been talking about your Ideal Self. We mentioned earlier that your brain holds not only images of the outer world, but images of yourself. These self-images are very important. A bad self-image will not harmonize well with the exalted goals you seek for yourself. In other words, the pieces won't fit well together, and you won't get what you are working for.

Your internal image of yourself is not only built upon ideas, but also upon observations. This is crucial, since you really can't hide anything from yourself. If you lie all the time, your internal image will contain that information, and you will have a hard time trusting yourself. How much integrity you have or don't have may or may not be displayed to the rest of the world, but you yourself know, even if you'd rather not. If you are untrustworthy, you'll have a very hard time believing in yourself. And if you do not even trust yourself, the higher levels of action and growth are cut-off to you. Integrity matters – it matters a lot.

So, what if you don't have a great image of yourself, based upon true information? Well, you had better start there and start working on it seriously. If the central mechanism is untrustworthy, forget about the rest of it being reliable. Get true to yourself before trying to do everything else.

5.2.1.3 Reorientation

You may come across images and ideas that have a legitimate appeal to you, but really do not harmonize with your new goals. In such cases trying to simply uproot them is a problem; after all, they have legitimacy and real roots. A better method is to reorient them, or, as some say, to reframe them. That means to keep the roots, but to retrain the growth of the organism in a way that is supportive of the main goal.

As an example: A friend of ours had a lot of pleasant and formative memories from times when he lived in old tenement-type apartments. These were times when he reordered his life – the roots of his success were formed when he was in these places. So, he has a lot of good feelings and memories associated with the dark, old apartments. That is an image in his mind that is so deeply tied to things he highly values that it will not and should not go away.

On the other hand, he no longer wants to live in a tenement every day, even if he might enjoy revisiting them every so often. Having the image of himself in the tenement would tend to bring him back to it (by teleology), and he certainly does not want that. So, what to do?

We suggested to our friend that he change what surrounds the good image and to give it a new look. Instead of seeing the dank apartment as a place to live, he could see it as his secret hideaway. He could buy a large tenement building as an investment and secretly keep one apartment for himself. This would be supportive of his financial growth and would not undermine the legitimately good feelings regarding the apartment.

There is another important visualization technique that we mentioned earlier in this chapter: Modeling. By modeling your life on someone else's, you can adopt a lot of their internal characteristics. This is another batch technique, like switching paradigms was for the force method.

There are many examples in history of one person becoming much like another through close and prolonged contact, plus a bit of hero worship: Moses and Joshua, Elijah and Elisha, and many, many others. Modeling works, but there are caveats.

5.2.1.4 Autosuggestion

Autosuggestion means talking aloud to yourself. In many ways this is similar to building expectations by visualizing goals, but we list it separately because speaking seems to have a separate effect associated with it.

Think of autosuggestion like exercise; developing and strengthening that which is desired and squeezing and displacing that which is no longer desired. For whatever reason, autosuggestion works. Again, you can expect to come across varied memes that have loosened moorings during the process and again, this is the perfect time to deal with them intelligently.

The classic objection to autosuggest is that "you're only lying to yourself." Well, that can be done, but we do not suggest it. As we mentioned above, self-honesty is critical. Lying to yourself generally just gums-up the works, but you *can* safely dream aloud and say where you are going. You can safely envision yourself in the future. In effect, you begin to create your future by speaking to yourself. Whatever the mechanisms, continued autosuggestion has worked so many times that there can be little doubt regarding its general effectiveness.

5.2.2 Upgrading

This is where we begin to postulate a bit. Sure, we have support for the things we are about to put forth, but less than we do for the things written above. So, since we decided to be very open with you on our thinking, we decided to let you know that we are getting a little bit more theoretical here.

There seem to be underlying brain structures and/or operations that give idea-organisms more power over us than they "should" have. Here are two big reasons why we think this is true:

1. A meme is only a packet of information, a mental tool. Yet removing or even threatening a meme can cause significant discomfort. That may indicate that it is somehow embedded deeply... too deeply. Certainly some of the discomfort comes from the brain building circuits that are based upon that meme. But unplugging the meme "shouldn't" be a trauma; it should be like removing an application program (think word processor) from your computer, not like changing an operating system.

(Yikes.) For us, however, it is a lot like an operating system change – difficult and time-consuming.

2. You are the "Decider." It is your function to decide which ideas you want in your head. However, when an Ideology is rooted, it takes over some of those responsibilities. When you question the choices made by this idea-organism, you experience significant discomfort. In effect (and probably in reality as well), the ideological parasite takes over one section of your psyche and runs it as an automated routine. Your job of analyzing and deciding is bypassed, given to another, and your obedience is enforced by discomfort. Does this sound right to you?

From the above, we postulate that by correcting the operations of whatever underlying mechanism is involved here; we can make everything associated with revising one's collection of memes much, much easier.

Exactly how might we do this? The same ways we've already mentioned:

Force: When you feel a sense of pain that says, "Don't even try," you say, "Tough, I'm doing it. I will not back down."

Teleology: Envision yourself doing all the choosing, and enjoying doing it. Feel the thrill of actually being in control of your own mind. Satisfy yourself that doing this will increase your happiness and effectiveness; after all, no outside party is going to make choices as benevolently as you will yourself.

Reorientation: When you start to feel worried about some aspect of this, slow down, identify the concern (could take seconds or hours; sorry), then see if you can reframe the essential need to have a different purpose or meaning.

Autosuggestion: Why wouldn't you want to say, "I am in control of my own mind"? Fear of responsibility is certainly a common reason, though not a good one. Do you really think that an autoresponder routine designed by others is going to help you? Feel the fear, say what you want anyway.

Remember also that being afraid to assert your own rights is a slave mentality. This is your brain, your psyche, your life. Don't be afraid of some "massa," who uses pain and intimidation to shut you down. (This is not intended as a slight upon real slaves, who have been subjected to horrible, warping physical and mental incentives. It is an analogy to the fact that idea-organisms can make slaves of us all.)

5.2.3 Removing the Hooks

We explained, in an earlier chapter, how ideological organisms are quickly accepted and inordinately held to by people, because they offer cheap, and easy, fast self-esteem. This type of self-esteem is inauthentic, coming from external sources rather than internal sources. (Self-esteem should come from self, not from others, and no one knows you better than you do yourself. Besides – it's called self-esteem – not other-esteem!)

In effect, cheap external self-esteem puts deep hooks into human minds. It really is very similar to drug addiction, though it can be cured quite effectively.

The cure, of course, is simply to run the sequence in reverse, and start building authentic self-esteem. The real thing is much more solid and satisfying that the cheap imitation.

How to do this:

1. **Reject cheap self-esteem**. If people say good things about you just because you are part of the group, don't allow yourself to be fooled by it. It's not real, and you can't consider it real.
2. **Analyze yourself and your actions.** Was what you did a good thing? Why? Were you being honest with yourself?
3. **Be honest with yourself.** Every mistake can be rectified, but if you are not purely honest with yourself, you will not recognize the mistakes and they will go unreformed.
4. **Change bad behavior.** Just stop doing it. Focus on good behavior and when you slip, correct yourself. You control your own body and you control your conscious mind. Do it!
5. **Accept your goodness**. Do not be afraid to admit that you have done well or that you are a good person. Perhaps it would be better not to tell everyone else, but do not neglect to tell yourself.
6. **Enjoy your goodness.** If you have legitimately done well, revel in it. Feel good about it. Replay the scenarios in your mind. Replay and savor your victories. Many people fear doing this; they think they'll turn into some type of braggart. This is unlikely. Besides, you are analyzing yourself now; you'd notice and correct it, right? So enjoy!

Also, remember your concept of Ideal Self? When you do a full honest review of yourself, your Ideal Self should be proud of you for some of the things you have done that live up to your Ideal Self Image. That pride is authentic self-esteem.

Your Ideal Self Image should include being proud of yourself for maintaining the mind you want to have and for learning to think clearly and correctly, according to your own desires.

6.2.4 Bits and Pieces

Before we leave this subject of cleaning up your mental landscape, there are some other scattered ideas that we want to make sure you have. These are not the core, primary ideas, but they can be helpful. Here you go:

5.2.4.1 Self-Interview

Remember that you can interview yourself. We suggest that you do this the way a lot of people do meditation – in a quiet, comfortable, interruption-free place. Ask yourself questions and expect to get an answer; see what thoughts and/or images float up to your consciousness. Again, no magic here, just using the brain.

5.2.4.2 Dreams

No, don't worry, we're not going to try to tell you how to interpret dreams, and we're not at all sure they are "the royal road to the unconscious," but they can be interesting at times. Occasionally they are windows into some internal operations or concerns. If so, use that information. Other times, they are reflections of daily events or simply errata floating off your hard-drive. Use dreams selectively, but if you get a good clue from a dream, take advantage of it.

5.2.4.3 Redefining Yourself

Remember that the image you hold of yourself will affect everything else. So, even if you do all the things we recommend, yet hold on to an image of yourself as "the hard-luck case", "the one who has to carry the burden for the others", or other such thing, your progress will become derailed at some point. Self-image, like character, is destiny. All the things we've written about will help revise your self-image, but you'll have to allow the change, even if your friends and family aren't comfortable with it.

5.2.4.4 Clan Discomfort

You'll have to disregard the expectations that other people have upon you. This is especially important regarding people close to you. They are used to you being as you are, and may have strong expectations. They may even be relying on you in a sort of survival strategy.

You changing will scare them, or perhaps just make them uncomfortable. (If you're very lucky, most of them will applaud your progress, but problems are too common for us to get your hopes up.) If you move forward too overtly it will make other people feel bad. They fear your progress because it makes them look inferior, and they already have more of that than they can bear.

Let's be very clear – you don't owe them anything, save to do them no harm. If you moving ahead makes others feel uncomfortable, that's their problem, not yours. Move on anyway. Decide whether improvement or acceptance matters more to you. It is likely that you'll have to choose what is best for yourself over the comfort of others – maybe multiple times.

Do not fear that you will lose all your ties to other people. Once you are secure in yourself, others will gravitate back to you – they will even compliment you on the very same choices they previously tried to discourage.

5.2.4.5 Acting

Most people don't really know themselves very well. They live the life they think they are supposed to, not their own consciously chosen life. Their actions are directed and even ordered by the approval of others, not themselves. They get loud and drunk to show other people that they are vital and alive. They go to all the right places - say and do all the right things at the right time. They may be known as pillars of their communities – loved by all. But they do not get approval from within. Many of them aren't even sure what it would be like to be proud of themselves.

This affects almost all of us to one degree or another, and you'll have to watch yourself and root it out as it appears. You may have adopted roles early in life. When you notice them, resolve to stop playing those roles. In this matter, inertia is not your friend. William James wrote three rules for changing your life:

1. Do it immediately.
2. Do it flamboyantly.
3. No exceptions.

5.2.4.6 Self-referral and Other Referral

Self-referential people get their esteem from within, and will do things because they, themselves, will feel good about it. Those who are other-referral get their esteem from without and do things when they get positive feedback from others. Be the first example, not the second. This goes very deep and is a very powerful thing. People who are other-referral are subject to being miss-led all through their lives and can be made to feel bad very easily. They also behave worse.

Self-referral people will usually do the right thing, simply because it is right. We call these people "solid" or "reliable." Not only is this an issue of honesty, but it is critically important in business and other areas of life where reputation matters.

People who are other-referral tend to do the right thing only when other people think they should – and only when other people are watching. That tends to make them unreliable and variable.

5.2.4.7 Status-Seeking

We all like it when people think well of us and respect us. And there's nothing wrong with enjoying that. There IS something wrong with requiring it. A great many people live all their lives seeking status and envying people who have more status than they do. It is neither healthy nor necessary to base one's self esteem on one's position relative to other people.

People who seek status also tend to take a zero-sum view of status and try to steal it from others by putting them down. If they can make you feel bad, they feel a bit more powerful. This is very pervasive and breeds bad conduct almost always.

The more you do the rest of the things we mention here, the more you should have legitimate self-esteem. You will be the kind of person *you* want to be, not what other people expect you to be. People will often think well of you, you'll enjoy it, and it will be real, solid, and enduring.

5.2.4.8 Fear of Responsibility

Bear in mind that most people arrange their lives so that responsibility will not stick to them. This leads them into a lot of stupid bargains. In actuality, the whole thing is a mistake. If you disavow all responsibility, you also remove yourself from taking credit from what you do well.

Don't allow yourself to fear responsibility – to run from it. Responsibility is inseparable from individuality. Take them both; you'll be better and happier... once you get over the shock.

There is a unique and odd comfort in blind acceptance. It removes all responsibility from you and places it upon the thing you accept to run your life. The same goes for complete submission to some religion or other ideology. There is a certain pleasure offered here; relief, actually.

Don't fall for it! It's false. Choosing to let others do your thinking for you is still a choice that you have made. You remain just as responsible, and your results will suffer.

5.2.4.9 Fear of Success or Failure

We have discussed how all wants and fears stem from the behavior of replicators – biological or ideological. This can cause us to fear things even if they will be good for us – because replicators fear change. This can cause you to fear things that are new, even when logically you know no harm will come to you. Harm may however come to certain ideas in your head. Those ideas will resist the change.

If you start your own business, ideas about being an employee in a company will die. If you get involved in a serious relationship, ideas about being an independent single person will die. This is the origin of both fear of success and also fear of failure.

If you try and fail, ideas you hold about yourself – that you can accomplish something – will be hurt, so to protect those ideas, you come up with excuses to not try. That way you can keep on "knowing" that you could be great if you wanted to.

Maintaining the status quo protects all the ideas in your head; shaking up your world can dislodge some of them, so they try to prevent you from moving forward.

5.2.4.10 Death of an Identity

Breaking up a relationship is a form of death for the identity of yourself in the relationship: "Relationship You." (You may catch our allusion to the old Seinfeld gag – but there is truth in this joke.) This is one reason why ending a relationship can be so hard. After living with this other person for a long time, part of your identity includes the other person. If you split, those Identities will be ripped out, which feels bad.

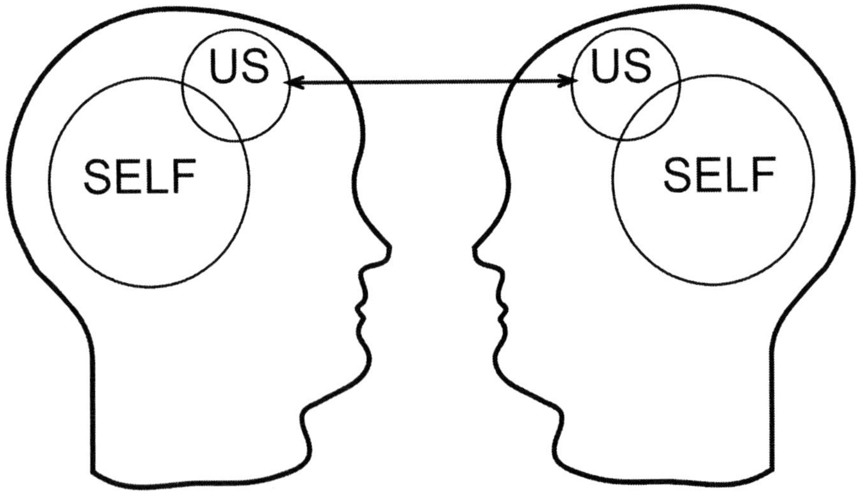

The same sort of thing can happen when changing jobs, leaving your home town, and in many other cases. It causes us a disproportionate level of pain, seeking to keep things the same. Remember that the discomfort you are feeling is due to idea-organisms seeking to prevent you from changing. If it's the right thing to do, do it anyway.

Note also that losing status is a form of death for Identities that are supposed to have a certain status. Rising in position is also a threat to a long-established status. Both fears of success and failure can be attributed to death of an identity that is part of your self-image. People can also be very mean to one of their local group-members who rise above them or falls below them in some way – so the Collective Identities in other people's minds are also an issue.

A marriage (or any relationship really) is a Collective. You really want to do something as an individual, and yet you find yourself not doing it, because you feel pressure from your idea of what you must do for your marriage. (This is not the same as rationally deciding on what is best among options.) Obviously this also happens for people with their families, social groups, racial groups, etc., but it really does extend down to the level of any simple two person relationship.

5.2.4.11 Fear of Error or Ignorance

We're all wrong sometimes, and we are all ignorant of many things. These are not things for which we should be ashamed.

For example: A boy is born in some backward, forgotten hill town. He grows up entirely ignorant of the modern world. When he finally does get to the city, he is woefully ignorant as compared to people raised there.

This is NOT a reason to be ashamed – it is an accident. On the other hand, if he sees the knowledge of the city and runs back to the village in order to avoid it, THIS is a reason for shame... or at least for guilt.

People who are willing to admit they could be wrong are MUCH more likely to actually be right.

Shame locks you down and prevents forward movement. Reject it.

5.2.4.12 Grouping Ideas

Every hot new ideology seems to start with a kernel of truth, then expand it and add a bunch of BS to attract more interest. People then tend to accept all or nothing. Just because you recognize BS, it doesn't mean there isn't a kernel (or more) of truth. Likewise, where you recognize truth, it doesn't mean that everything there isn't also a lot of BS.

Symbiotic ideas start well, but a lot of hype gets added to the mix in order to get them heard. Since this works, anything you are likely to hear has a lot of BS mixed in. That means you have to consider all of your opinions, not just adopt them.

This is also why intelligent folks can be radically divided. Each side has 50% BS built into their ideas. Falling for the fallacy of labels, they can target the weak parts of the each others' philosophy and dismiss it all as untrue based on its weakest links. Any time we accept labels – we are accepting 50% BS.

Labeling allows groups of ideas to be taken as one – and this allows parasitic memes to bundle themselves along with symbiotic and altruistic memes.

5.2.4.13 Substitutes

People tend to displace authentic virtues with cheap substitutes... a lot.

For example: A whole lot of people define themselves as "anti" something or another. Why? Well, do you remember building fancy toy buildings when you were a kid, then having your little brother or sister knock it over in a second? And do you remember when you did it too? Destruction gets fast and easy results.

Complaining is a whole lot easier than Planning. Destroying is easier than creating. It is much, much easier to be a critic than to be an artist.

And that's just one example. Authentic things are harder to find and develop. But, damn... it's wonderful to know you have the real thing! It's really, REALLY nice.

5.2.4.14 Easy Ideas

When people replace thinking with the memorization of slogans, ideas get repeated for all the wrong reasons. What really gets ideas around is when they are easy to repeat. Rhyming and rhythmic phrases, catchy tunes, use of alliteration – all these things are memory aids, but also make the memes that the words carry more likely to be believed and passed along. Madison Avenue ad agencies use those catchy jingles for just this reason. This is what passes for knowledge in the heads of many people – cute slogans that are easy to remember. Do you really want the most dumped-down slogans of past loudmouths running your mind or do you want ideas that are logically consistent?

5.3 Logical Thought

Logical thinking and the scientific method are tools that can be used to analyze ideas and conduct useful experiments. However, it takes some degree of mental discipline to use these tools effectively. It is often easier to assume that other smart people have done the thinking for you and just take it on faith that what they tell you is true.

Even when you do start on the path to thinking things through for yourself, you may often stop when things become difficult. When logical thinking calls into question a long held belief, it often seems easier to dismiss logic than to work backwards and untangle all the interdependencies that you have built up.

If you are willing to take the time, the tools we discuss in this section will be useful to you.

5.3.1 Axioms

We would all like to have the answers all the time. But if you don't really have the answers, the only way to work around your ignorance is to make something up. You may think this seems like cheating – it would also seem to be a possible source of false information. We have been talking about not taking things on faith – this sounds like doing just that. However, if done properly, it's not. The way to do it properly is by saying this:

> We promise to always remember that we just made it up. We also continually strive to reduce the number of things that we are holding in our mind as ideas we can't prove. But we will give this idea the benefit of the doubt for now.

That is what an axiom is. It is something that we can't prove and we know we can't prove, but we act like it is true anyway. It is a working assumption. This is a very useful tool as long as we are willing to discard an axiom if we ever manage to prove it is false. In fact, in logical thought, we don't even think of our axioms as being true or false – we think of other statements as being true or false based on a given set of axioms. We must discard an axiom not only if we prove it false, but also if we prove it true. If we prove it true, it stops being an axiom and becomes a statement that we can prove or disprove based on our other axioms. We don't stop believing the provable ones – we just no longer consider them axioms.

We can only prove a statement true or false in relation to other axioms. We need axioms, but we try to keep this set of made up stuff as small as possible so that we can remember that it might just be bullshit.

It might help to look at your set of axioms as a logical tool kit – you want to keep your tool kit as small as possible because it is something you have to carry around with you all the time. You don't want it to be too heavy. (The metaphorical additional weight is the extra mental energy it takes to remember that each axiom is something that may need to be discarded.) On the other hand, you want to have the tools you need available when you need them, so you want your kit to contain enough axioms to tackle any particular thinking job.

So where do you get these axioms from? How do you start assembling a tool kit?

The most common way to create an axiom is to try things that seem universally true to us. Axioms are just assumptions that we make – and you know what happens when you ASSUME – that's right, you have heard this one before, it means you consider something to be true which is not necessarily true.

This can be dangerous, so we should look for axioms that seem to accurately reflect the real world, and that we think will prove useful to our continued survival and growth.

So far this is pretty easy. The hard part comes when we start working with our axioms. Continuing to use axioms just because they seem true sounds like a recipe for a logical train wreck, however, we also require that they cannot be proved false. If a path of experimentation and logical reasoning, using our set of axioms, produces a logical contradiction, then those axioms cannot be used together. This process allows us to see which axioms can work together to form a particular world-view, and that can be applied consistently to the observable world around us.

For Example:

Axiom 1: GOD is omniscient (All knowing)

Axiom 2: GOD is omnipotent (All Powerful)

Axiom 3: GOD is omnibenevolent (All Good)

Experimental evidence: Bad things happen to good people

This is a classic religious mystery – a case where the axioms which a religion asks us to take on faith seem to disagree with observed reality. If GOD can see all evil, has the power to fix all evil, and does all good, then why is there still evil in the world?

Logic dictates that such a conflict be resolved by either modifying the axioms, or further experimentation showing that our evidence is faulty. Some possible resolutions include:

- Change or remove axiom 1 – GOD isn't always watching. In The Bible it says on the seventh day GOD rested. Perhaps he is still asleep and isn't currently in omniscient or omnipotent mode.
- Change or remove axiom 2 – GOD'S powers are limited in some way. For example, we might decide that GOD can not have two different contradictory things happen at the same time, or must allow some rules of causality. If faced with a choice of having some evil now lead to greater good later, or allowing some small evil now to avoid a greater evil later, then GOD will make a choice in favor of the greater good or the lesser of two evils.
- Change or remove axiom 3 – GOD doesn't feel the need to be good all the time. Some or all of the time GOD leaves it up to us to be good or evil while just observing us. God does not always get involved.

Sometimes GOD just gets caught up in watching the show. (This is probably an easy thing to have happen when you are all seeing!)

- Question the experimental evidence – are we sure that bad things happen to good people? Perhaps those people were really bad, and we just can't see as deeply as GOD. When your grandmother was hit by that bus – is it possible she was on her way to a secret meeting of Satan worshipers? Or perhaps the evil that we perceive is actually good for us. Nietzsche said that which does not kill us makes us stronger. Maybe GOD is just helping us build up some good spiritual toughness.

There are even additional unstated axioms here that can be questioned. Is their only one universe? Perhaps GOD created all possible universes – with all possible events happening. If so, then His powers are even bigger than we might have imagined in Axiom 2 – given our unstated axiom that we exist in the only universe. Then from our single universe point of view it would appear that GOD was not omnipotent, whereas GOD would actual be more omnipotent than we can even imagine.

So when you see how fun and complicated these theological debates might get, it makes it all that much more understandable that Priests are willing to give up sex to just stay up all night talking about GOD instead.

The upshot of all this talk about axioms is that logic is not useful for proving anything to another person with whom we have absolutely nothing in common. One needs a common consistent set of axioms in order to argue logically on any topic. We cannot use axioms that they do not share with us to prove our point.

If the level of disagreement is so fundamental that we can not agree on the axioms, we can only try to convince the other person that it is more useful to some shared goal to see the world in a different way. We can only suggest that another person try out our axioms – we can not offer any proof for them.

This is another way in which a set of axioms is like a tool kit – it may be that there are different logically consistent sets of axioms that are useful for thinking about different topics. While it would be nice to have one set of super tools that could handle any job, axioms, like the tools for building a house, end up in the equivalent of special kits like plumber's tools, electrician's tools, carpentry tools, etc.

Changing someone's world view is not so easy and the great conflicts in the world are not always caused by arguments within a single world view. They are often caused by conflicting sets of axioms. Resolving such conflicts is only possible by showing that there exists no need for conflict, that actions taken by the believers of one world view do not affect those believing in the other, or that some course of action is available which is acceptable to both.

Surprisingly often, the actions are not influenced by axiom choice so much as bad logical thought. So let's take a look at what passes for good logical thought. How do we build new truths from our axioms?

5.3.2 Syllogisms

The standard way to build new truths from known truths is called a syllogism. This is a fancy word for combining two statements into a conclusion.

Here is the standard example:

Premise 1: All men are mortal.

Premise 2: Socrates is a man.

Conclusion: Socrates is mortal.

The general pattern of each syllogism is, as you can see, three statements. Each statement contains a subject, a predicate, an assertion or negation ("is" or "is not"), and a degree of certainty ("some" or "all"). In any syllogism, there is a term that is shared by each premise that is used to connect the other two terms that end up in the conclusion.

Given the 2 possible positions of the connecting term in each of 2 premises, and the 4 possible combinations of certainty and assertion/negation in each of 3 statements – some fairly basic math (2 x 2) x (4 x 4 x 4) shows us that there are 256 possible forms for a syllogism.

As it turns out, only 19 of the 256 produce logically consistent conclusions, so it is important to be aware that just stating something in the above manner does not make it correct – indeed if that is all you have to go on, the odds of it being correct are small.

Here is an example of a faulty syllogism:

Premise 1: Most politicians are veterans

Premise 2: Most veterans are honest

Faulty Conclusion: Most politicians are honest

This "three uncertain" example does not work because the uncertainty in each of the premises produces the possibility of no overlap at all. This is made more obvious by using the same form of syllogism with two true premise statements that produce a nonsense conclusion. For example:

Premise 1: Most cats are milk drinkers

Premise 2: Most milk drinkers put milk in their coffee

Faulty Conclusion: Most cats put milk in their coffee

Trying to create a nonsense conclusion using the same form of syllogism is a good way to test if it is valid form.

5.3.3 The Scientific Method

So far we have talked about deductive logic, in which results are obtained from the logical combination and progression of axioms. Perhaps an even more powerful form of logical thought, however, is called inductive logic. Inductive logic is the type of reasoning employed by the scientific method.

In inductive reasoning one starts with observations then formulates a hypothesis concerning how such observations are produced. Experiments are then created and formed to attempt to either demonstrate or invalidate the hypothesis. Only after a hypothesis has remained unchallenged for quite some time does it obtain the status of axiom or "scientific law" – and even then it may still be struck down or altered by new evidence. Francis Bacon, one of the fathers of the scientific method, wrote:

> *There are and can be only two ways of searching into and discovering truth. The one flies from the senses and particulars to the most general axioms, and from these principles, the truth of which it takes for settled and immovable, proceeds to judgment and middle axioms. And this way is now in fashion. The other derives axioms from the senses and particulars, rising by a gradual and unbroken ascent, so that it arrives at the most general axioms last of all. This is the true way, but as yet untried.*

If science has been at war with religion, then this is the reason. Science uses a chain of logic in the opposite direction from religion. The most basic axioms are not written in stone until every possibility has been explored. It discovers specific small truths first, arranges them into larger theories, and comes to its most general truths last of all. This is quite backwards from a religious philosophy. Religions ask one to accept the big answers on faith and to hold to that faith in the face of all opposition.

The scientific method asks that observation and experimentation should be taken as the ground upon which to build a structure of logical reasoning – that such grand ideas as the source of all creation should be a pinnacle to be reached only when the structure below is completely solid.

Religion, conversely, starts with fixed ideas about GOD and heaven, and builds down towards the Earth we can observe and test. Where the logical structure is not quite able to reach the ground, it is declared that some things man was not meant to know, or that divine mystery is beyond us, or that GOD will never supply proof that would make faith unnecessary.

Some have argued that science is just a different religion, and this claim is strengthened because some who call themselves scientists will often become fixed in their beliefs, or project beyond what they can actually demonstrate through experimentation. Quite a few scientists have a hard time saying, "We have evidence that this is true," rather than "We know this is true."

The scientific method demands that when new evidence is found which contradicts the existing structure, the whole structure MUST be shaken to the ground and rebuilt brick by brick. Some scientists become very attached to a long-standing logical structure, becoming quite fond of standing on its loftiest peaks. When new observations require demolition and reconstruction, such scientists can be found lying in the mud in front of the bulldozers, extolling the greatness of the thinkers that came before them, much the same way the faithful would speak of the prophets of their religion.

Other supposed scientists are drawn into the "either or" fallacy. When they see some logical error, or contrary evidence, in a religious argument, they forget their logic and jump to the conclusion that this proves the atheistic position, without recognizing all the possibilities in between. Or they decide that religious people are wrong to have faith in unproven ideas and that because the faith is wrong, the ideas must also be wrong.

They fail to recognize that to deny something without proof is as much an example of blind faith as it is to believe something without proof. It is as much an act of faith to declare that you know that there is no GOD, as it is to be a true believer.

The correct application of the scientific method allows a scientist to build up a structure of ideas based upon an experimentally testable hypothesis. One can not leap to any conclusions that one likes without the supporting experimental evidence; one must find repeatable experiments that prove the conclusion.

Likewise, one can not reject such a structure simply because one does not like the conclusion. Instead, we must create an experiment that shows its weakness. This gives a logical structure great strength – in that each brick in its foundation has been built logically, is testable, and need not be taken on faith. But it is also a great weakness, in that any given brick can also be falsified and removed, and this can bring the whole structure crashing down.

If there is a war between science and religion, it is like a robot fighting a ghost; they can not touch each other; they do not share the same axioms.

If you are one of the faithful, real scientists do not reject your religious observances to your God as being false. They reject your religion as being ill defined, imprecise, not adequately tested or testable. They ask to see falsifiable claims that can be tested. To them the key to truth lies in the opportunity to prove falsehood. Unless and until you create quantifiable experiments that show that through your prayer and faith, something testable happens, they will always see your faith as irrelevant – not false, but if not potentially falsifiable, not worth consideration.

If you are a scientist, the truly faithful do not reject your scientific methodology. They reject your science as being incomplete, of not reaching out to embrace the whole universe. They want to have all the answers, to have a complete understanding of the universe, and to know that their lives hold true meaning. Unless and until your structure of logic reaches the final theory of everything, and unless that final theory produces deeper meaning, they know they will be happier having faith in their understanding. If your theories do not give their lives meaning, they will be seen as not worth consideration.

The two viewpoints are not incompatible. However, any attempt at combining the two is an attempt to bridge the missing gap between the growing mundane foundation of a structure on the ground and the peaks of a lofty magical castle in the air. One can be a scientist and have faith in things one can not see. However, when one starts either rejecting scientific models based on religious convictions, or gaining or losing faith in universal meaning based on scientific methods, one is practicing bad science, bad religion, or both.

Some of the greatest scientists in the world have also been very religious, but it is not an easy thing to look at the world both ways, and many have committed errors of both science and religion in trying to do so. Einstein rejected models based on probability theory, saying, "GOD does not play dice with the universe." It just so happens that the end product of the probability-based models that he rejected (Quantum electrodynamics) is a theory that has resulted in the most accurate predictions concerning the physical world that humanity has ever been able to make.

Why was this a sticking point for him?

We don't know.

Surely Einstein did not believe that when he was at the craps table, GOD could not predict or control his next throw of the dice. Then why did basing physical predictions on probability theory at the sub-atomic level cheapen his concept of GOD? His failure to allow his deity Omniscience and Omnipotence that could transcend our concepts of uncertainty was bad religion, and his allowing this to affect his pursuit of logical thought was bad science.

5.4 Fallacies

Logical argument is actually kind of mechanical; mathematical, really. It uses structured thinking to explain how a conclusion has to be drawn from a given set of assumptions.

It is sometimes possible to create arguments that appear to logically prove something, but really don't. Such an argument is said to be based on some sort of fallacy.

It is important to be aware of the logical fallacies because they are found at the heart of almost every deception you will ever face. That means that you hear them on a daily basis. You will notice that a lot of these fallacies are still called by their Latin names. This is because they were first noted as examples of faulty logic a couple of thousand years ago. Despite the amount of time that people have known them to be examples of invalid argument, people still fall victim to them every day.

We will not go into a full list of all the identified fallacies here, but we will cover the ones that are most commonly used. A fun drinking game to play is to listen to any political or theological argument and whenever you hear and name a fallacy, everyone else has to take a drink. Sadly if less that 50% of the statements made in an argument contains a fallacy, it is a very well reasoned debate.

(This drinking game may well be the reason that philosophers are also often notorious drunkards.)

5.4.1 Fallacies of ambiguity

Fallacies of ambiguity are used to create a false conclusion by confusing the terms of the argument. Sometimes a term is used in a different way in one premise than in another, or sometimes tricks of language are used to suggest something false without actually stating it clearly.

By the way, a *premise* is anything that your argument presumes to be true. (The tricky thing about premises is when they are assumed, but not stated.)

5.4.1.1 Accentus

A fallacy in which ambiguity arises from the emphasis (accent) placed on a word or phrase, or choice of words, in order to say something without actually saying it. For example:

"He is telling the truth *this time*."

The implication here being that he usually lies, but since no direct argument has been made that this is the case, it can not be directly challenged, nor can the speaker be said to be lying based on the actual words spoken.

5.4.1.2 Grouping and Dividing

- SWEEPING and HASTY GENERALIZATON
- COMPOSITION and DIVISION

These are related fallacies that rely on the human mind's tendency to think in groups of things. Each of these fallacies attempts to confuse people by mixing up a group and its parts. The trick is to improperly apply the attributes of the group or situation to a specific example, or visa versa. Division example:

> "That Justice was on the supreme court when the court ruled in favor of abortion, therefore he is pro-abortion!"

However, based simply on the person in question being a member of a group that through its internal rules expressed a certain opinion, does not mean that the person held that opinion. The Justice might have been the author of the minority opinion, or abstained from voting.

A similar example of the Fallacy of Composition would be to say:

> "Judge Smith is one of the judges on the panel, and I know that he has expressed sympathies for the defendant's cause, therefore the defendant will get a fair trial."

Of course, the other Judges involved could easily all share an agenda that would be best served by having the defendant strung up by his thumbs, making the fairness of the trial unlikely at best.

Political arguments regularly make use of the confusion of properties of groups and individual members. This can even lead to the deliberate creation of new group words and phrases that are specifically designed just so this logical "error" can be exploited. For example:

> "We know that they have Weapons of Mass Destruction!"

In this political example, the classification of a set of many weapons allows a politician to say, "truthfully," that they know a certain group has access to "Weapons of Mass Destruction." However, the intention here is, without actually lying, to incite in the public the fear that would accompany saying that the group had access to the most dangerous weapons on the list (nuclear weapons with global delivery systems) even though the group is in fact known to have only the very least dangerous weapons included in the WMD category, and possesses no reasonable delivery system whatsoever.

5.4.1.3 Equivocation

This is an argument in which an expression is used in one sense in a premise and in a different sense in another premise or conclusion. Or (and you see this a lot in politics), terms that mean the same thing are used as if they are not the same. Some silly and obvious examples would be:

> "He removed some sand from the bank of that river; therefore he should be arrested for bank robbery."

"I did not have sexual relations with that woman." (She just gave me a blowjob...)

A less silly, though perhaps just as obvious example would be:

"We would never invade and occupy another sovereign nation. We simply intend to liberate the oppressed people and stabilize the area for as long as may be required."

Neither obvious, nor silly is the argument:

"It is murder to kill a human. A fetus is human. Therefore it is murder to kill a fetus."

In this case, the word "human" is used to mean both a fully realized thinking individual, and a collection of human cells that has the potential to be such an individual. A fetus does have a certain level of potential, and it may indeed be enough to make abortion immoral, but this argument doesn't make that case for immorality fairly.

The rest of the Pro-Life group thought that these guys were maybe just a little bit too "Hard Core."

Both sides of the debate certainly feel that killing a baby is immoral, even though a baby still only represents a certain level of potential to be a fully thinking individual. However, this area – the span between potential and realization of humanity – is precisely the issue that is open to debate. The above argument does not prove anything by trying to linguistically bridge the difference between realized and unrealized potential.

To show why this is true, consider that the same argument could just as easily be applied to individual sperm cells. They are human too – and each one represents a potential thinking individual given the right circumstances. Even the most radical pro-life activists have some cut-off point where they find the frustration of genetic potential not enough to be called killing.

If they did not, you would see people standing outside high school proms with protest signs like the ones pictured in the cartoon.

5.4.1.4 Reification

(Also ANTHROPOMORPHISM)

These are fallacies of applying attributes to an idea or thing that they do not in reality posses. Commonly, this means treating an abstract idea or inanimate object as if it had the qualities of an animal or human being. Example:

> "This country gave birth to you. You should therefore show it the same love it feels for you, just as you would your mother."

Obviously a country does not have the same feelings as a mother, and did not give birth to you in the same literal way.

This fallacy is particularly interesting to us, in that it is the fallacy that we and our book could be accused of. When we speak of ideological Higher Powers possessing an agenda, this might be seen as reification or anthropomorphism.

However, one must remember that a central argument of this book is that the information that makes up complex ideas is semantically no different than the information that makes up genetic organisms. This is why we hold that governments and religions can indeed be thought of as having "wants" and "fears" that are at least as valid as those of a low level biological life form, if not those of an actual complex animal or human being.

We also believe that this shows the concept of having a "want" can be viewed as just the result of an evolved replicator promoting the behavior that has given it survival value in the past. It does not matter if the replicator in question is genetic or memetic.

We are not attempting to invalidate this fallacy completely. In fact we feel that anyone who believes that some Higher Power is considering their best interests is falling for this fallacy. Higher Powers can not think the way we do – they just evolve such that they end up doing the things that benefit their continued existence and replication. Any higher thought that helps them is done by individual human beings in their service.

However, we are suggesting that a full understanding of information systems should redefine the concept of life to address the memetic as well as the genetic. Then real understanding might be gained concerning the level of life that idea-organisms can really have.

5.4.2 Fallacies of Misdirection

These fallacies are based on distracting one's opponents with issues that are not really logically related to the proposition being argued.

5.4.2.1 Appeal to Consequences

This is a fallacy in which the consequences of believing a proposition are introduced, rather than information concerning the truth or falsehood of the proposition. Examples:

> "If we decide that it is a constitutional right for everyone to carry a handgun, we will live in a world of Wild West gunslingers, with people dying in the streets every day."

> "If we decide it is not a constitutional right to carry a handgun, only criminals will have guns, and honest citizens will not be able to safely walk the streets."

Neither of these statements have anything to do with the issue of constitutionality. Rather than logic, they appeal to the listener to imagine the effects of a given decision, and influence that decision based on the claimed effects. These particular arguments are appeals to fear, which is very common for this fallacy.

Another classic example would be a common religious argument that makes use of this fallacy:

> "Believe that what we tell you is true, and in the next life you will be rewarded; do not believe and you will be punished."

Note that the act of considering the consequences of an action is not the fallacy here. The fallacy is in appealing to the consequences as a way of sidestepping some other rational standard of the truth of the argument. If the nature of the argument is to choose between two courses of action based on their relative merits, of course the consequences of each action are important and applicable. If the nature of the argument is to determine the truth or falsehood of a premise, however, the consequences of thinking one way or the other can not replace a rational decision about the premise itself.

5.4.2.2 Argumentum ad Nauseum

This fallacy works on the belief that the more times something is said, the more likely it is to be true. This is used in advertising where radio and television commercials are run over and over again until you know the jingles by heart. In politics, talking points are passed out to the faithful media mouthpieces so that the same ideas can be repeated in the same words again and again and again and again. In religions, the same prayers are recited and the same songs are sung, so the ideas sink in through massive repetition of the words.

It may seem obvious that lies can be repeated just as easily as truths, but a lot of folks are still regularly suckered by this technique of repeating falsehoods.

Perhaps even more problematic is the fact that this repetition is not always caused by any evil intent to spread bad information, but sometimes simply because the bad information is particularly interesting or easy to repeat.

> In the United States, many people decide what they should be afraid of based on the information they get from the mass media. (TV news, radio, newspapers, etc.) The problem is that the mass media has a commercial interest in being interesting as well as informative. To avoid being boring, they regularly report on uncommon occurrences rather than normal everyday events. This means that deaths from things that kill people every day (like heart disease and automobile accidents) get almost no media coverage, while things that are actually very rare (like terrorist attacks or deadly infectious diseases) receive a great deal of media attention. Common threats are mostly ignored while rare threats are talked about endlessly. This has the effect of projecting a threat model that is exactly backwards from any reality of the dangers in our world. Unfortunately people also regularly vote based on these media inspired fears and this affects the lives of other people, even those who have more rational threat models.

5.4.2.3 Interrogation

This fallacy is based on asking questions that presuppose some fact, such that the interrogated party must either seen to be accepting the fact, or evading the question. A classic example is the question:

> "Have you stopped beating your wife?"

5.4.2.4 Poisoning the Well

This fallacy is used to discredit an argument before it can even be heard. Example:

> "Only an idiot would agree that..."

5.4.2.5 Straw Man

This is also known as the fallacy of misrepresentation. The "Straw Man" is so called because he is easily defeated. Where a real man requires a real victory in battle to knock down, a straw man is easily pushed over.

One amusing example of this fallacy can be seen in modern TV commercials, in which an entirely fictitious competing brand is invented to highlight the features of the advertised brand. A humorous example of such an advertisement would run something like this:

> "At Good Guys Car Rental, we treat you with class!" Smiling agent opens door of luxury car and hands keys to smiling man. "Not like those other guys." Ugly clerk pulls lever and customer falls down chute into tiny economy car.

In modern political debate it is routine to hear politicians talking about their political opponents' plans and goals. When this happens, you can bet that their version of their opponents' plans do not match what their opponents would say.

This fallacy has also been used throughout history by religious groups who made claims about other religious groups that were not true. In some cases such lies were used to incite violence and genocide against whole cultures.

Almost any argument that has people killed also includes the next fallacy.

5.4.2.6 Two Wrongs

This fallacy supposes that some proposition is true or correct because it acts against some other false or wrong thing. This is the classic fallacy used to justify horrific behavior. Example:

> "We had to kill those innocent civilians because we are fighting against global terrorism."

5.4.2.7 Bifurcation

(also "False Dilemma" or "Excluded Middle")

This fallacy presents only two possible alternatives when many actually exist. People are very susceptible to this. Our minds seem geared towards thinking in these terms – True or False, Wrong or Right, Black and White, Us and Them. Collective idea organisms encourage this sort of binary thinking and exploit it. For Example:

> "Either you support the policies of The Great Leader, or you are a traitor who hates this country."

This type of thing gets said a lot, even though clearly you could love the country and still feel that the "Great Leader" isn't doing such a great job of leading it. In fact greater love for the country would mean more concern if you thought the leader was doing a poor job – someone who did not love the country would not care that it was being misled. A common religious example is:

> "I know that GOD is my father and watches over me in heaven, because I refuse to believe that I am the meaningless product of random chance."

Of course there are many more possibilities than just the two presented. There are many more creation ideas than just the one presented by a single religion, and if there is no creator, how does that make us meaningless? There are many possible ways we can have both existence and meaning. It is not logical to put forth only two choices – the God of one particular religion or an empty random meaningless existence.

5.4.3 Fallacies of Source

These fallacies derive from the idea that the source of an argument affects its validity. This is very easy illogic for people to buy into. We tend to think in terms of labels, credentials and brand loyalty. However the source of a statement has no direct bearing on its truth. A proposition is not true because it comes from a credible source and is not false because it comes from a non-credible source.

5.4.3.1 Age

- ARGUMENTUM AD ANTIQUITAM
- ARGUMENTUM AD NOVITAM

These fallacies suggest that something is true just because it is old (or new). They are opposites of each other, yet both used regularly. Examples:

"It was good enough for my grandfather – it's good enough for me."

"You're not still using that old technology are you? Version 2.0 was released last month."

5.4.3.2 Wealth

- ARGUMENTUM AD CRUMENAM
- ARGUMENTUM AD LAZARUM

Again these are opposites. The first fallacy suggests that someone is correct because they are rich – the second because they are poor. Examples:

"He must know what he is talking about; he made millions in the stock market."

"He grew up on the streets, so he really knows where it's at."

5.4.3.3 Popularity

- ARGUMENTUM AD NUMERAM
- ARGUMENTUM AD POPULUM

These fallacies put forward the idea that because a lot of people believe something, it is true. Example:

"90% of the people on the planet believe in some sort of afterlife. They can't all be wrong."

Of course 100% of the people on the planet also used to think the sun went around the Earth – and they were all 100% wrong.

5.4.3.4 Argumentum ad Hominem

This fallacy gets right to the root of all fallacies of source – it is a direct attack on the person doing the arguing, rather than the argument itself. It is an attempt to disprove a proposition by discrediting its source, rather than actually disproving it. Some political examples:

"My opponent is a typical 'Tax and Spend' 'Bleeding Heart' liberal."

"My opponent is a typical fascist conservative."

5.4.4 Fallacies of Correlation

- CUM HOC ERGO PROPTER HOC
- POST HOC ERGO PROPTER HOC

These fallacies are attempts to show causation based on association. "Cum Hoc" shows two things that happen at the same time, while "Post Hoc" is even harder to spot as being false because one thing actually follows the other.

Things that happen at the same time might be related, but they might not either. Things following each other might be related or might not be. Because things are somehow associated doesn't prove that they one causes the other. They might both be caused by something else.

As usual, these fallacies show up in political and religious argument, but they are also the source of many bad scientific studies that are used politically. For example:

> "Gun control laws don't work. In fact they can even make things worse by disarming victims. Studies show that states with the strongest gun control laws have the highest crime rates."

The argument here is that the gun control laws caused the high crime rates, however, without more information; it could just as easily be that the laws were passed in response to the high crime in the state. These laws may indeed not work, but it might also be the case that crime would be worse rather than better without the laws – nothing is proven by the simple correlation that was presented.

Even if the crime rates went up after the laws, the laws may have been passed with expectations of a rise in crime based on some other factor. A proper scientific study would make use of a control group – showing what happened in a similar area that did not pass the same laws. Did crime go up there too?

5.4.5 Paradox

A paradox is not really a fallacy, but it can be used to support faulty thinking. Paradoxes arise in any system that allows self reference – and concluding anything based on finding a paradox is an error. A paradox is neither an affirmation nor a contradiction. Its existence should neither confirm nor deny the usefulness of any system. To make either claim would be a fallacy.

A paradox occurs whenever a new idea can be proven false if it is assumed true, and can be proven true if it is assumed false. This excludes it from adoption in your current set of axioms but does not mean that your current set of axioms is flawed. In fact, if your set of axioms does not generate paradoxes occasionally, it is probably not complicated enough to be useful for most things.

Actually, the concept of paradox is apparently not well understood if one goes by famous examples. Here are two examples of supposed all time great paradoxes:

1. Epimenides the Cretan said, "Cretans always lie." Was he lying?
2. Can GOD create a stone so heavy that He cannot move it?

Neither one is actually a paradox.

The first is trying to be an example of the simpler paradox, "I am lying," or, "This sentence is false," but fails to complete the logical loop. The escape is that Epimenides is lying as he does occasionally because the truth is that, "All Cretans sometimes lie" and/or "Some Cretans always lie." His lying on this occasion does not imply that, "All Cretans always tell the truth," which would prove him not a liar and thus create a paradox.

The second is asking "Can an Omnipotent Being give up Omnipotence?" The answer is trivially, "Yes." Giving up omnipotence is doing something, and an omnipotent being can do anything – and can therefore do that. There is no logic loop here. Giving up omnipotence does not refute that there was ever omnipotence to begin with. It is no more a paradox than asking, "Can a guy holding a pencil put it down." After he puts it down he is no longer holding it.

Even if you eliminate the passage of time between the two states of omnipotence and denied-omnipotence, such as, "Can GOD do something that GOD can't do?" you don't have a true paradox such as, "This statement is false" – merely a fallacy of interrogation where the assumption of the question (that there are things GOD can't do) conflict with one of the axioms about GOD, namely that GOD is omnipotent (can do anything).

A true paradox can arise only from self reference in the system. It can be shown false if assumed true and true if assumed false, and is therefore neither true nor false, without contradicting any axioms.

This is particularly intriguing when you consider that being human is all about self reference. Our brains model the world and ourselves, while at the same time our brains are part of the world and ourselves.

Now that is a thought worthy of being an all time great paradox.

5.5 Bias of Our Culture

Since this book is about identifying, analyzing and sorting the ideas that float through our brains, it seems only fair that we should come clean about our own. This may allow you to better understand our ideas and make use of them, should you choose to do so. It may also be helpful to you if you are reading a translation, have a different religious/cultural background, or even have a different academic or professional background.

On the other hand, cultural differences only really matter in terms of communication, not as regards the ideas themselves. The rightness or wrongness of an idea has nothing to do with what culture it arose from, only whether or not it stands up to a comparison with reality. If it explains reality well, then it is a good idea, and where it came from is unimportant. If we do our job of communicating well enough, our cultural background shouldn't matter.

All of that said, this book is the product of a specific cultural heritage that both of the authors share. In this section we'll explain exactly what that is, and we will try to lay out the assumptions (axioms) that underlay the arguments in this book.

5.5.1 English Speaking

This book was written in the English language. If you are reading it in another language, the accuracy of what you are reading involves the mind and skill of a translator. This cannot be helped, but it does make the translator something of a coauthor, which you may wish to keep in mind.

A second issue is that your language and English may differ as to specific words and expressions. Translating is difficult. For example, in English, a non-violent situation can be described as "peaceful," even if many aspects of it are highly chaotic. In several other languages, "peaceful" would clearly imply that everything is under control. In most cases a good translator will deal with this appropriately, but you may want to verify this for yourself.

5.5.2 Judeo-Christian American

Our culture is American (United States) and Judeo-Christian. Many examples in the book will be based on this. For example, when we discuss God we are mostly referring to the Judeo-Christian God. In other words, we're talking about the big guy who sits on the heavenly throne. When we discuss laws, we are referring to the idea of Common Law or to the American law that sprang from it.

Since Judeo-Christian American covers a lot of specific ideals, we'll list what we think are the most central and unique of them:

5.5.2.1 Allegiance to Ideas

The ideas we share are held to be more important than geography or ethnicity. America was (and to a large extent still is) far more of an idea than it is a place or a race. There is no specific American gene pool, and American territory has changed greatly over time (though not recently).

The central idea of America is that people give the government permission to do things – not vice-versa. However manipulated and mangled this idea has become, it still has moorings. We feel that holding to a good idea is far more critical than fidelity to geography or ethnicity. Ideas make or break us, but dirt is for walking upon and ethnicity is an accident of birth.

5.5.2.2 Merit is Paramount

Or, stated differently, only the effectiveness of an idea or technique matters, not its origin. Shakespeare wrote, "Adopt a virtue and it is yours." That is really the golden core of Western civilization. The Greeks copied the best ideas from the Egyptians, the Romans borrowed wholesale from the Greeks, the British took the best ideas from several sources, and the Americans borrowed wholesale from the English. "Take what works, wherever you find it, and use it for best effect." would be an excellent description of our stance.

5.5.2.3 The Common Law

We believe in fairness and progress. One great tool for this is, and always has been, the Common Law that we inherited from the English. The two central statements of the Common Law are this:

1. Individuals should keep their agreements, and not defraud others.
2. Individuals should not aggress against, or encroach upon others.

The Common Law is based upon self-reference and integrity. Integrity and reason trump everything else and all people are equal in the sight of this law.

5.5.2.4 Co-Dominance

We are comfortable with co-dominance. We do not engage in an endless struggle to feel dominant over our friends, coworkers, etc. We tend to reject purely dominant-submissive relationships. We may accept hierarchies in our workplaces, but we do not accept this as applicable to the rest of our lives. Where we accept authority, we do so only by voluntary choice.

5.5.2.5 Cooperation

We are the descendants of farmers, and from them we learned that helping your neighbor works out best for all involved. We may not actually be obligated to help our neighbor, but mutual assistance makes life better for both of us over time. We are confident in our own abilities and do not have to snatch the last piece of pie before our neighbor sees it. We can both make our own pies, and we can both do it better if we help each other.

5.5.2.6 Delayed Gratification

We also learned from our farming ancestors that you have to save some of the corn for next year's seed. We have learned to restrain ourselves. We can take less now in order to get more at a later date, even if "later" is quite a long way off.

5.5.2.7 Individuality Above Clan

While we expect mutual kindness to arise in families, we do not require the submission of the individual to the clan, or even to the immediate family. (This obviously does not apply to young children, who must be closely controlled by their parents merely for their own safety.) We regard close family associations as a good thing, and sometimes even as a thing of beauty, but we reject family control over the individual.

5.5.2.8 Reality Above Philosophy

Philosophy is a wonderful study, but it only becomes valid if and when it helps us better deal with reality. The "beauty of an idea" is highly subjective and may not have anything to do with the rightness of that idea. Ideas that match reality are right, ideas that do not match reality are wrong, regardless of their "beauty."

5.5.2.9 Rejection of Class

This is an American concept that we hold dear. We believe that class boundaries are a great evil, holding humans in a sort of slavery to the accidents of birth. We tolerate no class restrictions.

5.5.2.10 Basic Freedoms

Freedom of choice, thought, association and speech are sacrosanct. No one touches these without offending, period. We hold that individuals are responsible only to do no harm. Not only should they be free to live independent, unique lives, but in doing so they make best use of their individual talents. The end result is a world that is a better place than it would be if they had served some mandatory cultural ideal.

5.5.2.11 Comfort with Inequality

While all men ought to be equal before the law, we do not expect them to produce equal results. Some of us are stronger, some are faster, some think more rapidly, some work harder, and some of us are more usefully trained. Our upbringings vary widely. Our results will never be equal, nor should they be.

We are comfortable with that. We each, through both success and failure, build our own lives as best we can. We are self-referential regarding our success. What other people think of us is not our primary concern; what we think of ourselves matters more.

5.5.2.12 Failure is not Permanent

We do not hold it a stain upon our souls to try and to fail. If we fail, we try to understand why our venture failed, to improve our ideas, our methods, and our personal virtues – then to begin again. We see even multiple honest failures as little more than obstacles, and we deeply admire the man or woman who has gone through multiple failures yet soldiers on and eventually succeeds.

5.5.3 Technical Professions

Our backgrounds include scientific education and engineering occupations. This gives us a set of ideas that we live by and, indeed, feed ourselves by following.

5.5.3.1 The Scientific Method

We rely, fearlessly, upon things that have been verified and shown to be repeatable. When used correctly, the scientific method works. We'll stick with it.

5.5.3.2 Logic

Logic is the science of non-contradiction. Self-contradictory statements have shown themselves to be untrustworthy so many times that we choose not to waste our time with them. In fact, we work hard to avoid them.

5.5.3.3 Confidence in Technology

We love technology. It keeps us comfortable, preserves and cooks our food, and in general frees us from many of the mundane concerns of survival. We have seen it blow through, work around or make irrelevant so many obstacles that we doubt it little.

5.5.3.4 Non-Worship of Nature

Not only is Mother Nature a fairy tale, but Jack Frost regularly kicks her ass. Nature kills almost as much as it nurtures. It's almost funny to see Nature's idolaters clinging to their heating, air conditioning, cleaning and refrigeration devices, desperately avoiding the glaring contradiction.

5.5.3.5 Linear Time

Time moves forward. While we are open to theories that predict a possible backwards movement, we have yet to see proof. And we have certainly never seen proof of circular time. Such concepts may be useful for unprovable religious theories, but they have no useful place in our reality – at least not yet. Until then, we assume that time is linear.

5.5.3.6 Objective Reality

We presume that we are applying our technical formulas to things that are real and which will respond consistently. So far we have not been disappointed.

5.5.4 Our Axioms

We discussed axioms earlier in this chapter, as things which we hold to be true even though we can't exactly prove them. At first this may sound like a stupid thing to do, but it really is necessary. For example, our first axiom is that reality is, in fact, real. This is very probably true, but can we really prove that reality is not some bizarre, cosmic video game? We don't know how that could be done without stepping outside of our universe. So, we accept, as an axiom, that what appears to a sane man to be a rock is indeed a rock. If we ever gain the ability to step outside of our universe we can verify this axiom; then we can call it either a truth or falsehood. Until then, it is something we choose to accept without proof.

5.5.4.1 Reality is Real

This has to be the most overwhelmingly accepted idea ever to exist on Planet Earth. In fact, it's hard even to imagine an existence where this wasn't axiom number one. We are 100% reliant on reality being real every time we decide to focus our eyes on something, take a bite of food, or even take a breath of air. The guy who actually believes that reality is not real lives in the psycho ward. He's curled up in the fetal position because he thinks that the world is made, alternately, of prune juice and silly putty.

5.5.4.2 Our Perceptions are Accurate

The knowledge we get through our senses is good, even though it is limited. When we see a rock, our perceptions are right, even though they may not tell us everything about the rock. X-ray, infrared or other forms of analysis may tell us things that our naked eyes cannot, yet that does not make our eyesight wrong, just limited.

We must use our perceptions with sound reason in order to be sure. For example, merely seeing the sun go up and down makes it appear to be moving around the fixed Earth, but appearance does not make the simplest explanation true. In this particular case, further observation and analysis provided a better answer.

5.5.4.3 Humans are Individuals

This is another one of the things that is so overwhelmingly held, that to think otherwise is hard to imagine. Why even bother to communicate if we are not separate beings? We are so obviously separate beings that actually believing otherwise would earn us a quick trip to a padded room. (Of course this would only happen because we were defying a collectively held idea ;-)

5.5.4.4 Reason is Our Best Tool

Reason has led to all of our advancements, and no other source has really come close. Even when inspiration provides some good clues, reason must be used to bring the new thing into actual existence.

6
Beheading Leviathan

Reading this book, you may have come to accept the idea that the ideological equivalent of multi-celled organisms can and do exist in idea-space. Further, you may understand that these ideological replicators have evolved to influence us in ways that are not beneficial to us as individual human beings. Even if you succeed in eliminating Collective Identities from your own mind, the effects of such parasitic idea-organisms will still be all around you. Other people, who still believe in Higher Powers, will try to impose the will of those ideological entities upon you.

Your next thought may be, "Well what can I do about it? How can I help to free these other people from mental bondage?" Or, if you are a little more self interested, your first thought might be "How can I use this knowledge that other people don't have to make myself rich and famous?"

One answer is that you try to teach those around you. Maybe you could even write a book about it – we did it already, but don't let that stop you, maybe you could do it better. Also, movies, comic books, claymation cartoons, Doctor Seuss style children's books – all of these would probably be useful for spreading such an important idea.

But maybe writing and teaching are endeavors that are a little too abstract and/or intellectual for your tastes, and/or you are not the artistic type. Well then, you can always teach by example. Live your life in a way that reflects your refusal to surrender your individuality to any Collective.

Collective Identities resist certain technologies (seeing them as threats). Perhaps such technologies can actually help peacefully shrink the influence of collective thought. Why not give it a try? Embrace those new technologies and ways of doing things that Collectives seem to fear. If you are a technological type yourself, you can even work on the invention and improvement of such technologies, as well as just being an early adopter.

Perhaps the most important thing to do is not to hide your love of individual liberty. Don't keep your head down or your mouth shut.

When you hear someone talking about how we all have to pitch in and make sacrifices in a time of crisis, be the one saying that you are more than willing to help people in need on a one on one basis, but you are not putting on a uniform and goose stepping to marching music.

When your leaders call for you to suspend your right to think or have opinions, and to simply follow them faithfully, you be the one to remind those leaders – and everyone else who's eyes are glazing over – that those leaders work for you; they are supposed to be representing your ideas, not telling you what your ideas should be.

When those leaders try to scare you with hypothetical dangers, you can be the one to rationally ask them, "Will this terrible new danger kill more or less people per year than lightning strikes? Bee stings? Automobile accidents? Eating fatty foods?"

When those who worship the status quo trot out hypothetical horror stories that could result from the new ideas, just speak up and say:

"Shouldn't we let those who are brave enough to try new things, do so unopposed? If it works it could be great, and we will never know unless we get out of their way and let them prove their ideas!"

Anything that empowers individual people and reduces enforcement by central authority is going to help. Ideas that do not produce value can not survive in a free market for long. If you want to shrink the Collective, then that is your goal – more freedom – less restrictions on communication and exchange of value.

Perhaps we can someday shrink the Collective Identity to the point that it is an amusing anachronism, and individual values and liberties are the driving force in the world. But until then, there is a battle going on. The bad news is that it has been going on for a long time, and the collective idea-organisms are still with us. The good news is that we just might be winning.

What follows in this chapter is a collection of our best ideas on what you can do to change the world to one of greater freedom for individuals. Give each of these ideas some thought. If you like them, consider how you could help make them a reality. And feel free to come up with your own even better ideas.

Don't ask us what you should do – figure it out for yourself.

6.1 Who Should I Vote For?

Up till now we have been looking at collective idea-organisms academically. Now we are taking a look at the Collective from the point of view of reducing the bad effects it creates. We want to see if there is anything we can each do personally to reduce its effects.

In the United States and other representative democracies, your personal power over the government is your ability to vote for your leader of choice. But how do you know who to vote for to increase your personal liberty and reduce the strength of the Collective?

Let's start by clarifying the central issues of collective idea-organisms:

The first goal of any organism is to survive. The central issue in the eyes of any collective is to keep humans as hosts. If the humans ever seriously turn against it, the Collective is finished. This has already happened to a lot of particular collective idea-organisms. History is littered with them. But this basic type of idea-organism is still around and still hurting us.

Even deeper than issues that relate to any single Collective, is the strategy of all Collectives. After all, parasitic idea-organisms exist only as free-riders inside of human brains. If the humans ever figure out that their minds are being used without their consent, there is a very real chance that they will rebel and then the whole game will end. That would mean that all Collectives, everywhere, would have to either justify their existence rationally, or fade into nothingness.

The central mechanism of using human minds without proper information and consent is the one thing that Collectives must maintain. Nothing else matters in comparison.

6.1.1 How Do They Think and Evolve?

And, while we're at it, how smart are they? I mean, if we are seen carrying this book around, should we be afraid?

Idea-organisms reproduce and grow by taking over the operation of human minds. To use an understandable (and quite accurate) analogy, they install their software, take over a certain amount of memory space, and use the central processor from time to time.

So, even if an idea-organism performs some adaptive operations in an individual mind, this is only one node of a Collective with millions of nodes. How, exactly is an idea-organism to communicate this new thought to the rest of the Collective?

Collectives develop new thoughts in a slow-motion process. It goes like this:

1. The little nodes (software running in a million individual minds) are constantly exposed to new ideas from other humans.
2. When an idea comes along that gives the idea-organism some sort of advantage, the node (again, this is the software running in any individual brain) lights up. Its energy level goes up and it is compelled to pass this idea along to other nodes.
3. The idea is then passed-along with increased energy and the first vestiges of authority. "Everyone in Ephesus is talking about this idea."

4. As the idea is passed along, the authority grows. The new ideas are recognized by the individual nodes, and each attaches some authority to them as they pass them along.

As the process shown above continues, a meme is added to the Collective. This is how Collectives think – in slow-motion.

Authority is the tool Collectives use to insure communication between nodes. Awarding a person (or story) the status of authority is to say, "Accept this!" Notice in yourself that the voice of authority comes with a strong discouragement to applying reason prior to acceptance.

Collectives have no mechanism to achieve any serious level of intelligence. They evolve like animals; they do not use self reference to cognitively adapt like we do. They evolve by replacing memes, not by replacing genes. This gives them a middle-speed pace of adaptation. Collectives adapt over decades, not over millennia like genes, and not in moments like human minds. (Seriously changing one's mind is high-speed evolution.)

There may be good reason why communist states always resorted to 5-year plans. That may be close to their shortest basic adaptation time.

6.1.2 How Do they Control People?

OK, how does this little outpost in someone's mind make them do what it wants?

Frighteningly enough, it isn't that hard and it's really effective.

Remember we talked earlier about self-esteem and how it influences people? Well, this is how Collectives force people into obedience.

Above we spoke about how new ideas that fit well with the Collective get passed slowly from mind to mind, and how new collective ideas turn their originators into "voices of authority." New ideas that do not fit well with the Collective receive just the opposite treatment. If an idea or behavior of some individual does not fit in well with the collective mindset – other members of the Collective give feedback that stifles the idea. If the person persists, they label that person as an outsider – a geek – a social outcast – perhaps even a criminal.

In fact this stifling of new ideas starts before the idea is even out of the potential innovators mouth. Before a person can even voice a new idea, to see how other people will react, it has to get past that person's own filters – the images in the person's mind of how other people are *likely* to react.

These are the Distributed Identity Models that we discussed previously. They act as a filter over what ideas the person is ever even able to express. In this way, most people avoid even the slightest risk of public shame by not speaking up when a new thought arises. They put new ideas quickly out of their minds for fear of public ridicule. Only those with very weak Collective Identity infection ever do speak up, and they are often subjected to huge societal pressures to shut up again.

Humans are hyper-sensitive to shame, as well as being wildly overly-sensitive to guilt. They are driven to cover these tender 'wounds' with whatever salves and bandages they can find.

Collectives are only too happy to provide such bandages.

Notice two important things from your own life experience:

1. At some point, you were almost certainly hurt very badly by being publicly exposed as shameful. You were embarrassed by saying something wrong, especially in front of an authority and his/her group of followers. You felt small, weak, and vulnerable. (And God bless you if you only experienced this as a child and were able to work out of it.)
2. Your first instinct when facing this situation was probably to say, "Everyone else did it too!"

Now, think about that for a moment. Stop and re-read those two points. Are they true? Was your defense from shame to hide in collective behavior?

This is one of the main hooks that the Collective uses to secure obedience.

As we said above, Collectives are only too happy to give humans a fast, easy salve for their shame. And that salve is the shelter of authority. Earlier, we called it "external self-esteem." If many people are doing something, we are confident that we will not be shamed if we go along with them. Voices with mass acceptance are safe.

Conversely, there is almost nothing more frightening than standing alone. You'll notice that public speaking is always mentioned as one of the greatest fears experienced by humans. And being "afraid to speak alone" is perilously close to being "afraid to think alone."

Self-esteem and shame are the carrot and stick that collective idea-organisms use to control their hosts.

Notice also that this is what prevents people from changing their minds. Once this self-esteem band-aid is in place, they cannot bear to have it ripped off, much less rip it off themselves. If you consider yourself a "good person" based upon your political affiliation (and many folks do), then rejecting the ideas of your party can be like ripping off the band-aid. And it can get worse if people will say bad things about you after you express your change of opinion.

This applies to all Collectives, not just the political parties mentioned above: Religions, tribes, families, all of them.

This is how people are forced to remain in their place.

Changing your mind takes guts, and may come at a price.

You will notice that the majority of humans make decisions based upon the criteria above, far more than they do on the actual merits of any particular choice. After all, their internal pain or comfort is all too obvious. Unfortunately, the thinking of many people stops at somewhere close to this point.

There is one meme worthy of particular attention that is used for control by almost all Collectives: The condemnation of "selfishness." The technique of making individuals feel selfish and guilty is a great master-stroke for the Collective. It makes them unwilling to defend themselves as individuals and afraid to act in their own self-interest. There is an old martial arts phrase – "De-fanging the snake." This is when you strike an opponent's weapon-hand, rather than just blocking the weapon. The opponent loses the weapon and "the snake is de-fanged."

In the same way, instilling a fear of selfishness is to de-fang the human mind. Give this a bit of thought. Acting in self-interest is NOT the same as abusing or exploiting others. But allow your self-interest to be removed "for the good of the team" and you are sure to be abused and exploited.

(Of course the Collective – selfish in both nature and practice – is always fully immune from such criticisms of selfishness. Cute, huh?)

6.1.3 Which Candidate?

From the standpoint of the Collective, any political candidate's stance comes down to a single issue: Increased Control or Decreased Control. Nothing else really matters to a Collective. If they get more control, they can express their nature freely. If they have less control, they will be restrained.

In the eyes of the Collective, political movements always break down into High-control factions versus Low-control factions. What the Collective "wants" is a mass society; all being conditioned the same way, feeding on a unified stream of information, and being kept away from serious thinking by the same flashing stream of entertainment.

Animals develop hunting strategies, and so do Collectives. For example, every political party is the "party of liberty." For God's sake, Hitler and Stalin said they were pro-liberty! Why? It convinces hosts that the party is on their side. (If everyone had read this book, maybe the slogan would be, "We're Pro-Host!") A promise of liberty makes the hosts more willing to sacrifice their own interests for the cause.

People and ideas are promoted by the Collective when they do service to the Collective. The candidate that voices the best way of making people "all pull together" (especially if uncritically) becomes the new hero. The intellectual who develops the strategy becomes a "leading voice."

In one of his darker moments, one of our favorite authors, Ben Hecht, declared that "thinking makes us monsters." Well, not exactly. Thinking the ideas of a Collective makes us monsters. Listening to Hitler's logic, to Stalin's, to Castro's... these thoughts make us monsters. Thinking as an individual – rare though it may be – makes us useful and beneficial to our fellow humans. It angers brains that are controlled by Collectives, but it improves the world we live in.

Collectives were much more comfortable in Dark Ages Europe than they are today. So long as the hosts continued to reach the age of reproduction, all was cool. Past that hurdle, ideological stability was about all that really mattered. It has taken a lot of brave men and women, sometimes lashing out erratically, to get us to where we are now. Bless their memory.

You might also watch for this: Authority figures for the Collective tend to speak in terms of abstractions, rather than in terms of concretes. They talk of "upholding the law," rather than of "locking people in cages." Or, they speak of a "democratically-elected leader," rather than of a "thug who attacks dissenters." This can be pretty hard to pick up when these guys are talking fast, but you may find a useful tool for reviewing written arguments.

Abstraction can be useful, but is not to be preferred over concrete reality. Abstraction is only a tool, not a super-reality.

"Once again I am asked to choose between a fat beast with a long memory for revenge and some braying jackass. Why never a real human being?"

So, who should you vote for?

We suggest that you vote for the candidate who talks less about the team and more about the individual players — less about menacing groups of evil doers and more about specific tangible wrongs. Vote for the people who see the world in terms of many individual human beings trying to get through life, rather than huge ideological constructs that must be either worshiped or defeated. Vote for the ones who are really about allowing free behavior, not the ones who turn freedom into an icon for which you must sacrifice the things you really want to do.

Vote for less control by the Icons over the individuals.

Vote for humans!

6.2 Fighting For a Free Market

We have spoken about the nature of the Icon Problem: That once people have a group of ideas in their head under a single name or image, they have trouble examining these ideas individually for validity. This allows bad ideas to ride along with good ideas.

This basic concept is what is wrong with collective governance and authority. Bad government "services" receive spill-over good will from people who are taught that the government as a whole is good. And since there is no competition in these services, people may not even be able to see an example of how things could be better.

If the government tells people that it is protecting them by not allowing unlicensed, unregulated, operators, who are just in it for profit, why wouldn't people believe them? Especially without visible examples of people who are "in it for profit" doing it better and cheaper than people who do it because they get a kick out of controlling other people's lives.

6.2.1 Hard Choices

If you want to beat back the creeping Collective, even just a little bit, one of the best ways to do this is to either start or use free market alternatives to Collective controlled services.

Even just using such an alternative service is a hard choice to make, because what this means is that you will have to pay for something that is already being given to you for free. (Well, they are actually stealing money from you and then using it to pay for a service they are offering for free, but they are going to steal the money from you anyway, so that makes the service seem like it's free.) Or, you will have to use a service provider who is not paying the licensing fees, and is therefore illegal – and you are risking fines or worse for your voluntary economic arrangement. You may need to both ignore the free government handout, and risk the government punishment to actually engage in free economic behavior. This is the classic "carrot and stick" scenario that is so effective in motivating people. There is a good chance that both parts of it are being employed in an attempt to control any given industry.

It is unclear that you will necessarily be rewarded for this behavior, even if you avoid being punished. Engaging an unlicensed, unregulated, unauthorized, non-governmental, practitioner of some trade may cost more than the government version or it could be that the service is inferior, and the reason that the person doesn't have a license is that they are not very competent.

The only saving grace is that it should almost never be both. If the goods or services in question are things that the government supplies for free, any provider that is charging you will have to be much better than the government. If it is just the case of an industry that is burdened with licensing and regulation, any unlicensed provider is going to be much cheaper than those that are required to foot the bill for the regulation of their industry.

If you are careful, you can do better working outside of the Collective approved system.

However, the Collective is doing everything it can to make sure this is not the case. In an earlier chapter we talked about problems in the free market, such as the "tragedy of the commons problem" or the "prisoner's dilemma" that were caused by incomplete information. We mentioned that "altruistic memes" sometimes enforce good behavior in such situations. Here we see the other side of the coin. When it is an evolutionary advantage to the collective idea-organism to make things worse for everyone, it will enforce behavior that causes bad economic situations. Where the Collective is functioning properly in its own interest, it will make sure that the best move for you to make in your own self interest is in line with what it good for the Collective, even if some other path would be better for everyone on average, should enough people resist the Collective long enough to realize that better situation.

Actually starting a free market alternative business is hard. The Collective is guaranteed to impose higher penalties on the entrepreneur for not doing things the way the Collective wants them done, than it would impose on someone who was just a customer of such a business. This is a necessary strategy for the Collective, as the rewards to the individual who works around the Collective's rules (and create greater value for everyone) are very significant, thus the deterrents to such behavior must be stronger. Where a customer might just be reprimanded, the business owner will be fined. Where the customer would be fined, the business owner jailed. Where the threat to the Collective is great enough that a customer would do jail time, the entrepreneur might be permanently incarcerated or even killed.

It is not impossible for the free market to take back an industry from the Collective. In the United States, it was illegal for any private concern to deliver packages and compete with the US postal Service. This did not stop FedEx from doing it anyway, and getting the laws changed. Now there are numerous package delivery services that have raised the standards of package delivery back to free market levels. In principle, this could be done in any industry where some company was willing to take the risk of violating existing law to provide a better service and benefit everyone in so doing, and could demonstrate that obviously better service before getting shut down by thugs with guns.

So, working outside the system is not going to be easy. But if you are willing to try, there are things that can be done. The key thing you can do is to use your voice. Your power of communication is your best defense and offense when it comes to doing battle with The Leviathan. Remember that the Collective is a creature of information, and your best weapon to weaken the beast is the right information spread to the right people.

6.2.2 Lazy Minded People

OK, this is the section where we tell the ugly truth.

People always complain about lying, deceiving politicians. (Heck, we do it too.) But in any type of half-functional republic or democracy, that is misplaced anger. The people who elect the lying politicians are the guilty parties.

Most people do not think much. They follow the patterns set by folks around them and remember slogans that get them nods of approval. If you are thinking a little bit here, you're tying a couple of things together... keep going... That's right! They serve the dominant DIs of their place and time.

All of the things mentioned above – which you must know that people do – makes those people... suckers! Dupes. Chumps. That may seem like unkind terminology, but what shall we do? Make it so soft and smooth that no one ever really gets a kick in the ass?

Until those (many) folks start to think and to take control of their own minds, they will remain suckers and will continue to do the same self-defeating things. And because you must share a world with them – you will suffer the consequences along with them!

It is time for you to start telling people that they are acting stupidly – living by auto-pilot and fearing to be themselves. If you think you are not like that, then it is time for you to start kicking those other people in the ass (metaphorically speaking of course). If you fear you might be like that yourself, then it is time to kick yourself in the ass – to start making some changes.

6.2.3 War of Words

If everyone realized that freedom of individual choice was superior to using collective force, the world would be a better place for all. Since that is not where we find ourselves, the real key is convincing people. That is done by talking about it, and by demonstrating that it is true.

Educate people in the science of economics. Where economic principles disagree with "common wisdom," we find that common wisdom is speaking the words of the Collective – calling for more rules and less freedom. Economic science shows that freedom of thought and actions produce the most good.

If you use a non-governmental or unlicensed product or service in lieu of one authorized by the Collective, and it works out well for you, tell people about it. Recommend the solution to your friends, and tell everyone how superior it was to the authorized alternative. Let people know that options exist for them beyond what the Collective wants them to know about.

When people do things that demonstrate individual liberty, tell them how proud you are of them – make them feel good. A Collective Identity expressing itself in people will cause just the opposite reaction, and this must be combated. Instead of telling them how foolish they are being, compliment them on how brave they are being. It is your liberty they are extending too.

When someone argues the position of the Collective mindset, argue back. Argue for the importance of personal liberty and freedom. Those infected by the Collective will be jealous and resentful of those working outside of it. Express your displeasure to anyone that is perpetuating the idea that conformity is more correct or safer than free will. If someone is trying to degrade someone for being weird or different, laugh at them and ask them why they are so insecure as to need to be normal.

Weirdness breeds new ideas, and new ideas are the best way to retain individual freedom. Freedom is most easily found by creating new situations to which the Collective has not yet had a chance to adapt. Economic freedoms, having been removed, can be regained with new business ideas and new technology.

6.3 Engineering Freedom

One of the major themes of this book concerns the fear of technology that is exhibited by collective idea-organisms. Different technologies frighten different Distributed Identities for different reasons. Communications systems, however, are of particular interest to all Ideas that cause collective behavior.

Communications systems are the nervous system of the Leviathan. Without them it can not maintain its identity across multiple minds. On the other hand, communications systems can also carry competing ideas, allowing them to grow strong enough to overthrow the dominant ideas. Communications systems are therefore both required and feared by the Collective.

We have talked previously about different types of communications systems, and how they affect the ability of collective idea-organisms to control the flow of information in a society. Central broadcast of information favors the growth and survival of collective Ideas. Central control of information gathering likewise increases the power of central authority. Central authority is weakened when people can communicate easily person to person, and when people can easily gather their own information.

Even more dangerous to central authority are communication systems that easily let any individual communicate a message to multiple interested parties at the same time – to broadcast their message. We see evidence of this in the way central authority has controlled such technology as radio and television. Either of these technologies could be used by any individual to communicate with many interested listeners. To prevent this free proliferation of uncontrolled ideas, almost every government on the planet has strictly controlled and licensed these mediums, turning them into central point technologies with a few State approved broadcasters and many mute listeners.

Even the United States, a country with the concept of free speech written into its founding document, has decided that new technologies allowing far reaching speech must be controlled and licensed.

The First amendment of the Constitution of the United States says "Congress shall make no law ... abridging the freedom of speech, or of the press..." Yet somehow, congress routinely passes new laws controlling speech that are enforced by the F.C.C (Federal Communications Commission), and new copyright legislation that abridges freedom of the printing press, record press, CD press, DVD press, etc... One has to wonder what part of "shall make no law" they do not understand.

If you want more liberty, greater freedom of communications is a fine place to start. If you are an engineer or entrepreneur, you should work to develop systems that increase the abilities of individuals to control their own information, and to exchange information with whomever they wish. If you are not in a position to create such systems, then you can at least be an early adopter – using and spreading such systems quickly. Do not let central authority tell you that using such systems is wrong. Stand up and demand your right to free communications. This is almost certainly a path to greater freedom.

6.3.1 The Internet

The Internet is a distributed system that denies central control. Ironically, the protocols that allow it to operate in a decentralized way grew out of the fear of atomic war that the United States Government was using as its current boogeyman to keep the people scared. Conflict between Collectives allowed freedom to creep in.

Collective idea-organisms are currently adapting as fast as they can to try to control this system that was designed to defy centralization. Whether it can be controlled will depend on what individual applications are invented and used by people everywhere.

6.3.1.1 File Sharing

File sharing systems are a great way to share information. This technology is a natural growth of the interconnectivity of computers that is the Internet. Almost by definition, what it means to connect two computers is to be able to share files between them.

So what is the problem? Why the controversy? How could anyone consider this sort of activity illegal?

The problem lays in the obsolete idea of Copyright. Before the invention of the printing press, authors wanted people to copy their content and share it freely, as this increased their fame and made it more likely that they would receive commissions and or patronage. This was the business model for the creation of art for a long time. But with the invention of the printing press, governments began to try to control the growing spread of information.

> Copyright law was actually first invented as a means of controlling the publication of religious ideas. During this time the "patent" was a tool of central market control that granted monopoly rights for the selling of a certain good or service. The first copyrights were based on patents granted to printers' guilds. The concept of "intellectual property" was created later as an attempt to maintain these controls in a time of greater individual rights and freedoms. As the idea of "property rights" came into its own, the idea that these regulations protected a different non-physical kind of property was encouraged.
>
> Labeling the central control of ideas as "intellectual property law" distracts from the fact that it is actually a system for reducing property rights. Each copyright or patent granted by the government places yet another limitation on the patterns into which you can legally arrange your own personal property. It would be both more accurate and historically appropriate to call such legislation "pattern monopoly law."
>
> The economic idea of "property" applies to scarce resources. Patterns are not scarce resources. They can be infinitely repeated. Such a system of regulation creates artificial economic scarcity and gives collective idea-organisms a way to slow and discourage the new ideas and technologies that threaten them.
>
> The only scarce resource involved in authorship or invention is the ability to claim credit for one's work. Plagiarism might be viewed as theft of intellectual property. But making copies of an existing work without claiming credit does not resemble theft in any way.

If the first printing presses had been as fast and as far reaching as the current Internet, the idea of copyright would never have even come into being. That being the case, trying to enforce such systems now that the Internet exists is foolish. However, progress in information reproduction technology was once slow and business models developed back then that only work if control over the reproduction of a given work is treated as a legal property right.

These business models have continued to the current day when our technology for reproducing information has grown to the degree that this business model is untenable. As the ease of reproducing information increases, the cost of enforcing an unnatural control on information flow increases. This is why we see Corporations in various media publishing businesses lobbying the government to try to make good, useful technologies illegal.

This case of corporate Collectives trying to prevent technological change is not unusual. The business models of many industries often find themselves threatened by environments created by new technology. Another type of Intellectual property – "patent law" – is more commonly used to repress new technologies for a time. A Corporation fearing certain technology that targets its ability to sell a product to people is no different in principal from a Nation State's restriction of transportation technology that threatens to reduce people's territorial instinct, or a religious idea-organism resisting medical technology that reduces people's fear of death.

In the end, because the technology is, in fact, symbiotic, and useful to individuals, the technology wins out. In the United States, more people already use file sharing systems than vote in the elections for the congressmen who pass laws trying to make file sharing illegal.

To truly understand how ridiculous it is to continue to attempt to enforce the artificial scarcity that copyright creates, first imagine a world where we all decided that each atom of CO_2 that you breathed out of your lungs was your property because it had been created by you. No one else could use it in any way without paying you. If a farmer's plants absorbed it, he would have to pay you, etc... Now try to imagine the costs of enforcing such a system.

Enforcing intellectual property law is like that, but even worse. Individual molecules of CO_2 are at least discrete items that never spawn more molecules of CO_2, and they travel through the atmosphere relatively slowly. Whereas we now have technology that allows information to spin off nearly unlimited multiple copies of itself at a rate measured in encyclopedia sets per second, and that information can travel around the globe at the speed of light.

As the speeds of our information technology increase, the costs of enforcing Intellectual Property Law are increasing exponentially – going toward infinity.

The current state of the art in file sharing is the Bittorrent system designed by Brahm Cohen. The beauty of this system is that bandwidth load is shared among all the users downloading the file. This allows crucial information to be quickly distributed to the whole world, without requiring the original source of that information to have large bandwidth capabilities.

Kudos to Brahm and all the other people who worked on Bittorrent! They have created exactly the kind of information system that makes life hard for collective idea-organisms. Check it out at www.bittorrent.com

The next step in file sharing technology may be Internet distributed file systems – with every user's data spread across multiple computers all over the world, and with cryptographic solutions that make it impossible for agents of collective authority to trace where a specific file is actually stored, or find out whom is accessing what.

Every new file sharing system that increases the number of interested "listeners" a single individual can easily and cheaply communicate information with simultaneously, or reduces the ability of any central authority to monitor or obstruct information flow, increases our level of free communications – our freedom of speech.

6.3.1.2 Cutting the Wires

Currently the wires, through which the Internet is connected, are mostly owned by government or corporate entities. These entities will naturally try to use this to facilitate information good for their survival and replication – to restrict information deemed bad for their purposes.

This has lead to the fight for "network neutrality" in which legislation was sought to prevent the owners of the wires from charging different rates based on what information was contained in the packets they routed. This legislation was not passed, which is not surprising, as it is a rare law that increases freedom.

It also might be argued that whoever owns the wires should be able to use any pricing model they want. Perhaps then, a better path towards free information flow is to just stop using those wires.

Wireless routers have been created that can find a path to route packets from one side of a city to another, without ever "going to ground" through land lines. If there was a way to make the operation of such wireless routers commercially good for those operating them, they might proliferate across the entire world, creating an Internet run by the end users, with no larger entities trying to control any part of it.

At the least, having such an alternative would put pressure on the owners of the wires to not adopt pricing strategies that would cause their customers to want to use a different system.

The key to such an arrangement would seem to be a routing system that allowed electronic payment information to be passed along with the packets, so that everyone would pay a small amount to the owner of each hop on the network route to have their packets forwarded. Such "micropayment" systems have been one of the ongoing goals of developing electronic currency systems.

A system that would instigate the growth of private node wireless networks across every major city would prevent Collectives from throttling the communication of unapproved information.

6.3.1.3 Free as in Beer

Another way that collective idea-organisms are fighting for control of Internet communications is by using "Intellectual Property" law to control the protocols that Internet systems use. This is equivalent to telling people that they can not say certain things, because you own the language that they are using to speak, and you refuse to license it for the speech they want to use it for.

Consider email – one of the most popular uses of the Internet. Servers that exchange email can be run by anyone. No one pays a licensing fee to exchange email. Every server is an equal participant in such exchanges. This makes email extremely powerful and useful, but it was only possible because no Higher Powers were there to try to keep this protocol from equally empowering everyone. It was developed by geeks for other geeks when no Collective was interested in what they were doing.

Now collective idea-organisms are very interested in the Internet. Any new protocol must be filtered through collective ideas about business models, national security, etc... If email were to be invented today, rather than being a free protocol that everyone could use on every server equally, various corporations would all be creating their own proprietary version of email, and insisting that they were going to win over the market so that all electronic messaging would eventually take place only on their servers.

Government would get involved too – having seen that the Internet was the future of the world, various government agencies would all want to have a piece of it. The post office would say that email was letters, and insist that people use electronic stamps and pay the government for each email. Law enforcement would demand, in the name of national security, that a copy of each email be sent separately to each interested enforcement agency. It would be impossible to create the email system we have now, while paying any attention to these collective interests.

The email system that we currently use could not be invented today. Ten years after the modern Internet started to be widely used; you could not get people to think in terms of free distributed protocols.

Later protocols, such as instant messaging, and IP telephony, show the infiltration of the idea-organisms. Rather than a single protocol that anyone can use, providers want everyone to use their own system and servers, and actively resist any attempt to bridge the systems and make them inter-operable. These technologies will never truly come into their own until any new provider can use the same common protocols without fear of legal action, and no one entity controls the "center" of the system.

Richard Stallman, founder of the GNU project (a precursor to Linux) in 1983 and also founder of the Free Software Foundation in 1985, recognized that software protocols that were monetarily controlled tended to damage the shared experience of computer use. That the concept of monetized "Intellectual Property" just slowed down the progress of computer technology.

For the Internet to continue to evolve as a tool of individual freedom, rather than a tool for information control by the Collective, this flawed concept of Intellectual Property must be ignored by innovators. It is bait used by the Collective to gain control over information flow. The trick is to convince people that it is in their own best interest to be able to control their inventions. This provides a handle for central control and suppression of technologies that would otherwise increase individual freedom.

In the world of Open Source Software, the analogies "Free as in Speech" and "Free as in Beer" are often used to distinguish between "without restrictions" and "without cost." The protocols for any electronic communications system must be "free as in beer" in order that the system also be "free as in speech."

There is even individual financial self-interest in seeing past this collective control trick. If you are a programmer, and you give away your protocols, they are more likely to be widely adopted. It is quite possible for you to do very well financially based on your reputation as the creator of a protocol that everyone uses. On the other hand, if you patent a protocol and no one else ever uses it, you gain nothing.

6.3.2 Surveillance and Location Monitors

In order for central control to be effective, good information must be available concerning the people to be controlled. Additionally, the people must also be denied such information about their controllers.

In his book, "1984," George Orwell described a State that kept its citizens under constant video and audio surveillance. This imagined dystopian nightmare state was a place of harsh central control and almost zero personal liberty.

Many have paid attention to the cameras pointed at the citizens in this fable, and blamed them for the problems of such a system. However, the lack of cameras pointed at the rulers is also an important part of the story, and one that seems less frequently pointed out.

However, the idea that the problems of central authority lay in the lack of ability of the regular individual to monitor the actions of the agents of central control is a very old one. It is classically embodied in the Latin phrase "*Quis custodiet ipsos custodes?*" or "Who watches the watchmen?"

6.3.2.1 The Watchmen and the Watchers

Cameras continue to become cheaper and more abundant. Walking in the downtown area of any large city in the United States, one is almost always on camera. Many are quick to point to this and predict that Orwell's nightmare society is becoming a reality. However, the truth may be exactly the opposite.

Instead of cameras controlled only by the State, we are seeing an explosive growth of personal cameras. Every cell phone has one now. Every private business has its own security cameras. Instead of a world with increasingly draconian law enforcement made perfect by constant surveillance, more often than not, it is the bad behavior of law enforcement that is caught on camera by individuals.

On March 3rd, 1991, L.A. Police stopped Rodney King for speeding, and when he failed to comply with their instructions, beat him severely. It is debatable whether or not this particular beating was justified based upon standard police procedure, but there is little doubt that such beatings for failure to respect police authority were quite common at the time. What made this particular beating so extraordinary was not the degree of injustice or severity of the beating, it was the fact that the public got to see it blow by blow.

More and more such cases of authorities being caught "on tape" doing something wrong have happened since then. Also, more and more cases of individuals committing crimes have been recorded, and the offenders have been punished based on this evidence. As cameras get cheaper and more plentiful, bad acts are harder to hide. This is true whether such are committed by cops or private citizens. This may be leading to a world where there is no difference between a cop who does something wrong and a private citizen who does something wrong. Both will receive proper feedback in the form of punishment that fits the crime committed.

It does not matter that each time this sort of thing happens it receives less national attention. The attention can be very local, and the effect will be the same. When people are under observation, or might be under observation, they will not often do things that they would not want other people to know about.

In a 1994 Wired Magazine article, noted libertarian Sandy Sandfort suggests that police be monitored when on duty, both by cameras and by positioning systems tracking the motions of each individual part of their bodies:

> *Today's audio-video technologies make it feasible for juries to vicariously relive police actions. Imagine the courtroom scenes if a police helmet was equipped with a tiny video camera, perched like some mystical third eye in the center of the officer's forehead. Add a supersensitive microphone next to each ear and, sprouting from the top of the helmet, various communications antennae. Imagine if everything the officer saw and heard was captured for later review ... single-chip, coin-sized versions of their [motion detection] units will be made cheaply enough for each officer to wear several on their uniforms and equipment – wrists, elbows, ankles, knees, heads, torsos, hips, guns, nightsticks. An officer's every move will be captured. Unlike video, this technology works in the dark and does not depend on the direction the cop's camera is facing. With such a recording, many crucial questions can be answered*

The technology to do this exists today. It is just a matter of properly developing the system and using it. If we are going to allow a government to police us, trusting them to properly use the violent powers we grant them, shouldn't we also require that we all be able to carefully watch these watchmen?

6.3.2.2 Security without Authority

We should need fewer police as individual surveillance increases. Fewer crimes are likely to be committed when everyone knows they are always "on the record." Technology that allows people to call for assistance from anyone willing to help also decreases the need for police presence.

Cell phones are starting to become equipped with positioning systems. These systems are useful for letting your friends know where you are, but could also be useful to bring you help when you are in trouble. Every mobile phone could be, equipped with a distress button to be pressed in an emergency. Such a panic-button could send a call out to nearby phones of registered "Good Samaritans." This could provide help to the scene of any crime or accident faster than any central authority.

This kind of technology has the potential to reduce the need for central authority. It allows the return of a situation where every person has equal rights again, and none are promoted to higher class citizens by virtue of carrying a badge. It allows everyone to be both protected and a protector as they choose. This technology could lead to a safer world.

Do you want to increase liberty? Build systems like the ones described here and make them popular to use.

6.3.2.3 Physical Privacy

"But what about my privacy?!?" you ask, horrified by the above description of a world with more and more cameras and mobile phones that keep track of your every move.

Author David Brin, writing on this topic in his book "The Transparent Society" suggests that as cameras become smaller and cheaper that privacy will have to disappear – but that it is ok, we will learn to live with it – just as long as everyone has access to the cameras, and not an elite few who control us. He describes citizens living in the future world like this:

> *They realize that -- out of doors at least -- privacy has always been an illusion. They know that anyone in town can tune in to that camera on the lamp post over there... and they don't much care. They perceive what really matters... that they live in a town where the police are efficient, respectful, and above all accountable. ... Above all, one thing makes life bearable -- the surety that each person knows what is going on, with a say in what will happen next. And rights equal to any billionaire or chief of police.*

Brin's idea is that the need for privacy dies away in a world where transparency becomes the norm. People who are thought to be keeping secrets are shunned, and everyone becomes more accepting of all forms of behavior.

There is some evidence that this is already happening. Our standards of acceptable levels of nudity and profanity in public media constantly slide towards the more permissive. Famous people are caught more and more often with their pants down (both literally and figuratively) and this changes the opinion of the average person about what is acceptable behavior.

It is even starting to seem that you can not be a real celebrity until you have a private sex tape released to the public.

Do we think that privacy will die, and that this is a good thing? Not completely. We think that private communications might be able to stick around, even in a world of cheap and tiny cameras, and that they probably should. We see communications privacy and physical privacy as two different issues.

6.3.2.4 Communications Privacy

Remember when we talked about simplifying possible viewpoints erroneously into some single axis, when multiple axes could be involved? This is such a case. The fight of Privacy vs. Transparency does not need to be a single axis. Physical actions and communications can have entirely separate levels of privacy or transparency.

The physical world of actions is not necessarily the same place as the intellectual world of words. While cameras get smaller, cheaper, and more plentiful, this does not necessarily stop people from communicating secretly. In the world of information encryption and security, there is a concept called a "trusted computing base" or TCB which is the area that needs to be secure in order to exchange information privately. This TCB could conceivably get smaller and easier to hide just as fast, or even faster than the cameras.

Currently, if you want to send a secure encrypted text message, you must type it in a room free of cameras which might record your computer screen or the motions of your fingers on the keyboard. You must also have a screen that is not producing radiation that can be read through walls, or special walls that block any such radiation. Your computer must be free of malicious software, and your encryption program must produce an unreadable message for anyone but the intended recipient. The area that must be controlled and secure is the size of your office and perhaps even some area beyond the walls.

This is a very big space to try to secure against cameras that become cheaper, smaller, and more plentiful. Eventually, cameras the size of specks of dust may be floating around in the air and clinging to your skin like microscopic burrs. It will be very difficult to regularly use encryption, if its successful use requires a trip through a chemical wash down and into a special chamber that prevents any information escaping via sound or electromagnetic waves of any spectrum.

If privacy ever becomes this difficult, we will have a similar, if inverse, situation from the 1984 scenario. Rather than a case where only Big Brother has spy cameras, it will be that only Big Brother has the defenses to stop the cameras that we all have.

Fortunately, the answer to this problem is already in the works. As the trusted computer base gets smaller, it also gets harder to compromise. Eventually, people will have computer screens built into their glasses, and then after that, feeding the display directly into their brains. With no visible display, it will be impossible to covertly read over a persons shoulder, no matter how small or well positioned the camera. Eventually no keyboard will be necessary, with finger motions, sub-vocalizations, or direct brain connections. As we blend computers with our own minds, we should be able to retain private communications even as cheap small cameras mean that we lose all physical privacy.

The end product of this could be the world of totally physical transparency with total intellectual freedom. In such a world, you could never kill someone and get away with it. You could not publicly claim that you despise certain behavior, while secretly doing what you claim to hate. But you could speak your mind anonymously, and argue academically for the validity of any behavior – thus (hopefully) increasing tolerance for all consensual human behavior.

Are you looking to increase liberty? Why not create systems to make sure that no central authority can ever stop people from communicating freely and privately? Or at least try to use existing encryption systems. (Check out www.pgp.com)

If you are more ambitious, think about the effect it would have on the world if easy to hide computer/phones could link up to low level satellite network. Imagine if people all over the world were to receive these devices for free, and could suddenly all access a variety of ideas from around the world, rather than just listening to what their local government officials and/or religious figures were telling them.

For much less than the cost of one "regime change" the United States Government could afford to create such a network and distribute the necessary personal communications devices around the world. This would bring free speech to countries that badly need it and provide a crucial tool for people everywhere to reduce bad government. This would truly be a gift of liberty, rather than hypocritically trying to force a more libertarian culture at gunpoint.

Such a world-wide private and personal communications network would be very cheap on the scale of what large countries spend on their military – and used world-wide, it would make a lot of that military unnecessary.

If you want to bring better governments to the whole world, maybe you should work on making this kind of system a reality.

6.3.3 Online Money

Technologies for private communications – encryption and anonymity – are very important when it comes to the idea of online financial transactions. In this day and age, money is really just a form of communication. Its all about promises of payment made by one person to another that are understood to be freely transferable to any third party.

Free value exchange is a form of free speech.

Before understanding how electronic currency can be different and better for our freedom, one must first understand the history of currency and how collective idea-organisms have exploited it from the beginning. In fact, Higher Powers have been so completely intertwined with the history of money that some of the first banks were also religious orders. Jesus was even noted for chasing money lenders out of the temple.

6.3.3.1 History of Money

The concept of money is old indeed. Currency is defined as whatever thing is commonly accepted as payment for goods and services in a society. Tobacco, alcohol, seashells, and various metals are all examples of things that have been currency at one time or another in various places throughout the world. Standard measures of a currency commodity have often been produced by trusted authorities for ease of trade – the minting of gold and silver coins in certain denominations is one of the longest standing traditions in this regard.

Very early on, idea-organisms discovered that control over currency helped them survive and replicate. A couple of thousand years ago, when asked if government taxes were justified, Jesus Christ is reputed to have pointed to the Icon of The Caesar on a coin and said "Render unto Caesar what is Caesar's..." meaning that if these coins that people accepted as currency were issued by the government, and people chose to use them, then the government could make rules concerning their use – including asking for tax payments in such coins.

The next form of currency to become popular, and supersede the use of coins, was that of promissory notes. This was based on the idea that an organization who had gold in two cities, far apart in travel time, could accept gold from a client in one city, and issue them a note to have gold paid to them when they reached the other city. This made the client less prone to theft, and carrying around paper was much easier than heavy sacks of metal. It soon became convenient to just trade the paper. To do this, the paper currency was marked to be paid to the bearer rather than any specific individual. Money became 'stealable' once again.

Photo credit Richard Beale - used with permission

6.3.3.2 Modern Money

Higher Powers were involved in this system almost from the beginning. Religious orders, as well as governments, have issued paper currency. Why did the authorities take over so quickly? Because of two things:

1. Controlling people's money helps control people's actions.
2. Authority lent credibility to the new system. When new things arise, people fear to approach. But if the great (insert Higher Power name here) backs this... well, it must be OK.

There was actually a free market in paper currency until the prevailing governmental Collectives realized that minted coins were no longer the currency of choice, and started driving other organizations out of this business. Then, as usual, without any competition allowed, governments began to destroy the product.

In many nations, hyperinflation was caused by issuing currency without controls, and today, perhaps still the strongest currency in the world, the United States dollar, is no longer a promise of anything, other than being accepted as payment of United States taxes. (For the record, this occurred in 1971. Richard Nixon signed a law removing the link between the U.S. Dollar and silver metal.)

Today almost every nation-state has laws declaring that only they may issue currency. But what does this really mean? Currency is not controlled by edict of the state, but by what the people are willing to accept in payment.

Any promissory note is a form of paper currency. Coupons from the local donut shop that entitle the bearer to a free donut are a currency backed in donuts, and in theory, a thriving economy that accepted these coupons as payment could spring up if the local government currency became degraded enough and no other useful alternative existed.

In fact, the lawyers of the local donut shop are aware of how perilously close they are to violating law here, and there will often be fine print on the coupons declaring that they have no cash value, to make them somehow "non-monetary." This is a legal fiction. There is no qualitative difference between a coupon backed by delicious fried sugared dough product and a pre 1970s U.S. dollar backed by silver.

Government issued currency that is not backed by anything is, in fact, less intrinsically stable than the donut coupon, assuming that the donut provider is as reputable as the government (not necessarily a particularly huge stretch in the case of some governments).

6.3.3.3 Future of Money

Today, electronic information systems offer a possibility of a new kind of money. Paper money is really just information about who is promising what to whom. This information does not need to reside on paper. Value can be stored in digitally-signed contracts or held in account balances on computers. In fact, electronic account balances on the computers of government licensed banks, already account for a huge percentage of the US currency "in circulation."

However, just as file sharing allows people to communicate freely with each other outside the information distribution channels approved by the government, church, or corporation – the Internet also makes it possible for people to freely exchange information concerning who owes what to whom. It is only a matter of time before the proper electronic systems are available, and people realize that they can do business with each other quite well using exchanges of electronic contracts and account balances, without resorting to anything created by the government. The ideal electronic currency system would have no hierarchy built into it, and anyone should be able to act like a bank, a mint, or simply an owner of electronic contracts.

Once we have a free electronic currency system, people will no longer have a moral obligation to "render unto Caesar." The currency won't be Caesar's anymore – it will be ours.

Want to free the world from enslavement by the Collective? Help develop a distributed system that allows people to exchange value freely and privately without restriction. Make the protocols freely available to anyone who might want to use them.

6.3.4 Markets and Wagering

Modern business ventures are often made possible only by purchasing insurance to remove risk from the project. There is no discernible difference between the insurance industry and any other wagering on an unknown outcome of events. However, in many countries an artificial distinction has been drawn between insurance industries and other wagering businesses that are prohibited.

To make this a little clearer, consider that a professional football team in the United States is a business, and this business does better if the team wins. Therefore, it seems likely that Lloyd's of London would be willing to mitigate a team owner's financial risk by allowing them to buy insurance against a losing season. However, looked at from the point of view of United States law, this team owner would be betting on the outcome of a sporting event – in fact, betting on their team to lose which is considered particularly bad.

Government prohibitions on gambling offer an excellent insight into the hypocrisy of the Icons of central authority. In the United States, because gambling is said to be bad for people, private numbers games have been made illegal. However, once private numbers games were criminalized and run out of existence, the government was quite happy to step in and offer state run lotteries that offer worse payouts than the numbers games had. Additionally, note that churches are allowed to run bingo games and some other wagering events that a private individual would be fined or jailed for offering to the public.

Even the stock market is just another type of wagering. When you buy a stock you are betting that the price of the stock will go up – when you sell you are betting that it will go down. Such markets are a source of great economic good in the world, by providing liquidity to property holdings of all sorts. They have been around for a long time, and have long ago fallen under strong central controls.

But there are some other interesting types of markets that are on the verge of being constructed. These new types of market may lead to changes in the world that no collective idea-organism is prepared to face.

6.3.4.1 Idea Markets

Price feedback is a key factor (perhaps THE key factor) in the outstandingly positive results of free markets. The individual values of all participating individuals combine to set the value of any given commodity.

People with a strong opinion are generally either quite knowledgeable or brainwashed on the subject. The influence of idea-organisms can cause this brainwashing and distort the market, but only for a very short time where no force is used. This is because the brainwashed quickly lose their shirts, while the knowledgeable do quite well and continue to play the game. Thus we can expect in a free market that the price of any given commodity reflects an extremely accurate evaluation of this commodity's real value. It is probably even accurate to say that this is the definition of real value.

A free market can not only point out the correct valuation of a commodity, but with a little economic trickery, can be turned into a sort of oracle to answer difficult questions. The trick involves creating a commodity that represents each of the possible answers to a given question, and letting everyone trade shares in these commodities. Where the market settles is an indication of the relative probabilities that the group as a whole assigns the answer to the question.

While an idea market "oracle" is not by any means supernaturally accurate, it can be superior in predictive capabilities to ANY other method of making a decision. This is so because anyone with a potentially better predictive system benefits by entering the market – thus lending their expertise to it.

The more people who are allowed to participate in an idea market, the better it works. When everyone is allowed to play, no system can make better predictions.

Polling a group in any other way does not have the same effect of separating claims of confidence from actual confidence, as the market system does. When people have to "put their money where their mouth is" the best guesses of the most knowledgeable people come to the forefront, without any need for some central authority to decide who is the most knowledgeable. These results lead directly to the idea that a larger group can make better decisions than any smaller representative group, or single leader, no matter how the representatives are chosen.

This means that we do not need leaders at all, just free open markets set up to ask the right questions in the right way. The questions asked need not even be issued by any central authority; they can be posed by any party willing to pay to seed the market for the answer to a given question.

Are you looking to build something of value for all of mankind? Why not this?

6.3.4.2 Disaster Markets

In 2003, DARPA (a US government research agency) started working on a system for placing wagers on terrorist activities. The idea was that it would help forecast these very difficult to predict acts. When the press and various politicians got wind of this, it was shot down, being generally criticized as an incredibly ill-conceived idea. However, none of the people talking against the idea demonstrated any knowledge of why it might or might not work. They just seemed to think that two bad words like "terrorism" and "wagering" when put together must make a really extra bad idea.

Not only would such a market have been very likely to produce useful information, but it might have had side effects of a world-shaking nature. These effects would certainly be bad from the viewpoint of collective idea-organisms, but perhaps very good effects for individual liberty everywhere.

The world-shaking side-effect would be that these markets would interfere with the events they were set up to bet on. In much the same way that the existence of fire insurance leads to some unexplained fires (from which people collect insurance money), the existence of a market in which people can bet on the outcome of specific real-world events, leads to some different outcomes for those events.

People who are in a position to influence a particular outcome will bet on the thing that they can make happen and then will act to make it happen. Therefore, people who want a certain thing to happen need only bet against it to increase its chances of happening – they are "sweetening the pot" for those who are in a position to influence events.

This is why the NFL doesn't want people betting on football – they want the players, and not the betters, to determine the outcome of the game. Of course these "side-effects" are totally counter-intuitive from a betting standpoint – you would bet on the team you want to win, right? But from an insurance or market economics standpoint it makes perfect sense to receive money when something you don't want to happen occurs and to pay money when things happen the way you want them to. This is hedging your value – it's what insurance is all about.

It turns out that the creation of general wagering markets that allow betting on "bad" things like people's deaths and acts of terrorism, or on good things like the invention of a new technology, may be an incredibly powerful use of market forces. Such markets might allow groups of free individuals to exert more power in the world than any system of law and government would ever allow.

Let's look at the story of one man's ideas about how that might happen.

6.3.4.3 Assassination Politics

In August of 2001, James Dalton Bell was sentenced to 10 years in federal prison for the crime of "stalking." In 1996 he had released an essay on the Internet entitled "Assassination Politics." One might think that these two facts are unrelated, except that if you read the trial transcripts and the applications for search warrants in the development of the case, Bell's writing on this topic is mentioned repeatedly. There is little doubt that Bell's writing of this essay played a significant role in both the fact that charges were brought and the extremely harsh sentence he received for offenses of an entirely non-violent nature.

The charges that he was convicted of (and received a ten year sentence for) were two counts of "stalking a federal agent." Bell's defense was that he was conducting his own investigation into illegal conduct by the agents in question, whom he claimed were engaged in an illegal investigation of him based on his political ideas. The question of whether Jim Bell is now a "political prisoner" of the United States Government is certainly open to interpretation. However, it bears mentioning that no one has ever been jailed for more than three years for stalking a US citizen who did not carry a badge or hold political office, where no restraining order was violated. Also that, based on their own testimony against Bell, the agents in question were in fact following Bell before he started following them – and were perhaps surveiling him initially with no legal authority to do so.

In Bell's controversial essay he argues that a free market using untraceable electronic currency and allowing wagering on the time of death of any person could replace the need for any other use of force in the world – that armies would no longer be needed – that the concept of Nation State might even fade away, leaving us all just free individuals living in a better world.

The mechanism by which this would occur is a grim one. The betting pools being a way of sanctioning the assassination of leaders who do not really serve the will of the people. However, his hypothesis is quite compelling and one can't help but wonder if a world in which very bad leaders were routinely killed might not be a better one than a world where young people are routinely sent to their deaths in uniform.

It is also interesting to note that a distributed market system, calculating who deserves to die, does not set up the kind of cycle of violence that a system of nations trying to police each other does. There is no obvious way to retaliate against millions of unconnected individuals worldwide who all voted against someone, each with small amounts of money. Hence this kind of violence would not beget more violence – it would not go on and on in countless retaliations for retaliations for retaliations...

Furthermore, the power of the idea is such that one can't help but wonder if a related, but less violent mechanism, might not be developed – a system that might use market forces to depose bad leaders without actually killing them.

Regardless of whether you believe that Bell's idea is a "good" one, it is certainly an interesting one. It may not be something that could be done morally, and certainly never legally, but it is also something that is illegal for the wrong reasons. It is illegal (or would be made so as soon as anyone tried to implement it) because it threatens the status quo of the Collective, not because it is by any real measure a worse system than what we have now.

Our current world legal and political systems certainly contain a large dose of violence. There is no reason to believe that Bell's system would be worse as measured in number of deaths. In fact, there is logic to the idea that it would be better. It would shift the feedback of violence away from the innocent and onto the people who actually start the trouble. Of course, it is not easy to get the people who make the rules to allow for a system that makes them pay the price for their bad choices.

Optimizing the equation of power is all about maximizing control while minimizing accountability. Those who would develop systems to do just the opposite are a bigger threat to the collective idea-organisms than any number of human deaths.

If you really believe in liberty over central authority – maybe this is the system you should develop. But before anyone is killed, we suggest first trying out a market for hitting people in the face with a cream pie. It would provide some negative feedback without the finality of an assassin's bullet. Maybe it would be enough to just embarrass bad political leaders rather than killing them. Maybe it would be enough to just hurt their reputations.

6.3.5 Reputation Capital

Reputation has always been a major force in the world, and it is just gaining more power as information systems become more extensive.

We already live in a world where anyone who is about to do business with someone else can type a name into a search engine to find out what other people have to say about that person. In certain cases, there are already agencies that distill this information into an easy to digest number – credit agencies being the most obvious that comes to mind. If someone wants to lend money to another person, a credit score is a good indication of how likely they are to be paid back. Feedback from previous business transactions is used to evaluate them to other potential business partners.

Other societal problems can certainly be solved in this manner. One method that does not exist yet, but would seem to help society greatly, would be a rating for how litigious a person is. That is to say, how likely they are to sue another person or business.

Many people complain about the increase of frivolous law suits, and this would seem to be a good way to deter them. People who might otherwise engage in frivolous law suits would have to consider how it might affect their ability to do business in the future.

Of course if it reduces the amount of work for lawyers, they will almost certainly try to make it illegal. Their claim will be something along the lines of how it deprives the little guy of its right to sue the big corporations, never mind the fact that big corporations would seem to have more at stake in protecting their reputations than any little guy.

Evil can be reduced by penalizing misdeeds through loss of reputation. Good can be increased by rewarding correct behavior through increased reputation. It therefore makes sense that a very efficient reputation system could replace centrally controlled systems of law enforcement.

In a small tribe, a transgression punished by making the transgressor an outcast was almost the same as a death penalty. We live in a complex world with a lot more people, but we all still need other people to survive. If information flow became nearly perfect, and a person was truly and justly tagged with all their misdeeds, the societal market feedback should provide a commiserate punishment in terms of lost opportunities for any transgressor.

A truly heinous offense might even lead to the offender dying from lack of ability to trade for necessities, all without any enforcement cost, other than the loss of whatever value that person might have provided. But in the less extreme case, that person would just be required to provide more good to make up for any offense, and that extreme case could only happen when a person was deemed incapable of producing further positive value.

We have looked at a couple ways for central authority to be successfully replaced by equal individuals all acting freely, at the right time, with the right information. If information technology can make sure that the right information is available to the right individuals at the right time (and perhaps you can help make this a reality), then all we would have to do is reduce bad laws until all individuals are free and equal.

6.4 Rolling Back

Even if we are correct that new technology and individual action can effectively replace central law enforcement, the systems that are already in place will resist this technology. If they can't control it, they'll make it illegal.

Collective force will tend to be used against any system that would replace collective force.

While it is obviously better for us to replace expensive systems that don't work well with cheap ones that do, the collective idea-organisms that have grown up within those old systems will fight for their lives. In fact, even as these technologies are becoming available, rather than government shrinking, it is growing larger, sometimes by inspiring fear of the very technologies that could help replace it.

How can we stop the growth of the Collective, let alone roll it back?

6.4.1 Revolution

The classic answer to the question of how to roll back bad laws is revolution. Power systems get set up to perpetuate and grow (evolve to survive and reproduce) and when they start to do more harm than good, people get angry. If the system does not have the proper feedback methods for that anger, such that real change can be accomplished when it becomes clear to people that it is necessary, then working outside the system becomes the only way. However, getting enough people behind the idea of a revolution, such that they can act together to make it happen, can only really occur in one way – that is with the growth of another Collective Identity.

This is why, when a Collective does have a revolution, it immediately becomes a mythical thing – itself an icon. The leaders of the revolution set up shop, start creating their own bad rules, and continue to operate in the name of The Great Revolution. Anyone who opposes them is labeled ”counter-revolutionary” even years later when they are someone again in the position of wanting to change a bad system – just like the founding fathers of the current system were.

Of course the worst thing about revolutions is that they are rarely bloodless. Even non-violent protest usually results in quite a few deaths before the powers that be get the idea that breaking heads won't get these people to go back to work for them. So where a slower, more peaceful method of reducing government and rolling back laws can be found, it is almost certainly preferable to one that involves killing people.

We should add that “revolution” is mostly just a word that people toss about to make themselves feel important or enlightened. An actual revolution is almost always an excuse to seize an existing system and to become the new boss. This is much easier than building something that is new and better.

But should you ever find yourself in a situation where a whole new set of laws can be re-written, a really good place to start is to write a constitution that specifically limits the powers of the government. Experience shows that it will only be a few generations before your words are being interpreted to mean exactly the opposite of what you were trying to say, but that is a few generations of freedom that people would not have gotten otherwise.

When you decide to grant power to government, start by thinking "What powers would I allow the government to have over me if I knew that my worst enemy in the world was going to be in charge of this government?"

This is the only reasonable way to look at it if you want a society where it is legal to be different. The people who end up in charge of government are always the people who take great pleasure in controlling the actions of others. This is because the center of authority holds the greatest reward for such people or, more accurately, for the ideas they carry. Allowing the center of power to be a place from which ideas can be imposed on others turns it into a magnet for parasitic ideas.

This means that your leaders are either the people who are most infected by some Collective Identity that wants to use the center of power to replicate itself or they are entirely unscrupulous people that don't really believe in the system but enjoy the feeling of exercising power over other people's lives. Sadly, the latter are almost preferable, as they at least have understandable human wants and fears.

6.4.2 Political Reform

Let us assume that you live in a place that can be changed without resorting to violence. You should first consider yourself very lucky if, during the last revolution in your country, the new government was set up with some feedback mechanism by which you can do something about out of control bad government. Next, consider the following items as possible places to use that mechanism to start reforming your government.

6.4.2.1 Changing Political Incentives

Politicians and Police are just like anyone else; they are trying to make the world they live in a better place for themselves. If the system in which they are required to work aligns their self interest with making the world a better place for everyone else, then things will get better. If it does not, things will probably get worse.

If you have any say in government at all, then some sort of incentive system is already in place, but it is probably not directly tied to the results you want. For example, you may be able to vote to elect politicians who you think will do a better job. However, this incentive is not linked directly to the results, but rather, to what the average person *thinks* the future results will be.

You may want to live in a city without crime, but the politicians and police may find that their jobs are actually better rewarded when there is a lot of crime to scare you into voting for them and spending a lot of money to get rid of that crime. If the crime goes away, you may forget why you need them.

The political argument will be that the more crime there is, the more money you need to spend to get rid of it, but this is actually a reverse incentive. You actually end up paying the politicians and police more when there is more crime. Basic economics would tell you that this is not the way to reduce crime.

Instead, think about setting a fixed law enforcement bonus. Now, if there is no crime, or all crimes are solved, all the police and politicians involved get that whole bonus. However, if there is crime, or unsolved crime, that bonus is reduced according to some formula. (Of course you would need independent crime statistics; else the police and politicians might just under-report crime.)

A bonus like this presents a direct economic incentive to your employees (that's right, they are your employees) to perform the task for which you are employing them. This is the way results are encouraged economically.

The additional benefit is that it also sets limits on the government in terms of how much they can ever do. They do not get more money when enforcement costs are rising; they get less. They are forced to give up on ideas that are not working rather than just spending more money on them. This is a very good thing, as it prevents runaway government.

6.4.2.2 Applying Limits

Some other ways to put direct limits on government are "term limits", "time limits", and "word count limits":

Term limits prevent any politician or policeman from serving in office for longer than a set period of time. This is done to ensure that government is being conducted according to a system of limiting rules and is not based on relationships between the specific officials. From a memetics point of view, what this accomplishes is to help break up the formation of smaller Collective Identities within some portion of the government.

"Sunset clauses," are time limits on laws. If every law is required to expire after a short time period, politicians are kept busy re-arguing the case for old laws, rather than passing a lot of new ones. Old laws can die away gracefully when they have outlived their usefulness, without the issue having to be specifically addressed. Laws can be tested for a while and then allowed to die out if it is not working well – and this can happen without anyone having to seemingly be in favor of the problem that the law was originally intended to cure. (Could anything be more eminently sensible?)

Anyone who has ever made a real attempt to read through all the law of any modern country knows that there is way more law than there needs to be. In practice this means that only some of the law is ever enforced, and that people are constantly doing things they don't even know to be illegal. This gives police a great deal of power, through selective enforcement, to harass people that are different. They can enforce laws against "outsiders" that they would never even think of enforcing against their friends. Sunset clauses would help to reduce law to just what was actually always worth enforcing.

> If you have never actually read a piece of legislation, you really should do so. Trying to muddle through the legal-eze of even the simplest bill is a real eye opener. It is also fun to note how little the content of the law can resemble the title of the proposed bill – sometimes the law seems to be the exact opposite of the title. Its like they are deliberately trying to be confusing and long winded. Your representatives almost never actually read the laws they vote upon. They have people to tell them what to vote for – how to do their jobs.

Another method of limiting the amount of law is to actually limit the number of words that can be used. Some historical tribes were said to have had a single man who had to memorize all of the law and recite it at a meeting once a year. Anything he forgot was no longer part of the law. This put the effective limit on the word count of all laws within that which a single man was able to memorize and recite in a reasonable time period.

Word count limits or clause limits on each particular law are also a good idea because they prevent laws that are so long as to be unintelligible, as well as preventing laws from being passed in groups, where riders are constantly added. Such riders allow two laws that only 26% of the people in the country would agree with to get 52% of the vote when they are packaged together. This is how special interest groups get legislation passed that almost no one is happy about. Each political representative says, "I'll pass this for your constituents if you pass that for mine." Bundling the laws makes sure that the politicians don't have to trust each other on this. It is likely that a lot less bad legislation would be passed if they did have to trust each other.

6.4.3 Reducing the Bureaucracy

Picture the Leviathan. How much of the beast is teeth? Not much as a percentage, huh? The teeth are the scary parts, but they are small parts. Most of Leviathan is bone and soft tissue.

In the same way, most of government is not what you think of as "The government." There are dozens – hundreds – of bureaucracies. There are buildings full of unionized, impossible-to-fire people, each getting a paycheck, insurance, and a pension. THIS is government. THIS is what takes roughly half of every productive person's labor.

Certainly many government employees are decent people who are kind to animals and call their mothers regularly. But if they were working for any other type of entity, they'd never survive as they do. If the bureaucracy were reduced, they would have to find work with employers who were actually able to fire them if they failed to produce. Actually, that would be the compassionate thing to do for these folks. They'd feel a lot better about themselves in the long run – even in the medium run.

Leviathan's mouth grabs the food, but the rest of the body demands it of the mouth. Until these armies of unfireables are disbanded, Leviathan's hunger will be undimmed, and we might all end up in its belly.

6.4.4 Local Laws

Government systems are based on a hierarchical structure of power – the idea that laws at the top level overshadow laws at the lower level. This is terrible for individuals. The smaller the group for which a law is intended, the more likely it is to actually be in tune with the feelings of all the individuals in the group concerning what should and should not be illegal.

An ideal system of law would let each person select the things that should be illegal. Then you would be bound to respect both your own law and that of any other person you interacted with. Of course such a system would involve a multitude of complex interactions that we probably don't yet have the information systems technology to deal with, and would still have all the usual problems with publicly shared resources.

The next best thing would be to just reverse the current system of jurisdictional hierarchy. Having the laws of smaller jurisdictions override the laws of the larger jurisdictions is a general recipe for liberty. For example, in your own house, you would automatically be allowed to do whatever you wanted to do. If your local community was OK with you walking around naked, then you could do that too, even if the average community in the country did not like the way you look naked.

When the Constitution of the United States was ratified in 1787, it gave certain limited powers to the U.S. federal government, but it continued to allow the individuals States to make almost all of their own laws. In fact, the understanding was that the States of the union were, in most respects, still individual Nation States.

This ability for citizens to choose the laws that they wanted to live under, simply by moving to another nearby State, created some competition between States to actually have the laws that the people wanted. It also allowed laws to be tried in one State, and the effects of the law, good and bad, to be observed before being adopted elsewhere – and before they became part of the Distributed Identity of "The Law" in everyone's minds.

There is no doubt that this ability to have competing lower level laws played a part in the great success of the United States. However, the seemingly inevitable process of central government strengthening its power has lead us to the more historically usual centralized power structure, in which the Federal government tries to claim the right to override State law in every situation.

Getting from the current top down system to the reverse would be difficult (see revolution above) but local laws that explicitly refute higher level laws can still be used as a political tool to express a smaller Collective's dissent against the higher governmental structure. It is even possible to pass local laws making it illegal to enforce the higher level laws, although, like any effective tool for liberty, once discovered, the higher Collective will make this additionally illegal.

Your best chance for liberty might be to move to a local jurisdiction with other people who share the same opinions that you do. This will allow you, and those of like mind, to become a shining example for the rest of the world of how your perfect system can work. If the rest of the world will leave you alone that is.

If the structure of law were bottom-up rather than top-down, experimental communities could test new systems of law. This would allow many attempts to produce better laws, rather than one giant experiment that hurts everyone whenever it fails. Letting different people try lots of different ideas is the best chance we have to find better ways to do things. Of course the collective idea-organisms do not want new ways – they want to enforce *their* status quo.

6.4.5 Planned Libertarian Communities

One way to achieve liberty is by getting together with a bunch of like-minded people, and forming your own community, where you all agree never to allow collective thinking to get in and mess with your freedom. The idea of such a planned libertarian community is that with like minded individuals, a minimum of government would be allowed, and when the society did better because of it, it would be a shining example to everyone. (Of course there have been quite a few historical examples of the benefits of limited government, and yet government keeps growing everywhere.) Some people have suggested creating a new town, but others think bigger, wanting to buy a small semi-defunct country.

The idea of taking over one State of the United States has even been suggested.

6.4.5.1 The Free State Project

Beginning as an article entitled "Announcement: The Free State Project" published in 2001 by Jason Sorens, The Free State Project has a membership of over 7000 people (as of the time of this writing). The stated intentions of the project are to move 20,000 libertarian-minded people to a single small state where their political activities could be enough to swing the political climate of that state towards true free market capitalism. The initial article even suggested that the end goal could be succession from the United States to create a new country, although that has not been seriously promoted as one of the goals.

If you are interested in getting involved with the Free State Project, visit their web site at www.freestateproject.org

As of late 2006, the Free State Project has yet to reach its goal of 20,000 people, and (unless motivated people like you decide to get involved) it may never actually get there. But the idea has certainly taken hold in many minds. Once New Hampshire was chosen as the state, splitter factions that liked other states better immediately began to advertise their own Free State initiatives.

Even Non-libertarian groups borrowed the idea. A group called "Christian Exodus" declared that it would make South Carolina the "Christian state."

In an essay entitled "*The Most Sincere Form of Flattery*," Amanda Phillips, President of the Free State Project, wrote:

> *The Free State Project (FSP) is worthy of imitation. It has had a remarkable life so far. Begun as the brainchild of Jason Sorens in a discussion forum, it has grown into the full-fledged movement for liberty it is today. The FSP forums are an unending source of discourse on liberty and discussions on how to attain it. Across the country, members work on spreading the word.*

Needless to say, if you don't like Libertarians and happen to live in New Hampshire, or you don't like Christians, and happen to live in South Carolina, these calls for mass migration to your state are probably somewhat annoying.

That said, we can't resist getting in on this act. So here is our suggestion for a mass migration of like minded people:

6.4.5.2 Free D.C.

Washington D.C. (District of Columbia) is the capitol of the United States. It is not a state, nor is it inside any state, having been set aside so that no state would receive favoritism by being the home of the national capitol. It has no senator and only has one non-voting representative in the House of Representatives.

Now it would seem counter intuitive, as this might be considered the "belly of the beast" by libertarians, but here are some reasons why we think all libertarian activists should immediately get together and move to Washington D.C.:

- **Population** – D.C. has less than half the population of New Hampshire, so any influx of libertarians would have more effect.
- **Taxation Issues** – Libertarian activists could immediately stop paying taxes and fight the IRS under the slogan of "No Taxation without Representation" – which should still be a fairly popular slogan, even if it hasn't been used since the Revolutionary War.
- **Publicity** – things that happen in the capitol make the news more. While the US congress has the power to override the district local government, if it had to do this every time it was in session, it would make a continuous point about local laws. Also, the cameras are already there and during a large part of the year the press in D.C. is bored and just looking for something to do.
- **Access** – By being there at the heart of things, libertarian values might rub off on politicians. If young DC politicians only had libertarians to socialize with, they would at least have to pretend to be libertarian, and some of it might stick.

If the libertarians did it successfully, the Christian exodus people might decide they had to go to D.C. too, and then other groups with any sort of ax to grind.

Wouldn't it be great to see United States political big wigs have to live and work in a city full of libertarian activists, interesting religious groups, and who knows what other strange and wonderful people trying this same trick to their own purpose – also an over 50% racial minority population. Imagine being a federal level politician in a city that became a magnet to all sorts of people with fringe viewpoints. It would not be easy to have to always play the "straight man" in such a crazy environment. This could change the character of the average type of person who sought out high level political office – almost certainly for the better.

But if moving to a new town and getting involved in local politics seems like a lot of work to you then you ain't seen nothing. How about starting your own country?

6.5 New Frontiers

If changing your current government is not an option, perhaps you should consider starting a new one somewhere else. This might do more than just give you more freedom. It might make more freedom for everyone.

In David Friedman's book "The Machinery of Freedom," he talks about the idea of government services being absorbed into the free market – including the use of force to protect individuals from crime. His idea is that central authority could disappear if overlapping jurisdictions for the legitimate use of force became normal. This amounts to private police forces protecting their customers based on a set of rules their customers choose. He uses the following analogy to describe the effects that might be observed if there was a real market in government services and citizens could easily switch providers:

> *Everyone lives in a house-trailer and speaks the same language. One day, the president of France announces that because of troubles with neighboring countries, new military taxes are being levied and conscription will begin shortly. The next morning the president of France finds himself ruling a peaceful but empty landscape, the population having been reduced to himself, three generals, and twenty-seven war correspondents.*

That example may seem a little weird, but to some degree there is actually a market in governments today. Governments can be considered as businesses that provide a certain set of services for a price. Governments vary in quality and price paid for these services in Property, Liberty, and sometimes even Life.

It is theoretically possible to go into the government business yourself, but there are significant barriers to entering the industry. You need to do something as costly as overthrowing an existing government – or find some unclaimed living space (or in some cases space claimed by people with inferior technology to your own will do) and colonize it. In the former case, you inherit the old government's customer base; in the latter case you will have to start marketing right away to build a new clientele.

The cost of switching service providers in the government arena is very high, so you have to offer a significantly better deal to start winning customers (citizens) over from other governments. Your potential new citizens will need to see a large advantage to your new way of living that is worth paying this high cost of changing providers. Governments claim monopoly rights for providing their services in a certain geographic area. Barring some way of breaking that monopoly, a physical move is required to change providers. In the worst cases, dodging bullets and climbing over barbed wire topped walls will be a necessary part of the cost to switch government service providers.

For the moment, only rich people are in a good position to switch countries in search of a better deal. But despite these significant economic barriers, if a better government exists, and the citizens of other governments know about it, it does put some pressure on all governments everywhere to provide better services and/or reduce prices.

6.5.1 The Frontier Effect

There is historical precedent for this competitive pressure in the government market. Whenever in history there has been an accessible frontier for people to move to, older governments have had to relax their controls or lose citizens.

The most recent significant instance of this was the "New World," in which people moved to the western hemisphere in great numbers, seeking new land and new liberty. During this migration, not only did they set up freer ways of living where they went, but the countries that they were moving from also showed a significant trend towards increased liberty as well. For a large part of its history, The United States of America was a frontier in which liberty thrived. Only when there was no frontier left did things start to move in the other direction and a national Collective Identity based on geographical boundaries starting to gain significant strength.

6.5.2 Start-up Countries

Within the past hundred years, just about all the land on the planet has been claimed by one nation state or another. As a result we have a handful of large nations capable of exercising military control over other countries – a larger number of nations that could not field such a military effort, but could probably resist any larger invader indefinitely, at great cost to that invader – plus a scattering of very small countries that exist only at the pleasure of larger nations.

At this point in history, new nations arise only through revolution or civil war in existing countries. Efforts to start a new country from the ground up like a small business have, in almost all cases, met with failure. For those interested in startup countries, the book *"How to Start Your Own Country"* by Erwin Strauss is an excellent collection of case histories of various start up country projects.

These case studies show the difficulty of finding places where making new land is possible, or of navigating the global political climate. From the point of view of looking at government as an industry, this indicates a very high barrier to entry, as well as a high cost for customers in changing providers.

Experimentation in this area seems to indicate that building a new country from scratch and then attracting citizens is not a particularly doable thing. This is not really surprising, considering that this is not the way it has ever been done historically. The usual way is for a bunch of people, who don't even know they are starting a country, to move into uncharted territory in an attempt to make a living. Such pioneering homesteaders, setting up their lives in the new world, created new freedom for themselves – and through the effects of competition between governments, also increased freedom for every one else.

It would be nice to recreate this effect, but as it was pointed out earlier, all the available land has been claimed by governments – even where they are not using it, and no one lives on it. Governments are not interested in experimenting with new ways of living. Even though such experimentation could offer new information to us about what is good and what is bad about the ways we currently live, from the point of view of the Collective Identities that steer governments this would be very dangerous. It would allow competition and might lead to the creation of new competing Distributed Identities.

So if there is no land to homestead, where are today's pioneers to go?

6.5.3 Seasteading

A number of the ideas for startup countries have had to do with colonizing the oceans. However, they have mostly all suffered from the idea that you need to build a new country all at once. This causes all their plans to look like:

1. Get enough money together to build floating inhabitation for 10,000 people. (A billion dollars is the usual figure mentioned.)
2. Build a floating city-state.
3. Declare nationhood.
4. Wait and see if anyone else wants to move there, to live under your new improved government system where only you are royalty.

Obviously, they all fail at step 1.

The Seasteading concept is a little different. The idea behind Seasteading is to make the technology available for a single family to move to the ocean, and make a living, for something near to the cost of a small building on the land.

Floating "houses" would allow pioneering seasteaders to just "hit the trail" and find their spot on the ocean to start farming fish or engaging in any sort of work that does not require too much space or dirt. They don't have to declare "nationhood." They can just start living their lives and see how it works out.

The Seasteading plan looks more like:

1. Get enough money to build your own floating home (maybe $100,000? That is 1/10,000 of the billion dollar figure above.)
2. Build your floating home.
3. Move to the ocean.
4. Wait and see if anyone else decides to follow the example of living freely and become your neighbor.

Any plan that only requires people to get involved a few at a time, and invest reasonable sums of money is, of course, far more likely to see some real results.

With modern information flow, the lives of any pioneering seasteaders would become well known to landlubbers. Their increased freedom would become a standard to measure land based governments against. If and when there were a lot of seasteaders, they would quite likely link together in larger groups. However, because each seastead could be moved easily, they would have exactly the conditions described by David Friedman in "The Machinery of Freedom" excerpt above with his analogy of a nation of house-trailers.

For seasteaders this would not be an analogy, it would be real. They could all literally float away from any government that tried to enact bad laws, leaving the bureaucrats to fend for themselves with no citizens to tax. This is exactly the sort of freedom of movement that a Collective Identity based on physical territory can not tolerate. Therefore no similar Collective Identities would likely ever develop in a seasteader community.

Seasteading could be highly beneficial for individuals everywhere, forcing governments to compete with better services (including more freedoms) at lower cost (fewer taxes).

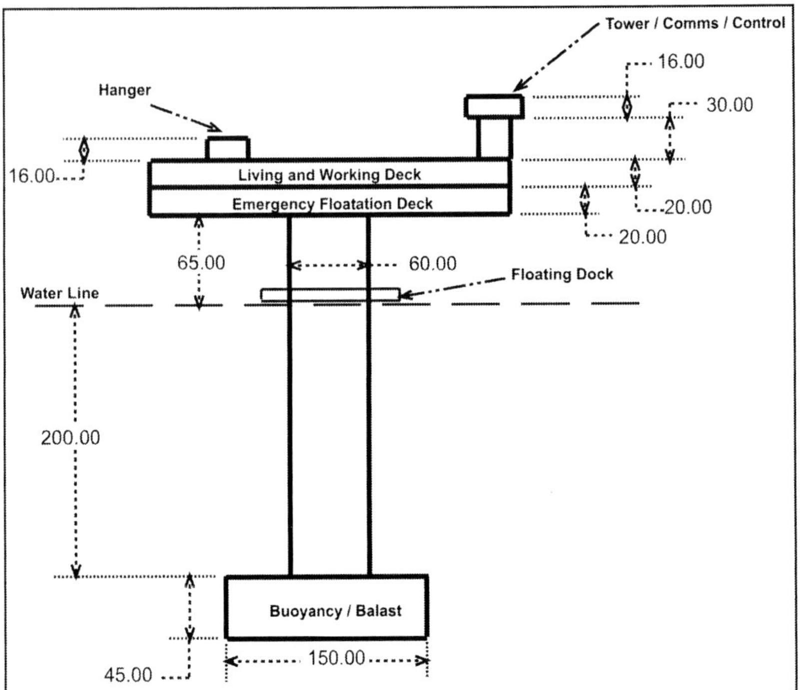

Seastead design with "mushroom" top by architect Andrew House

Each seastead would be like its own mini government, and seastead owners would be "captains of their own ships." In terms of the analogy we made above – looking at government as a business with a high barrier to entry and a high cost of switching providers – the advent of seasteading could vastly reduce both of these costs. Should seasteading make it cheap to start a new government, and cheap to switch to a new government, all governments would feel pressure to provide better services at a lower cost.

Seasteading might also help change the paradigm of legal jurisdiction and central authority. Unlike collections of sovereign states on land, collective bodies that were the equivalent of the governments of Seastead cities, or nations, could not apply top down laws, but would, rather, have to concern themselves with interactions between sovereign Seasteaders.

This is the way the United States Government started out, with its authority over sovereign states filled with sovereign individuals, limited to interactions between those states. However, the federal government eventually extended its power over the States, because there was no way for the States to easily "float away" (as was proved with a bloody civil war). In "The Machinery of Freedom," David Friedman writes:

> *It took about 150 years, starting with a Bill of Rights that reserved to the states and the people all powers not explicitly delegated to the federal government, to produce a Supreme Court willing to rule that growing corn to feed to your own hogs is interstate commerce and can be regulated by Congress.*

But perhaps the idea of seasteading can change all that. If the current highest power Collective Identities are based on the idea of Geographical control of real estate, they might well be influenced by the culture of a place that has fluid connections between properties. There is some reason to hope that this might work out well; after all, most of our planet is actually covered in water. It is also worth noting that many of us expect the human race to get off this planet some day, and any political systems we find that work for living on that water will be more applicable to the large open areas of outer space than are the current rules of central authority known to dirt dwellers.

The Founding Fathers and Mothers of Seasteading might be known farther into the future than the Founding Fathers of any nation, as the political systems they create for pioneering the "Next Frontier" will be far more likely to fit the needs of the pioneering spacesteaders on that "Final Frontier" – certainly more so than the rules of any dirt-bound nation.

Some possible candidates for inclusion in the group of "Founding Fathers" of Seasteading are Wayne C. Gramlich, Patri Friedman, and Andrew House, (See their intellectual work in this area at www.seastead.org) but it remains to be seen what pioneering spirits will actually be the first to make the move to the high seas, and to set up the first systems for self government there. Anyone who wanted to throw a large chunk of money at this idea might well be buying immortality. (The kind where your reputation lives forever – we will talk about the much cooler kind of immortality, where you *actually* get to live forever, later in the book.)

Interestingly, Patri Friedman is David Friedman's son, and Milton Friedman's grandson. If a line of great libertarian thinkers can be, unhypocritically, called a "dynasty," they have one going.

6.5.4 Space Colonization

Beyond living in every possible climate and terrain, on land, sea, or floating in the air, human kind seems likely to eventually leave the planet of its birth and move on to the rest of the Solar System. Perhaps, eventually even other stars and other galaxies. If this exodus does indeed occur, it should be a time of unprecedented liberty. Expanding in three-dimensional space, the frontier only gets larger as you move outward. And those who choose to live in the gaps, between planets and stars will never lack for a place to move if the neighbors get too "noisy."

The first step in this process is to have some group of brave people lift civilization out of its gravity well by its own boot straps. A community on the moon at 1/6 Earth gravity would be a start, but a community living in orbit would solve more of the general issues for survival of our species in space.

We hope to live long enough to see this process – and if we can slip some increases in the right technologies past suppression by the Collective, we just might. God Willing...

In the next chapter we will talk about some possible future technologies that might help humankind get to the stars, and might let you live long enough to see it happen. These are technologies that we may never see unless we can reduce the suppressive effect of collective idea-organisms.

On the Death of Friends

[Shortened Version]

And there was a time, not long ago
When the dream was young, we would go
Together. The stars would be ours
And all the planets, even Mars.

But time was wasted, getting there.
We trusted others and had no fear
That they would work to open space
Not just for us, but the human race.

We watched and waited, helped and worked.
But in the program, corruption lurked.
Pork and fools, timidness and more,
Not opening space, they were the door.

Years went by and little got done,
And still we waited, children of the Sun.
We knew somehow that real soon
We would go together, dancing on the Moon.

But time was passing and took its toll,
In years, and lives, and parts of our soul.
Our friends are dying, one by one,
No more to ride with us and share the fun.

We still will go, though they will not.
And those that delayed us should be shot,
For stealing the dream and taking away
The friends who were going with us someday.

-- Jim Davidson

Full version of this poem at
www.indomitus.net/ondeathfriends.html

7
Playing God

Scientist and science fiction writer Arthur C. Clarke's three laws of prediction:

1. *When a distinguished but elderly scientist states that something is possible, he is almost certainly right. When he states that something is impossible, he is very probably wrong.*
2. *The only way of discovering the limits of the possible is to venture a little way past them into the impossible.*
3. *Any sufficiently advanced technology is indistinguishable from magic.*

This chapter is about the development of new symbiotic memes taken to the extreme – to the point where they might seem magical.

The technologies we discuss in this chapter may seem like far out science fiction, but most of the reason they seem unbelievable may be because they idea-organisms in your mind are afraid of them. Such fantastic future science will at least shake things up for your idea-organisms, and may in fact kill many of them. Therefore, you may find yourself not wanting to believe that these things are possible, or thinking that they are somehow bad things.

However, they are not only possible, but might even happen fairly soon, so long as we don't let the Collectives suppress or control technological development.

Since the quest for fire, mankind's journey has been one of gathering knowledge and developing new technologies. New technologies are developed to fulfill a wish. We are constantly striving to make our environments more comfortable, and to enable us to do things better, easier, and at less cost/effort. This quest has lead to technology so advanced, that if a boy scout, with his full kit packed for a camping trip, were transported back in time, primitive man would probably worship him as a god, and if one of those primitive men was brought forward in time to view a modern city, he could easily be convinced that he was getting a look at heaven.

Our urge to extend our individual capabilities and improve our lives through harnessing new, symbiotic ideas, has lifted us to great heights as a civilization. However, the very ideas that bind us together into a culture have a natural tendency to resist new ideas that upset human limitations. Some idea-organisms replicate themselves by claiming to fulfill wishes that technology has not yet fulfilled, or in ways that go against wishes we might have, and such idea-based entities fear the progress of knowledge in directions that will actually fulfill such wishes.

In this chapter, we will discuss some of the technologies that human beings are currently developing, or may be able to develop, and the good that they can do. We will also discuss which DIs will fear those technologies the most, why they will fear them, and how they attempt to suppress them through unwarranted fear, disapproval, and collective force.

In the previous chapter we ended with the idea that mankind's future may be to colonize outer space. However, the technologies required to get there will be quite advanced, and not all of them will meet the approval of all the prevailing idea-organisms.

Certainly nature worshipers will find it unnatural to leave the home planet, abandoning Gaia. Nation states will worry about which country will control the territory of the moon, mars, or even all of outer space. No doubt racial and ethnic groups will complain about an imbalance of representation among astronauts. And many of the necessary advances in technology, that we will need to take this next step into space, are certain to have those of religious faith worried that we are "Playing God."

7.1 Suspended Animation

One technology that may be necessary for mankind's eventual journey into outer space – and one that has certainly played a part in many fictional stories that feature future technology – is the idea of suspended animation. Interstellar distances are so great that even light, which travels faster than we could ever travel according to current theories of space-time, can take many years to travel between even two "close" stars. So, authors who wanted to set stories in civilizations that traveled between stars have often used the idea that human beings could temporarily be "turned off" for the duration of an interstellar voyage. The idea was that if a person could be put into Suspended Animation, even if the trip took many, many years, no time would pass for the person at all, and they wouldn't have aged a bit when they were revived at the end of the journey.

7.1.1 Annoying God

As long as such technology had remained purely fictional, it would not have bothered anyone. However, making this technology actually work is sure to anger certain religious idea-organisms. The reason for this is that one of the biggest replication strategies for religions involves removing fears about what happens after death. This usually takes the form of some sort of idea about an immortal soul that goes someplace else when the body dies.

The idea of suspended animation blurs the line between life and death.

If it is possible to suspend human beings, and then at some later point reanimate them, in the interim, are they alive or dead? Even more intriguing, is the idea that it might be possible to use some method of suspension before the technology that would allow reanimation has yet been invented. If you have people in suspension and the technology to revive them exists in theory, but has not yet been made to work in practice, are they alive or dead?

In this case, the answer to whether or not they are really dead has to be that it is unknown. If they can ever be revived, then of course they were never dead. However, if they can never be revived, or will never be revived, you can make a pretty convincing argument that they were dead all along. It is therefore impossible to say if they are dead or alive. They exist in some in-between state. Like Schroedinger's cat, they are caught in an uncertain situation.

There is actually no theological reason why such technology should bother any religious person or institution. There are several possible theological answers to this question. Perhaps the soul knows the outcome of the experiment, and leaves the body only if the person will never be reanimated. Perhaps GOD knows the outcome and removes the soul if the body is actually dead. Maybe the soul can even leave for a while, and then come back if the person turns out to not really be dead.

Catholic dogma seems to suggest that the soul lies in the grave with the body, and only goes to heaven after the dead rise on judgment day. So Catholics in particular should have no problem with frozen bodies that might be either dead or alive. They will either be reanimated before judgment day by some new technology, or will rise with the rest of the dead on judgment day – should that day happen to come along before such technology is invented.

Additionally, the Catholic Church has already strongly condemned the destruction of cryopreserved human embryos, indicating that a soul is present in those embryos. If they believe that embryos in cryostasis are still viable living human beings, how could they not believe that an adult human being in cryostasis is not also still a viable living person?

However, it is quite likely that despite these quite logical points, religions will do everything in their power to resist this technology. (That is, if it becomes popular enough to warrant their attention.) The reason for this is that any hope of forestalling death in this manor has the potential to cut into the mind-share of any religious idea-organism.

If people believe that future technology can revive a person who has been in some way suspended, the next idea is to use this to cheat death. If you are going to die of something, you can just have yourself suspended in the hope that in some future time the technologies to reanimate you and to also cure what is killing you (even if that is just old age) will be invented. This idea opens a potential doorway to physical immortality.

Furthermore, once you grant that such is possible, does this not morally compel us to make the attempt to suspend each and every dying person? As long as there is a possibility that they can be returned to healthy life, are we not ethically bound to try to save them?

There is no good reason why GOD would have a problem with immortality; however, the idea of GOD (which we are referring to as God) is going to have a big problem with it. God the idea-organism is promising an afterlife in exchange for believing in him. Any alternatives for avoiding death are a threat to God's ideological existence. If everyone starts thinking that technology can make them immortal, they will have less reason to host the God idea-organism.

God certainly still has some other tricks, like maybe saying that Armageddon will come eventually, so you can't use any technology to escape judgment forever, or suggesting that without God you have no true purpose, so you had better believe in God or feel like everything is random and meaningless. But even with those other replication strategies, Suspended Animation is a technology that would do some harm to some of God's current ability to continue to survive and grow. It also certainly doesn't help that being suspended almost sounds like a burial ritual, which is something that religions consider to be their domain.

7.1.2 Experiment in Progress

On one hand, our theories about collective behavior brought about by Distributed Identities predict that religions should come out strongly against this technology. On the other hand, there is really no good theological reason for them to do so. This is the first verifiable prediction that we have made. Previously we have just been talking about the history of collective ideological organisms, not predicting what events their existence should cause in the future. Theories that any good scientist might previously have dismissed as being not "falsifiable," even if somewhat compelling, are now real science. An experiment is in progress.

People are working on suspended animation, and making regular breakthroughs. This technology is becoming a very realistic possibility. So now we can just sit back to watch, and wait, and see how God will react to this threat.

If religion is really about following GOD, then suspended animation should by seen as pretty harmless stuff. There is no reason why this technology would threaten GOD. However, if it is God the Distributed Identity (the living idea-organism with its own reproductive agenda) whom religious people are really listening to, then at some point they should start to get seriously upset about this sort of technology.

If we are right about the nature of God and other collective idea-organisms, we should soon see some serious public disapproval, and probably an attempt to make this technology illegal.

7.1.3 Early Thoughts on Suspension

Throughout the ages, various great thinkers have speculated on whether it might ever be possible to preserve a corpse well enough that it might some day be returned to life. Benjamin Franklin, one of the founding fathers of the United States of America, had this to say in a letter to another scientist:

> *I wish it were possible... to invent a method of embalming drowned persons, in such a manner that they might be recalled to life at any period, however distant; for having a very ardent desire to see and observe the state of America a hundred years hence, I should prefer to an ordinary death, being immersed with a few friends in a cask of Madeira, until that time, then to be recalled to life by the solar warmth of my dear country! But... in all probability, we live in a century too little advanced, and too near the infancy of science, to see such an art brought in our time to its perfection...*
>
> -- Benjamin Franklin, April, 1773

The idea of suspending a human being after death for later reanimation may actually predate the historical record. It seems that ancient Egyptians had some notion that this is what they were doing for the bodies of the Pharaohs, through the process of mummification. (Hollywood movies with walking mummies give us proof that the idea of the Pharaoh's return, if not the actual Pharaoh, did survive.)

7.1.4 Rethinking Death

Religious miracles aside, many people have been brought back to life throughout history. As early as the 1500s, it was known that inflating an apparently dead person's lungs with hot air from a fireplace bellows could sometimes revive the person. Drowning and hypothermia have come to be known as ways of dying that are not necessarily permanent if the right techniques are applied to a victim. Children drowning in cold water have sometimes been returned to health after over an hour with no heartbeat or sign of body heat.

As our understanding of the ways in which the human body shuts down in response to trauma have increased, it has become obvious that many people who were once thought dead, were actually in a state from which they could have been revived – with more knowledge – with better technology. Modern medical technology often allows us to keep patients alive on machines indefinitely. We continue to hold out hope, as long as there is any reason to believe that the functions of the brain are still working, or might start working again. Modern declarations of death are often just a case of deciding when it is too much effort to continue the fight.

We now pull people back from the edge of death so regularly, that there are even common stories of near death experiences. People brought back from the brink talk about seeing a tunnel of light. Some religious people point to this phenomena as evidence of an afterlife, claiming that such people are seeing the "tunnel to heaven." Oddly they don't point to a supernatural cause for other similar shared experience caused by nerve trauma. The phantom limbs that amputees experience are not called "Soul Limbs," the tingling after a loss of circulation is never explained as "Angels dancing on the skin," and no reference is made to the "bells of heaven" ringing in one's ears following a painfully loud noise.

Brain death is more of a realistic modern indicator of death than a lack of heart beat. A modern doctor will still not declare time of death on a patient whose heart is beating but this is a holdover from an older definition of death. Just as new knowledge and technology have lead to past definitions of death being invalidated; even newer technology will almost certainly do the same thing to our concept of brain death.

One possible answer to this question of "When is dead, really dead?" lies in the concept of "Information-theoretic Death."

Information theory expert, Ralph C. Merkle, Ph.D. defines death this way:

> *...if the structures in the brain that encode memory and personality have been so disrupted that it is no longer possible in principle to restore them to an appropriate functional state then the person is dead. If the structures that encode memory and personality are sufficiently intact that inference of the memory and personality are feasible in principle, and therefore restoration to an appropriate functional state is likewise feasible in principle, then the person is not dead.*

As long as the information that describes you completely has not been lost, some theoretical future technology might be able to restore you to life.

For Example, if you were to fall into a machine that is designed to cut pigs into precisely sized cubes of meat so that they can be included in cans of delicious brown sugar baked beans, you are in much better shape than your friend who falls into the machine next to it, which happens to be set to puree. Since the chop setting follows predictable patterns, it might be possible to determine where each cube belongs. With some theoretical technology, you could be glued back together alive and well. Your friend, however, has probably been agitated to the point that no amount of computing power could figure out which bit goes where.

Obviously you are both screwed in terms of current medical technology, but in terms of some future medical technology, you are not information-theoretically dead. Just because all the King's horses and all the King's men can't do a job now, doesn't mean that *nobody* will *ever* be able to do that job. (Horses have never been very good at performing medical procedures anyway – so including them in any attempt would no-doubt be a mistake.)

If someone has the presence of mind to shovel the pieces of you into a time machine and transport you to a 25th Century hospital, you might be put back together there with little difficulty. Unfortunately, there is rarely a time machine available when you need one, and after your heart stops the clock is ticking. Some time shortly after circulation ceases, the body starts to decay. Sometime after that Information Theoretic Death is going to be reached.

However, we have learned something from revived hypothermia victims. The colder the brain gets, the longer it takes for Information Theoretic Death to occur. This is because what we think of as heat is really just the motion of molecules. The more they are moving around, the sooner they can get from an ordered pattern of information to a chaotic arrangement that can no longer (even information-theoretically) be returned to that ordered pattern.

We have found our time machine. If you need access to 25th Century medical technology to cure what ails you, your best bet is to be frozen. But you need to be frozen colder than the average deep freeze.

You know how if you leave food in the freezer for a long time, it ends up tasting funny when you cook it? That is because molecules are still moving around. Chemical reactions are still occurring. The food is still going bad, just very slowly. Likewise, if your brain is not being kept much colder than the average deep freeze, you are still dying – just more slowly.

Fortunately, it turns out that technology already exists to get you cold enough. Liquid Nitrogen can be produced fairly cheaply, and is so cold (-195 C) that if your body is cooled with it, all chemical reactions stop. As long as you remain at that temperature, it is possible to preserve the information in your brain forever. You are in suspended animation. This technology has been named "cryonics."

Photo credit Sean Hastings 2002

Pictured here is one of the earliest cryonics storage tanks ever built. It has kept patients suspended at The Cryonics Institute in Michigan, since the late 1970s. We are pretty sure that the little electric fan on the right hand side of the picture has nothing to do with the process that keeps the patients cold. Sean visited the facility in June of 2002, and he swears that there is a giant tank of liquid Nitrogen in back of the building that could keep this tank – as well as the many other patient storage tanks – cold for months between refills.

Liquid Nitrogen can be brought in by truck from anywhere, so power outages are never an issue.

7.1.5 History of Cryonics

The modern quest for a real world technology for suspended animation began in the last half of the 20th Century. Some historical milestones in that quest have been:

- In 1956 Robert A. Heinlein writes the novel "The Door Into Summer," in which the main character journeys into the future through a process of being frozen and revived.
- In the 1962s, physics professor Robert C. W. Ettinger publishes "The Prospect of Immortality," in which he lays out the arguments for a means by which people could be suspended at liquid helium temperatures, and kept in suspension until some future technology might be able to return that person to life, full health, and perhaps even youth.
- In 1965, the word "cryonics" is coined by Karl Werner to describe suspended animation through extremely cold temperatures, and is used in the name of the first cryonics organization, the Cryonics Society of New York (CSNY) founded by Curtis Henderson and Saul Kent.
- In the mid 1960s, several other Cryonics Societies are also founded in the United States – one in Michigan and several in California.
- In 1966, Japanese scientist, Isamu Suda, demonstrates that cat brains could be frozen, using glycerol as a "cryo-protectant," and when carefully warmed, months later, EEG readings demonstrate a degree of continued brain functions.
- In 1966 Walt Disney dies at age 65 of lung cancer. While he is not actually cryonically suspended, he apparently talked about the possibility of cryonics, and this leads to a long standing rumor that his body is being "kept on ice."
- In 1967, Dr. James Bedford was the first human being to be cryonically suspended by the Cryonics Society of California using liquid Nitrogen.
- In the mid 1970's several non-profit organizations are started in California, and Michigan to provide long term storage of suspension patients.
- In 1986, in the book "The Engines of Creation," K. Eric Drexler describes how a future medical nanotechnology might someday be used to heal tissue damage and reverse aging. He also mentions that such a technology might be used to revive people from cryonic suspension.
- In 1996, Timothy Leary, famous advocate of psychotherapeutic LSD use, while dying of cancer, publicly states that he is going to be cryonically suspended. He changes his mind at the last minute, and is finally cremated instead, but as with Disney, there is an ongoing rumor that he is in suspension.
- In the late 1990's cryobiologists discover methods of perfusing tissue with certain new cryo-protectants such that they can be cooled to

extremely low temperatures in a glassy vitrified state with minimal crystallization.

- In 2000, existing cryonics organizations begin to take advantage of vitrification technology to significantly reduce freezing damage in cryonics patients.
- In 2002, Ted Williams, American Baseball legend, dies and is placed in cryonic suspension. This is the first time a very famous person is actually suspended, and a media circus ensues (see below).
- In 2005, a company called 21st Century Medicine announces the development of a new cryo-protectant for vitrification that allows them to successfully vitrify a rabbit kidney, lower the organ to stasis temperatures, then later warm the kidney and transplant it into a living rabbit as a functional organ.
- As of 2006, over 100 human beings have been put into cryostasis, and well over 1000 persons world wide have made arrangements to be suspended with one of several existing cryonics organizations.

7.1.6 Growth of an Idea

The idea of cryonics is certainly still new. (A few thousand people signed up for cryonics worldwide constitutes a very small minority opinion.) But good ideas tend to take off exponentially – growing amazingly quickly.

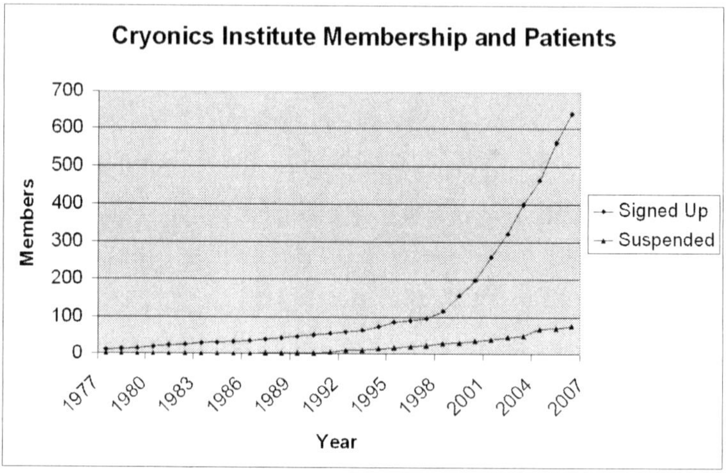

Take a look at this graph of members of "The Cryonics Institute," which is just one of several cryonics organizations in the United States. The graph shows two curves. One curve is for patients who have actually been suspended, and one is for people who have made suspension arrangements – that is, have prepaid or otherwise arranged funding for suspension with a life insurance policy, or the like.

Membership data for a cryonics organization should certainly be a good indicator of the rate at which the idea is catching on. Looking at this graph we see the familiar "hockey stick" shape for an idea that is taking off exponentially. If the growth of the idea is indeed exponential, then being "frozen" in liquid nitrogen should very shortly become a quite normal third option for funeral arrangements, along side the more usual current options of being buried or burned.

7.1.7 Media Spin

The case of baseball legend Ted Williams being placed in cryo-stasis sparked a lot of media controversy. Because Ted Williams himself, as a famous person, had an extended Distributed Identity, many people felt that they "knew" that Ted Williams would never do something so out of the normal. This may have seemed like "bad press" for cryonics. However, when your ideas are different than the main stream, it is hard to get good press, and it is often said that "any publicity is good publicity." In the end, this attention to cryonics only increased the number of people signing up for such services.

It is the nature of media to magnify the impact of any set of events. This means that the spin they put on a story, will be based on what will attract the most attention. This is not necessarily even a factor of purposeful distortion on the part of the media. When many various slants on a set of facts are offered, the one that attracts the most attention, quite naturally, gets repeated often.

In the case of Ted Williams, suggestions were made along the lines that he was only being frozen to preserve his famous DNA so that it could later be sold. His son, who had arranged the suspension with the thought that he might be saving his father's life, was painted as a villain who was taking advantage of his father. It was as if Ted Williams, as a "national treasure," somehow belonged to all of America, more than he belonged to his family, or even to himself. No media source bothered to research cryonics organizations, and find out that preserving DNA for later retrieval was not the purpose of such a suspension.

Because the media slant will always be towards the most interesting, any media piece on cryonics that is initiated by the news that a celebrity has signed up, is bound to be slanted towards the idea that it is some sort of scam, and that the poor beloved celebrity has been duped. The one exception to this rule would be if the celebrity in question was famous for being universally hated. If a "bad" celebrity was known to be undergoing cryonic suspension, then the exciting slant would be towards the idea that this bad person was going to live forever. In such a case, the idea that cryonics might be something that actually worked would be the far more interesting slant for the media to portray.

It is only a matter of time before some death row inmate, guilty of horrible crimes, asks to be cryonically suspended after the state executes him. When this happens, the TV news will suddenly start assuming that cryonics is a sure thing. We will see them asking some poor member of a victim's family "How does it feel to know that your loved one is gone, but that this killer is going to live forever?"

When this happens, we will see both a surge in people signing up for cryonic suspension and also the start of efforts to make cryonics illegal.

There is something odd about the way people think. They are often more willing to believe that something is possible when it means that something bad will be the result; that someone else is getting away with something. If you present it as good news, saying "A scientific path to immortality has been discovered!" people will not believe it. But if you tell them that some villain is escaping a death sentence, they will inexplicably find the possibility much more credible. People just seem more willing to believe bad news than good.

Whether it is professional baseball players or convicted felons, the media exposure of cryonics is bound to increase, and more and more people will find themselves considering the Pros and Cons.

7.1.8 Calculating Cryonics

So what are the Pros and Cons in the cryonics equation? What are the costs? What are the Odds? How do you decide if it is worth it for you to sign up to be frozen someday?

Robert Ettinger, often called the "Father of Cryonics," had this to say:

> *Clearly, the freezer is more attractive than the grave, even if one has doubts about the future capabilities of science. With bad luck, the frozen people will simply remain dead, as they would have in the grave. But with good luck, the manifest destiny of science will be realized, and the resuscitees will drink the wine of centuries unborn. The likely prize is so enormous that even slender odds would be worth embracing.*

This sounds something like a poetic version of Pascal's famous Wager.

7.1.8.1 Pascal's Wager

Famous mathematician Blaise Pascal said that since doing the things required by the church to get into heaven took up only finite resources, but the reward of eternal paradise was infinite, that it made sense to "bet on GOD" from a risk-reward point of view. However, Pascal's assumptions are faulty. The main flaw in his logic is that there exist more than just one religion, and therefore, multiple ways to "bet on GOD." In fact, there is no guarantee that any existing religion has it right. In theory, the choices of behavior are infinite, thus the cost of doing all the things that might work is also infinite.

It gets worse – some of the things that religions ask you to do may contradict each other. Behavior that one religion says is required for infinite reward may, according to another religion, bring you infinite suffering. Pascal's conclusion should therefore have been, with no other reason to believe in a particular path to GOD, that any such cost would be too much.

7.1.8.2 The Cryonics Equation

Below is a commonly presented logic diagram for the choice of cryonics.

	Cryonics Succeeds	Cryonics Fails
With Cryonics	You Live	You Die
Without Cryonics	You Die	You Die

It looks pretty simple when presented this way, but the real question is "Is the chance of living worth the cost of betting on Cryonics?" Unlike Pascal's Wager, the reward being offered isn't some infinite reward – it is just more life.

Some people's gut reaction is that any amount of life has infinite value, but that just isn't true. You make economic decisions every day in which you place a finite value on your life. When you chose to get in the car and drive to the movies, rather than staying home and watching TV, you are calculating that the additional value you receive from watching a movie is worth the additional chance of dying on the road. Staying home is definitely safer, so if you really placed infinite value on your life, you would never choose a ride to movies over watching TV at home.

On the other hand, there is probably no amount of money that someone could give you in exchange for a 100% chance that you would then immediately die. This is because the scenario where you are dead and rich offers you no additional value. What's the difference between dead and rich, and dead and poor?

So when your life is thrown into the pot, some weird things do happen to the value equations of the bet. This is simply because you need to be alive to appreciate any value gained, and death may be legitimately regarded as a loss of all value you have. Even if you value the idea of what may happen after you die, based on your actions today, money is still something that you can only appreciate while you are alive.

Ultimately, the amount you should be willing to pay depends on how much your life is currently worth to you and how likely you think it is that cryonics will work.

7.1.9 What Does It Cost?

The current (2006) cheapest price for cryonics storage is about US$30,000. This buys you the cryonics storage procedure, plus indefinite storage time until revival becomes possible. The most expensive option on the market, which includes additional bedside support team, possibly faster emergency response, and the satisfaction of knowing that you are spending the most you can spend, runs about US$160,000. This may sound like a lot of money, but when paid for by an insurance policy, it does not come to very much money per month.

Cryonics is particularly cheap when you consider that many people are willing to regularly tithe 10% of their incomes to the competing afterlife provider of their choice.

Using an online Life insurance calculator, we find that a 25 year old female in the United States can cover the minimum cryonics option with $30,000 of life insurance for a price of $22.80 a month. A 25 year old female is not the average case. The cost to buy such insurance increases if you are male, and if you are older. Fortunately, the amount of money you make also statistically increases if you are male, or older. Cryonics looks to be very affordable, unless you wait until the last minute to make arrangements.

If you have a lot of money, think about this: Maybe you can take it with you after all, despite what everyone says. Some of those who are signed up for cryonics have worked out legal trust arrangements to hold onto their assets while they are inconveniently dead.

If you don't have a lot of money now, who knows – maybe that thing about putting a penny in a bank account for a few hundred years earning compound interest really does work, and you could wake up super rich.

We doubt the "untold riches when you wake up" theory, but the prospect that one might wake up at all intrigues us.

7.1.10 Legislating the Afterlife

The cost of cryonics is currently very affordable to the average first world citizen – and would seem to be well worth it if you believe there is even a small chance that it might actually work.

Of course cryonics is a relatively new idea, and the government hasn't had a chance to really start regulating it yet. When this happens, there will be rules and regulations, licensing, and maybe even prohibition. Government regulations already play havoc with the costs of medical care, prescription drugs, and all sorts of other things that people sometimes need to stay alive longer. If they can literally "tax us to death," why should we not expect them to also be able to keep us from having an afterlife?

Actually, one jurisdiction in Canada has already made cryonics illegal. In 2004, British Columbia passed a bill which contained the following section:

> *A person must not offer for sale, or sell, an arrangement for the preservation or storage of human remains that is based on:*
>
> *(a) cryonics,*
>
> *(b) irradiation, or*
>
> *(c) any other means of preservation or storage, by whatever name called,*
>
> *and that is offered, or sold, on the expectation of the resuscitation of human remains at a future time.*

Earlier we predicted that religions would work to have cryonics outlawed. However, the above law seems more geared towards preventing what the writer of the law must have been too close-minded to see as anything but fraud. Although perhaps that law writer's religious beliefs did play a role in the thinking (or lack there of) involved.

But we are not going to declare that "we called it" yet, as there is reason to believe that the law was not instigated by religious beliefs.

Any lawyer who gave this law a close read would have to agree that it not only outlaws cryonics, but also outlaws the burial ceremonies performed by most churches.

If a Catholic Church (or any other religious institution) charges money to have the body of a believer buried on "holy ground" with the idea that this will somehow aid in that persons resurrection and journey into the afterlife, they have certainly violated this law in terms of its prohibition against *"any other means of preservation or storage, by whatever name called ... that is offered, or sold, on the expectation of the resuscitation of human remains at a future time."*

We wonder what the British Columbia police will do when people start filing complaints against churches for violating this law.

The reason that such "future science" is objectionable to religion is that it treads in some of the same territory claimed by religious beliefs. This also makes it quite difficult to enact impartial sounding legislation against scary new ideas that does not also criminalize more popular (but maybe just as scary) ideas. How can government fairly suggest to any group of people that their ideas, about what should be done with their bodies after death in order to obtain an afterlife, are less valid than those of anyone else?

From a legal standpoint, it is hard to distinguish between different beliefs about an afterlife. Some people believe that when they die they will later rise up from the dead and ascend to the heavens to sit on a semi-solid cloud where they will play the harp and be at peace for all eternity. Some may think that when they die they will go to the center of the Earth to experience eternal torment in liquid fire. If we happen to believe that when we die we will go to the suburbs of Detroit Michigan, to be suspended in liquid air until we can later rise from the dead, does that really sound very different?

Can the law actually discriminate against our belief just because it is based more on science than superstition? Should the government really be allowed to pass laws making some groups' burial practices criminal, solely on the basis that the majority of society holds different beliefs about the possibility of an afterlife?

Of course, whether they "should" or not, they probably will. But if we are lucky, even better technology will come along before we die, and we will get a shot at living forever, without ever being put in a vulnerable state of being suspended and subject to the will of other people while we can not defend ourselves.

7.2 Nanotechnology

Of course, the big question in cryonics is, "How can we reverse the suspension process?"

Current suspension technologies are almost certainly holding people out of the hands of Information Theoretic Death, but this is only because the Information Theoretic Reaper is a very picky fellow indeed.

Current cryonics patients are not in stasis via some time stopping technology, they are in molecular stasis because they are being stored in a place where there is not enough heat for their molecules to move around. At that temperature, no change of state is occurring, but the process of getting them there did not leave them undamaged. In the early suspensions, previous to vitrification techniques, a lot of ice crystals formed and a great deal of tissue fracturing occurred. Although such damage is of a predictable nature and thus reversible by the standards of Information Theoretic Death, no technology currently exists that can reverse it.

However, technology that might do the job has at least been envisioned. Not long after the idea of suspended animation through cryonics, the concept of fantastic new technologies through miniaturization of machinery started to gain mind-share. Cryonicists now envision tiny little machines on the molecular scale that could repair tissue at the cellular level.

These tiny little robots could be built to cure any medical problem, including such extremes as reviving someone who had been frozen solid. But the applications for such technology are not just medical. Every field of human endeavor could probably make use of a technology that operates on a scale too small for human beings to be aware of, and thus would seem indistinguishable from magic.

7.2.1 From Micro to Nano

In 1959, the famous physicist Richard Feynman gave a talk entitled "There is Plenty of Room at the Bottom," in which he discussed the possibility of information storage and the creation of machines on a scale smaller than had previously been commonly thought possible. He pointed out that we were a long, long way from the theoretical limits of miniaturization of technology.

Proof of his ideas about the shrinking of machines has been demonstrated by ongoing progress in the field of computers. This lead to Gordon E. Moore's 1965 observation that transistor based technology was progressing exponentially, with the number of transistors available for fixed cost, doubling every two years. This has become known as Moore's law, as information technology has continued to keep an exponential pace ever since. (See graph.)

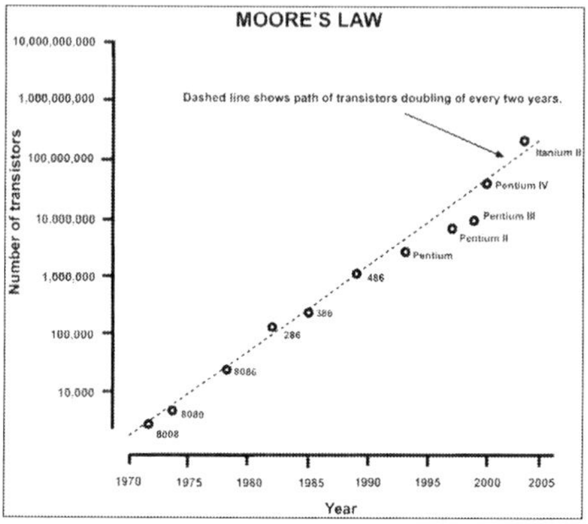

Feynman's claim that machines with actual moving parts could also be continually made smaller and smaller, with the theoretical limits being far ahead of us, has also born some fruit. Although the ideas for such tiny machines have mostly been theoretical speculation, once it is seen that something worthwhile *can* be done, it is usually only a matter of time until it *is* done. Feynman said:

> *What would be the utility of such machines? Who knows? Of course, a small automobile would only be useful for the mites to drive around in...*

Just a few decades later machinery is being created with gears so small that they are perhaps the right size to be used in such a tiny car for mites. Here are a couple of pictures zooming in with a microscope on a mite who is inspecting just such an array of tiny gears:

Courtesy Sandia National Laboratories, SUMMiTTM Technologies, www.mems.sandia.gov.

The mite shown here is too small to be readily visible with the unaided eye. The magnification of these pictures is in the range of 100 to 500 times. However, these microscopic machines represent just the start of what is possible in making use of the plenitude of room that Feynman suggested was available at the bottom.

Where the gears pictured here are measured in micrometers (thousandths of a millimeter), such technology could theoretically be reduced to the scale of nanometers (millionths of a millimeter). It is possible to build machines on such a scale that the smallest parts, for example, a ball bearing in a tiny engine, might be composed of just a single molecule of just a few dozen atoms – perhaps even smaller.

In 2005, a single molecule shaped like a car, was designed and built by a group at Rice University led by Kevin F. Kelly and James Tour. This mono-molecular "car" has a chassis, axles, and wheels that actually turn as it moves over a surface. This is true technology on the scale of nanometers.

The "nano-car" is not only too small for mites to drive, but at a size of under 4 nanometers, even the smallest of viruses couldn't slip behind the wheel and take this baby for a spin. (That is if it actually had a steering wheel – or an engine. The prototype was apparently not equipped with all the options one might expect to find on display in the showroom).

The journey of reducing machines from the scale we are used to, down through the micro, to the nano has been demonstrated as not just theoretically possible. It has actually been done. But why should we care? What can we do with such tiny machines, beyond building cars so small that even mites with advanced circus clown training can't fit inside?

Nano-Car

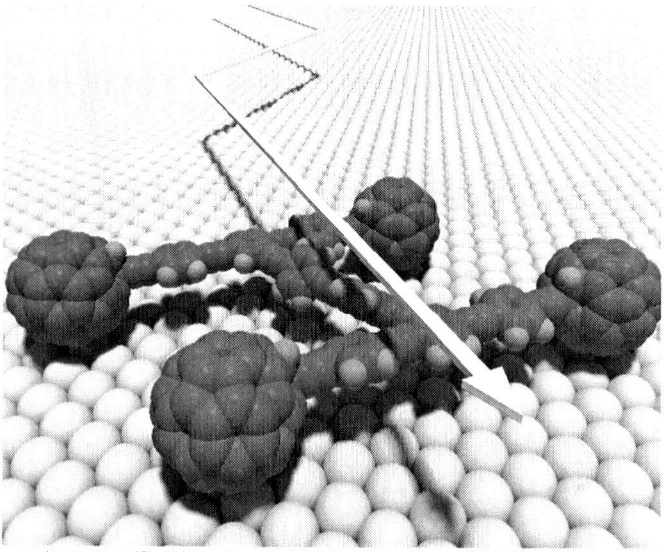

Image courtesy of Rice University Office of Media Relations and Information. Credit: Y. Shirai/Rice University

7.2.2 The Magic of Nanotechnology

In the early 1980s, Eric K. Drexler first coined the term "nanotechnology" to describe the application of machinery built on the nanometer scale. He also opened up a world of fantastic possibilities, with his description of these near magical technologies, in his book "Engines of Creation."

Such tiny machines can not do much to affect the world at our scale of observation, unless there are a whole bunch of them working at once. So it would seem necessary to create vast numbers for any real world application.

Feynman suggested the possibility of building many machines simultaneously with a multitude of tiny remotely-controlled "hands." Drexler, however, borrowed John von Neumann's ideas of machines that could recreate themselves. Drexler imagined tiny factories that could assemble any other nano-machine, and could even assemble themselves. He called such machines "universal assemblers."

In a world with such nanotechnology, you might build a house simply by piling a certain amount of raw materials on a lot, and dropping a nanotech house seed into the pile. When activated, the seed (actually a large number of nanotech assemblers) would start reproducing itself, as well as making specific nanomachines designed for moving the necessary materials to where they needed to be. Towards the end of the task, the general assemblers might start taking each other apart, so that when the house was finished, no remaining active nanomachines would remain.

It is even possible to envision a scenario where no raw materials need to be delivered, and the nanomachines find what they need in the soil and rock of the Earth below the house as they build it.

You may think that such a magic process as dropping a seed in the ground and growing a house might take a long time, after all, it can take a century to grow a large tree, but in theory this need not be the case. Bacteria can be considered to be naturally evolved nanomachines, and under the right circumstances, with a continued supply of food, and nothing to kill them, bacteria can double their numbers in under a half hour. If a nanotech seed were capable of this kind of growth rate, it could start out weighing only a few grams, and build a house weighing a hundred metric tons during the daylight hours of a single day.

7.2.3 New Bodies

The tiny size of nanomachines will allow them to operate at the same scale as our own cellular machinery. This makes them ideal for medical use. Surgical precision was once limited by the size of the scalpel and the doctor's hands. Fine surgery is already being controlled through magnification and tools that translate the larger motion of a surgeon to a much smaller scalpel. However, doing things like reconnecting severed nerves would take a single surgeon far too long, where millions of tiny surgical robots could do it quickly and safely.

Additionally, there is no reason not to integrate nanotechnology into our bodies. Such devices could wait inside our bodies unnoticed, ready to fight specific bacteria and viruses that might otherwise outwit our immune systems, or rebuild broken bones as soon as the happened, even replace damaged tissue temporarily until the body could catch up. Imagine if after an accident, your internal array of nano-surgeons could heal your broken bones, and patch your wounds within minutes. Imagine a world where a gunshot wound closed almost immediately and was never even close to being life threatening.

If they work better than our cells, why not just replace all of our cells with them? Why cling to an obsolete evolved organic platform at all? The machines could replace our cells one at a time so as to preserve our consciousness throughout the entire process. What would stop us from having new, better, indestructible bodies?

Depending on how infected you are with the idea-organism we call "Nature," thinking about the idea of replacing every cell in your body with tiny machines that do a better job either sounds perfectly reasonable, or it is really giving you the heebie-jeebies right now. And if you are hosting religious ideas about a "soul," you may also feel strongly that your soul couldn't live in a nanotech body.

But why not?

A soul is supposed to be a powerful magical otherworldly supernatural force. If it can live without any body, why not in a different kind of body?

Emotional reactions to ideas come from defensive idea-organisms, not rational thought.

7.2.4 What Color is Your Goo?

Drexler was also kind enough to invent possible disaster scenarios along with his ideas about this new technology, rather than wait for the environmentalists to come up with them on their own. The worse-case scenario is that out of control assemblers, capable of the kind of growth rates described above, envelop the entire Earth, turning mankind and all our works, into a gray goo.

Why a *gray* goo? No particular reason. Other more colorful scenarios have been suggested, although they are just as gooey. In the book "How to Mutate and Take Over the World" by R.U. Sirius and St. Jude, it is a *green goo* scenario. The world ends with an industrial accident at a nanotech bakery that turns the entire world into key lime pie filling.

Of course, every new technology seems to have a story about how it is going to destroy the world. This may be because we are all a little bit infected with a Distributed Identity of Nature. The idea of something man-made that so closely resembles a living organism in the way it can eat and grow is probably the most frightening thing in the world to an idea-organism with a core meme of "natural is good and artificial is bad."

Why should we be afraid of molecular level machines, when, in actuality that is precisely what our bodies are? We are already nanomachines constructed from carbon based chemicals. Every living thing on the planet can be viewed as a complex collection of nanomachines. No molecular machine that evolved naturally has ever been so effective at multiplying itself that it has managed to cover the entire Earth, so why should we be concerned that man made molecular machines could ever accidentally do so?

The fear of the artificial is especially strange when you understand that it is a war between the genetic and the memetic. The idea that "natural is better than artificial" is a meme, and memes are artificial. Therefore, fear of the artificial is a self hating meme.

There is definitely a strange war going on in people's minds between the memetic and the genetic. The same people that might express distress at the thought of us integrating advanced technology with our bodies are probably also squeamish about facing the reality of what our bodies are. Some people don't like the idea of evolution, because they don't want to think that we are related to animals, but we are made up of the same stuff that other animals are.

Many of life's realities seem to "gross people out" – the clothes we wear have sometimes been treated with urine, our food is grown in dung, tiny little insects too small for us to see crawl on our bodies all the time eating our dead skin. These truths are unpleasant because ideological constructs in our mind, concerning how reality "should be" are at odds with how reality really is. Ironically, many people have very artificial concept of what is natural.

Even the most primitive slime molds are collections of cells – just like we are. Our cells have just learned a few more tricks, like secreting strong calcium compounds in long sticks and acting together as different organs, including muscles to prop those sticks up and walk around on them. Just like every other animal, the code that creates our entire body is inside each and every one of these tiny little creatures. What we think of as a body is really just a shape that all those slimy little creatures, clinging together, happen to enjoy forming.

Those worried about being related to monkeys may dispute the theory of evolution, but they cannot dispute the fact that our bodies are made up of the same slimy little creatures as other animals. (snakes, snails, and puppy dog tails...) But they don't like to think about it, so they just stop thinking.

Inside we are all made up of the same slimy goo.

7.3 Augmented or Artificial?

Every four years, the nations of the world compete in the Olympic Games. The quest for each athlete is to be the best, and by doing so, contribute to the pride of their nation. Interestingly, the rules of the Olympic Games have had to be modified consistently over the years, in an effort to "keep them pure." That is to rule out the use of any foreign substances or other technology to enhance athletic performance.

This amounts to an attempt to ensure that only genetics play a part in who is the strongest and fastest, which seems very strange, as these games are not being conducted between racial groups, but between countries. A country is an ideological construct, not a biological one, and if one country's ideology produces better performance enhancing technology than another, shouldn't that strength be represented in these games as well?

Also, consider the Special Olympic Games that are often held for disabled people. There are regularly held foot races in which the contestants are double leg amputees. Since the 1980s, the development of prosthetic limbs has improved rapidly, and now the fastest man, with no legs, is knocking on the door of records set by two-legged runners. How can you tell a man that has come back so far, from such adversity, that he will never be allowed to compete with "whole" human beings, because he has an "unfair advantage" from having lost his legs?

But if you do allow a legless man to win an Olympic Gold Medal for sprinting, how long before athletes are having their legs removed on purpose, just to compete at the same level? On the other hand, why shouldn't they? If artificial legs are better, why would we not all want them?

7.3.1 Drugs

Our contests of athleticism currently outlaw the use of foreign performance enhancing substances. However, it is getting harder to decide what substances are foreign, as people find ways of using naturally occurring chemicals in the body, in greater doses. If existing hormones, like HGH (Human Growth Hormone) can be used to augment muscle growth, how does that really differ from eating a diet that contains all the precursors for the body to make more HGH?

And what if the body actually produces the drugs, through stimulation of the glands, or gene therapy to make the glands that produce adrenaline or other performance enhancing biochemicals more active? How is it different to select for winners from among those who have natural mutations for more active secretion of certain natural chemicals, and those who have undergone therapy to cause those same glands to become more active?

Academic competition is about brain competing against brain, rather than body competing against body. In the world of science, people work to discoverer new answers, not just to increase all of our potential knowledge, but to distinguish themselves personally. A great part of the quest for new knowledge is the learning of previous knowledge. Having an understanding of the science that has come before, and the proper library skills to research previously gained knowledge, have always been a part of being a great scientist. Should we ban drugs that help the learning process as being unfair to academic competition, or should we embrace them as something that can only accelerate the discovery of new knowledge?

7.3.2 Telephony

The library skills that we mentioned above were once a vital part of research. Now every mobile telephone has a connection to the Internet, and a search engine can quickly pull up the knowledge one is looking for on any topic. You would not expect contestants on jeopardy to be allowed to access the Internet, but connection to a network of combined human knowledge is becoming a part of our culture. If you were interviewing someone for a job, you would pick the candidate that can find answers the fastest, you would not care whether those answers came out of personal memory, or off the Internet, just that they were the best answers in the shortest time.

Soon, with the right technologies, the difference between accessing your own personal memory, and that of remote data stores, will be unnoticeable.

7.3.3 Virtual Reality

They say that the best teacher is experience. Artificial experience, if indistinguishable from the real thing, should be just as good. With electro-neural interfaces, it should be possible to experience anything you chose, at anytime.

This will be the best teaching tool ever, but it will also be the best drug ever. In fact, since it would allow you to feel any way at all, it is not just a drug, it is all drugs. Certainly there will be people that crawl into their fantasy worlds and never come out. With the lure of being able to have a perfect life in a perfect fantasy world, why would you ever want to return to a flawed reality?

There is no doubt that someone somewhere will try to outlaw virtual reality, even as it becomes the best tool for educating people that was ever invented.

7.3.4 Cybernetics

And with direct machine brain connections, we are back to artificial limbs, with artificial muscles. Instead of looking like well-designed machines, these limbs will look like well designed bodies, but able to work hundreds of times harder and stronger. When a person who chooses to become an armor-plated cyborg can crush an un-augmented person without even breaking a sweat, everyone will want to use this technology, or they will become second class citizens with second class bodies. Any DI that is horrified by this "unnatural" change in humanity will fight like crazy to have this technology outlawed.

7.3.5 Bush Robots

If you add nanotech to this picture, our natural bodies might disappear completely. In the book, "Mind Children," Hans Moravac described a future synthetic creature, called a "bush robot" that had smaller and smaller branches down to the level of nanometers. The evolved human body has limbs that can supply powerful lifting force, that branch into hands and fingers for finer control, but imagine if you had fingers on the ends of your fingers, and more fingers on the ends of those, and so on down to the smallest scale. You could manipulate small objects on any level, with your smallest fingers doing the work of nanotech assemblers.

Would such a creature be a robot, or could it be something that you could do with your own body?

The question of whether we might be creating robots with fantastic new capabilities that will one day rise up and replace us, or whether we are engineering ourselves to have those same capabilities, is a question of how much we are willing to embrace augmentation technology.

What is human and what is machine may soon just be a mater of personal opinion and choice.

7.3.6 Evolving Simulations

Computers can already do many things that, before their creation, could only be done by the human mind. Some people believe that the barrier to self awareness, to true personhood, can be crossed just by the process of increasing the complexity of these thinking machines – when the computers are complex enough, they might just "wake up" and be people just like we are. Others think that the creation of true thinking machines will require a greater understanding of our own brains. But some believe that such knowledge is unobtainable, that it is simply not possible for any system, including the human brain, to ever fully understand itself.

One way around the problem of having to actually figure out how a mind works before you can build one, is to put a brain together the same way that nature did. If you could set up an experiment where a simulated "creature" could interact with its environment and reproduce with some random variance. If you tailored that environment towards rewards for displaying increased intelligence, then you would theoretically, eventually produce an intelligent creature.

You do not have to know how intelligence works, just be able to know it when you see it.

7.3.7 Turing Tests

The term "Turing test" refers to the interaction with a system, in order to ascertain its level of intelligence. The idea comes from Alan Turing, a famous British mathematician and early computer scientist, who proposed that the only way we know other people are intelligent is that they convince us that they are by their words and actions. He suggested that computers might someday be intelligent, but the only way to know if they were or not, was to communicate with both computers and people, in such a way that you could not tell which were which (perhaps through written messages). When you could no longer pick out the people from the machines, he said, the machines would have to be considered to be as smart as the people.

Interestingly, you can also use the concept of a Turing test to determine when people are acting as individuals, and when they are acting on behalf of a Distributed Identity. The next time you are on the phone with the representative of a government (or large corporation) trying to get something done, and they are in a position of having to follow some internal policy, ask yourself, "Does it seem like I am communicating with an intelligent being, or could this be a badly programmed machine?"

7.3.8 Brain Scans

Another way to create artificial intelligence might be simulating a human brain at the molecular level. If you could take a picture of a brain with a technology like MRI (Magnetic Resonance Imaging) but with much finer resolution than is currently available, you could then feed that data into a computer, and have it simulate the processes of the brain on a molecular level. This would create a functioning artificial brain, without any need to understand how the brain works; you would just be copying a known working model.

This is, of course, another pathway to avoid Information Theoretic Death. Like cryonics, where the information stored in the brain is preserved in a frozen brain, the information required to rebuild a brain is certainly preserved in a brain scan of enough resolution. Does it make any difference if the original brain is repaired, or if the brain is just rebuilt atom by atom? Each atom of a given type is the same, after all – it is the pattern that makes you who you are, not the individual building blocks. It is even said that over the course of a number of years, you replace every single atom in your brain with a new one anyway, as biological processes bring new materials in, and flush old materials out. If so, how can any individual atoms be more important than others, if they are in the same pattern?

Another interesting kind of immortality might exist through the technology of a brain scan. If a recording were made of your brain, and it was never turned back into you, but everyone on the net had access to all your information and processes, you would live on through all your ideas, but would not really be alive. Anyone could determine what you would have to say on any subject, even though you would not be there in any sense to actually say it. Existing as passive data, rather than as an active simulation, would be somewhat like "living on" through your works. Greater beings that came after you would have access to your knowledge and mental processes, much the way you now can read the written works of authors that died before you were born.

> Anders Sandberg, a noted transhumanist, once said that he would rather evolve into a post human being that had a functioning copy of himself as he thought now, at its core, rather than just one that had a copy of himself in memory for access as needed. But of course that is just his perspective now, as a human; as a post human, he might find his current personality to just be annoying extra baggage.

7.3.9 Duplicates

Some people deny that a copy of your mind could ever actually be "you" in any real way. One thing they point to is the problem of duplicates. If two copies of you exist at the same time, they can't both be the real you, can they?

The simple answer to this problem is that, once created, they are certainly different individuals, but from your point of view now, looking forward, they are both you.

To understand this, consider that you think of you 10 years from now as still being you, even though that person may be made up of entirely different atoms. It is not the material that the future you is made of that matters, it is the fact that the pattern of your current consciousness, your memories of now, are preserved in that future version of yourself.

Looking forward to a time when you are duplicated, there is no way to decide which you is the "real" you. Both contain your mind and memories. Both are you. The fact that they consider themselves to be separate people at that point should be of no concern to your feelings about them now. It is the continuation of memory from now to then that preserves identity – and it preserves it in both copies equally.

Interestingly, if making copies of oneself becomes easy, then human beings as a unit will have become replicators. Those who are actually able to see themselves, not as individuals, but as part of a larger whole, will do better than those who cling to individuality. If one duplicate is willing to sacrifice his life for two copies, this is a good sacrifice. Those that can do this will survive better than those that can not. Since all copies will be the same, this will not be like the case of sacrificing yourself for your country – no individual information will be lost.

This will be especially true if duplicates can actually re-synch their memories, or are in constant telephonic mental communication. A world with such technology is bound to have larger collective creatures with more than one body. Individual human minds will then be able to be what collective idea-organisms have always aspired to – a single person with multiple bodies.

Here's a mind-bending thought: Technology that allowed multiple bodies to act with a single mind could set the stage for a most ironic showdown. A collective idea-organism based on the idea of individualism – one mind one body – could find itself at war with individuals who wanted the freedom to compete on a level previously reserved to Collectives by having multiple bodies at their disposal.

7.3.10 The Singularity

We might augment our own minds until they become upgradeable hardware that runs the software of our consciousness. Or we might create machines that have their own intelligence. Either way, once intelligence is running on upgradeable hardware, something very interesting can happen; intelligence can start working on the design of its own hardware.

Let's say you have transferred your mind to a bush robot. You can think faster than you did in your human mind, but not as fast as you would like to be able to think. So you go to work at designing a faster brain. As soon as you finish and implement that new design, you start again to work on an even faster design – but this time it takes a lot less time to finish Brain Mark IV because you are working with your smokingly fast Brain Mark III. And then Brain Mark V could be developed even faster, and so on.

It turns out that this sort of feedback of ever increasing development speed, that occurs once a mind is upgradeable, creates an exponential effect that goes to infinity in a finite period of time. You reach a point, in theory, where you can do an infinite amount of mental work, in a finite period of time. The time at which this occurs has become known as "the singularity" in science fiction and technical cultures. This is the equivalent of Kingdom Come for the believer in artificial intelligence – the end of the world, although not necessarily in a bad way. It is the point where artificially intelligent life vanishes into its own navel.

Why there has to be an end of the world scenario associated with any new technology, is an interesting question. It probably says more about the way people think than it does about any real end of the world possibilities. Then again, we have been listening for radio signals from the stars for quite a while now, without hearing evidence of another civilization like ours, so we either just happen to be the first in a large volume of space, intelligence like ours is very rare, or creatures like us just don't last very long in our current form.

In 1998, Robin Hanson wrote an essay entitled "The Great Filter – Are We Almost Past It?" in which he explores all the improbable events that have to come together to produce intelligent creatures like us, and contrasts it to the amount of empty space time we have observed without detecting evidence of creatures like ourselves. Can we calculate the probabilities concerning whether this filter, that prevents us from seeing many other intelligent species like us, is in the past or the future? Have we already cleared the big hurdle that a species such as ours must get past? Will we now go off and easily colonize the universe or is the biggest challenge still in our future? Are we unknowingly facing imminent destruction? This essay is online at hanson.gmu.edu/greatfilter.html

7.4 Life Extension

Myths of the Tree of Life and the Fountain of Youth have existed throughout human history. Young people do not like getting old, and old people wish they could recapture their youth. Some say they are happy with their allotted life span, but there can be no doubt that such legends play to wish fulfillment. Throughout the centuries, those who have had everything else, have always at the end wished they could trade it all for just a little more time.

Don't Lie Down

You say you're glad one day you'll die
though not tomorrow or today.
I say that's just a clever lie
you tell yourself so you can play.

For should you ever come to know
that soon might be your time to go.
You will work hard for a new lease
not just lay down to rest in peace.

And though you think it only fair
you leave your place to someone new
how would you feel to learn they knew
a way to stay but would not share?

-- Sean Hastings (May 2002)

7.4.1 Medical Science

The history of medical science has always been one of battling disease and death. While medical professionals may hesitate to say that the history of their profession has been a quest for the fountain of youth, or a search for immortality, that is certainly what it amounts to. The goal of medicine is to cure sickness and infirmity, and now that medical science has developed cures for most of the problems caused by external organisms such as parasites, bacteria, and viruses, it has begun, quite naturally, to examine naturally occurring failings of the human body.

Hereditary diseases are still considered to be diseases worth fighting. The fact that such weaknesses are encoded into your genes does not make them any less painful or urgent than health ailments that come from external causes. Problems caused by unwanted behaviors of our own bodies, such as multiple sclerosis, hemophilia, sickle cell anemia, Alzheimer's disease, cystic fibrosis, muscular dystrophy, lupus, and cancer, despite their genetic nature are all still thought of as terrible diseases to be battled by modern medicine.

It is only a matter of time before doctors everywhere start to look at the aging process itself as a hereditary disease that might just be curable.

In fact, age is already considered to be a disease when it happens faster than normal. Progeria is a hereditary disease that causes much faster than usual aging in human beings, causing an average lifespan to be approximately 1/6th of the normal human lifespan. This is considered to be a horribly tragic disease when it takes the life of sixteen-year olds who look 90 when they die. But because it is so normal for ninety-year olds to look 90 when they die, people don't seem to notice that it is really just as horrible a way to go.

There is no rational reason not to consider aging a hereditary disease. It is just a disease that we all happen to have. A disease that actually now takes more lives than any other. More people die from age and age related illnesses now than any other single cause. Just because we all have it, is no reason not to address the problem. Logically, the fact that it affects so many people should make the problem seem more urgent, rather than less. The only reason it does not seem urgent, is that the problem has existed for so long that it is the expected norm, and that collective idea-organisms always embrace the norm.

A disease is still a disease, even if everyone has it. If everyone on the planet suddenly contracted a new ailment that cut their lifespan by half, people wouldn't just say "Well, everyone has it, so I guess that's ok." They would be very upset. If cutting all of our normal life spans in half would be a very bad thing, doesn't it then make sense that the doubling of our normal lifespan would be a very good thing?

The majority of people don't yet seem to think so. But, some people have the good sense to see our limited lifespan as a problem worth solving.

7.4.2 SENS and Sensibility

When asked why many people do not see aging as a bad thing, Dr. Aubrey de Grey sometimes answers that they must all be in some sort of a "trance" or "hypnotized."

Dr. de Grey is one of the lead voices in a call for a "war on aging," and the originator of SENS (Strategies for Engineered Negligible Senescence), a plan for approaching the task of curing aging from an engineering standpoint.

He thinks that it is quite obvious that aging causes a great deal of human misery, and that anyone of a humanitarian mind would want to stop all that suffering. How it is that so many people seem to think, that all that pain and misery caused by aging could ever be a good thing, is quite beyond him.

> *I have bitten my tongue and given earnest, sympathetic answers here to the many concerns I encounter when the prospect of defeating aging is raised – but I don't pretend that it has been easy to do so. I make no secret, here or elsewhere, that I have a low opinion of the reasons people give for defending aging – and an even lower opinion of the fear that people seem to have of thinking about the topic even faintly rationally. I think that apologists for aging are in a 'pro-aging trance' – that they are victims of a mutually-maintained collective hypnosis on the topic, a flight from normal rationality that resembles nothing so much as the behavior of participants in a stage hypnotist show.*
>
> -- Aubrey de Grey (www.sens.org/concerns.htm)

When you think about this strange pro-aging/pro-death sentiment from the standpoint of evolved memes, the reason for this collective "trance" becomes a lot clearer. We have previously discussed the idea that collective idea-organisms of a religious nature specifically make use of our fear of death to propagate themselves. This makes it quite understandable why such religious ideas will likely fight any technology that threatens to remove, or even significantly reduce, human mortality. Secular Collectives have also evolved in an environment where humans age and die, so even when aging does not play directly into an idea-organism's replication strategy, it has certainly played a role in the shaping of every Higher Ideological Power.

For example, almost all Collectives have some sort of top down power structure, and part of the reason that the less brainwashed members of the lower levels tolerate orders from the higher is the idea that they might someday fill those higher positions. Aging leads to retirement or death of people in the higher slots, and allows advancement even is cases where advancement by merit has been made impossible. Eliminate aging, and the incentive structure for competent individuals at the lower levels of such a structure falls apart. This could easily kill any given Collective.

Consider such constructs as corporate pensions, and national social security. Increased longevity threatens the basis upon which these systems were founded. These systems evolved with an understanding that those drawing money, based on the obligations of the system to them, will someday cease to do so.

The reason why idea-organisms evolve to fear new technology is that new technology changes the capabilities of individual human beings. Complex idea-organisms are adapted to certain rules about what people can and can not easily do. In the specific case of aging, almost all Collectives will have adapted their systems to a finite human lifespan. Changes to that particular human limitation might bring about a new situation for which the existing Higher Powers are not properly adapted. They might not survive such a change.

Furthermore, even on the level of individual thoughts and actions, the intellectual concept of inevitable future death, cries out to be accepted. Death is something that our biology both instructs us to avoid at all costs, yet puts us in a position of making it inevitable. As a creature intellectually capable of seeing the end, but (at least in the past) not capable of avoiding it, you either have to find a way of rationalizing it or you will go crazy. Crazy is nonproductive and therefore non adaptive, so evolution soon makes sure that we find some way to not think about the problem.

We would not be surprised if some sort of biological mechanism exists that causes any ongoing fear, with no immediate escape, to eventually fade into acceptance. This would solve the mind body conflict that an understanding of aging and death creates.

In fact, the steps of coming to terms with death have been well documented by many psychologists. When people find they are dying of an illness, they go through 5 stages: Denial, Anger, Bargaining, Depression, and Acceptance. Please note the similarities with five stages that people go through in the course of their lives, concerning their personal relationship to their own mortality:

- **Adolescence – Denial.** Kids seem to believe they are immortal.

- **Young Adulthood – Anger.** Angry young men (and women) compete to find happiness, meaning, and prosperity in a life they realize is finite.
- **Middle Age – Bargaining**. Mature people develop life goals. They want to get certain things done before they die – make sure their kids are taken care of financially, accomplish things of lasting importance, etc.
- **Late Middle Age – Depression.** Mid-life crisis. People transitioning into old age often become depressed and question the direction of their lives.
- **Old Age – Acceptance.** Retirement-aged people often return to previously forgotten religious beliefs to allow them to accept death.

The disease of aging takes decades, rather than months, to kill. So this process also spans decades, but the reaction to death by aging is really no different than the reaction to being struck down at any age by terminal cancer.

It would be interesting to do a psychological study on people who have come to an acceptance of a terminal diagnosis, to see if they are as resistant to the idea of a new possible cure as some people are resistant to the idea that aging might be cured in their lifetimes. (Psychologists seem to like tricking healthy people in the name of science; maybe they would be ok with lying to dying people too...)

The reason we are programmed this way is that when you really can't do anything about a problem, it's better to not think about it than to let it cause you ongoing distress. It is more productive to ignore the unsolvable problem than to waste effort on something that is, in fact, unsolvable. However, the fact that at the gut level people still badly want a solution makes this dilemma a great hook for idea-organisms to infect people.

Recently medical technology has gotten a lot better and we understand the aging process in ways that we did not just a few decades ago. Perhaps we have reached a point where there is a more sensible approach to the problem of aging, than to just ignore it. Maybe we can finally do something about it.

There are certainly more people around now that believe that aging might be a curable disease. People who were young enough to have seen the possibilities of new medical technology before succumbing to the acceptance process outlined above - people who never really picked up any collective Ideas, because of their tendency to analyze ideas for their useful content.

Photo courtesy of the Methuselah Foundation. - Credit Kevin Perrott

We spoke earlier about how such people may not have good social skills, lacking the ability to blend into groups so well, but they also make all the greatest scientific leaps because their minds are free from the Collective. Consider this picture of Dr. Aubrey de Grey:

Dr. de Grey was born in 1963, so he is young enough to be of a generation that would not be surprised by any new scientific miracle. His improbably long beard, and highly questionable fashion sense (at least based on the one picture we have of him) indicate that he is not swayed by collective ideas. He is not afraid to say "aging is a disease – let's cure it!" even though this is not yet a popular position to take among his scientific colleagues.

So some other scientists might think he is a little crazy,

and he may even look the part, but his approach to the fight against aging is really quite sensible.

7.4.3 The SENS Approach

The idea behind the SENS approach is to consider the task of combating aging as if it were an engineering project, rather than an exercise in pure scientific inquiry. The reasoning behind this approach is that medical practices are a technology, an application of science, rather than a science itself, and technology can often run ahead of science in its usefulness.

For example, the Wright Brothers didn't have to understand the physics of a wing (something that is still argued about to this day), or the mathematics of thrust and lift, in order to build a working airplane. They just had to find the combination of things that worked to achieve their goal. Throughout history, a lot of medical technology has been developed this way. For example: Willow bark was known to provide pain relief, long before the mechanism by which acetylsalicylic acid affects the human nervous system's pain signals was fully understood.

Dr. de Grey is not just suggesting trying random drugs to see if any of them reverse aging. He is using the mental tools of an engineer to approach the problem; identifying the best place to act on the problem, breaking the overall problem down into discreet parts, and exploring reasonable pathways for research into the proper technology for solving each part of the overall problem individually. This has led him to a qualitatively different way of approaching the science of aging inhibition than any used by other medical research professionals.

7.4.3.1 Different From Old Approaches

The medical field of aging research was previously divided into two disciplines, Gerontology and Geriatrics. Gerontology is a study of the causes of aging, while Geriatrics is the study of the diseases that arises from aging. The focus of each field confines their thinking on the problem to separate, non-overlapping, areas of aging research.

Dr. de Grey's insight, in his initial survey of the best place to work on the overall problem of aging, was to realize that given two non-overlapping fields of research there must exist a middle ground not covered by either.

Reasoning as an engineer, Dr. de Grey thought out the problem this way:

1. Metabolic functions cause damage.
2. The damage builds up.
3. This build up causes pathology (disease).

So Gerontology is the science working on the problem posed in #1 above, trying to prevent the highly complex workings of the metabolism from causing damage to the body. And Geriatrics is working on the problem posed in sentence #3, trying to prevent this damage from causing disease. But no scientific effort had yet been made to look at aging as an engineering problem by trying to repair the existing damage – to reverse the effects mentioned in sentence #2.

He diagrams the fight against aging this way:

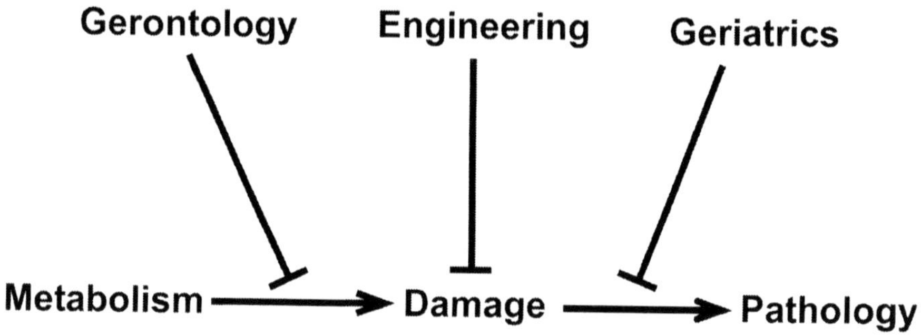

It turns out that acting to reverse the damage caused by aging may be easier than the other two approaches.

Gerontology is difficult because the metabolism is very complex. While it is a very worthy field of study, the results of gerontological science in combating aging are likely to be slow in coming and hard to implement, as they would require changes to existing metabolic processes. Also, because many different metabolic issues may contribute to the accumulation of metabolic damage, it is difficult to isolate any one place to start.

Geriatrics is just as difficult because there are so many different pathologies that can arise from metabolic damage. Curing them all may be ultimately impossible. It too is a very worthy field, in that it works to alleviate the suffering of people already advanced in the disease of aging, but it can never hope to halt aging, only to combat specific symptoms.

However, the Engineering approach is one of doing repair work on a system to keep it functional – reversing damage, rather than trying to prevent it completely or waiting to tackle the many problems that it can lead to. Dr. de Grey writes:

> *The engineering (SENS) strategy is not to interfere with metabolism per se, but to repair or obviate the accumulating damage and thereby indefinitely postpone the age at which it reaches pathogenic levels. This is practical because it avoids both of the problems with the other approaches: it* ***sidesteps our ignorance of metabolism*** *(because it does not attempt to interfere with metabolic processes and their production of side-effects) but also it* ***pre-empts the chaos of pathology*** *(because it repairs the precursors of pathology, rather than addressing the pathology head-on).*

It turns out that where the causes of metabolic damage are not fully known or not well understood, and the diseases that such damage can cause are incredibly numerous, the actual types of metabolic damage that build up over time, are both finite and fairly well understood.

7.4.3.2 Seven Deadly Sins

In creating the SENS plan, Dr. de Grey sought to quantify all the possible types of metabolic damage that could lead to age related disease. He found that there were only seven categories of metabolic damage:

- Cell loss, atrophy (Cells not being replaced as they die)

- Mutations of cell DNA (Cancer and other mutated cells)
- Mutations of mitochondria (a separate part of the cell with its own DNA)
- Unwanted Cells (fat, bad cartilage, bad immune system cells, etc)
- Extracellular protein damage (hardening of arteries, and the like)
- Extracellular junk (plaques and other build up of bad materials)
- Intracellular junk (cells that divide slowly can fill with junk and fail)

All known geriatric disease is a product of one or more of these types of metabolic damage. These seven types of damage make up the total known causes of aging and no additional factors for age related diseases have been discovered in the past 25 years of geriatric research, indicating that this is quite probably the whole list.

Dr. de Grey believes that good theoretical techniques exist for repairing or neutralizing the effects of each of these types of damage. With the right research initiatives, real world therapies for dealing with each of these causes of metabolic damage might be implemented in fairly short order. Given funding for research in the areas he describes, we can have a cure for aging within decades. Not just in some future world of science fiction, but soon enough for the majority of the people currently alive to see the first real treatments for the effects of aging.

The biggest problem right now seems to be the aversion that people generally feel, when asked to think about this issue. This causes people to either dismiss the idea without thought, or even to actively oppose it. This makes funding for such research scarce. To combat this problem, Dr. de Grey came up with the idea of a prize for the keepers of the longest living mouse on the planet.

7.4.3.3 The Methuselah Mouse

The Methuselah foundation began raising donations in 2003 for the Methuselah Mouse Prize, a way to bring attention and funding to SENS research. There are two categories, one for the longest living mouse by any method and one for the longest living mouse with treatments started at middle age. The later prize is intended to encourage research in the direction of a SENS type engineering solution to the longevity problem.

There are several reasons for such a prize: Firstly, prizes such as this have been known to attract funding to research greatly in excess of the amount of the prize. This is because the prestige and publicity of winning such a prize is greater than a scientific breakthrough for which no prize is being given. Perhaps more importantly, however, the ongoing nature of this prize will, by publicizing an older and older mouse every year, continuously draw attention to longevity research and infect people with the idea that it might be possible to achieve the same sort of life extension effects in human beings.

Because a mouse is both a normally short lived creature and a cute fuzzy mammal that people seem to be able to identify with, when mice receiving SENS treatments can be shown to living many times the lifespan of mice without treatments, people will not be able to help themselves from making comparisons to human beings. They will think about how long they might live once such treatments were available to people.

While clinical trials with longer lived animals would take a much longer time to show results, the effects of successful treatments on mice will be obvious quickly and visible to the public immediately, bringing in further funding for such research. Hopefully, when people start to see evidence that it could really work, this will not only increase funding but will also help dispel some of the thoughts that it might not be a good thing to do, since such thoughts may well just be defensive reactions to something unpleasant that people think of as inevitable.

As of the time of writing this (December 2006), the oldest mouse to date, with a single type of gene therapy, lived to be about 66% longer than the average laboratory mouse of the same type. This is slightly longer than results that have been achieved previously with calorie restriction.

To read more on the topic, visit www.mprize.org

7.4.4 The CRON Diet

Calorie restriction is an idea championed by the late Dr. Roy Walford, as a lead researcher of Gerontology at the UCLA School of Medicine. CRON is an acronym for Calorie Restriction with Optimal Nutrition. It is a diet based on Walford's findings that almost every type of animal on the planet has a low calorie persistence mode built into their genes.

When times are good, and food is readily available, animals live in a normal mode of reproduction and exhibit a normal life span. However, when less food is available for a significant amount of time, most animals experience a shift in metabolism. The animal's reproductive systems are inhibited and their metabolisms run at a somewhat slower speed, allowing the animal to live longer. In the case of some types of animals that have evolved in environments that regularly experience such periods of famine, this can be a much longer life span.

Walford showed that this effect translates to mammals and quite probably to human beings. He claimed that the right low calorie diet, specifically designed to still provide the correct essential nutrients, could cause a human being to experience a degree of lengthening of their natural life span.

His research predicts that a man, who might otherwise naturally live to be 80 with no other intervention, could start a program of 25% calorie restriction with optimal nutrition, and expect a 10% increase in lifespan to age 88.

Compared to the fantastic technologies we have been talking about – some of which might lead to immortality – this may seem somewhat mundane. However, those technologies don't exist yet, and this one does. Extending your lifespan through clean living and eating right is a very important thing to do, for one very important reason.

7.4.5 Every Year Counts More than the Last

At the current moment in history, the capabilities of the human race seem to be expanding at an exponential rate. Maybe they have actually been doing so since the invention of language, but the way an exponential curve grows, it can seem to be rising slowly for a long time before it really starts to take off. There is every indication that we are now living in that period of time where it really starts to take off. Technology is advancing faster than ever before.

Even if the capabilities of the human race were remaining fairly constant, there would be some small chance every year of a scientific breakthrough that could stop you from moving ever closer to the grave.

So let's say you are 40, and with your current life style you will live approximately another 40 years to die around the age 80. If you live 8 years longer through proper eating, then you would increase your odds of never having to die of old age by 20%, with 8 more years in which an "immortality drug" could be invented.

However, if the capabilities of the human race are rising exponentially, the chance of such a discovery might be increasing by some factor ever year. (This seems pretty likely to be the case.) Let's suppose that the chance of someone discovering the "Fountain of Youth" is only going up by small fraction, say 10% every year. If that is true, by living the extra 8 years, you do not just increase your chance of surviving by 20%, but by over 200%.

Additionally, consider the idea that the results of longevity research are likely to be available in incremental jumps of technology. An admittedly overly simplistic way to look at this might be as follows:

Suppose that every 10 years SENS researchers come up with a new treatment that is capable of reducing your age better than the last treatment. Now imagine that the first treatment can only take 1 year off your age and each new treatment is 1 year better than the previous technology. So if you start at age 40, in ten years when the first treatment is invented, you can have your biological age reduced to 49, ten years later you will be biologically 57 while chronologically you are 60, and so on.

The progression goes as follows, with the first number being your actual chronological age in years, and the second number (in parenthesis) being your biological age helped by SENS treatments. 40(40), 50(49), 60(57), 70(64), 80(70), 90(75), 100(79), 110(82)!

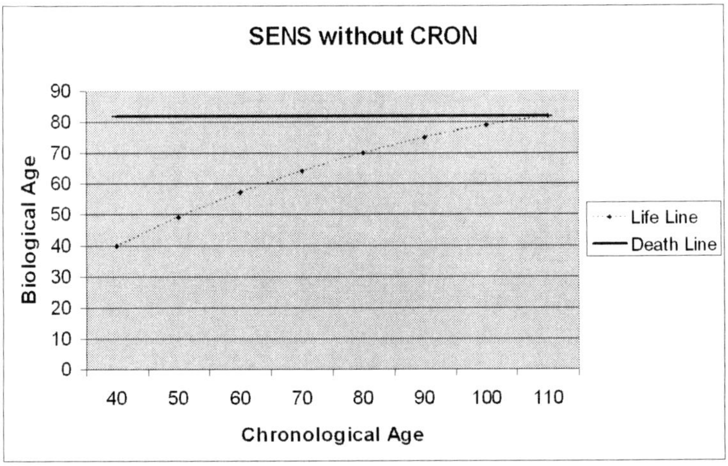

Oops! We decided that you were only going to live to be biologically about 80, so you dropped dead between chronological age 100 and 110, but you did live 20-30 years longer than you would have without new medical technology. Where a natural lifespan, unassisted by medical technology, would have been a straight line on the graph above, your SENS assisted lifespan curves away from the "Death Line." Unfortunately, in this case, it does not curve fast enough to escape the "inevitable."

However, if you had just managed to live a little bit healthier life style, perhaps by using Walford's calorie restriction techniques, you could have pushed that "Death Line" up a few years. If you pushed it far enough, the new medical technology might have gotten to the point where you actually started to age backwards! Such a life span progression might look like this:

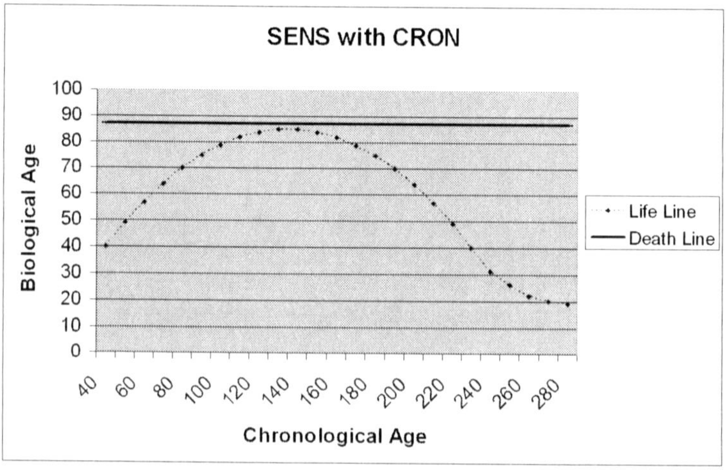

We can't say definitely that calorie restriction will mean the difference between dying at 110 years old despite all the best new medical technology available, or celebrating your 300th birthday in the body of a 19 year old. However, you can see how the few more years of life that a healthy life style could give you, might really make a big difference in your lifespan as new medical technologies are developed.

Because medical technology is improving, we are now living in a time where a healthy lifestyle has a bigger payoff than ever before in history. Where healthy living may once have meant the difference between dying at age 50 or age 60, today it might be the difference between dying at 60 or 120. Or maybe even the difference between dying and not ever dying!

Your chance at immortality all depends on how fast scientific progress is allowed to happen, and how long you can stay healthy enough to see the fruits of new research.

Think about it. How does giving up your biggest vice, be it smoking, unprotected sex with strangers, or French Fries, weigh in against the chance for immortality?

(Mmmmmmmmm French Fries... maybe we'll just have to take a chance on that cryonics thing working...)

7.5 Where is My Flying Car?

In this book we have been predicting some pretty remarkable near future technology. It is not uncommon, when you are predicting future technological miracles, to have someone ask the question "So then where is my flying car?" This is because flying cars were one of the items predicted frequently by futurists in the 1950s and 1960s.

The path of technological progress is uncertain, and rarely correctly predicted. Predictions of specific technologies to come are rarely correct. But dismissals of technology as being impossible (or many lifetimes away) are likewise rarely correct.

In 1903, the New York Times ran an article about the prospect of heavier than air flying machines that predicted it would be over 1000 years before such a thing was possible. On the exact same day that this prediction appeared in print, Orville Wright was noting in his journal that the Wright brothers had just begun the assembly of such an aircraft.

Clearly the Wright brothers were visionaries who defied the popular opinion, and would not let anyone tell them what was impossible. However, just a few years later, Orville Wright is quoted as saying "No such flying machine will ever fly from New York to Paris." This shows that, when it comes to technological progress, even the previous visionaries are often wrong about just how far and fast things will go.

Even those who shatter the previously believed barriers of science tend to erect new barriers in their own minds for someone else to come along and break later – and usually not very much later.

So, do we know for sure that immortality is right around the corner?

No, we do not.

But we do know that those who would claim that it is an impossibility, or that it will only be developed in the far far future, don't know what they are talking about either. There is good evidence that it can be done – therefore it most probably will be done. And probably quite a bit faster than most people would think possible.

How soon will it happen? Well, that may just be a factor of how soon we let it happen – whether we let collective idea-organisms get in the way, or we fight them for what we want.

So, where then *is* your flying car?

Let's take a look:

The most recent flying car project is the Moller Skycar in the United States. Here are the specifications listed for the Moller Skycar design:

- Passengers: 4
- Maximum speed: 380 MPH
- Cruise speed: 290 MPH
- Range: 900 Miles
- Size: Large automobile

- Best mileage: 25 MPG
- Useful payload: 900 lbs
- Can hover with one engine failed
- Can use automotive gasoline

The prototype Skycar was built, tested, and did indeed fly as of 2003; however, it was only ever tested while tethered to a crane for legal reasons. The reason for it not being allowed free flight is that the FAA has not approved it as a flying vehicle. Originally that was supposed to happen in 2005 – but instead, the SEC filed charges against Moller in 2005 for fraud in seeking investment for such a preposterous thing as a flying car.

Even though Moller could demonstrate that his prototype did indeed fly, he was still forced to settle, pay a fine, and also stop seeking investment until such time as the FAA approved the manufacture of flying cars. This is something they are unlikely to ever do.

Even if they did approve such a vehicle, they would, without a doubt, still require operators of such a vehicle to go through full pilot training. In fact, there have been several previous "flying cars" (cheap personal sized flying vehicles) but none have ever sold well because only licensed pilots have ever been allowed to fly them. And flying licenses are much harder to get than driving licenses.

The nature of government is to insist on the normal and prohibit the unusual. Until flying cars are normal and popular, they will be strongly regulated or forbidden. Until they stop being regulated or forbidden, they will not become normal and popular. This is the "Catch 22" by which governments regularly suppress new ideas and technologies.

So you see – the government is really the only thing preventing the flying car from taking off.

Flying cars are also particularly troublesome technology to certain idea-organisms that have a large influence on government. We have talked previously about how Geography is the Distributed Identity that currently most influences the government and how this causes the government to strongly secure borders and control travel. If the average citizen had a vehicle that could travel almost 400 miles per hour, controlling travel would be much harder. This means that personal flying cars are not likely to get any bureaucrat's stamp of approval.

(Just think of all the scary things people could do with all that individual freedom of movement! Eeeeek!)

With the current political climate in the United States, including the current bogeymen of terrorism and global warming, it is more likely that the government will be outlawing regular cars than it is that they will be approving flying ones.

We now have an answer to the classic question, "Where is my flying car?" It remains tethered firmly to the ground, pending government approval.

Will we let the collective idea-organisms do the same thing to our chances of becoming immortal? We hope not, but we are not overly optimistic.

For us to have a real shot at immortality, more people will have to wake up to the fact that slowing down the future may very well be the equivalent of killing everyone that is alive today. If they don't, it will happen without anyone ever noticing. Technological progress will be slowed by the collective idea-organisms. People will continue to die when they would normally be expected to die. It won't be considered a terrible loss of human life – just the "normal" and "natural" course of events.

People don't miss what they never knew they could have.

Or even if they do miss the unrealized potential of the future a little bit (as seems to be the case with the flying car) they eventually just assume they were wrong to ever think it was possible.

8
Final Thoughts

We have covered a lot of territory in this book – perhaps too much for a single volume. But the scope of collective idea-organisms is wide indeed, encompassing all of human life. So it seemed appropriate to follow these ideas everywhere they went.

In this last chapter, we want to relate a few final messages that you can take away from this book – messages that may help you live a longer, healthier, more empowered life, while helping those around you to do the same (or maybe they will just make you laugh... that is always good too.)

8.1 The Last Generation

If you believe that any of the technologies we have talked about are possible (and there certainly are some good reasons to think so), then it would seem that we can look forward to a very interesting future. It may be that we are destined to be a race of immortal beings with powers that we would previously have described as godlike, or maybe we will just create the machine creatures that will replace us, or even something in between as our technology becomes more and more a part of us. Alternatively, we may still be heading for some sort of end of the world scenario, in which we, and all of our works, will come to some cataclysmic end.

Every technology we have talked about holds immense promise for bringing us all a much better life, however, every technology also seems to have some end of the world scenario associated with it. This could be because any power can be used for good or ill, or it could just be the way we tend to think.

There have been many 'end of the world' scenarios before, and we have survived them all without even breathing very hard. Here is just a small sampling:

- A couple thousand years ago, there were people predicting that all civilization was doomed by the military practice of the time of salting the Earth of a defeated nation, so that no crops could be grown there again. The theory was that eventually all farm lands would be salted, through ongoing warfare, and then everyone would starve.
- The year 1000 AD brought the first millennium crisis, with people believing that Christ was sure to return and Armageddon would follow.
- In 1798, Thomas Malthus predicted overpopulation and mass starvation was just a decade away, and it has continued to be thought to be "just a decade away" by many others, ever since.
- In the 1970's with global temperatures having fallen steadily for 40 years, some concerned environmental scientists predicted the start of a new ice age, and told people that global cooling (yes *cooling*), caused by our modern industrial practices, was going to freeze us all – unless we shut down all the factories.
- In the 1980's we were going to be annihilated at any moment by a nuclear war between super powers, perhaps started by computer error or a computer hacker.
- There was another millennium scare in 2000, and this time, there was the millennium bug with computer date stamps not registering properly past Y2K – it was certain to threaten modern civilization with a massive global computer shutdown.

However we have not survived the entire list of imagined world ending disasters – not by a long shot. Just for fun, here are a few additional possible scenarios: (This is the short list. Many more available at www.exitmundi.nl):

- cosmic ray burst
- super volcanism
- drastic climate change
- another big bang
- deadly new mutant animal species

- super virus or bacteria
- black hole

Now here is an interesting thing about all the scenarios we just listed: they could all be natural occurring phenomena. At any time, we could all be killed by a completely natural disaster according to the plot line of any of these scenarios. However, most people do not seem worried about the world suddenly coming to an end through natural forces.

Now take a look at the list again, but this time put the words "New technology causes..." in front of each of them. Do the scenarios now seem more likely? To a lot of people, the prospect that science could cause some of these things seems far more likely, and/or worrisome, than the idea that they might occur without a human cause.

Now take a look at the list again, but this time, put the words "New technology saves us from..." in front of each. Does that make you feel better? Most people don't seem to think about the fact that we create science to shelter us, and to serve our needs, and that this should make a scenario where science saves us, more likely than one in where science accidentally destroys us.

The point we are trying to make is that there is no particular logical reason to believe that such a disaster will occur soon, let alone that we will somehow cause it with our science. However, the idea that this might be the case seems to be in a lot of people's heads. Most people seem to believe that the idea of science causing such a disaster is more likely than it occurring naturally. The only explanation we can find for this bias is that certain idea-organisms have reasons to want us to resist technological change.

These idea-organisms will continue to promote disaster scenarios to slow our technological progress. More such scenarios are always in the works. Some people point to prophecies that foretell our immediate doom, saying that the Mayan calendar predicts a "new cycle" in 2012 and that our technology will destroy us then. Some predict that the "real" millennium computer bug will happen in 2038 when the UNIX date time format runs out of space. Global warming has us burned, flooded, or frozen (pick the one that scares you most) sometime in your lifetime. And there is the nanotech earth eating goo scenario.

This all seems very scary doesn't it? But you can probably always find a prophecy to say whatever you are scared of, if you just look hard enough. For example:

If you believe in prophecy and are afraid of nanotechnology, have you ever considered this registered trademark of The Sherwin-Williams Company? Perhaps they should never be allowed to use nanotechnology in their paint factories...

If we were to allow this to happen, after being so clearly warned by this obviously prophetic logo, wouldn't our faces be red?

(We know, the joke isn't as funny in black and white, but color printing costs being what they are, what are you gonna do?)

It is always more interesting to say that the world is about to end than it is to say that the world will continue on and be just fine. It will always grab more attention. It will always produce more newspaper headlines and teasers spots for later news programs. ("There are three common household products that are probably in your home right now, and could suddenly cause the end of the world! Tune in at 11 O'clock to find out what they are.") Such fears are exactly the kind of thing that Collective Identities use to gain control. The message they send is that you will be safer if control of such dangerous matters is left to some Higher Power.

But why should we believe that the Collective can protect us from ourselves? We know that a free market works to give us the things we want, and that the Collective almost always does a worse job. When it comes to deciding what technologies will be pursued, the free market has a record of producing things that benefit individuals, while large collective entities, in competition with each other, have given us things like atomic weapons and genetically engineered diseases. There is no reason to believe that central control will not do more harm than good.

It may be true that as individuals get more powerful, a single very upset person might one day have the power to destroy everyone and everything. However, a Collective is more likely to create the technology that would make that possible, and keeping someone from using it, once it is created, will be a real trick. Also consider that the only people who ever seem to be willing to commit such acts of murder/suicide are those infected with the urgent cause of some Collective Identity.

If we allow collective Higher Powers to decide what technology is developed and what is suppressed, it is more likely to create harmful dangerous technology, and suppress good uses for advanced technology, such as giving us all longer healthier lives. This could actually make the difference between you living to see some incredible future world, or dying of old age just decades before things really get interesting.

If we can control the future in any way, reducing collectivism's drag on scientific progress is probably our best bet. As a person living in the early part of the 21st Century, you may well be part of a truly unique generation of human beings on the planet Earth. But which unique generation are you a part of?

You might be part of the last generation that has to die, or the first generation of immortals.

Whether you let the development of new technology be influenced by individual hopes and dreams, or controlled by some collective mindset, could well make the difference of whether or not you get to witness the future of mankind.

We can't tell you if the future will be hell on Earth, or heaven, or something more mundane in between. All we can say is that we think it would be a real bummer for you to die of old age just before it becomes clear what is actually going to become of humanity. And it would be especially annoying if the only reason you were not saved was because some group of people, hosting idea-organisms based on writings that are thousands of years old, denied your right to life by slowing the progress of medical technology.

Do your best to stick around. You don't want to miss the punch line, do you?

8.2 Rethinking Atheism and Anarchy

Atheism and Anarchy are not really ideologies, in that they are not complex ideological organisms. Each of these words represents opposition to a particular type of complex collective idea-organism. They both claim that the Idea-organism they are fighting is not necessary in order for people to lead good lives. There should be one word for both of them, but there is not, mostly because Church and State are not generally recognized as being the same sort of "multi-celled" ideological organism we have described in this book.

Atheism is the idea that a collective religious construct is not necessary.

Anarchy is the idea that a collective political construct is not necessary.

"Individualist" is perhaps the closest word we have to describing the autonomous human, standing apart from any collective mindset. A strong sense of individualism leads us to conclude that no Higher Power has any right to control our minds.

Because both atheism and anarchy stand opposed to a number of large, popular, complex ideas there is a tendency to try to cast these (much simpler) ideas into the same mold; to make them into larger ideological constructs than they are, and to attach other ideas to them; In short, to turn them from simple ideas into complex idea-organisms.

Because of this, those who believe in the ideas of atheism and/or anarchy are often actually convinced to end up doing strangely contradictory things – like having strong *faith* in their Atheism – or forming Anarchist *groups* to fight the powers that be.

The typical atheist or anarchist seems to only see half of the concept involved in denying Higher Powers. The funny thing is that they each see different halves of the big picture. This is actually kind of useful, because all they need to do is borrow from each other to get the whole picture.

8.2.1 Atheist

Richard Dawkins is a famous, modern, self-proclaimed atheist. He is also the person who came up with the concept of memetics, but this does not seem to have saved him from going down a typical atheist path. He sees the pain and suffering that hosting religious ideologies has caused in the world, and it angers and saddens him. He sees the "myth" of God as the root cause of this suffering, and decides to fight it. This is a brave choice to make. However, he allows the ideological construct of God to define his fight against it, and misses any real opportunity to reduce the bad effects that the idea of God causes in the world. Here's how:

Like most all Atheists, Dawkins obsesses over the issue of whether or not God exists. He applies his logic to the issue, and comes up with every reason you can imagine why you should not believe in any sort of Supreme Being who created the universe. He tells people that a belief that gives them great comfort is false. This, of course, causes these people mental pain, and makes them close their minds to Dawkins' arguments. The more widely he manages to spread his message, the more he sets himself up as a visible opponent to faith, and this increased opposition to faith may actually help to strengthen the hold of religion on people's minds. In the end, he may actually cause greater pain and suffering than if he had stood mute.

Since God, if he exists, does so outside our physical world, the question of existence will always be debatable. You can make your points about evolution all day, and all you are doing is winning an argument about where God has intervened in the world, not the argument of whether God actually exists or not. However, there is another class of argument, one that the average Anarchist embraces but the average Atheist seems to ignore – possibly because it is really a theological argument. That argument avoids the issue of God's existence and instead argues the idea that man need not worship anyone or anything. It runs something like this:

> Why should it be automatic that, just because a higher being created the universe, that you should worship him? OK, so you are told that GOD is bigger, more powerful, and more knowledgeable. But there are people right here on Earth that are bigger, stronger, faster, and smarter than you. You don't automatically worship them. You don't consider yourself to be obligated to do their bidding, and to serve their interests. Why should a god or GOD be any different?
>
> Why would anyone ever assume that GOD would want you to do everything he said? It's all supposed to be about free will right? GOD would want you to use that brain he put in your head. He would want you to make your own mistakes and learn from them. Maybe when you do bad things, it really does make the baby Jesus cry. But he is probably crying more about the people who always do what they are told without question. It is this blind obedience without thought that causes most of the horrible shit that happens in the world.
>
> If GOD exists, he doesn't want you to worship him. He is confident enough in his omnipotence not to need that kind of ego boost. He is certainly going to be pissed off if you don't think for yourself and choose to have someone else tell you what to do. He gave you that brain and he wants you to use it!
>
> And if you are one of those people that have a need to tell other people what they can and cannot do, stop it! Don't try to prevent other people from exercising the Free Will GOD gave them, he would want them to come to the right decisions because they figure it out for themselves, not because you prevented them from doing the things that you think are wrong. Find a better place to get your self-esteem from than controlling others.

Now it seems odd to say that this is an Atheist argument, since it starts by saying "OK, let's suppose there is a GOD" and this is a statement that the 'faithful' Atheist can not easily allow himself to make. However, no being, no matter how powerful, is really a god unless people worship him. If they do not then he is just another sentient creature who is bigger, tougher, smarter or whatever. Atheism means not having gods, it does not mean believing that there is no creature in (or outside of) the universe that is more powerful than any or all human beings.

If you have faith in yourself, in your right to choose your own actions, and make your own mistakes, then you can allow for the possibility of a more powerful being, maybe even a creator of the universe, and still be an atheist.

So we would suggest that atheists everywhere stop trying to prove there is no supreme being, and start asking people to look at the consequences of handing their choices over to other people's versions of what that supreme being wants us to do. Ask people to question why a supreme being would ever want them to do anything to increase his, her, or its glory. Any ideas that say that a supreme being needs a human to do anything for it are the product of either unscrupulous individuals taking advantage of faith, or an ideological organism with its own agenda.

8.2.2 Anarchist

Timothy McVeigh was a recent, infamous, self-proclaimed Anarchist. As you probably know, he was involved in the bombing of a United States Federal building in Oklahoma City, on April 19th, 1995, and was ultimately executed for his crimes on June 11th, 2001.

If someone tries to tell you why McVeigh did this, you may find yourself arguing that he was a monster or a madman, and being unable to even accept the possibility that there were "reasons" for what he did. However, the ideas in your head that prevent you from opening your mind to McVeigh's reasons... are the same types of ideas that made it possible for him to do something so monstrous.

McVeigh had his reasons. He saw the pain and suffering in the world caused by clashes between central authority and people with different ideas about how to live their lives. Specifically, he was aware of the events of August 1992 at Ruby Ridge where a family was killed by US Marshals and FBI agents on their own property. He also had in mind the events of April 19th, 1993, in Waco Texas, where, after a 51 day siege, 76 people were killed by ATF agents burning their homes.

These events bothered him greatly. He saw The State as the source of the death of innocent people, and he decided to fight it. This was a brave choice to make. However, he allowed the ideological construct of The State to define his fight against it, and missed any real opportunity to reduce the bad effects that the idea of The State causes in the world. Instead he brought more death to innocent individuals – these deaths by his own hand.

Like most all Anarchists, McVeigh was obsessed with the idea of Freedom. He believed that The State should not be able to control his actions through the threat of violence. He may well have tried talking about this over the years, telling people that the beliefs that make them feel safe are false, and that the State offers no safety, only control.

But most people will not understand such a message, or are frightened by it. In the end he decided to retaliate against state violence, perhaps hoping that his retaliation might mitigate violence by The State in the future. Of course, his own violent actions only served to increase people's sense of danger, and strengthen their feeling of need for The State's protection.

McVeigh's own concept of The State allowed him to see other people as evil parts of an evil State, rather than fellow individuals, just because they worked in a government building. He probably did not even understand that other people would see his actions in terms of the individual deaths he caused and not as an act of revenge against The State for the killings at Ruby Ridge and at Waco. Violent actions will never weaken a Collective that exists, for a large part, to give people a sense of safety. Rather, such actions will strengthen that ideological organism.

There is, however, another way to go about things, if one wants to expand personal liberty. It is a method that atheists are very familiar with, even if it is unknown to anarchists. Rather than fighting with violence, or even trying to make people feel that they don't need the protection The State offers, instead we can challenge the actual existence of The State icon. The argument for this runs something like this:

> What is the Nation State? Is it a set of lines drawn on a map? Why should we feel loyalty to some cartographer's scribbling? We are all individual people, responsible for our own actions. Those that believe that acting on behalf of a piece of Geography automatically makes their actions correct are simply delusional. No one should have greater rights than anyone else, and no one claiming to represent a piece of Geography should ever even be taken seriously.
>
> This is not to say that people shouldn't make rules about how they interact. However, if these rules are to be enforced with violence, they should always reflect the actual feeling that, on average, individual members of the group would be motivated to use violence to enforce the given rule. In addition, anyone enforcing behavior on behalf of others should be able to point to specific victims of the prohibited action, who would themselves have been willing to use violence if they were so equipped.
>
> The injured party should never be a mythical entity like The State or Society. Nothing should be declared a crime unless it is done so to defend real victims against what they could reasonably define as harm worthy of using violence to prevent. Also, the size of "the group" for whom laws are made, should always be as small as possible to keep things individual and personal, in contrast to having a hierarchy of laws that are enforced downward from the level of a mythical Nation State.

It may seem odd to say that this is an anarchistic argument, as we have just allowed justification for a system of laws. However, the claim can be made that we are all just individuals living in anarchy right now, that some people choose freely to believe in The State, and these believers fear that violation of The State's rules – by anyone – puts them in danger.

If people believe that your actions are a threat to them, then they are simply acting in self defense when they try to stop you. If there is a set of rules that they believe should be enforced, and these rules are very important to their own happiness, then how can any good anarchist suggest that they should not be allowed to act accordingly?

However, the authority for enforcement of such rules does not arise from the land we stand on, or from a symbol like a flag, or from some mythic concept of national identity. It arises from the values of specific individual human beings. If everyone fully appreciated that fact, it would be all that any real anarchist could ever ask for.

When you start believing in the authority of a geographic jurisdiction, and lend credence to "the law of the land," you elevate these things to the status of Higher Powers. Once this happens, laws that individuals would never otherwise choose to have enforced with violence are imposed upon everyone. The myth of the Higher Power makes people think that this is all OK – or at least to accept it all without thinking about it very much.

It is possible to allow people to choose their own laws in small groups. It is possible to dismiss the idea that anyone can ever be acting on behalf of The State or any other icon. It is possible for rules to be enforced only on the behalf of specific individuals. There is no need to believe in The State.

Provided you recognize that everyone has the right to believe in a different system of rules, and realize that no system of rules stems from any higher authority than individual thought, you can go ahead and believe that some limited system of rules is a good thing, and still be an anarchist.

We would suggest that Anarchists everywhere stop fighting The State with bombs and guns, or even with words about how terrible The State is, and come to understand that The State that they oppose is just a fictional construct. Instead, try to teach people that it is evil to believe in the existence of The State – that patriotic loyalty to a flag, a set of lines on a map, or to anyone claiming to be a voice for such imaginary symbols, is the root of most of the violence in the world.

8.2.3 Individualist

We would also suggest that all atheists be anarchists and that all anarchists be atheists and that everyone should be both. But be both in a non-combative way that stresses Individual free will over collective thinking. That is, everyone should be an individualist and also respect everyone else's individualism.

Feel free to believe in a supreme being, and to respect the sets of rules that other people expect you to live by in their company. Just don't believe in Higher Powers. An actual existing supreme being need not be conceptually superior to you, and a human being claiming to represent some icon is definitely not.

Feel free to impose rules of conduct on others, and allow them to impose rules on you; just don't lend greater authority to a set of rules when it comes from someone claiming to represent a larger group of people. The only people who count, in determining what is and is not acceptable behavior, are those who are actually currently being affected by the behavior in question.

And everyone else should mind their own damn business.

8.2.4 Heroes and Villains

For the record, we have a great deal of respect for the work of Richard Dawkins, and a great deal of contempt for the actions of Timothy McVeigh. However, you will notice reading above that we criticize Dawkins, and cast nobility on McVeigh.

Being able to do this is what being a free thinker is all about. If you are not able to see the occasional truth among the lies of the people you hate, and the trace of evil mixed in with the good of those you love, then you are not thinking past the labels and icons.

Only when you allow yourself to both pity the weakness of your heroes and admire the strength of your villains, will you be seeing the world clearly in terms of individual ideas, rather than through the fog of illogic that is the life's breath of collective idea-organisms.

You don't know anything aright until you have favorably considered its opposite.

8.3 Spreading the Word

Let's say you really liked the ideas in this book, and wanted to spread them, but it occurred to you that some of the ideas might be dangerous, and you didn't want anyone to get hurt. We faced this same problem ourselves in the writing of this book. We had to ask ourselves the following questions:

How do you help potentially good but scary ideas along into the world, in such a way that they do the most good, and cause the least harm?

How do you pass along interesting information without it turning into Gospel and Dogma?

How do you make sure that people really understand ideas, rather than having faith in them?

If our ideas are correct, this all boils down to the following question:

How do you make sure that these ideas won't become the core of some new Collective Identity that starts feeding on individuals for its own survival and growth at the expense of their own?

8.3.1 Avoiding Collectivism

To answer this, we reviewed our thoughts on the ways in which simple memes become dangerous collective idea-organisms, to see if there were ways in which we might avoid that trap. As we have related elsewhere in this book, we believe that Collectives are born from three basic errors of logic:

A. Taking a set of ideas as being an inseparable whole.
B. Lending greater credence to ideas based on their source.
C. Putting forward an untouchable icon as the source of a set of ideas.

Thinking about how these points related to our book, and what we could do to address each of them, here is what we came up with:

1. In order to address the issue of ideas acting together, we decide to make it very clear that the ideas in this book are to be considered entirely separable. To this end we must be willing to change the text of this book as errors are inevitably discovered. If you disagree with any part of this book, and can articulate your reasons, please tell us why you think we are wrong. If we agree with your analysis, we will change the book. If we disagree, but feel your argument has enough merit to be addressed, we will include a discussion of the issue. You can direct such response to www.godwantsyoudead.com/feedback.html
2. In order to address the issue of source, we attempted to stress that nothing makes our ideas any better than your own ideas or anyone else's, beyond the content of the ideas themselves. We are just regular guys. (I mean, sure, we both happen to be smart, athletic, good looking, and incredibly well endowed, but we're still just regular guys...) We are not going to try to impress you with our credentials, noble ancestry, previous good deeds, IQ scores, or anything else – these ideas will stand on their own merits or not at all.

3. In order to address the issue of an icon, we had to give up one of our original ideas. One of our first thoughts in writing this book was to not use our real names. It occurred to us that someone who did not like our ideas might decide to take it out on us personally – whether that meant yelling obscenities at us on the street, or actually physically attacking us. So we had decided to use a fake name for the author of the book. His name was going to be "Lester Faith" or "LES" to his friends, as a play on the words "less faith." And "LES" was also going to stand for Life Extension Science, because the possibility of immortality through science is one of the specific themes of the book.

It was all really very clever...

Then it occurred to us that making up a fake but cool sounding name was playing right into criteria C above. While "LES Faith" couldn't be beaten on the street for his writings, this is also a big part of the reason that he might actually turn out to be a very dangerous fellow. He could become an icon, whereas a couple of regular guys probably could not. So we decided that the right thing to do was to brave the inherent dangers of using our real names.

So, if you do not like our ideas, and are interested in actively attacking them, we would ask that you do us a few good turns in consideration of the steps we took to introduce these ideas with an eye to being careful not to create a collective idea-organism to compete with the one you are hosting.

8.3.2 All We Ask

i. In consideration for us admitting that every portion of our thesis must stand on its own, please do not try to attack an idea that you do not like (but can not directly refute) by pointing out some entirely different mistake that we have made. It is all too common for people who don't like one thing that someone said to try to dismiss it by attacking some other thing they said. They then make the claim that, since the source of the ideas is not infallible; all the ideas are somehow suspect. Hopefully you will not stoop to that level. If you don't like a specific idea, attack that idea on its own merits, not some other stupid thing we said.
ii. In consideration for us not trying to claim that we are smarter than anyone else, please don't try to attack us based on who we are. Try not to make the argument that you are somehow better suited to judge the truth than we are. Stick to the merits or flaws of the ideas, and your arguments will be stronger than if you claim to know better because you have an advanced degree or lofty position in some organization. Show us your evidence, not your credentials.
iii. In consideration for us using our own names, and thus opening ourselves up to personal attacks, we ask you one last favor. If somehow, by our writing this book, you feel we have caused you some sort of injury, and that we need to be punished, we only ask that you first make very sure that we really deserve that punishment.

To this end, we ask (and we think not unfairly) that you have actually read this book from cover to cover. You should be sure that we really deserve your wrath. If you have not carefully read each word, and clearly understood all of our arguments, you can not be sure that we are wrong. (Also, you might have missed the bit where we admit that it was all just a big joke, not to be taken at all seriously.)

If after you have carefully read every word we have written, you still think we deserve to be punished, and decide that you need to yell insults at us on the street, or march back and forth in front of our houses carrying picket signs. Well... we are big believers in free speech. What can we say – yell and march as much as you need to make you feel better. However, if our words have hurt your feelings so much that you feel the need to hurt us back in a physical way, we would suggest that you carefully reconsider this extreme action, and think about an alternative.

Perhaps it is actually the printed words themselves that are at fault, and not us. Maybe what you really need to do, to get back at those words and to make yourself feel better, is go out and buy a very large number of copies of this book and burn them. Try it – it might just do the trick. (Repeat as often as necessary to make you feel better.)

If after trying that, you still really feel the need to throw one or both of us a beating, please consider jumping to the end of the book and looking at that whole list of people we have credited as helping us or being our influences. Maybe we were serious when we said we couldn't have done it without them. If that's true, this book might really be more their fault than ours. Seriously, now that we think about it, they are all totally to blame for this book! Go get them!

8.3.3 Things to Do for Fun

If on the other hand, you really like our ideas and want to spread them to other people, please also consider the possible downside of this. Be sure to take similar steps to the ones we did. If you want to get together to talk about these ideas, make sure that you don't form a group with leaders. Everyone should be an equal. Don't even let anyone be the "first among equals," or "more equal than others" to quote George Orwell's "Animal Farm."

Whatever you do, for God's sake, don't give your group a cool name!

Keep in mind that we do not condone the formation of even a non-group with non-leaders trying to promote the ideas in this book. We think it is a really bad idea. I mean, what kind of things would such a non-group do anyway?

Actually, we have thought of a few things that an atheist anarchist individualist non-group might decide to do for fun, and to advance the non-cause. We have recorded them here for information purposes only. If you think of any other such ideas that we might have missed, send them to us, and we will include them on this list without using your name, to protect the guilty.

Here is our current list of bad ideas, ranging from borderline acceptable to the very bad indeed, and from not even mildly amusing to the very funny. If these ideas all seem somehow negative, or controversial, this is only because that is what gets attention, and therefore, that is what spreads the word. (If we thought that a puppy petting event would be likely to help, we would have included it here too.)

In no particular order:

- Join the Libertarian party and/or the Free State Project.
- Raise funds to have the bodies of executed criminals cryo-preserved.
- Deface churches and governmental offices, signs, websites, etc..., with info-hazard symbols like the one on the back cover of this book. You can get Info-hazard stickers at www.godwantsyoudead.com/shop.html
- Start a political movement to privatize police protection in your local jurisdiction – allow multiple private justice services with overlapping jurisdictions to act based on contracts with Individuals.
- Take a page from the abortion wars, and set up an operation rescue style organization for cryonics. This would involve stealing bodies (or just the heads) from undertakers before they can be embalmed, cremated, or buried, and having them cryonically suspended. If cryonics works, you will be saving lives. You can also show up at pro-life vs. pro-choice shouting matches as the "anti-death" faction, declaring that corpses are important and should be saved, not fetuses.
- Spread the rumor that some other country (whichever country your government is currently trying to play up as a competing economic or military power is probably a good one to mention) is very close to curing aging. Say that you heard that soon people of that nationality will be living forever, but they are not going to let us have the technology.
- Have copies of this book delivered to school libraries or, labeled as social studies text books, sent to private religious schools and public school districts that decide to teach Intelligent Design Theory. Or leave the book on the shelf at Wal-Mart or any bookstore refusing to stock it.
- Wrap copies of this book up as "Suspicious Packages" and leave them in public places. Remember that the more flashing lights a package has, and the more beeping noises it makes, the more "suspicious" it is.
- Assault famous people by throwing copies of this book at them – especially while the cameras are rolling. Actors and singers are fine choices. Politicians and religious figures are more appropriate but they are usually harder targets. The more famous a person you hit with a copy of this book, the more people will want to read it. We seriously doubt that anyone will be clever enough to score a "bull's-eye" on a head of state – or pontiff of a religion – not that you should consider this a challenge, but we would be very impressed... oh, and any famous talk show host who has chosen not to include our book on her well-known book list would also make an especially good target.
- If you happen to be a famous person, avoid having copies of this book thrown at you by always carrying one with you, prominently displayed for cameras. This can also be useful when you are caught naked or in some other compromising situation by the paparazzi – this book is the perfect size to cover your face with at such embarrassing moments.
- Or, you and all your friends could all just shave your heads and stand around on street corners, and outside airports, passing out pamphlets and flowers, and asking for donations. To find out how to send us all your money go to www.godwantsyoudead.com/donations.html

But seriously – do have fun, but think carefully before doing anything to upset the brainwashed too much... **They just might kill you for it!**

8.4 The Hero/Coward Choice

> *You do not face these ideas head-on because you are afraid of them – you are afraid that you might have to agree with them. And then you would have to face the choice either to be a hero or to be a coward.*
>
> -- A Lodging of Wayfaring Men

If you have actually made it through this whole book, then you have been exposed to a lot of very powerful ideas. Some of them may seem right to you. Others may seem wrong. Or, perhaps, you disagree on the surface because an idea makes you uncomfortable, but somewhere underneath you fear that the idea may be right?

Never forget that shame and intimidation are your enemies. You have a functional mind, and you are to use it. We have done our best to make our arguments understandable. It is up to you to consider them for yourself. You have to decide. Yes? No? Hold for further review?

We won't even tell you that all of the ideas we have are necessarily right. We have almost certainly made some mistakes of fact or logic. We are just human beings, doing the best we can to figure things out, and then pass what we came up with on to other human beings. As human beings, we are prone to being right only just a little bit more than being wrong. The last thing we would ever do is tell you that our ideas are infallible or that you must believe in them because they come from some power higher than you. We will simply offer up what we think is correct for your consideration.

Do not take our word for anything. Do not take *anyone's* word for *anything.* If you do not rely upon your own mind for judging the rightness of our ideas, then you have not understood them at all.

Don't ask your minister.

Don't ask your relatives.

Don't ask anyone.

Ask yourself.

But there's a problem with this, isn't there? If you make your own decisions, you alone are responsible for them!

We are not going to help you here. Choose. Either you have the guts to use your own mind, or you don't. Pick one or the other.

If you want someone else to make your decisions for you, then you are a coward.

If you will rely on your own mind ONLY, you're a hero.

This is your chance to put a solid foundation under your feet. And understand – the foundation is not our book; the foundation is the choice to rely solely upon your own judgment. If you decide that everything we have said is wrong, but still decide to make all your own decisions, using your own mind, hereafter – you are a hero in every way that matters.

How you feel about our ideas is not important. How you feel about yourself and your own ability to think things through using your own mind is the most important thing in the world...

Do you want to improve? Then here it is! Do it! Take that step!

We told you that we weren't going to make it easy for you. We presented you with some big ideas. We think they are right. But you alone must choose for yourself.

This is how great men are formed. This is how great minds are set in motion. Do you wish to be that kind of person? It's all in the choice to stand alone – to make up your own mind and to hold it inviolate.

Right now is when you get to make that most important decision.

Right now is when you get to make the Hero/Coward Choice.

Choose for yourself!

Choose now!

Choose!

Credits

Contributors

A lot of thought and work has been done by a lot of individuals to see this book in print. Here are some of the people who made this book possible. We couldn't have done it without them.

Words, Ideas, and Editing

These people all contributed ideas, did proofreading, or helped out in some other notable way during the thinking, writing, or editing processes.

- Scott Banister- found a spelling mistake (on the cover) not sure if he opened the book
- Vincent Cate
- Coop – the angry drunken red-neck
- Katherine Tombeau Cost
- Sarah Curry
- Jim Davidson
- Aubrey de Grey
- Mathew DiBernardo
- Luke Farrugia
- S. Morgan Friedman – whose vision of this book was better than we could manage
- Patri Friedman
- Janet Hastings – tore her son's first book into three pieces (returning them corrected)
- Jo Hastings
- Leonard "Buzz" Hastings
- S. Alexander Jacobson – would have done more but could not make email work
- Aaron R. Johnson
- Charles King
- Allison C.S. Lewis
- John Kipling Lewis – John is also one of our artists (see below)
- Nicole Macieik
- Alexander J. Marsh
- Deirdre McDaniel
- Sameer Parekh
- Kate Ragsdale – Kate is also one of our artists (see below)
- Stanley Rosenkampff – because he asked for this credit and is big and scary.
- Joseph M. Saul
- Sandy Sandfort
- Alexis Stahl
- Matt Siegel – deserves special thanks for providing the most feedback
- Michael J.J. Tiffany – deserves special thanks for finding an artist for us.
- Anja Williams
- George "Loki" Williams

We are almost certainly forgetting someone and are truly sorry about it.

Artists

- Sean Hastings – www.SeanHastings.com
- John Kipling Lewis – www.QuitYourJobDay.com
- Joanne Mason
- Pinguino – www.PenguinPalace.com
- Kate Ragsdale

Pictures

The task of adding pictures to the book was almost entirely Sean's. He started with notes and sketches he had from his original 1996 start on the book, and in late 2006 he started to do his own final drawings. He found artists to handle the stuff he was not capable of drawing himself, but most all of the image ideas were his.

So if the art sometimes seems a little silly for the seriousness of the topics being discussed – that is Sean's fault and not Paul's – although we both certainly felt that the book should have some level of comic relief. Given the degree of emotional attachment some people can have with many of these topics, we think that while discussing them it is important to break the mood now and again with a little bit of laughter.

This is a list of the images that appear in the book by section, along with the people who helped create them, and any pertinent copyright information:

Front Cover

Image: **God With Gun** – Original Art: Michael Angelo, 1512 – predates copyright – Concept: Sean Hastings, 1996 – Image altered by Joanne Mason, 1998 – All rights purchased from Joanne Mason by Sean Hastings – John Lewis came up with the idea for a vertical layout of the cover.

1. Evolution of Higher Powers

Image: **Cosmic Hand** – Concept: Sean Hastings, 2006 – Art: Kate Ragsdale, 2007 – Caption: Sean Hastings, 2007 – All rights purchased from Kate Ragsdale by Sean Hastings.

1.1 Biological Evolution

Image: **Saber Tooth Rabbit** – Concept: Sean Hastings, 2006 – Art and Caption: Kate Ragsdale, 2007 – All rights purchased from Kate Ragsdale by Sean Hastings.

1.2 Ideological Evolution

Image: **Dawkins Fish** – Concept: Sean Hastings, 1996 – Art: Sean Hastings, 2007

Image: **Jesus Fish Family Tree** – Concept: Sean Hastings, 1996 – Art: Sean Hastings, 2007

Image: **Collective Stick Man** – Concept, Art, and Caption: Sean Hastings, 2006

1.3 Identities and icons

Image: **Identity Echoes** – Concept and Art: Sean Hastings, 2006

Image: **Distributed Identity Cloud** – Concept: Sean Hastings, 1996 – Art: Sean Hastings, 2006

Image: **Fame Identity After Death** – Concept: Sean Hastings, 1996 – Art: Sean Hastings, 2006

Image: **Collective Identity** – Concept: Sean Hastings, 1996 – Art: Sean Hastings, 2006

1.4 The Higher Powers

Image: **Icon Lineup** – Concept, Art, and Caption: Sean Hastings, 2006

Image: **Racial Yin Yang** – Concept and Art: Sean Hastings, 2006

Image: **Relationship as Distributed Identity** – Concept: Sean Hastings, 1996 – Art: Sean Hastings, 2006

Image: **Head Full of icons** – Concept and Art: Sean Hastings, 2006

Image: **Two faced Preacher** – Concept and Caption: Sean Hastings, 2006 – Art: Pinguino (www.PenguinPalace.com), 2007 – All rights purchased from Pinguino by Sean Hastings.

2.1 Down from the Trees

Image: **Stone Hand-axes** – Art: Cropped from illustration in "Victoria County History of Kent" Vol 1, p 312, published London, 1912 – Copyright expired, 1968

Image: **Cave Painting** – Art: Unknown artist, circa 15,000 B.C. – predates copyright

2.4 Democracy and Empire

Image: **What Kind of Jew are You?** – Concept and Art: Sean Hastings 2006

2.9 The Long Arm

Image: **Lady Justice Busted** – Concept: Sean Hastings 2006 – Art: Pinguino (www.PenguinPalace.com), 2007 – Caption: Sean Hastings, 2007 – All rights purchase from Pinguino by Sean Hastings.

3. Your Money or Your Life

Image: **Uncle Sam With Gun** – Original Art: Montgomery Flagg, 1915 – Original copyright expired, 1971 – Concept and Caption: Sean Hastings, 2006 – Image altered by John Lewis (www.QuitYourJobDay.com), 2007. All rights purchased from John Lewis by Sean Hastings.

3.1 Killing The Goose

Image: **Strong Central Authority** – Concept and Art: Sean Hastings 2006

Image: **Weak Central Authority** – Concept and Art: Sean Hastings 2006

Image: **No Central Authority** – Concept and Art: Sean Hastings 2006

4.1 Biology and Ideology

Image: **Times Square** – Photo: Sean Hastings, 2007 – Models: Nicole Macieik and Barney the Dog – Image used with the permission of Nicole Macieik (Barney the Dog, however, refused permission, and is threatening to sue.)

Image: **Oil Refinery** – Photo: John Mullen, 2006 – used with the permission of John Mullen

Image: **United States Lights** – Data: Marc Imhoff of NASA GSFC and Christopher Elvidge of NOAA NGDC, 2000 – Image: Craig Mayhew and Robert Simmon, NASA GSFC, 2000 – Copyright: NASA, 2000 - VisibleEarth.nasa.gov – Image is used in book free of licensing fees according to NASA requirements that they be provided credit as the owners of the imagery.

4.3 The Question of identity

Image: **Pirate Ninja Self Image** – Concept: Sean Hastings, 2006 – Art: Pinguino (www.PenguinPalace.com), 2007 – Caption: Sean Hastings – All rights purchased from Pinguino by Sean Hastings.

Image: **Homunculus Driving** – Concept and Art: Sean Hastings, 2006

4.4 Your Ideal Self

Image: **Faith in Two Axes** – Concept and Art: Anonymous, 2006 – image used in book with permission of anonymous creator

4.6 Bits and Pieces

Image: **Couple Identity** – Concept: Sean Hastings, 1996 – Art: Sean Hastings, 2006

5. The Art of Thought

Image: **Santa on Cross** – Concept: Sean Hastings, 1996 – Art and Caption: Sean Hastings, 2006

5.1 Free Your Mind

Image: **Fanatic Head** – Concept and Art: Sean Hastings, 2006

Image: **Group Head** – Concept and Art: Sean Hastings, 2006

Image: **Idea Head** – Concept and Art: Sean Hastings, 2006

5.4 Fallacies

Image: **Pro-Sperm Protesters** – Concept: Sean Hastings, 1996 – Art, and Caption: Sean Hastings, 2006

6.1 Which Party Should I Vote For?

Image: **Elephant and Donkey** – Concept, Art, and Caption: Sean Hastings, 2006

6.3 Engineering Freedom

Image: **Roman Coin** – Photo: Richard Beale, 2007 – Image used in book with the permission of Richard Beale

6.4 Rolling Back

Image: **Free State Project Logo** – Copyright: Free State Project, 2004 – Image used in book with the permission of the Free State Project

6.5 New Frontiers

Image: **Seastead Blueprint** – Concept and Art: Andrew House, 2003 – Image used in book with permission of Andrew House

7.1 Suspended Animation

Image: **Cryonics Storage Tank** – Photo: Sean Hastings, 2002

7.3 Nano Technology

Image: **Moore's Law Graph** – Created by Wikipedia user: Wgsimon. – Modified by Sean Hastings – Image is used in this book with no specific permission, but with the understanding that it has been released into the public domain.

Image: **Mite on Nano Gears** – Image is used in this book with no specific permission, but with the understanding that it may be used in exchange for including this statement: "Courtesy of Sandia National Laboratories, SUMMiTTM Technologies, www.mems.sandia.gov"

Image: **Nano Car** – Image is used in this book with no specific permission, but with the understanding that it has been released as part of a press kit by Rice University and may be used as part of a description of research work done at Rice, if credited as follows: "Image courtesy of Rice University Office of Media Relations and Information. Credit: Y. Shirai/Rice University"

7.5 Life Extension

Image: **Aubrey de Grey** – Photo: Kevin Perrot, 2004 – Image is used in this book with the permission of Dr. Aubrey de Grey and the Methuselah Foundation.

8.1 The Last Generation

Image: **Sherwin Williams logo** – Image used without permission – Not sure exactly what our legal position is on this, but it was a funny joke that just would not have worked without actually showing the logo. This would seem to qualify as "Fair Use" if any such concept is still recognized in the continuously growing realm of copyright legislation.

Back Cover

Image: **Infohazard Symbol** – Concept and Art: Sean Hastings, 1996 – Caption: Sean Hastings, 2006

Reading List

This is a list of some of the books that the authors note as influencing their thinking in the creation of this book, and recommend for your further reading.

- *The Bible* (Any literal translation.)
- *Hitchhiker's Guide to the Galaxy*, Douglas Adams (five-book trilogy.)
- *The Origins Of Totalitarianism*, Hannah Arendt
- *The Psychology of Self-Esteem*, Nathaniel Brandon
- *The Transparent Society*, David Brin
- *The Discourse of Voluntary Servitude*, Etienne de la Boetie
- *How I Found Freedom In An Unfree World*, Harry Browne
- *The Richest Man In Babylon*, George Clason
- *The Origin of Species*, Charles Darwin
- *The Sovereign Individual*, James Davidson, Lord William Rees-Mogg
- *The Selfish Gene*, Richard Dawkins
- *Engines of Creation*, Eric Drexler
- *The Lessons of History*, Will and Ariel Durant
- *Principles For A Free Society*, Richard Epstein
- *Surely You're Joking Mr. Feynman!*, Feynman, Leighton, Hutchings
- *The Machinery of Freedom*, David Friedman
- *Free to Choose*, Milton & Rose Friedman
- *Civilization And Its Enemies*, Lee Harris
- *The Road to Serfdom*, Friedrich A. Hayek
- *A Child of The Century*, Ben Hecht
- *Think and Grow Rich*, Napoleon Hill
- *Gödel, Escher, Bach*, Douglas Hofstadter
- *War Before Civilization*, Lawrence Keeley
- *Freedom and the Law*, Bruno Leoni
- *The Reawakening*, Primo Levi
- *Whatever Happened To Justice?*, Richard Maybury
- *Human Action*, Ludwig Von Mises
- *The Evolution of Civilization*, Carol Quigley
- *Atlas Shrugged*, Ayn Rand
- *Great Mambo Chicken and the Transhuman Condition*, Ed Regis
- *A Lodging of Wayfaring Men*, Paul Rosenberg
- *The Demon-Haunted World*, Carl Sagan
- *Envy*, Helmut Schoeck
- *How to Start Your Own Country*, Erwin Strauss
- *The Market For Liberty*, Morris and Linda Tannehill
- *The Third Wave*, Alvin Toffler